D0908306

Real Folks

REAL FOLKS

Race and Genre in the Great Depression

Sonnet Retman

DUKE UNIVERSITY PRESS   DURHAM AND LONDON   2011

© 2011 Duke University Press
All rights reserved
Printed in the United States of America
on acid-free paper ∞
Designed by C. H. Westmoreland
Typeset in Minion Pro by Keystone
Typesetting, Inc.
Library of Congress Cataloging-in-
Publication Data appear on the last
printed page of this book.

For my parents,
Martha, in loving memory of Eb,
Frank, and Roselle

And especially for Ava, Sylvie, and Curtis

Contents

Acknowledgments ix

Introduction 1

PART I: THE FOLKLORE OF RACIAL CAPITALISM

1. "A Combination Madhouse, Burlesque Show and Coney Island":
The Color Question in George Schuyler's *Black No More* 33

2. "Inanimate Hideosities": The Burlesque of Racial Capitalism in
Nathanael West's *A Cool Million* 72

PART II: PERFORMING THE FOLK

3. "The Last American Frontier": Mapping the Folk in the Federal
Writers' Project's *Florida: A Guide to the Southernmost State* 113

4. "Ah Gives Myself de Privilege to Go": Navigating the Field and
the Folk in Zora Neale Hurston's *Mules and Men* 152

PART III: POPULIST MASQUERADE

5. "Am I Laughing?": Burlesque Incongruities of Genre, Gender,
and Audience in Preston Sturges's *Sullivan's Travels* 191

Afterpiece: The Coen Brothers' Ol'-Timey Blues in *O Brother,
Where Art Thou?* 241

Notes 251

Bibliography 287

Index 311

Acknowledgments

As I reflect on this book's numerous iterations, I am grateful to the many people who offered me mentorship, counsel, friendship, and support. The foundations of this project were really laid at Princeton University, where I had the good fortune of encountering Valerie Smith, who, with her brilliance, grace, calm, encouragement, and humor, has opened up the world to me, far beyond the realm of academia. She has read every word of this book. One of the great joys of my life is counting Val as a mentor and friend for over two decades now. Officially, this project began when I was a graduate student at UCLA in the English Department and had the opportunity to study with an extraordinary group of professors, including Kathryn Hayles, Arthur Little, Ken Reinhard, Valerie Smith, Eric Sundquist, and Richard Yarborough. Ken Reinhard and Richard Yarborough, in particular, illuminated the political possibilities of documentary and satire with great insight and wit. Thank you for introducing me to *Sullivan's Travels* and *Black No More*: these texts haunted my dissertation and they now occupy much of this book's focus.

The research for this book was funded early on by a Greenfield Research Fellowship at the Roosevelt Presidential Library during the summer of 1997 and by a University of California Humanities Research Institute Postdoctoral Fellowship in conjunction with the "Microcosms of Knowledge" Research Group (1997–98). I am grateful to the intellectual vision of Microcosm's organizers, Mark Meadows and Bruce E. Robertson, and the scholarly engagement of fellow participants, Ken Arnold, Rosemary Joyce, and especially Rebecca Lemov. More recently, I have benefited from a faculty fellowship with the Walter Chapin Simpson Center for the Humanities at the University of Washington, which provided me with time for writing and an opportunity to circulate work in progress among a terrific group of fellows. The director, Kathleen Woodward, and the associate director, Miriam Bartha, have created an exemplary interdisciplinary scholarly community to which I and many others are indebted. A Woodrow Wilson Junior Faculty Career Enhancement Fellowship during the year 2006–7 couldn't have come at a more crucial stage; that fellowship made it possible for me to complete the book under the formal mentorship of Valerie Smith.

At the University of Washington, I have found a home for my work in several locales both on and beyond campus. My home department, American Ethnic Studies, and the departments to which I am adjunct, Women's Studies and English, have each provided me with the intellectual and emotional sustenance of good colleagues and administrators. Thanks to Angelica Hernandez-Cordero, Dalia Correa, Lauro Flores, Erasmo Gamboa, Tetsuden Kashima, Seyed Maulana, Ellen Palms, Devon Pena, Elizabeth Salas, Connie So, and especially, Rick Bonus, Gail Nomura, Tyina Steptoe, and Steve Sumida in AES. Thanks also to many other scholars and friends at the University of Washington: Francisco Benitez, Marisol Berrios-Miranda, Stephanie Camp, Zahid Chaudury, Eva Cherniavsky, Laura Chrisman, Shannon Dudley, Juan Guerra, Mae Henderson, Moon-Ho Jung, Tom Lockwood, Joycelyn Moody, Chandan Reddy, Caroline Chung Simpson, Nikhil Singh, and Stephanie Smallwood. I am indebted to the forward vision, expert advice, and institutional support of Ana Maria Cauce, Luis Fraga, and Judith Howard. I am grateful to the three-campus interdisciplinary working group, Women Investigating Race, Ethnicity and Difference (WIRED), the brilliant brain child of Habiba Ibrahim, Ralina Joseph, and Janine Jones. Thank you Julia Aguirre, Rachel Chapman, Frances Contreras, Michelle Habell-Pallan, Alexes Harris, Trista Huckleberry, Suhanthie Motha, Naomi Murakawa, Leilani Nishime, Ileana Rodriguez-Silva, Manka Varghese, Wadiya Udell, Sasha Welland, Beth West, and Joy Williamson-Lott. Every aspect of my scholarship, including this book, has profited from the always astute and generous commentary of a writing collective that includes Rachel Chapman, Susan Friedman, Susan Glenn, Angela Ginorio, Michelle Habell-Pallan, and Shirley Yee. I am particularly indebted to Michelle for her mentorship even before I arrived on campus. A more informal, yet no less vibrant, writing group with Gillian Harkins and Alys Weinbaum pushed the manuscript into its final form. Several graduate students at the University of Washington have made this project's stakes clearer to me: Zakiya Adair, Melanie Hernandez, and Andrea Opitz, as well as the students in the courses "African American Satire," "The Literature of the Harlem Renaissance," and "Exhibiting Culture, Performing Race." From a more oblique angle, the Experience Music

Project Pop Conference has served as a community of inquiry focused on some of this book's central concerns—authenticity, racial masking, and satire among them—and I thank Eric Weisbard and Ann Powers for their commitment to the pop project and their enduring friendship, as well as all of the conference regulars, especially Daphne Brooks, Michelle Habell-Pallan, Maureen Mahon, R. J. Smith, Gayle Wald, and Oliver Wang. Michael Mann's "Ali" gave me the chance to work with Lydia Cedrone, Sean Ilnseher, Kathy Shea, and Mann himself, introducing me to aspects of film production that later informed my research.

A number of brilliant interlocutors have given me feedback and opportunities that shaped the intellectual trajectory of this book: Herman Beavers, P. Gabrielle Foreman, Adam Green, Brian Johnson, George Hutchinson, Jon Lohman, and Jean Wyatt. Several people, whom I am lucky enough to also count as dear friends, read the manuscript or portions of it and offered key critiques, suggestions, and clarifications: Mary Pat Brady, Daphne Brooks, Nico Israel, Gillian Harkins, Rebecca Lemov, Heather Lukes, Kate McCullough, Raphael Simon, Valerie Smith, and Alys Weinbaum. I radically revised and expanded the manuscript with the incisive guidance of the developmental editor Edward J. Blum. I am indebted to *PMLA Journal* for publishing an earlier version of chapter 1 in its special issue on *Comparative Racialization*, edited by Patricia Yaeger ([October 2008]: 1448–64); it appears here in revised and extended form. My editor at Duke University Press, Ken Wissoker, has been a model of patience and encouragement, helping me pull the book's argument more sharply into focus. My copy editor Maura High made this book far more lucid and my managing editor Neal McTighe seamlessly steered it through production. Priscilla Wald and my other anonymous reader at Duke University Press were extraordinary, giving my manuscript the kind of close reading that one can only dream of: I am ever indebted to them for their scrutiny and care.

I have been sustained during the writing of this book by friends and family who generously discussed its central questions and many others over dinner, runs, dog walks, and just about every other social occasion. Los Angeles will always hold me in its thrall because of a most amazing group of friends, more like family: Philip De Leon, Ken Ehrlich, Carla Eisenberg, Heather Lukes, Molly McGarry, Rita Rothman, Shirley Rothman, Rafi Simon, Janet Sarbanes, Bill Stavru, and Michael Udesky. I thank you all not least for your exquisite senses of irony and always knowing the place where politics enters. In the Los Angeles diaspora, Mary Pat Brady, Daphne Brooks, and Lisa Thompson continue to keep me lifted, through humor and critical insight, each in her own way. I am indebted to my earliest group of friends, Jennifer Emerich, Anne Forester, Lesley James, and Jennifer Nelson for informing this book's very sensibilities. I am thankful to those who made Seattle feel like home again: Matt Aalfs, Amal Al Faiz, Faye Bathurst, Roberta Carlson, Tami Fairweather, Melissa Finch, Rachel Flotard, Sarah Flotard, Lucretia Granger, Michelle Habell-Pallan, Shelly Halstead, Gillian Harkins, Rich Jensen, Matt Johnson, Ralina Joseph, Julia Kellison, Alan Pruzan, Steve Retz, Nick Straley, Manka Varghese, Juliet Waller-Pruzan, Alys Weinbaum, Emily White, and David Williams.

For obvious and less obvious reasons, there would be no book without my family, particularly my parents. What might not be overtly apparent in its pages is the degree to which my blended family has shaped its content and direction as well as providing me with childcare, meals, and other crucial forms of support that enabled its writing. My siblings' curiosity about the project made me feel like it was worthwhile. And, at least to my knowledge, in the spirit of Schuyler, West, Hurston, and Sturges, they've never yet let the occasion for an outrageous joke or performance slip them by. Thank you, Alex Higgins, Eva McGough, Natasha, Nicole, and Zoe; Zach Jones; Mischa Retman and Jyothi Rao; Melissa, Jimmy, Jake, and Sam Standish; and Jenny, Drew, Noah, and Eli Zavatsky. For last-minute help in capturing the book's artwork and for getting the visuals and their humor instantaneously—like everything else—I am indebted to Mischa. My aunt Mary Beth Kelsey showed me that a doctorate was possible, along with many other things, and my uncle Todd Kelsey and my aunt Jill Levy always asked great questions. I thank my in-laws, Anne and Kent Bonney, Laurie Bonney, John Bonney and Erica Bonney-Smith, for welcoming me into their family so completely and for tolerating my basement writings during our visits with them at Cape Cod. I also thank the Bradys, Gareys, Gordons, Haxbys, and Smiths who have made those trips so much fun. My mother, Martha, has been there for me at every turn, offering me love, encouragement, knowledge, and financial help when I needed it. She practices a progressive everyday ethics of care that is kind and deliberate and we are its beneficiaries. Her partner, Eben Carlson, tempered his book lust and voracious appetite for questions of human consciousness with a wry sensibility that continues to inspire me. By way of her insight, confidence, and love, my step-mother, Rosselle Pekelis, has shown me the stakes of this book, always asking me that not-so-simple question, "What's it mean for the Jews?" My father, Frank, has been an anchor for me, helping me to stay focused on the bigger questions and let go of the rest. He demonstrates the possibility of a balanced life that keeps humor, love, pragmatism, social justice—and dogs—at its very center. (On that note, Jasper was integral to the daily life of the book, as was Stella, in spite of herself.) Each of my parents have helped me learn how to think, write, and speak about culture and politics more effectively and this book reflects their efforts as much as my own.

Finally, this book is dedicated to my daughters, Ava and Sylvie, and to Curtis. Ava and Sylvie have not brought me sanity but something better, a sense of the present in its rich absurdity, beauty, and promise. Though they are both tired of hearing me say "one more minute" at the computer, they have given new shape to my priorities. Curtis has lived with this book as long as I have. He has read its many drafts and debated with me about more than one of its claims. He opens up new ways of perceiving what is in front of us. With his wit, intelligence, tenacity, and love, Curtis makes everything possible.

Introduction

O honored folk, do not begrudge the sight / and rumor of reality.
—A. T. ROSEN, Federal Writers' Project, *American Stuff* (1937)

Here, in the vast granary of facts on life in America put away by the WPA writers, the documentary reporters, the folklorists preparing an American mythology, the explorers who went hunting through darkest America with a notebook and a camera, the new army of biographers and historians—here, stocked away like a reserve against bad times, is the raw stuff of that contemporary mass record which so many imaginative spirits tried to depict and failed to master.—ALFRED KAZIN, *On Native Grounds* (1942)

This book chronicles the search for authenticity in the United States during the Great Depression, which lasted from 1929 to 1941. Amid skyrocketing unemployment and spiraling deflation, in the wake of the stock market's collapse, various writers, ethnographers, documentarists, filmmakers, and reformers sought out something real, something genuine, with which to ground an increasingly tenuous sense of national identity. They found it in the folk. The folk's rural, artisanal know-how seemed to comprise the "raw stuff" with which to remake American identity.

While the search for the folk did not begin with the 1930s, its urgency, direction, and shape altered considerably with the onset of the Depression.[1] The folk and their premodern authenticity were represented with an immediacy borne of the era's most modern technologies: documentary photographs and books, sound recordings, films, and newsreels. They emerged as an incongruous amalgam, providing, in the famous words of Van Wyck Brooks, a "usable past" for an uncertain present ("On Creating," 219). Featured as stalwart protagonists in much of the period's documentary, the folk took center stage in various narratives of recovery across the political spectrum. In some of these stories, this folk embodied a purportedly precapitalist way of life, an enduring stoicism in the face of the marketplace's erratic excesses. In other accounts, they

represented an embattled group in need of government intervention—
"pseudo-peasants" on the verge of vanishing due to the ravages of capitalism and unpredictable forces of nature (Smith, *Making the Modern*,
298). Viewed either as relics worthy of preservation or as victims deserving of aid, the folk were perceived as a pastoral resource integral to the
nation's healing and crucial to the brokering of new deals.

Bearing the weight of so much consequence, the rhetoric of the folk
not unexpectedly became "folksy." Many of the era's documentary endeavors transformed the folk into populist, regional clichés of "real"
Americans and "real" America. In protest, a hybrid genre formed: documentary and satire merged in various ways to critique the fabrication of
folk authenticity and expose its patriotic and corporate exploitation in
the popular cultural narratives of the period. While many studies of
realism in the 1930s simply assume the folksiness of the folk, this book is
concerned with the "invention" of the folk in Depression-era politics
and culture. From this angle, the folk constitute a powerful "fiction" in
both senses of the term—as a falsehood and as a literary creation. *Real
Folks: Race and Genre in the Great Depression*, then, is about a search for
folk authenticity and also about hybrid forms of documentary and satire
that told a different kind of story about the folk in the most uncertain
of times.

With the specter of a second Great Depression haunting nearly every
discussion of a faltering global economy, it comes as little surprise that
the thirties hold the antecedents to our own cultural moment. As politicians attempt to speak plainly, their pronouncements often take on a
folksy quality. Some, like the former vice presidential candidate Sarah
Palin, talk of "real America," while others, such as President Barack
Obama, suggest "we dust ourselves off and get back to work." Former
president George W. Bush is famous for his appeal to "gut feeling" in lieu
of facts to explain his administration's flawed decision making, so much
so that the parodic conservative political pundit Stephen Colbert coined
the term "truthiness"—"not quite fact, not quite fiction"—to describe his
rhetoric. As in the thirties, we've seen a powerful response to the folksy
articulations of the last decade in the documentary of *Frontline* and, as
Colbert's coinage suggests, in our own hybrid form of satire and documentary, the mock news of *The Colbert Report*, *The Daily Show*, and the
Dave Chappelle Show. Indeed, when the satirist Jon Stewart was asked by
Bill Moyers, who specializes in documentary, if the work of satire and

documentary feeds into people's sense of helplessness, Stewart replied, "No. . . . this is how we fight back." Stewart's reply acknowledges the shared aims of these modes of address. In this dialogue and in shows like Stewart's, we glimpse the makings of a hybrid genre: satire and documentary coming together to expose the deployment of folksiness and its familiar appeal in the twenty-first century. By exploring the manufacture of the folk in conjunction with commercial capitalism and populist discourses of nation building, I hope in this book to shed light on our contemporary negotiations with mass-mediated identity and consumer culture, and our grappling with the "real" and the "authentic" in narratives of self, community, and nation.

It is no accident that the term "folksiness, the state or quality of being 'folksy'" originated in the United States in or around 1931, at the tail end of the Hoover administration (*Oxford English Dictionary*). Or that we've come to remember the tumultuous thirties through near-iconic iterations of the folk and the folksy: Walker Evans's black-and-white photographs of dispossessed tenant farmworkers; the Joad family in John Steinbeck's novel *The Grapes of Wrath* (1939) and the movie of the same name; Franklin D. Roosevelt's homey radio *Fireside Chats*; Alan Lomax's recordings of Leadbelly and Woody Guthrie housed in the national Archive of American Folk-Song; "Native" roadside attractions in the form of Wigwam motel courts, pay-to-visit tribal villages and Indian pageants, and totem poles commissioned by the New Deal's Civilian Conservation Corps, Indian Division; and regional folkways collected in the travel guides of the Federal Writers' Project's American Guide Series (Veitch, *American Superrealism*, xvi). In such a list, we see how the populist ideal of the folk was disseminated through modern mass media. And no form would deliver the folk more convincingly than documentary, its seemingly straightforward language of facts and its emphasis on the quotidian compounding the realness of its subject.

The United States was not alone in seizing upon mythical figures of authenticity and realist forms of representation to fortify its citizenry in the havoc of the global Depression. In the Soviet Union, Joseph Stalin advocated art that explicitly celebrated the life of the worker—the protagonist of a classless society presumed to be already in existence in the USSR—by institutionalizing socialist realism as the official artistic doctrine of the state in 1934 (Foley, *Radical Representations*, 162).[2] From another ideological platform, National Socialist German Workers' Party grounded its Nazism in "decontextualized ideas about folklore culled from Romanticism to the 1930s," conceiving *der Volk* as a figure of spiritual unity and racial purity, a gauge for state policies of racial cleansing (Bendix, *In Search*, 166). American conceptions of the folk would encounter and negotiate these distinct but contiguous cultural formations from Europe. As each of these iterations of the people show, such categories of authentic national personhood were invented, unstable, and shifting, and they served a range of political agendas on the left and the right. To what ends the folk and their pastness would be used—and abused—is part of the story I aim to tell.

Departing from a conventional literary history of the 1930s that couples nonfiction and social realism, this book traces the decade's convergent satirical and documentary genres in a set of unruly texts that bring to light alternative forms of cultural production and social critique around the figure of the folk: George Schuyler's *Black No More* (1931), Nathanael West's *A Cool Million* (1934), the Federal Writers' Project's *Florida: A Guide to the Southernmost State* (1939), Zora Neale Hurston's *Mules and Men* (1935), and Preston Sturges's film *Sullivan's Travels* (1941). As I argue, the satirical energies of the thirties have been largely overlooked in the steady focus on realism, an omission that has rendered the writings of Schuyler, West, and others at best anomalous and at worst inscrutable. In fact, these writings were by no means anomalies, but instead responses to the Depression era's representational crisis and its corresponding recourse to icons of working-class and rural authenticity. Through these novels, ethnographies, guidebooks, and films, I trace the foundations of the folk in a fraught, triangular racial formation of white, black, and native. As I show, a hybrid genre of satire and documentary formed a site of theorizing in which conventional epistemologies of the folk were both staged and queried (Lamothe, *Inventing the New Negro*, 11). This hybrid genre created a common discourse of moral truth-telling aimed at the patriotic and economic production of the folk in populist narratives promoted by the New Deal nation-state and corporate capitalism.

Real Folks is organized around two variations of this hybrid genre; the first I call *modernist burlesque* and the second, *signifying ethnography*. These terms are meant to suggest the text's ascendant genre and its interplay with apparently unrelated modes of representation. Both modernist burlesque and signifying ethnography theorize the construction of the folk by way of the literary and the visual. Both forms inhabit that which they mean to critique, using exaggeration, irony, and reversal to reveal the performative dimensions of the object of their scrutiny. Each form makes its readers aware of their own press for the authentic. By way of their complicity critiques, modernist burlesque and signifying ethnography offer their readers a resistant reading practice.

When Schuyler and West deploy the folk, it is always a parodic citation. This gesture helps define their modernist burlesque, a kind of satire that occupies its subject from the outside in by pushing its most theatrical and technological elements to spectacular excess.[3] Both Schuyler and West deploy modernist burlesque to dismantle the authentic aura that surrounds the folk and the "self-made man," an aura derived from these figures' central role in capitalism's story of limitless opportunity. In their burlesques, they illumine how the clichéd story of American class ascension—the bootstrap myth—depends upon impersonation, a performative making of the self into the upwardly mobile, white, and male rugged individual. Each character enacts this transformation on stage in front of large audiences. The reader witnesses how the audience who consumes the performance wholesale becomes reified, incorporated as white supremacist or fascist cogs in a mass-produced nationalist script. In this way, Schuyler and West disturb the dynamics of identification central to the rags-to-riches plot. By providing examples of all-consuming spectatorship and their violent outcomes in the voice of documentary, the actual audience is asked to distance itself from the textual audience. As readers distance themselves from these narratives of authentic personhood and nation, other progressive political configurations and possibilities emerge to fill the void.

The second variation of this hybrid genre, signifying ethnography, follows a structural logic similar to modernist burlesque, citing and inhabiting that which it means to question in order to instill in its readers a self-conscious critical reading practice. Whereas modernist burlesque implicates the performing protagonist and his multiple audiences in the perpetuation of insidious nationalist dramas, signifying ethnography implicates the ethnographer and the reader in the activity of searching for "the authentic." In so doing, it shows the folk to be fluid, ephemeral, and impure. I draw upon Hurston's definition of signifying found in *Mules and Men*, one of the first definitions of the term in the study of linguistics, "to show off" (124n4)—and, I would add, "to show up."[4] As Henry Louis Gates describes it, *signifying* deploys the "use of repetition and reversal" to launch "an implicit parody of a subject's own complicity in illusion" (*Figures in Black*, 240). In regard to the popular nonfiction of the Depression, this illusion encompasses the desire for unmediated transcriptions of reality and a steadfast belief in their authenticity.[5] Within the signifying ethnographies this book treats, the reader is made aware of her own investment in the fiction of nonfiction's unmediated status.

The texts in *Real Folks* emerge within a particular juncture of *racial capitalism*, a term I use, following Cedric Robinson, to emphasize the ways race is always a foundational structure within the operation of capitalism in the United States (*Black Marxism*, 2).[6] In the first half of the twentieth century, Jim Crow, the federally mandated system of racial segregation, permeated capitalism's economic and social structures, resulting in unequal wages for workers as well as the segregation of places of consumption. These divisions also facilitated the growth of niche and crossover markets that cashed in on gendered, racial difference, such as Madame C. J. Walker's beauty products, designed primarily for an African American female clientele; and the race records of the 1920s, produced initially for African American consumers and then for a crossover market. Paradoxically, just as these niche markets grew, Fordist technologies of mass production ushered in the promise of standardized goods and a homogeneous "democracy of consumers" (Cross, *All-Consuming Century*, 2). As a consequence, singularity and homogeneity became mutually perpetuating market values. In this economy, the folk were positioned as unique artifacts, their difference made "real" through modernized media—the radio, records, concerts, newspapers, and movie newsreels—and its new ways of hearing, seeing, perceiving, and mediating (Filene, *Romancing the Folk*, 57). These technologies worked in tandem with commercial culture's commodification of the folk on a national scale. In this way, the folk were capitalized on as a tonic against American standardization and against the crisis tendencies of advanced capitalism as evidenced by the Depression. Through their variations of the hybrid genre of documentary and satire, each of the texts in this book expose the ways the folk were both called upon to evoke a precapitalist past and exploited in the form of nostalgic folk authenticity. In the end, the folk are revealed to be an anxious product of commercial modernity—not an antidote to it. By examining the ways that satire and documentary hybridize each other in this period, we see at once the means by which the folk were constituted within a nostalgic story of corporate capitalism and also the vigorous critique of that constitution made so powerfully in the cultural expression of the time.

OH HONORED FOLK!

What is the story of the thirties without voice-of-God narration, the booming male voiceover that introduced such classic documentary films as Pare Lorentz's *The Plow That Broke the Plains* (1936) and *The River* (1937)? An omnipotent narratorial device invented in that era, it self-consciously projects a sense of its story's importance for posterity, in part, by imposing coherence on its subject. The loud, commanding tones of voice-of-God narration attempted to make order of the Depression's chaotic devastation. Many parties across the political spectrum vied for this powerful omniscient voice. The din of these voices then, and the symbolic place of the thirties in the national imagination now, make it all the more difficult to grasp that decade's texture, complexities, and con-tradictions (Veitch xvi). The artists included in this book grappled with these didactic representations as they spoke to the many conundrums of a nation racked by economic crisis. At the forefront of their efforts lay the thorny problem of how to represent "the people" (Veitch xvii; Den-ning, *The Cultural Front*, 125). The folk provided one possible answer.

The economic free-fall of the early thirties destabilized prevailing no-tions of personal, communal, and national character. Fiscal chaos raised serious questions about what was "real" or "authentic." Banks failed by the hundreds; businesses cut back on production and payrolls; wages went down and unemployment went up. The so-called American Way of life was frequently revealed to be an American Dream.[7] All the while, President Herbert Hoover and his administration denied that there was any depression at all, insisting instead that the "downturn" was only temporary. In 1930, when a delegation came to Hoover seeking the im-mediate expansion of federally sponsored public works, he informed them: "Gentlemen, you have come sixty days too late. The Depression is over" (Levine, "Historian," 18). In spite of Hoover's denial, the plight of those who had long constituted and haunted the borders of the nation's economic order—the "ill-housed, ill-clothed, ill-fed," as Franklin D. Roosevelt later put it—now took center stage.

Populist and regionalist formulations of American identity reverberated in the shock waves of the crash of 1929. As a skeptical public grew increasingly more cynical, politicians, social reformers, journalists, and artists invoked various images of "the people" to render coherent the badly splintered imagined community of the nation. Yet, in the cautionary words of Michael Denning, "If language were politics, we would all be populists" (125).[8] One of the more infamous debates within the communist-leaning Left occurred in 1935 at the American Writers' Congress, when the literary theorist Kenneth Burke, in his speech "Revolutionary Symbolism in America," argued for the use of the term "the people" instead of "the worker," for its more "basic" address and mobilization (Burke 89).[9] Though Burke received a less than enthusiastic response for this suggestion, his speech augured a shift toward a more populist appeal: "If 'Third Period' communism talked incessantly of 'the proletariat,' the Popular Front tended to speak of 'the people'" (Alpers, *Dictators*, 11). Burke's semantic suggestion is but one instance of the period's populist turn. The ideological battles over "the people" were fought vociferously on the right and the left by demagogues such as Louisiana's crooked populist Huey Long and the fascist Father Coughlin, liberal centrists such as the New Dealers, and radical antiracist labor activists such as the Congress of Industrial Organizations (CIO) and the larger Popular Front—in Denning's useful terminology, the "cultural front"—the affiliation of leftists and radicals who aligned themselves with New Deal liberals against fascism (xiii–xx).

Within these competing expressions of the people, the folk were often posited as racialized relics of American authenticity and purity, the ballast from the past that anchored present imaginings of the national collective. Such usages were indebted to earlier iterations of the folk that emerged within the growing field of ethnographic folklore in the 1890s, and it is worth tracing that history briefly here for its relevance. Though its own distinct discipline, American folklore studies was built upon a European model originating in the counter-Enlightenment romantic nationalism that began to flourish in late eighteenth-century Germany. Folklore's most famous early interlocutor, the German philosopher and poet Johann Gottfried Herder, espoused the centrality of der Volk, "the people," and their language and customs in the organic, authentic development of the folk-nation (Herder, *Another Philosophy of History*, xxv). Articulating a vision of the nation-state that was patriotic but also culturally relativistic, Herder argued that folklore and other expressive forms best represented the "spirit of the times" (*Geist der Zeiten*) and the shape of national character in its particular historical moment (Bunzl, "Franz Boas," 20; Bendix, *In Search*, 41).[10] Herder's philosophy concretized "the modern invention of the 'folk' category" at the naissance of industrial modernity (Bendix 35).

Inspired by Herder's valuation of the folk and tradition as key to the creation of world history and national unity, Jacob and Wilhelm Grimm—the famous Brothers Grimm—set about preserving and promoting German folk poetry and lore against the encroachments of modernity (Bronner, *Following Tradition*, 190). The brothers viewed such material as cultural treasures presumed to contain a purity, simplicity, and vitality particular to the rural regions of Germany, such as Hesse, where the Grimms themselves had deep family roots (188). Entwining Romantic longings for authentic folk artistry with a desire for scientific method and rigor, the Grimms annotated, edited, and categorized the tales they compiled, successfully "artifactualizing" their collections for a growing audience of scholars and popular readers (Bendix 49; Stewart, *Crimes*, 105–6). In an adjacent movement, British Romantics such as William Wordsworth and Samuel Taylor Coleridge concentrated their poetry on common people of humble and rustic origins, attempting to narrate their passions in a "language really used by men" (Wordsworth, "Preface," para. 5). The embrace of peasant protagonists and a corresponding pastoral aesthetics provided part of the impetus for the study of folklore internationally in the nineteenth century. In 1846, the British antiquarian William Thoms coined the term *folklore*, bringing together such German and English precedents to propose "a good Saxon compound, Folklore,—*the Lore of the People*," as a replacement for Latinate terms such as "popular antiquities" and "popular literature" (qtd. in Emrich, " 'Folk-Lore,' " 361; Bronner, *Following Tradition*, 219). In particular, Thoms hoped to enlist "some James Grimm . . . who shall do for the Mythology of the British Islands the good service which that profound antiquary and philologist has accomplished for the mythology of Germany." Thoms's coinage espoused the Anglo-Saxon revivalism and its particular concept of Englishness that he hoped the practice of folklore collecting in England would further advance (Abrahams, "Phantoms," 9).

In the United States, Ralph Waldo Emerson and other American Romantics in the mid-nineteenth century drew upon similar ideas in their notion of the "common man," a seemingly classless, unspoiled, and democratically inclined individual—a self-reliant white man—who undertook the task of building the republic, be he learned or illiterate (Bendix 72–74). While Emerson and Henry David Thoreau aspired to the authentic simplicity of the common man in the 1830s and 1840s, others located authenticity in marginalized communities of the North American continent through a concept of the savage folk, following the evolutionary model of the day (McNeil, "Pre-Society Folklorists," 3).[11] By 1888, the year the American Folklore Society was first established, Emerson's "common man" had been granted a national history that included several intersecting folk populations who bore the imprint of the so-called New World rather than the Old. Hence, in the inaugural volume of the society's *Journal of American Folklore*, its editor, William Wells Newell, outlined their objectives: to spur "the collection of the fast-vanishing remains of Folk-Lore in America, namely . . . Relics of Old English Folk-Lore . . . Lore of Negroes in the Southern States of the Union . . . Lore of the Indian Tribes of North America . . . Lore of French Canada, Mexico, etc." (Newell, "Field and Work," 3). The folk were thus primarily conceived of as white Americans of "Anglo-Saxon" descent, African Americans, and Native Americans (Becker, *Selling Tradition*, 54–55; Grider, "Salvaging the Folklore," 26). This unstable tripartite racial formation was already under construction in the work of Americans who were folklorists before the inauguration of the society, local-color writers, and collectors who amassed the songs and stories of each group.[12]

W. E. B. Du Bois improvised upon this popular concept of the folk as he made the case for African American inclusion in the modern nation in *The Souls of Black Folk* (1903): "There is no true American music but the wild, sweet melodies of the Negro slave; the American fairy tales and folk-lore are Indian and African; and, all in all, we black men seem the sole oasis of simple faith and reverence in a dusty desert of dollars and smartness" (7). Here, too, Du Bois drew upon his knowledge of Herder's Romantic formulations of the folk's "cultural gift . . . as the foundation of national character," most likely gleaned from his postdoctoral education in Berlin at the Friedrich Wilhelm University (Allen, "Reading of Riddles," 59). At this point in his development as an intellectual, rather than assert the formulation of a discrete African American nationality and risk its suggestion of black political separatism, he would deploy the notion of racial ideals (Allen 62). He advocated "fostering and developing the traits and talents of the Negro, not in opposition to or contempt for other races, but rather in large conformity to the greater ideals of the American Republic, in order that some day on American soil two world-races may give each to each those characteristics both so sadly lack" (*Souls* 7).[13] By locating evidence of these racial gifts bequeathed to the nation in the music and folklore of African Americans and Native Americans, Du Bois asserted a rootedness in a folk past for groups left out of the nation's charmed circle. In this way, the claim to a folk past functioned as a persuasive bid for true national belonging.

Yet the folk were just as often used to demarcate the grounds of exclusion, as seen in the immigration debates over "real" Americans and "real" Americas in the 1920s. In tandem with an expanding Ku Klux Klan membership that included as many as four million members, concerned citizens encouraged Congress to take into account the fate of the "American race"—"a blend of various peoples of the so-called Nordic race"— against the encroaching threat of "mongrelization" (qtd. in Roediger, *Working toward Whiteness*, 139). The cry of "race suicide" issued from the fear that if (white) "American" families did not increase their birthrate, as Alys Weinbaum puts it, "the United States would quickly become a land comprised of the darker-hued progeny of prolific foreign-born immigrants from Southern and Eastern Europe and the descendents of African slaves" (*Wayward Reproductions*, 188). Such beliefs led to the passage of the xenophobic Immigration Restriction Acts of 1921 and 1924, which excluded Asians and all but prevented the immigration of Southern and Eastern Europeans. Such nativist sentiments shadowed the populist rhetoric of the folk in the Depression era.

The discourse of the folk emerged at the intersection of the decade's populism and regionalism, their imaginary local communities expressive of no single ideological orientation (Denning 132–33; Veitch 166n5). The folk were not synonymous with the people; rather, they were construed as regionally located ancestors or native others in competing conceptions of the people. Just who the folk were in the period's many regionalisms depended on whether you were listening on the radio to Father Coughlin, FDR, or John L. Lewis. Indeed, in right-wing diatribes, the folk were made to be representatives of rural, small-town values, the Protestant work ethic, and the great White Way, a group threatened by the recent influx of immigrants, African Americans, and women in the wage-labor workforce. From a liberal angle, the folk stood for the legions of dispossessed agricultural workers who had fallen victim to mechanized farming practices, greedy lenders, and a series of catastrophic natural disasters, a group cast white or "without race or ethnicity" (Denning 134). In the period's most radical formulations, the folk represented a regional touchstone for an antiracist labor movement, their industrial folklore emblematic of the transition from agriculture to industry.

Communist conceptions of the folk in the 1930s overlapped with such radical formulations, though they were often hampered by a kind of nationalist romance (Jarrett, *Deans*, 93). In the communist thinking of the period, the folk comprised a laboring preindustrial peasant class from the past, a basis upon which to build a socialist nation. During the Third Period (1928–35) in particular, the Communist Party USA offered the history of rural southern black labor and culture as evidence for its Black Belt nation thesis. That argument proposed that black people living in the Deep South constituted an oppressed nation within a nation deserving of recognition and sovereignty (Foley 173–76; Holloway, *Confronting the Veil*, 3). Some Marxist commentators presumed that rural black folk culture was oppositional by nature, a repository of proletariat feeling from an authentic American peasant class (Foley 184). In the same years, Stalin turned to Russian folk culture to locate "pre-proletarian folklore" expressive of the attitudes of "working masses from the past" (Dorson, *Folklore*, 18). The prerevolutionary laboring peasant functioned as a heroic antecedent to the modern-day peasant-cum-worker and "folklorism—politicized folk adaptation—became a major industry in the Stalin era" (Dorson 18; Stites, *Russian Popular Culture*, 78).[14] In the United States, a folksinger and fellow traveler such as Woody Guthrie would mine traditional folk songs for their revolutionary potential. Figured as precursors to the worker, the folk and their premodern popular culture—people's culture—were understood to express the stirrings of a nascent movement toward proletarian sovereignty and revolution.

As such examples demonstrate, the politics and cultural production of the thirties were shaped by competing conceptions of collective identity and the folk's central place within them. Roosevelt's New Deal attempted to steer the country out of its misery, not just by introducing a host of new social programs but also by strategically entering into this revived debate over the definition and identity of the nation and its citizenry. As Priscilla Wald observes, "Official stories constitute Americans" (*Constituting Americans*, 2). No administration understood this better than Roosevelt's. His New Deal seized upon the issue of the authentic folk to solve the problem of how to represent "the people," developing programs that set out to display the vernacular traditions of historically marginalized groups to tell a story of national fortitude and exceptionalism. Among these official forays into folk culture, the president and first lady personally hosted nine folk music concerts in the White House between 1934 and 1942 (Filene 134). These events mirrored the administration's cultural endeavors in the shape of the Farm Security Administration's photographic section, its funding of the Library of Congress's Archive of American Folk-Song in 1937, and the invention of Federal Project Number One. Under the auspices of Federal One, the Federal Writers' Project would unearth and recount the regional folklore and culture of the nation's states, towns, cities, and rural areas in its American Guide Series, publishing over a thousand books and pamphlets (Weigle, "Finding the 'True America,'" 62; Stott, *Documentary Expression*, 111).

With the radical folklorist B. A. Botkin at the helm of the folklore division of the Federal Writers' Project, Charles Seeger in charge of the Federal Music Project, and Alan and John Lomax directing the Archive of American Folk-Song, the New Deal officially joined in the decade's folk revival (Filene 137). Taking a cue from the fields of anthropology and folklore studies, these government agencies focused their rhetoric and their actions on cultural loss, adopting an updated model of salvage ethnography, the same imperative that inspired the founding of the American Folklore Society some forty-five years earlier. Each of these projects sent photographers, folklorists, ethnographers, and fieldworkers out to gather images, interviews, lore, and songs from the nation's local folk populations (Filene 136). As these professionals took up the project of many progressive reformers before them, investigating the assimilation process and "living lore" of recent immigrants, they redoubled their efforts to record the vulnerable dignity of "native-born" workers and "traditional" populations. Federal folklorists and others placed particular emphasis on groups who were viewed, in the words of the critical race theorist Devon Carbado, as "foreign in a domestic sense"

("Racial Naturalization," 639). Such groups were accorded a racially and temporally liminal status, subject to an "inclusionary form of exclusion," positioned both inside and outside the national imagination as "original" peoples (Carbado 638).

Within this iconography, Native Americans, African Americans, and poor rural whites were conscripted to embody an organic, precapitalist past seen as apparently antithetical to commercial modernity. Whereas Native Americans were often depicted as highly marketable relics of an already vanished frontier, impoverished African Americans were often represented as exotic, domestic "others." Poor rural whites, alternatively, were made to symbolize a nostalgic and "traditional" Anglo-Saxon identity. Each group may have been assigned its specific place in the Edenic past but the groups certainly were not treated equally. These representations shored up white privilege, providing a folksy precapitalist antecedent to the white figure of the "standard" citizen-consumer in the 1930s. Though African Americans and Native Americans were included within the imaginary purview of the nation's original peoples, they were still denied the material prerogatives of proper citizenship. In *Real Folks* I demonstrate, in part, how these purportedly disappearing groups were used by New Dealers and others to tell a story of capitalist progress, to show just how far the country had come.

The production of the folk was not simply ideological, but economic in scope. Though the Federal Writers' Project was legally prohibited from making a profit from its publications, the project was certainly intended to stimulate the nation's economy (Szalay, *New Deal Modernism*, 63). The New Deal, along with various vectors of popular culture, promoted America to Americans. Four out of the five bestselling novels of the thirties explored the search for security in history or on the land, with repressive gender and racial hierarchies firmly in place: *The Good Earth* (1931), *God's Little Acre* (1933), *Gone with the Wind* (1936), and *The Grapes of Wrath* (1939) (McElvaine, *Great Depression*, 221). Cultural loss and its preindustrial folk iconography thus became the occasion for a lucrative nostalgia, a nostalgia that ironically fortified capitalism, the very agent of "authentic" culture's destruction. Robert McElvaine, a historian, observes, "The past, like the ownership of a piece of land, offered a refuge for people distressed with the present and fearful of the future" (221). People bought into this strain of nostalgia, ideologically fixing and fixating on a stability that never was.

DOCUMENTING THE FOLK

The folk emerged in many articulations of populism and regionalism expressed primarily through the medium of documentary. As several critics have argued, the folk were an animating subject within the documentary movement of the thirties and the New Deal grasped the potential power of this icon and this medium. Alfred Kazin observed in his literary history *On Native Grounds* (1942) that the unprecedented crisis of the Depression precipitated a "literature of nationhood, beginning with the documentation of America . . . and reaching a thunderous climax in an effort to seek out the American tradition" (485). Kazin argues that documentary, in providing "a living record of contemporary American experience," constituted a means of "collective self-consciousness" and "national self-scrutiny" (485, 486). In his groundbreaking cultural history *Documentary Expression and Thirties America*, first published in 1973, William Stott built upon Kazin's work to launch his claim that "the primary expression of thirties America was not fiction but fiction's opposite . . . documentary . . . the communication, not of imagined things but of real things only" (xi). Stott made a powerful case for the centrality of documentary and its visual language of facts in the Depression's social reforms and conceptions of collectivity, and his account has become a touchstone in the study of the thirties. In this book, I reassess Stott's documentary synthesis, departing from his analysis in several ways: as he makes the case for documentary's preeminence in the thirties and its concern for marginalized groups, he overlooks other genres—the hybrid forms that, I will show, take up this cause with equal fervor (cf. Denning 119). As important, Stott discounts the degree to which documentary contains various fictional modes within it.

Nevertheless, I am indebted to Stott's critical formulation of documentary as a genre. Beginning with the coinage of the term *documentary* in 1926 by the British filmmaker John Grierson, to describe the "creative treatment of actuality," Stott undertook the task of establishing documentary as a genre unto its own, "as distinct as tragedy, epic or satire" (ix).[15] He convincingly linked together a vast range of cultural projects that manifested, in his words, a documentary motive and imagination, including Edward R. Murrow's radio broadcasts; popularized social worker case histories and other social science writing; serialized soap operas; the wpa's travel guides; picture magazines including *Life* and

Look; Martha Graham's ballets *American Document* and *Appalachian Spring*; and documentary books such as Dorothea Lange's and Paul Taylor's *An American Exodus* and Margaret Bourke-White's and Erskine Caldwell's bestseller *You Have Seen Their Faces*. For Stott, these texts illustrated documentary's conventions: its appeal to emotion as a means of persuasion; its tone of immediacy; its "cult of experience," to quote Philip Rahv, from his article of that title (8); its embrace of the visual record as its primary forms of evidence; its function as a form of populist propaganda for various social and political causes; its romantic and sentimental focus on the common people, the proletariat, and the folk, or in Stott's words, "the worker, the poor, the jobless, the ethnic minorities, the farmer, the sharecropper, the Negro, the immigrant, the Indian, the oppressed and the outlaw" (53), people presumed to be "more real" (56) than the celebrities and elites who occupied so much of the media's attention. As Stott's list suggests, the featured subjects of thirties documentary shared a hazy class-based association: each group was presumed to be "the salt of the earth," authentic by virtue of their representativeness as members of the urban industrial working class, the rural poor, and the racially and economically disenfranchised (53).

Kazin and Stott were surely right about the fixation within documentary on these groups as the lifeblood of American identity—its nationalist protagonists—and the genre's concomitant preoccupation with authenticity. In a sense, the link between documentary photography and the folk is so established that it is often taken for granted. Specifically attending to the camera in their discussions, both Kazin and Stott identified documentary's central role in the creation of the folk, illuminating a crucible of new technologies, disciplines, and institutions in the 1930s that made this representation possible (Kazin, *On Native*, 512).

Indeed, if photography provided one means of recording the folk and the primitive for the incipient disciplines of folklore and anthropology at the turn of the century, by the thirties, the camera had become the primary tool through which the folk were visualized. Technological innovations almost guaranteed the ubiquity of the still and moving image in the Depression era. The convenience of smaller, hand-held cameras fitted with built-in viewfinders and less cumbersome flash units, the invention of faster film, and improvements in photomechanical reproduction, as well as the availability of more affordable automobiles, enabled a new way of accounting for America by rendering its places and people more easily accessible and visible (Solomon-Godeau, *Photography*, 62). A more agile style of photography became possible, giving rise to the large-scale expansion of street photography and photojournalism and the inception of the first big picture magazines (Tagg, *Burden*, 181; Scott, *Street Photography*, 57). Terry Smith describes how, as photography "became the dominant visual media in the United States, not just within the imagery of reform but within visual culture as a whole. . . . it became more and more harnessed to the job of circulating images of products and ambience, to promoting the spectacle of consumption" (*Making the Modern*, 286). The cinema promoted such images as well. In the late 1920s, motion pictures gained sound and color, a flourishing production industry, and modern theaters for screening, advances that augmented their quality of indexical realism and their popularity as a form of leisure entertainment and civic edification (Muscio, *Hollywood's New Deal*, 11–12, 68, 71). Through the Hollywood studio and star system of the 1930s, the film industry consolidated into a "national cinema" that articulated a new Americanism across classes and regions (2, 65, 74–77). The iconography of the folk materialized somewhere in the improbably shared terrain of social reform, leisure entertainment, and the marketplace—the space between realism and fantasy.

As the broad contours of Stott's study suggest, the communication of "real things only" was never entirely independent from the realm of fiction and its representations of the imagined. In contemporary film studies, the degree to which documentary and fictional forms inhabit one another has almost become a truism (Renov, *Theorizing Documentary*, 3; Rhodes and Springer, *Docufictions*, 3–6; Rabinowitz, *They Must Be Represented*, 24). Michael Renov argues: "Fictional and nonfictional forms are enmeshed in one another—particularly regarding semiotics, narrativity and questions of performance" (2). Given the considerable scholarship devoted to the discursive modalities of documentary, the study of documentary's enmeshment with particular *kinds* of fictional genres and tropes may be more to the point. Bourke-White's and Caldwell's documentary book *You Have Seen Their Faces*, for example, exploits a range of fictional modes including sentimentality, melodrama, and stereotype to depict its subjects—poor southern sharecroppers—as nonthreatening, even comic castoffs from an unjust and outdated economic system. The affective registers of these fictional modes—be they sympathy, estrangement, humor, outrage, or guilt—establish the parameters through which the reader encounters the work's central characters. And those characters represent an iteration of the folk.

In Stott's version of the thirties, social realism and documentary rule the day as they petition for liberal social reform on behalf of "[society's] most deprived and powerless subjects," the folk among them (56). But, as I have suggested, this account largely ignores the complex fictional elements *within* documentary, much less the presence of hybrid genres perhaps more difficult to categorize, modes that also cohered around the figure of the folk to lodge a form of social protest. It would be easy to set up documentary as the earnest purveyor of the folk and satire as its wayward foil. Yet that explanation doesn't make room for the many documentaries and ethnographies of the period that undermined the authentic aura of the folk they set out to represent. Nor does it allow for the ways that the satires often delivered their final punch through the reportorial straight face of documentary. Such an opposition ignores the methods of social persuasion shared by these genres, their live wire of irony and their delight in overturning the presumed spatiotemporal distance that structures the gaze of the ethnographer, the middle-class observer, and the folk.

Something more incongruous is afoot. As Bertolt Brecht explains, "Indignation at inhuman conditions can be stimulated in many ways, by direct description of a pathetic or matter-of-fact kind, by narrating stories and parables, by jokes, by over- and understatement" ("The Popular and the Realistic," 110). Brecht's insight encompasses both documentary and satire. What Michel Foucault observes of the "historical disciplines" applies to the presumed divide between documentary and satire in the thirties: "We must not imagine that these two [forms] have crossed without recognizing each other. In fact, the same problems are being posed in either case, but they have provoked opposite effects on the surface" (*Archaeology*, 6). Indeed, both genres are dependent upon realism for their articulation and authority, documentary presumed to be a transparent transcription of nonfictional reality and truth, and satire, a deeply exaggerated, fictional representation of reality that nevertheless conveys a highly mediated commentary about the status of the truth. In this way, though manifestly different in tone and style, they are each fundamentally propelled by the enunciation of a set of truth-claims, however provisional and incomplete.

The genres of satire and documentary are porous and expansive, unfinished, impure. They inhabit one another. As Wai Chee Dimock suggests, "The membership—of any genre—is an open rather than closed set, because there is always another instance, another empirical bit of evidence, to be added. . . . [Literature] will never solidify into a congealed shape. Its force of incipience pulls and strains against all taxonomic regimes. The spilling over of phenomena from labels stands here as an ever-present likelihood, a challenge to any systemizing claim" ("Introduction," 1378). Dimock then asks what would happen if literary studies were "organized by genres, in this unfinished sense, with spillovers front and center?" In its "unfinished sense," genre becomes hybrid and refuses the containment of the very taxonomic regimes from which it seems to issue. This generic propensity actively undermines the production of the folk as ossified type. It is no wonder, then, that the issue of genre, a taxonomy of representation, comes to the fore in an interrogation of the folk, a taxonomy of personhood. In her own performance as simultaneous folk informant and folklorist, an ethnographer such as Hurston enacts a tangible "spilling over . . . from labels." The hybrid texts in this study necessarily trouble the notion of genre as fixed. With the concept of hybridity—texts that enact their satire, in part, by adopting the tone and subject of documentary reportage and texts that document by way of satire's insurrectionary methods—I intend to place the "spillovers" between these two modes of representation front and center.[16] The "impossible purity" of the folk is rendered visible through the impurity—the hybridity—of genre (Brody, *Impossible Purities*, 11).

TOWARD A RADICAL COMPLICITY

In deposing social realism's hold on the thirties by highlighting a previously obscured hybrid aesthetic, my study joins other recent scholarship. In his important work *The Cultural Front*, for example, Michael Denning argues for the predominance of a kind of "social modernism" whose aesthetic innovations conformed to the logic of the oxymoron (122). Following the ruminations of Kenneth Burke on the political work of the grotesque, Denning equates social modernism with the revolutionary symbolism of the "proletarian grotesque." The proletarian grotesque is a trope that deploys the grotesque, such as "the gargoyles that open *Citizen Kane*, the accident-victim photographs in Weegee's *Naked*

City . . . the gigantic head of Mussolini in Peter Blume's *Eternal City*," in order "to wrench us out of our repose and the distance of the 'aesthetic'" (122–23). It is a way of seeing that potentially realigns our class allegiances. Denning's proletarian grotesque offers a broader insight into the Popular Front's strategies of representation: it shows how the arts of the Popular Front pushed genre into excess as a vehicle for protest, how they burlesqued, dismantled, and refigured typical narrative formulas and codes to shake their readers and viewers loose from a practice of passive reception. This strategy of disillusion through illusion moves away from populist oversimplification, toward a critical reading practice and a possible reconception of progressive politics. Given their penchant for burlesque as a form of satire, Schuyler and West might be understood to anticipate the Popular Front's aesthetic strategies in the early 1930s, and Sturges might be understood to ironically reflect upon them in the early 1940s. In their modernist burlesques, each artist pushed genre into excess, combining high with low.

In modifying *burlesque* with *modernist*, I name a distinct formation of burlesque that satirically and politically unmasks popular narratives of self-making as conveyed through the latest modernized technologies of mass production and media. I choose the word *burlesque* for its grotesque, imitative, and overtly theatrical meanings: as a noun, it is a form of literary or dramatic caricature or a "grotesque imitation of what is, or is intended to be, dignified or pathetic, in action, speech, or manner" (*Oxford English Dictionary*). Although in its current usage, *burlesque* is linked almost exclusively with "girly shows"—an association that began with the burlesque "leg" shows of the nineteenth century and was solidified at the famous Minsky brothers' nightclub in the 1930s—as the usage patterns in the *Oxford English Dictionary* suggest, in the nineteenth century and the early twentieth this genre of performance was far more diverse and complex (Lewis, *Traveling Show*, 195; Glenn, "Taking Burlesque Seriously," 93). Susan Glenn explains that burlesque connoted a "mocking, irreverent humor" wrought out of "parodic imitation of literary and theatrical texts and styles . . . as well as contemporary social, cultural and political fashions and foibles" (93).

While its earliest usage extends in Europe back to the seventeenth century, burlesque has more recent ties to specific forms of American popular theater, such as vaudeville and minstrel shows and other ambivalent acts of impersonation and self-making. Such acts naturalized (and denaturalized) authentic identity through visual performance. Within this era of theatrical spectacle, burlesque emerges as a parodic citation of the performative. Each text of modernist burlesque in this study knowingly features a protagonist whose deployment of performativity in front of an audience consolidates rather than undoes the power of racial discourse and other discourses of authenticity.[17] The performative as it works *within* each plot fulfills this conservative function. Yet, in a secondary register, the actual readers of the text are made critically to *see* this operation in action. We are made to comprehend just *how* the open dramatization of performativity shores up discourses of authenticity by way of a triangulated dynamic of looking whereby we watch the textual audience as they watch the performance on display. In this way, modernist burlesque demonstrates the ideological workings of performativity in cultural narratives of authenticity.

Indeed, George Schuyler seized upon the burlesque and its performative dimensions to describe his own satire, *Black No More*: "I have tried to deal with [racism] as a civilized man; to portray the spectacle as a combination madhouse, burlesque show and Coney Island" (qtd. in Mills, "Absurdity," 2). Around this time, in 1931, the folklorist Constance Rourke, in her groundbreaking book *American Humor: A Study of the National Character*, forecast Bakhtinian notions of the carnivalesque as she reflected upon the "lawless" energies of burlesque that had overtaken American theater one hundred years earlier: "To sustain burlesque something more than grotesquerie is needed. Satire enters into its attentions; once a territory is invaded by burlesque, all its objects are likely to look puffed and stretched, pinched and narrowed. But pure satire stands aloof, while burlesque wholly possesses its subject and wears the look of friendship" (110, 101).[18] Rourke underscores the edge and the danger of burlesque, that by inhabiting the subject of its mockery, it risks giving the initial appearance of sanction, of perpetuating the inanities it means to upend. Along these lines, Fred Moten reminds us that "modes of radical performativity or subversive impersonation are always already embedded in the structure they would escape" (*In the Break*, 2). In its strategic imitation, burlesque both invokes and forecloses the affective structures and desires that cohere in the subject of its derision; such are the friendly, even erotic, energies of burlesque as it lays its subject bare.

The burlesque disturbs. The authors' distance from their "material is always a bit uncertain," and the same goes for the readers, who are temporarily transported into the grotesque spectacle through the surface plot's drive toward revenge or sympathy (Marcus, *Mystery Train*, 102). In the examples of Schuyler's and West's novels, each plot attempts to manipulate the reader through affect in its twisted denouement: Schuyler's *Black No More* enjoins its readers to wish revenge on the white supremacists in the scenes leading up to their lynching, and West's *A Cool Million* elicits a momentary tinge of sorrow for its protagonist Lem as he is assassinated and then mourned as a martyr for the fascist party at the rally that concludes the novel. At the peak of violence in each text, readers must recoil from the duped majority—from the crowds, audiences, and dominant communities represented in each text—the people who (perhaps unwittingly) "buy into" the ideological system under review. Only the readers' unfolding recognition of their own manipulation within this scene prevents their interpellation within a white-supremacist, fascist script. Notably, modernist burlesque accomplishes this alienation effect when it most closely imitates documentary, adopting a reportorial tone and perspective that recounts such atrocities in graphic detail, a mode in stark contrast with the grotesque absurdities that surround it (Brecht, "Alienation Effects," 91). These novels avoid populism's temptation, its collective unification of "the people" against an "external enemy," an oversimplified "us" versus "them" (Žižek, "Against the Populist Temptation," 557).[19] By advocating a critical insider/outsider position for its readers, these texts espouse socialist ideals while taking an antipopulist stance. Moreover, they disallow any easy recourse to a liberal politics of empathy.[20] For these reasons, burlesque is often a risk the Left feels it cannot afford. Schuyler and West took that risk and, as a consequence, their work has been largely ignored or unrecognized in accounts of the leftist aesthetics of the thirties.

Neither Schuyler nor West situates himself or his readers *outside* of mass culture, where they both worked in other capacities, as a journalist and a screenwriter respectively. Theirs is a complicity critique in which the reader is implicated (Pfister, "Complicity Critiques," 610, 620–23; Stott 26–30; Marcus 114). In Schuyler's and West's positioning of their readers, they reenact a familiar modernist plotline but with a crucial difference: in the standard account of modernism, as Douglas Mao and Rebecca Walkowitz observe, it was "a movement by and for a certain kind of high (cultured mandarins) as against a certain kind of low (the masses, variously regarded as duped by the 'culture industry,' admirably free of elitist self-absorption, or simply awaiting the education that would make the community of cognoscenti a universal one)" ("New Modernist Studies," 738). Schuyler's and West's burlesques replay the story of modernism from a progressive political perspective. In their critique of commodity culture, the masses *are* duped by the "culture industry" along with the patriotic slogans of the nation-state and the racist, misogynist spectacles of advanced capitalism. Yet, the community of cognoscenti is not composed of apolitical, cultured mandarins who stay above it all through the transcendence of high art. Rather, in the destructive clearing of modernist burlesque, this community is made up of those who are able to perceive the ideological implications of uncritical consumption by way of their own *proximity* to that practice.

Undeniably, this is a chastening model. West and Schuyler produce a reader who in the words of Matthew Roberts "is 'critical' by way of his [or her] very complicity in the ideological mechanisms of mass culture" ("Bonfire," 65). What we are left with in these works, then, is a self-conscious reading practice, a perspective from which to reenvision progressive imaginaries and enact new alliances. It is not for nothing that Schuyler's and West's leftist activism in the early thirties—Schuyler's founding of black consumer cooperatives and West's efforts at unionizing Hollywood—coincided with the writing of these novels.[21] Arguably, these efforts were mutually reinforcing. Proceeding with the knowledge of their own complicity within the intractable conduits of commodity culture they criticized, a position that might lead to resignation, Schuyler and West instead strove to transform the structural frameworks of production and consumption they confronted on a daily basis.

In a sense, modernist burlesque plays with an insider/outsider paradigm central to the discipline of anthropology's embrace of participant observation fieldwork at this time. If modernist burlesque proceeds from "the look of friendship," from intimate proximity to critical distance, the ethnographies based upon participant observation most often move in an opposite direction. They trace the journey of an outsider-become-insider who alternates between both positions to achieve the experiential authority of the ethnological informant coupled with the critical objectivity of the ethnographer-observer. Hurston's *Mules and Men* is a tour de force of signifying ethnography: Hurston plays herself as an anthropologist outsider and a folk insider, entwining these stock roles into a Möbius strip of authenticity and performativity. A mediator between her subject and her audience, she signifies on the colonial and imperialist entanglements of anthropology and her readers' concomitant expectations of a preindustrial folk, real in their simplicity, out of time and removed from the circuits of modernity. By the book's end, her readers become most aware of Hurston's performance in staging the folk and their own press for authenticity. As Daphne Lamothe argues, Hurston and other "native ethnographers" like her deploy "a black modernist gaze"; they insist upon "a way of seeing that dislocates ways of [anthropological] knowing" (2, 3). Citing the conventions of modernist anthropology, particularly its emphasis on participant observation fieldwork, wherein the researcher forms personal relationships with community informants and participates in the life of the group, Hurston shows her readers how these conventions produce the image of the folk—and she makes them aware of their own complicity in the process.

EXTRAVAGANT INCONGRUITIES IN THE ARCHIVE

Though the racial and regional identities of the folk shift from text to text, the logic of the folk, their commodification, and appropriation is the thread that binds these disparate works together in this study. Although each of these texts addresses the construction and deployment of the folk in the thirties, they have nevertheless rarely been brought into conversation with each other, because of the bounds of periodization, genre, and politics. In assembling this unconventional archive around the figure of the folk, I hope to dismantle some of the false distinctions that support the conceptualization of discrete cultural lineages emanating from the New Deal, modernism, and the Harlem Renaissance. By necessity, I am attempting to draw together more tightly several already overlapping conversations about the trajectory of black modernist production, the work of the cultural front, and the documentary thrust of the thirties. My thematic emphasis inevitably includes artists who fall both within and outside of the parameters of the Left. Though writers such as Nathanael West and George Schuyler were avowed if idiosyncratic radicals, artists such as Zora Neale Hurston and the filmmaker Preston Sturges are considerably more difficult to classify in terms of their personal politics. This constitutes but one productive incongruity within this book's own archive.

Such incongruous considerations and pairings are built upon revisionist scholarship that challenges the orthodoxies of academic inquiry into
the 1930s and 1940s, primarily the assumption of a one-to-one correspondence between communist political affiliation and social realism. This
book owes much to scholarship that breaks with this portrayal—work by
Rita Barnard, Sara Blair, Michael Denning, Brent Hayes Edwards, Barbara
Foley, Rena Fraden, Robin D. G. Kelley, William Maxwell, Bill V. Mullen,
Cary Nelson, Paula Rabinowitz, James Smethurst, Michelle Stephens,
Jonathan Veitch, Alan Wald and Mary Helen Washington—which instead
interrogates the vexed political identities and interracial and international
formations of the literary Left and its multifaceted mainstream and experimental cultural production.[22] Each scholar insists upon the imbrications
of class and race, a point often neglected in considerations of Depression-
era culture. Following these recent methodological innovations, my
work assumes that the literary and cultural practices of American class
conflict in the 1930s cannot be separated from their racial or their gendered dimensions.

I am also indebted to revisionist scholarship on the thirties which departs from more biographically oriented criticism to elaborate upon debates among an ideologically diverse, even politically antagonistic group
of writers and intellectuals—in the case of Susan Hegeman's *Patterns for
America* (1999), debates regarding culture and "regional diversity and
class-based artistic movements," and in the case of Michael Szalay's *New
Deal Modernism* (2000), debates regarding "the literary politics of the
welfare state" (Hegeman 13; Szalay 16). Following their labors, I pursue
the rhetoric of the folk as it is dismantled in the resistant reading practices of an unlikely set of hybrid texts and incongruous voices.

To illuminate the hybrid variations of satire and documentary as they
merge to query the folk, the book's chapters are ordered in three sections
intended to build on each other. I begin with modernist burlesque, then
turn to signifying ethnography, and conclude with a return to modernist
burlesque, a structure that might seem to reinforce the division between
satire and documentary that I mean to blur. What I hope to show,
instead, are variations of this hybrid genre in texts that individually
speak to one another in close conversation and that collectively tell a
quasi-chronological story of the folk and its critiques in the 1930s. The
first part of the book, "The Folklore of Racial Capitalism," examines
George Schuyler's *Black No More* and Nathanael West's *A Cool Million*,

two modernist burlesque novels that strikingly forecast the vexed role of the folk in the nation's racialized political economy. Following Jonathan Veitch's work on West, I use the title "The Folklore of Racial Capitalism," combining "the folklore of capitalism" (Thurman Arnold's phrase for the symbolism and mythology of capitalism) with the term "racial capitalism" to describe the cultural narratives that gird a Jim Crow economy (Veitch 88; Arnold, *Folklore of Capitalism*, 1). Schuyler and West suggest that the maintenance and profitability of the color line depend upon the violent production of raced and gendered bodies as spectacle and invisible threat for a paying audience. The book's opening chapter turns to *Black No More*, a burlesque of the novel of racial passing that shows how racial authenticity is both capitalized upon and produced within consumer capitalism. In a bid for social mobility, the novel's black protagonist, Max Disher, is turned white through a mechanical procedure called Black-No-More invented by a black scientist, and soon the rest of the country's black population follows suit. Once Max occupies the privileged position of white masculinity, he markets his skills as a public speaker to corporations and white-supremacist organizations, who hire him to advance racist propaganda among white workers. Tracing the manufacture, promotion, and regulation of race in the novel, I argue that *Black No More* illuminates new market possibilities for the trade of racial property in commodity form during the Fordist era. In this way, the novel augurs the period's enthusiastic commodification of the folk.

Schuyler's concerns dovetail with West's in his novella *A Cool Million*, the subject of chapter 2, which also makes visible the violent economics of white patriarchy and the myth of class mobility. In that novel, its plucky American boy hero, Lemuel Pitkin, is literally torn to pieces in his efforts to earn "an honest cool million." In a darkly comic way, both books give serious consideration to the menace of domestic fascism in the form of racial segregation and other modern racial systems several years in advance of the collective antifascist efforts of the cultural front in the mid- to late thirties. In a letter that Nathanael West wrote in 1939 to Saxe Commins, an editor at Random House, West made the case for his own prescience: "Did you ever read a book called *A Cool Million* that I wrote and that was published by Covici Friede? A lot of people think it is a pretty good one and that the reason it flopped is because it was published much too soon in the race toward Fascism. It came out when no one in this country except a few Jeremiahs like myself, took seriously the possibility of a Fascist America" (West, *Nathanael West*, 791). Schuyler's and West's books articulated this argument in the beginning of the decade and aimed it not just at the South, but at the nation as a whole. With stunning acuity, these novels not only skewered the racist populisms that prevented interracial working-class solidarity; they also prophesied the folk's patriotic function for the nation-state in crisis, as we see in the chapters that follow.

To be sure, the folk become decidedly folksy in the Federal Writers' Project's *Florida: A Guide to the Southernmost State*, the subject of chapter 3. This chapter opens up the middle section of the book, "Performing the Folk," initiating an exploration of signifying ethnography, this study's other hybrid formation of documentary and satire. Both chapters 3 and 4 examine the role of the folk in official and individual-authored texts as they perform competing narratives of regional and national identity. These accounts focus on the particular case of Florida and turn on the question of northern and southern reconciliation in the era of Jim Crow and the problem of the rural folk within "uneven modernity" (Hegeman 4). Precisely because the South was often viewed as a feudal exception to northern industrialism, it was also seen as a pristine, rural enclave of anachronistic folk cultures vanquished elsewhere by modern commerce. This perspective informs much of the Florida guide and its marketing of nostalgic temporalities. I turn to the guide then to track the ways it draws upon this iconography to formalize the folk's function in the New Deal's story of progress. The guide is this study's least hybrid but most polyvocal text in that it consists of sections authored by many different contributors. The chapter argues that the guide promotes the state's tourist appeal and the nation's economy through the lure of ethnography and the promise of a heretofore hidden folk tableau vivant composed of "crackers," Seminoles, and Negroes visible to the prospective automobile traveler. This pageant of authenticity conforms to the guide's strategy of populist synecdoche: the Yankee common-man visitor stands in for the modern white American collective, while Florida's native folk are relegated to the past and to the geographic margins of society.

If the Florida guide is the proverbial straight man of my archive, an example of what this study's other texts work against, it also performs something equally tricky: due to its polyvocality, the hegemonic depiction of the folk is contested within its own pages. The guidebook editors hired their staff of writers partly on the basis of where they came from and who they were, in hopes of efficiently employing ethnographers who were simultaneously informants. In this way, they would create a "native" travelogue of each region. Like almost every entry in the American Guide Series, the Florida guide is composed of chapters drafted by different writers; some of them—most notably, the sections penned by Zora Neale Hurston—contradict and complicate the construction of the folk advanced by other sections. Hurston upends the folk, drawing upon strategies perfected in her work of signifying ethnography about Florida and its black inhabitants, *Mules and Men*, published four years earlier, a text that elicits and refuses the reader's desires for the authentic folktale and teller. In an exploration of *Mules and Men*, chapter 4 contends that Hurston constructed herself simultaneously as a distanced anthropologist and an authentic representative of the folk as she collected the folklore of her home town of Eatonville, the camps in neighboring districts where African American laborers harvested turpentine, and finally, the voodoo subculture of New Orleans. As Hurston reenvisioned the geographical and gendered contours of her fieldwork, she created a modern narrative of her subjects. While much of the documentary and ethnography of the thirties asked where and how the folk fit into the nation, Hurston's text self-reflexively cornered its readers and the discipline of anthropology itself to ask somewhat rhetorically, "Just who wants to know?" In this way, her ethnography signifies on representations of the folk in the official populism of the New Deal.

In the third and last part of the book, "Populist Masquerade," I return to modernist burlesque in Preston Sturges's masterpiece *Sullivan's Travels* as it cycles through the mainstream conceptions of the folk by which the thirties are still remembered. Sturges reiterates Hurston's query and asks once more just *who* it is who wanted to *see* the folk. Chapter 5 picks up the question of spectatorship to analyze the ways the film contrasts and consolidates competing configurations of genre, popular desire, and audience. By attending to the protagonist Sullivan's masculine transformation and its relationship to genre and the racial and class politics of the Popular Front, my argument pursues an aspect of the film that has been largely ignored. In its genre crossings and its masquerade, the film parodies the most prominent populist tropes and folk iconographies of the Popular Front and the New Deal. As the film stages a dialectic between realist and antirealist genres, as it visibly enacts masquerade that fails, and as it depicts different movie audiences diegetically within its picture, the film preempts the actual audience's turn either to a posture of aesthetic distance, or, conversely, an attitude of liberal empathy. Instead, it encourages its audience to adopt a stance of critical distance that may or may not bring about a realignment of class allegiances.

These chapters home in on a powerful form of social commentary located in the performative dimensions and resistant reading practices of the hybrid genre of documentary and satire: they show how these hybrid forms undercut the thirties folk revival's claims of authenticity; how they reveal the manufacture of the folk in a narrative of commercial capitalism's progress; and how they expose the inner workings of populist and fascist ideology. By harnessing the force of the performative in the hybrid genres of modernist burlesque and signifying ethnography, these writers, photographers, and filmmakers set out to raze America's "folklore of racial capitalism."

All the while, they proceed from a question succinctly posed in James Agee's and Walker Evans's *Let Us Now Praise Famous Men*: "How was it we were caught?" (81). Agee repeatedly asks this question, first in the voice of one of his female subjects and then as a rhetorical mantra, transforming it into an existentialist plaint. As we see in the work of Schuyler and West, Hurston and Sturges, there are other ways of asking the question and other answers, too. All these artists begin with the assumption that they and their readers are caught—they are implicated— just as surely as the characters that populate their works and the folk who took center stage in the populist rhetorics of the Depression era. Enjoining their readers to ask, "How was it we were caught?," they call for a self- reflexive reading practice that perceives the seductions of the real and the authentic in narratives of self, community, and nation and the possibility that radical truths may be found in the most outrageous of fictions. It is this reading practice and its potential for a progressive critical politics that I pursue in the chapters that follow.

PART I
The Folklore
of Racial Capitalism

A writer who cannot completely embrace the cause of the oppressed racial minorities, Negro and Jew and others, will never be able to fight for or enter the new socialist order for which every civilized human being must contend.
—EDWARD DAHLBERG, "Fascism and Writers,"
American Writers' Congress (1935)

1. Ben Shahn, *Medicine Show, Huntingdon, Tennessee*, October 1935.
Library of Congress, Prints and Photographs Division, FSA-OWI Collection,
LC-USF33- 006165-M5.

Chapter 1.

"A Combination Madhouse, Burlesque Show and Coney Island": The Color Question in George Schuyler's *Black No More*

To be a poor man is hard, but to be a poor race in a land of dollars is the very bottom of hardships.—W. E. B. DU BOIS, *The Souls of Black Folk* (1903)

In 1934, both the *Daily Worker* and the *Negro Liberator* denounced George Schuyler as one of "the most vicious pen prostitutes plying his trade in the Negro press" (qtd. in Schuyler, *Black and Conservative*, 220). Schuyler earned this distinction by publishing in 1931 several articles deriding the Communist Party USA's legal support for the Scottsboro Boys, nine African American teenagers falsely accused of raping two white women on a freight run in Tennessee, and Angelo Herndon, the nineteen-year-old African American coal miner and leader of the local Young Communist League, who was indicted in 1932 under the charge of "insurrection" for organizing a hunger march of unemployed black and white protesters in Atlanta, Georgia. Schuyler believed that the Communist Party had "stolen" the *Scottsboro* case from the NAACP and cared little about its black defendants.[1] To him, their International Labor Defense committee capitalized on both trials as publicity-generating causes célèbres (187). At least this is what he gleefully recounts in his red-baiting, late-in-life memoir *Black and Conservative* (1966).

In spite of the far-right cast of his autobiography, the actual record of Schuyler's publications, activism, and affiliations tells a different tale, one more complex but no less outrageous. What Schuyler neglects to fully explain in his version of this confrontation with the communist press is his own reputation at the time as a radical, albeit a cynical and irreverent one. Throughout *Black and Conservative*, he downplays the fact that until the late 1930s he was very much a part of the African American Left: he became a member of the Socialist Party in 1921 (113); soon after, he joined the black socialist group, the Friends of Negro Freedom; he declared himself a "violent red" in a favorable review of an Upton Sinclair novel in 1925 ("New Books," 331), and he would describe himself as a socialist well into the 1930s; all the while, he wrote for radical publications (Ferguson, *Sage of Sugar Hill*, 5).[2] Although Schuyler was not a Marxist, he was a prominent progressive black intellectual, sometimes activist, for whom antiracist and class struggles were inseparable endeavors.[3] Surely, then, in 1934, the communist press scorned Schuyler so publicly due to their expectation of shared political sympathy, their expectation that at the very least, he would curb his famously caustic opinions in regard to the *Scottsboro* and *Herndon* cases.

Journalist, essayist, satirist, novelist, science fiction writer, street speaker, socialist, union member, advocate of "race mixing," atheist, raw foodist, affiliate of the John Birch Society—Schuyler was nothing if not unorthodox. The details of his life only add to his intrigue as a public figure. Schuyler came of age in the 1910s, having left behind his home town of Syracuse, New York, to enlist in the army. As a soldier traveling from base to base he was able to see a good deal of the United States, and he wrote his first satirical sketches for a military publication, *The Service*. Yet he bridled at the segregated constraints of military life and his shoddy treatment by civilians even when in uniform. Though he never spoke publicly of it, he eventually deserted and served nine months in prison before his discharge in 1918 (Ferguson 12–13). After working a variety of unskilled jobs in New York City, he returned to Syracuse to work as a hod carrier. There, he joined the International Hod Carriers Building and Common Laborers Union, Local 40, in 1922 (*Black and Conservative*, 117). He made his first foray into radical politics and public speaking when he joined the local division of the Socialist Party in Syracuse and became its educational director (113). Public speaking would become a lifelong and sometimes lucrative vocation for Schuyler. Among his many engagements, he spoke on behalf of the Brotherhood of Sleeping Car Porters at their inaugural meeting in August 1925, and in the 1930s and 1940s he toured the college and forum circuit addressing topics as varied as "Psychoanalyzing the

Negro," "Feminism and the Race Problem," and "Consumer's Cooperation" (113–15, 158, 164).

Notwithstanding Schuyler's newfound political alliances in Syracuse,
the place proved to be too sleepy for him. He moved back to New York
City, working once more as a manual laborer, wintering in a "hobohemian" community in the Bowery before landing a job at A. Philip Randolph's and Chandler Owner's journal, *The Messenger*, in 1923. He
worked there first as an office manager, then as a writer and a managing
editor until the journal folded in 1928. As an editor, he published literature and essays by Langston Hughes, Zora Neale Hurston, and other
luminaries of the Harlem Renaissance (Ferguson 17). In the 1920s and
1930s, he wrote for black publications such as *The Crisis*, *Opportunity*,
Phylon, and *Negro Digest*, as well as journals with large white readerships
such as *The Nation*, *Modern Quarterly*, H. L. Mencken's *American Mercury*, and Mike Gold's *New Masses* (Peplow, "George Schuyler," 21–22;
Ferguson 2). He also began writing for the *Pittsburgh Courier*, one of the
most popular black newspapers in the nation, a position that he would
hold for forty-four years until 1966; one that would provide a written
record of his political transformation as he gravitated toward the anticommunist paranoia of the Far Right in the 1950s and 1960s.

Around the time Schuyler became the "preeminent personality in Negro journalism" in the late 1920s, he married Josephine Cogdell, a journalist and former model who hailed from a wealthy, white Texan family
(Theophilus Lewis, qtd. in Ferguson 99). Wed in 1928, four months after
they met in the offices of *The Messenger*, the couple took up residence in
Sugar Hill, Harlem's most exclusive neighborhood. In 1931, they had a
baby girl, Philippa Schuyler, who would soon be known as a child prodigy, playing the piano at age three and a half and composing by the age of
five. Philippa's exceptional intelligence and achievements served as proof
of the couple's theory of "race mixing" as a means of attaining "hybrid
vigor," in their view, the biological trump card that would dismantle the
canard of white supremacy at the core of the nation's racist structure
(Talalay, *Composition*, 13–14; Ferguson 76, 151). The Schuylers tempered
their biological theories with a nod to nurture as well, believing that their
efforts to raise Philippa following the recommendations of the behavior-
ist John Watson and a strict dietary regime of raw food had fostered her
extraordinary abilities as much as her biological inheritance.

As Schuyler established himself both personally and professionally, he filed investigative reports on controversial topics in the nation and abroad. The *Pittsburgh Courier* sent him on a tour of the South in 1926 to document the living conditions of the region's black residents; the *New York Evening Post* commissioned him to go to Liberia in 1931 to report on the selling of young male laborers to Spanish plantations off the coast of Nigeria; and the NAACP sponsored a trip with Roy Wilkins to investigate the exploitation of black workers on the Mississippi Flood Control Project in 1932 (Ferguson 19–20; *Black and Conservative*, 198). For Schuyler, these excursions further illuminated the striking correspondence between domestic racism and fascism and imperialism in the international realm, providing the basis for his novel *Slaves Today: A Story of Liberia* (1931) and his later serialized epic fictions, "Black Empire" and "Black Internationale," published in the *Pittsburgh Courier* in the late 1930s.

Schuyler's international perspective would also sharpen the political bite of his best-known novel, *Black No More: Being an Account of the Strange and Wonderful Workings of Science in the Land of the Free, A.D. 1933–1940* (1931), a satirical work of science fiction published at the height of his long, remarkable career. That novel advanced Schuyler's critique of race as absurd but essential to the workings of market capitalism. Its plotline brought together the themes of many of his most vitriolic editorials, including his rants against the glut of skin lighteners and bleaches on the market for black consumers (Ferguson 111); his screed against the mob mentality that pervaded American social life and politics; his debunking of the propensity of white and black leftists in the Harlem Renaissance and the Great Depression to romanticize the folk (93); his wary assessment of the technological progress of "machine civilization" (Schuyler, "Views," 6); his contention that America's claims of spreading democracy would mask the importation of Jim Crow race relations to other regions of the world (Ferguson 136); and his overarching view that the United States was embroiled in nothing less than an "economic race war" (121).

Black No More begins with a black scientist's invention of a machine able to turn black people white and follows the twists and turns of a citizenry rapidly adopting "pork-colored skin" (19). For contemporary readers, this outline might seem to augur colorblindness and other "race-blind" policies advocated by present-day black neoconservatives such as Shelby Steele, Thomas Sowell, and Ward Connerly.[4] The novel

might even be read to exemplify the prediction by the progressive sociologist Orlando Patterson that in the new millennium, race will be
supplanted by class by means of "biotechnology," as he stated in an
editorial entitled "Race Over" in the January 2000 edition of the *New
Republic.*[5] Yet, Schuyler's text provides a conclusion that is radically
different from Patterson's priority of class as well as the black neoconservatives' promotion of colorblindness.[6] In *Black No More*, race cannot
simply disappear; rather, it is made and remade in the context of cultural
and social shifts. It is inextricably bound to capitalism, a relationship
constitutive of the nation's "modern racial regime."[7]

Most likely speaking to fellow leftists who prioritized class as the primary source of structural inequality over and above race, Schuyler anticipates and ultimately rejects "either/or" formulations like Patterson's
opposition of race and class.[8] Instead, he unveils the violence of race in
America as it is manifested in market-driven formulations of identity:
his story speaks to fantasies and anxieties about increasing urban industrialization, racial assimilation, and the reproduction of raced bodies
in the black modernist moment. This chapter investigates the ways in
which race is manufactured and regulated through several sites of reproduction in the novel, including theatrical staging, assembly-line mass
production, and biological procreation. In each of these instances,
Schuyler's protagonist capitalizes on race as a highly commercial, free-
floating sign: while passing for white, he sells blackness and whiteness for
personal gain. In his racial passing, he quite literally performs to collect,
a plot of impersonation that proves to be central to modernist literary
experimentation, whether in the realm of fiction or ethnography. Speaking more broadly, as Schuyler burlesques conventional narratives of race
by enacting them, his book's mocking impersonations are heavily indebted to the minstrel tradition as well as the novel of racial passing. In
making the theatrical workings of such performances overt, by underscoring their mass commercial appeal, and by showing how they are
animated by the era's new Fordist possibilities for mass production and
consumption, Schuyler works in a mode best characterized as modernist
burlesque. He alludes to this particular satirical method in a letter to his
fellow satirist H. L. Mencken: "I have tried . . . to portray the spectacle [of
the color question] as a combination madhouse, burlesque show and
Coney Island" (qtd. in Mills, "Absurdity," 2). As we shall see, this explanation illuminates the intersection between his satirical work and

Nathanael West's and their mutual debt to vaudeville's topsy-turvy staple of cross-class, cross-race, and cross-gender impersonation as a means of exposing the absurdity of their subject, racial capitalism, a debt the filmmaker Preston Sturges shares as well.

Given the critical role of masquerade and self-making in the plot of *Black No More*, it is not surprising that gender is a central node in Schuyler's critique. Harnessing performance and mechanically repro-ductive technologies to the making of race, the scientific invention of Black-No-More supplants and usurps the racialized function of mater-nal labor for entrepreneurial aims (Mullen, "Optic White," 77). In this gendered transaction, it is the male characters in the book who deploy theatrical and technological modes of making race in order to comman-deer the central role of female biological reproduction in the production of racialized bodies and narratives of national belonging and exclusion. Yet counter to this plotline of male appropriation and the misogynist cast of many satires, the skepticism of the black women characters in the novel provides a vital model of critical reception for the reader.

Tracing a series of financial transactions in the novel that center on the manufacture of race, I argue that *Black No More* illuminates new market possibilities for the trade of racial property in commodity form during the Fordist era. In this way, Schuyler's narrative offers a complex and pre-scient understanding of race, gender, and capitalism in the interwar period, one that allows us to reconfigure prevailing concepts of the cul-tural production of the Harlem Renaissance and the Great Depression, and that portends our contemporary negotiations with mass-mediated identity and consumer culture on a global scale.

Curiously, for all of its modern-day relevance, Schuyler's writing has often been neglected in the conventional historiography of the Harlem Renaissance and the Depression. In most accounts and collections of black literary production in 1920s and 1930s, Schuyler's work receives short shrift, except for his typically provocative exchange in 1926 in *The Nation* with Langston Hughes about the meaning of black art.[9] This may have to do with Schuyler's later renunciation of progressive politics and turn to the right after the Second World War, epitomized by his eventual membership in the ultraconservative John Birch Society. Though there are notable exceptions[10]—most recently, Jeffrey B. Ferguson's critical bi-ography *The Sage of Sugar Hill* (2005)—present-day critics who examine Schuyler's work in the 1930s have often read it through the scrim of his

Cold War conversion, a revisionist move Schuyler colludes with in his autobiography, narrating himself in the 1920s and 1930s as a spy busy keeping himself "abreast of the Communist conspiracy" (*Black and Conservative*, 147).[11]

Neither Schuyler's later political self-characterization nor his choice of genre—modernist burlesque—should prevent us from seeing the radical and iconoclastic politics of much of his own interwar writing. Indeed, a reading of Schuyler's *Black No More* that attends to its outrageous yet trenchant materialist critique opens up a fertile avenue of inquiry into the literary production of the Harlem Renaissance, a social movement described as "a cultural nationalism of the parlor" and famously criticized by Langston Hughes, for its failure to raise the wages of "ordinary Negroes," and by Richard Wright, for its corrupt "liaison between inferiority-complexed Negro 'geniuses' and burnt-out white Bohemians with money" (Lewis, *When Harlem Was in Vogue*, xxviii; Hughes, *The Big Sea*, 228; Wright, "Blueprint," 1403). In these assessments, the Harlem Renaissance emerges as a tepid, bourgeois, and largely unsuccessful exercise in accommodation across the color line. Yet where does black modernist satire fit into these accounts? Few would disagree that satire offers a powerful vector of protest, one that is raucous, caustic, and no less angry than the literary mode most commonly denoted by "protest"— urban realism (Dickson-Carr, *African American Satire*, 2). Perhaps African American satire and its hybrid forms have been overlooked because they forgo the realist expectations and heavy burden of veracity that have weighed down black writers since the evidentiary aims of nineteenth-century slave narratives. By unseating our conventional conceptions of politically engaged fiction—if we momentarily depose urban realism— we might transform our notions of the Harlem Renaissance and the literary Left of the 1930s. We might recognize how other forms of fiction such as modernist burlesque occasioned paradigm shifts in a progressive key, performing the more abstract but no less important work of making readers see anew with regard to the social and material aspects of their world. This criterion extends the category of literature concerned with capitalism and race relations beyond the parameters of the social protest genre and its explicitly proletariat focus to include works that traverse new labor processes and class forces through a deeply satirical or ironic lens, texts such as Schuyler's novel, Rudolph Fisher's *The Walls of Jericho* (1928), Nella Larsen's *Quicksand* (1928), Wallace Thurman's *Infants of the*

Spring (1932), Langston Hughes's own *The Ways of White Folks* (1934), and others (Schockett, "Modernism," 34; Dickson-Carr 10, 69).

If we take into account the modernist burlesque of the Harlem Renaissance and its often absurdist and violent truth-claims, an alternative genealogy of that period emerges, one that centers writing explicitly engaged with racial capitalism and the vagaries of race as commodity in the marketplace. This genealogy might also illuminate the ways that the antiracist, materialist narratives of New Negro writers were often international in scope and how, by the early thirties, their work had established a precedent for the antiracist, antifascist allegories of Orson Welles and other efforts of the cultural front later in the decade (Denning, *Cultural Front*, 394–402). This chapter locates bold continuities between the modernist burlesque of the Harlem Renaissance and the proletarian thirties, showing conventional periodization and canonization to be profoundly inadequate. As others have argued, new configurations of the literary Left emerge when we prioritize genre over periodization. Darryl Dickson-Carr observes in his *African American Satire*, "Although the Great Depression effectively ended the high times of the Harlem Renaissance, African American satire continued to flourish after the movement's zenith. In fact, some of the best work of the Harlem Renaissance was published well *after* the movement's heyday. If we recall that *Black No More* was published in 1931, while *Infants of the Spring* saw print in 1934, it becomes clear that the Harlem Renaissance was not immediately cut short by the economic horrors engendered by the stock market crash of October 24, 1929" (82). Though many of the black modernist satirists recalibrated their focus with the crash of 1929 and its devastating fallout for black people already living in poverty, these writers sustained an interrogation into the vexed place of African Americans within the nation's folklore of racial capitalism, its bootstrap myths of prosperity and citizenship thrown up against the stark realities of Jim Crow.

Schuyler debunked the folklore of racial capitalism though his performative critique of the racial and class inequalities of a Fordist political economy. In so doing, he participated in a larger discussion within the period about the changing circumstances and meanings of black cultural production and consumption vis-à-vis the manufacture and exchange of racial commodities. *Black No More* draws upon the popularity of the minstrel tradition, the black vernacular and primitivism along with the novel of racial passing to examine what it means to perform and sell notions of racial authenticity and purity in commodity form. Along the way, Schuyler's novel skewers the racial populisms that prevented inter-racial working-class solidarity in his day. Moreover, it predicts the nationalist capitalization of the folk in the New Deal cultural projects and other avenues and articulations of the folk revival. Schuyler's critique anticipates the mass production of the folk as well as the ways that construction would be questioned by fellow writers such as Langston Hughes, Nathanael West, Zora Neale Hurston, and others. By contextualizing *Black No More* in this manner, I hope to recapture a vigorous intellectual and political inquiry into racial capitalism that gathered shape in the 1920s and gained force with the urgency of the Depression and vibrant efforts of the cultural front in the 1930s, animating African American literary production well into the decades following the Second World War.

THE VOGUE IN THINGS NEGRO

The cultural historians Lizabeth Cohen and Robert Weems describe how in the years between 1900 and 1940, African Americans' position as consumers was enhanced by increasing "wealth and gains in education," as well as migration and urbanization (Cohen, *Making a New Deal*, 148; Weems, *Desegregating*, 2, 7–14). While there were many reasons for this demographic shift, the advent of Fordism was certainly one of them. Henry Ford's technologies of mass production created a growing demand for industrial workers in urban centers, a body of laborers composed not only of white ethnics but also of African Americans.[12] Assembly lines produced greater quantities of inexpensive goods, and, in turn, line workers were conceived of as potential consumers: "Workers [needed] wages adequate to buy the products they produced. . . . Mass production required mass consumption" (Holt, *Problem of Race*, 63). Government economic policy was geared explicitly toward achieving the ideal of a "consuming public" by adjusting production to consumption through state intervention (64). In ideological terms, the role of consumption was integrally linked to citizenship: the consumer became the privileged citizen within the polity.

As more than one and a half million African Americans left the South for work in urban centers in the North and the West, the country's major markets saw the emergence of a visible and expanding group of black consumers—"an urbanized proletariat" (Holt 65)—for which to target their products (Weems 7). How did these consumers fit into the new consumer society? Did they join a raceless "consuming public" or, rather, did they collide with an unnamed white "consuming public"? More specifically, to what degree were the privileges and prerogatives of citizenship amalgamated in the marketplace actually extended to black consumers? If Fordism seemed to promise a veritable "democracy of consumers" (Cross, *All-Consuming Century*, 2), offering standardized goods and lifestyles to working men and women of diverse backgrounds, Jim Crow segregated that same space of consumption, leading to the eventual creation of niche and crossover markets, such as the era's beauty products and race records, that capitalized on "racial difference" (Cohen 154–57; Weems 14–16).[13] Such niche markets were emblematic of the growing commodification of culture, enabled by new media technologies in radio, recording, film, and photography that allowed for rapid mass production and national and international distribution. It is no wonder, then, that the politics of race were increasingly played out within the realm of consumption and representation.

A host of writers in the Harlem Renaissance cited racial shifts in the labor market and consumer culture as either a cause for celebration or a cause for concern. The sociologist Charles S. Johnson and the philosopher Alain Locke saw urbanization, diasporic diversity, and increased class differentiation as a potential source of power for black people, the catalyst for a "great race-welding" (Johnson, "New Frontage," 278–98; Locke, "New Negro," 7). In Locke's formulation, an emergent group of black middle-class intellectuals could consort with their white equivalents, forging new understandings across racial lines. In contrast, writers such as Jean Toomer and Zora Neale Hurston grew anxious that the black working class's encounter with mass consumerism would destroy a distinctly rural vernacular culture.[14] As Hurston explained in a letter to the anthropologist Franz Boas during one of her collecting expeditions in the South in 1927: "You see, the negro is not living his lore to the extent of the Indian. He is not on a reservation, being kept pure. His negroness is being rubbed off by close contact with white culture" (qtd. in Kaplan, *Zora Neale Hurston*, 97). Local instances of black cultural production, she worried, would be assimilated within an ever farther-reaching commercial culture that was racialized as white.

Such differing perspectives frame the much anthologized debate between George Schuyler and Langston Hughes published in consecutive weeks in *The Nation* in 1926. They deliberated over the possibility of "a true Negro art" (Hughes, "Negro Artist," 1311). Strikingly, the terms of their disagreement center on the black artist's relationship to "American standardization" as manifested in national consumer culture. In his essay "The Negro Art Hokum," Schuyler argued against the essentialist tenets of primitivism, the vernacular and white supremacy, claiming that while differences in caste and region might contribute to the creation of unique artistic forms, "the literature, painting and sculpture of Aframericans . . . is identical to the literature, painting and sculpture of white Americans" (1221). Schuyler's line of reasoning comes undone, however, when he contends that black and white people are subject to "the *same* economic and social forces" (1221–22; emphasis added). As he describes the particulars of a day in the life of an average white man and black man, each of whom wakes up to "the jangling of his Connecticut alarm [that] gets him out of his Grand Rapids bed," he soon uses the qualifier "same or similar" (as in "he gets the same or similar schooling"). Ironically, Schuyler must qualify his account to reflect accurately the segregated structures of public life—signs of inequitable "economic and social forces" and political disenfranchisement perpetuated by Jim Crow that his thesis would seem to deny.

In Hughes's rebuttal, "The Negro Artist and the Racial Mountain," he invoked a concept of racial authenticity that equated class ascension with racial assimilation (Smith, "Authenticity," 67).[15] Romanticizing the black working class, Hughes asserted that "the low-down folks" escaped the stultifying effects of the market: as such, "they furnish a wealth of colorful, distinctive material for any artist because they still hold their own individuality in the face of American standardizations" (1312). Of course, at least some of the "low-down folks" would have constituted a segment of the post–First World War industrial labor force, working in factories located at the very center of this mass culture of standardization. Contrasting them to the black proletariat, Hughes castigated the "smug" black middle and upper classes for assimilating to a white standard of bourgeois respectability, a process they accomplished by reading white newspapers and magazines, by sending their children to "mixed schools," by attending white theatrical productions and movies, and by owning a house and two cars (1311). By investing in these mass-produced commodities and visions of lifestyle, Hughes suggested, the black consumer forfeited a position of racial distinctiveness that purportedly operated outside of the market, at least according to the dictates of primitivism and the folk. The black consumer joined a national body of consumers implicitly understood to be white. In other words, black middle-class consumers gave up one kind of raced commodity for another: foregoing "the racial individuality" of black cultural production, they purchased mass-produced commodities (coded as white) to join an allegedly raceless democracy of consumers (1312). In both Schuyler's and Hughes's essays, the question of "true" black art rests largely upon patterns of consumption and their attendant meanings in terms of race and social class.

Given the "vogue in things Negro," this anxiety about racial authenticity, class position, and consumption resonated acutely not just for Hughes but also for many of the black modernists who were being asked by white publishers and patrons to produce primitivist and vernacular forms of expression, in self-presentation and literary style and theme (Hughes 1313). The currency of primitivism and the vernacular occasioned a self-consciousness on the part of these writers about what constituted blackness and, moreover, what it meant to perform blackness for personal gain. Many in the Harlem Renaissance inner circle—from Thurman and Larsen to Hughes—grasped the central paradox of this imperative: that although primitivism and the vernacular were defined as something outside of the marketplace, they were nevertheless situated thoroughly within it. During the 1920s and 1930s, race was capitalized upon in a dialectical manner. In this economy, if blackness was commodified as unique and folksy, even exotic and primitive, then whiteness was consolidated as the unnamed national normative standard. This process was mutually constitutive but *not* equivalent: in particular, it shored up white privilege, rather than undermining it. Moreover, it revealed how race was (and still is) produced as a cultural commodity, a transaction dependent, in part, upon the construction of race through visual and discursive narratives.[16]

Elaborating upon modernism's conflation of blackness with primitivism and the vernacular, Paul Gilroy notes how "black feeling could be traded as a cultural commodity in a new market" ("Modern Tones," 104). By way of example, we might consider the valances of the period's black popular music, wherein jazz stood for the primitive and blues stood for the vernacular. In contradictory ways, both forms were promoted as preindustrial figurations of essentialized blackness. They were cultural commodities marketed as "authentic" in an era of mass-produced goods, commodities made all the more complex by the apparent collusion of some black artists in their production and circulation.

Certainly the injunction for black artists to produce and sell authentic blackness was not new. This market demand had a fraught history in minstrelsy and its contemporary manifestation in the popular black-face routines featured in 1920s Broadway musicals and cinema, such as Josephine Baker's blackface performance in the revue *The Chocolate Dandies* (1924) and Al Jolson's blackface performance in the film *The Jazz Singer* (1927).[17] One of the most popular forms of theatrical culture enjoyed by multiracial, working-class audiences in the rapidly indus-trializing Transatlantic of the 1800s, minstrelsy might be understood as the production and commodification of public "blackness" in the form of a "lore cycle" that comprised "fetishized gestures," what W. T. Lhamon refers to as "a group's informal cultural capital" (*Raising Cain*, 69). Michael Rogin explains how blackface "Americanized" its immigrant performers through a logic of disavowal—I perform what I am not—allowing them to lay claim to whiteness: "Racial masquerade . . . moved settlers and ethnics into the melting pot by keeping racial groups out" (*Blackface*, 12). Initially a form of entertainment controlled by whites in the 1830s and 1840s and of a piece with the mutability implied in Jack-sonian democracy's "self-made man," minstrelsy's entrepreneurial and theatrical dimensions were transformed by the appearance of all-black minstrel troupes in the mid-1850s and their sky-rocketing popularity in the post–Civil War period (Rogin 50).

Throughout its history, the minstrel "lore cycle" itself opened up a great variety of satirical possibilities in the unsettling performances of brilliant black actors who sent up its stereotypical images of blackness.[18] Daphne Brooks describes how "blackface minstrelsy bequeathed African American cultural workers the critical tools to transport themselves liter-ally across the country, to new economic heights, and imagistically out of the desert of blackface abjection" (*Bodies*, 214). In the postbellum period, even as minstrel shows gained a sizable black working-class audience, anxieties about the circulation of those images on the part of the black intelligentsia and the black middle class led to twinned charges of self-loathing and selling-out directed at black entertainers who performed in blackface. Given the legacy of blackface minstrelsy, Brooks suggests that at the end of the nineteenth century, "it was black theatre that perhaps waged the most ambivalent uphill battle to rewrite white supremacist constructions of blackness" (213). This ambivalence would wend itself into discussions of self-determination and representation on the part of the New Negro, notwithstanding Alain Locke's declarations of "shedding the old chrysalis of the Negro problem" (4).

The controversy over minstrelsy flamed already heated conversations about popular representations of blackness among African American intellectuals, artists, and patrons during the Harlem Renaissance. W. E. B. Du Bois panned Claude McKay's novel *Home to Harlem* (1928) for "cater-[ing]" to prurient "white folk for a portrayal in Negroes of that utter licentiousness which conventional civilization holds white folks back from enjoying" (Wintz, *Harlem Renaissance*, 4:187). Using a similar rationale, Countee Cullen praised Du Bose Heyward's *Porgy* (1925) "as the best novel on the Negro by a white author that [he] has read," in part because "in his humorous passages . . . he does not offend us with the buffoonery and burlesque of which we are rightfully sick and tired" (Wintz 4:138). In each of these reviews, critics measured the cultural output of their peers by the yardstick of minstrelsy, firing the charge of blackface at artists who had allegedly succumbed to the profits and perils of playing the primitive and the folk. This initial foray into the politics of "selling out" involved black cultural producers and, as we have seen in Hughes's argument against Schuyler, black consumers as well who "bought in."

Minstrelsy, primitivism, and the vernacular were related subjects in a larger conversation about the shifting circumstances and meanings of black cultural production and consumption for collective self-determination. In the interwar period, African Americans evaluated their own increasing visibility as consumers in political terms, conceiving of the market, paradoxically, as both a space for potential economic group determination and symbolic entry into a democracy of consumption.[19] If the marketplace held forth emancipatory possibilities, much of the time black consumers were forced to depend upon white-owned businesses when there was no black alternative. In many cases, no black alternative existed because black entrepreneurs had little capital at their disposal (Cohen 152; Weems 24). Within these constraints, mass consumer culture offered new opportunities for getting a "fair shake." For example, given the choice between frequenting corrupt, white-owned, family-operated stores or white-owned chain stores that sold brand-name goods, African Americans most often chose the latter. In fact, black people patronized the sites and products of American standardization more readily than any number of white ethnics who still shopped at local stores and bought bulk goods as a means of holding on to the "old country" (Cohen 152). Setting Hughes's charge of bourgeois aspirations aside, these consumer choices were motivated in a pragmatic sense by the promise of regulated prices and consistent good quality.

In cases where standardized products designed for a unified mass consumer (read: white and middle-class) failed to meet the particular needs of black consumers, savvy entrepreneurs, both white and black, seized upon these untapped opportunities, generating an array of goods and services such as black beauty supplies, funeral homes, and life insurance companies to capitalize upon this new market.[20] Some goods specifically manufactured for black consumers—most notably, the period's race records—began to attract a small crossover market of white consumers as well (Cohen 152). While Black Swan Records was the first widely distributed black-owned record company in U.S. history, most of the other labels such as Columbia, Okeh, Paramount, and Victor were white-owned (Weems 15–16). Thus, while a few black stars benefited in monetary terms from this burgeoning market (those who were not bound by exploitive contracts), it did not translate into a financial windfall for black producers. Nevertheless, as recordings of African American blues and jazz began to bridge "styles across regions" and to receive air play on the radio, black popular music began to shape the national sound of youth culture.[21] In this way, for recent black migrants, consumption provided a means of asserting a "new black urban identity" that was national in scope.[22]

If the marketplace offered a degree of self-fashioning to black people by way of cultural expression, it also served as a space of overt contestation. Black consumers "seize[d] upon the citizen consumer role" as a vital form of political engagement, especially during the 1930s (Cohen, *Consumer's Republic*, 13; Weems 27–30). Given the devastating consequences of the Depression for African American employment, it makes sense that black people would deploy "the power of the purse" to make advances in racially segregated sectors of the labor market (Cohen, *Consumer's Republic*, 41). (One must first have a job to effectively conduct a labor dispute.) With "Don't Buy Where You Can't Work" campaigns as well as other consumer boycotts, African American consumer activists demanded jobs and better treatment from white store owners (44). Throughout the decade, grassroots organizations worked in concert with black leaders, politicizing black consumers so as to attain a more equitable position within the Fordist economy. Of course, this critique of the marketplace was predicated upon one's activist participation within it. Testament to the rapacious workings of capital, the consumer, no matter how vigilant, was always on the verge of being consumed, a point to which I will return later in my discussion.

In response to this dynamic, left-leaning theorists and activists such as W. E. B. Du Bois and George Schuyler used the idea of the citizen consumer to critique capitalism and formulate more radical and egalitarian economic models based upon socialist cooperatives and labor collectives (Cohen, *Consumer's Republic*, 49–53). In Du Bois's thinking, a "new social order" would begin with the economic power and cooperation of the consumer: as he explained in 1931, it was inaccurate "to think the economic cycle begins with production, rather it begins with consumption" (49; as qtd. in Cohen 47). In keeping with Du Bois's ideas about black economic self-sufficiency, Schuyler founded the Young Negroes' Cooperative League (YNCL) in 1930, which would organize groups in urban black neighborhoods to "study the principles and practices of consumers' cooperation, form buying clubs and eventually open stores" (Schuyler, *Black and Conservative*, 171; Cohen 50). (In 1931, a youthful Ella Baker served as the Young Negroes' Cooperative League's national director.) Schuyler debated Vere Jones, one of the Harlem leaders of the African American consumer boycotts in the mid-1930s, advocating instead for "the mutual aid of consumer's cooperation": "Everywhere today progressive workers are turning wearily from the trite old racial, national and religious slogans and controversies toward this scientific mutual aid; this enlightened anarchism pointing to a rational society free alike from parliamentary chicanery and the goose-stepping brutalities of dictatorship. Not by embarking upon futile and disastrous economic civil wars but by intelligent mutual aid in cooperation with white workers can Negroes improve their economic status" (*Black and Conservative*, 217). As Cohen makes clear, in the African American consumer movement "blacks used consumer power primarily as a means to secure their rights as producers" (*Consumer's Republic*, 52). Perhaps most striking about Du Bois's and Schuyler's conception of the citizen consumer is

their complex understanding of the reciprocal relation between producers and consumers in terms of race, capital, and power. Schuyler's
Black No More literalizes this conception by providing us with a scenario
wherein consumption turns black people white, thereby bestowing them
the rights of citizenship accorded whiteness.[23]

CONSUMING THE COLOR LINE

Schuyler's *Black No More* is a narrative of passing, part of a genre which
subverts basic epistemological assumptions about race and identity.
Passing unmasks the juridical, economic, and social structure of race. In
particular, it reveals the function of whiteness as a kind of property.
The critical race theorist Cheryl Harris contends that "the concept of
whiteness—established by centuries of custom and codified by law—may
be understood as a property interest" ("Whiteness as Property," 1728).[24]
She illustrates the extent to which race cannot be uncoupled from the
workings of capitalism. Valerie Smith expands upon this analysis, offering the important caveat that while racial passing is traditionally coded
as a desire to be white, the impetus for passing is often the increased
social and economic opportunities that accompany whiteness ("Reading," 43). If passing centers on the transfer of racial property—usually the
seizure of whiteness and its privileges—Fordist technologies of mass
production and their ancillary modernist others, primitivism and the
vernacular, give rise to a particular imaginary around the manufacture
and exchange of race as commodity. Put differently, Fordism instigates
new market possibilities for the trade of racial property in commodity
form. Thus, in much New Negro fiction that focuses on passing, race is
often produced and inscribed through purchasable objects, techniques,
and procedures—a kind of "identity prosthesis" that alters the consumer's body (Nakamura, "Race in/for Cyberspace," 712–20). To amplify this
corporeal dimension, the pass is always predicated upon some kind of
trespass, a fact that underscores the inherent mobility involved in the
transaction, specifically, the passer's reliance upon bodily performance
in the production of visual narratives of identity. Hence, Amy Robinson
suggests that "the apparatus of the pass" should be viewed as a "spectatorial transaction" rather than one that is ontological ("It Takes One,"

721, 726). Not only does passing manufacture whiteness through non-biological means, it also reveals the ideological foundations of "biological" race.[25]

These aspects of passing come together in *Black No More*, a novel that deploys a literal "mechanics of passing." The novel begins with Dr. Junius Crookman's invention of a machine called Black-No-More, which turns black people phenotypically white. He has just returned from Germany, where he has successfully conducted his experiment on a black man from Senegal, now "a pale white youth" (12). Crookman has developed this new scientific process in response to the edict that black people "either get out, get white or get along," an imperative that implicitly links the United States' fascism in the form of Jim Crow to Europe's fascist and Nazi movements (11). The transatlantic export of Black-No-More signals the international exchange of eugenics technology and its sinister uses, portending both the speed and traumatic consequences of such racialized processes and products on a global scale. (Schuyler would write of the eugenics movement in his "Views and Reviews" column in 1927: "At the present time the eugenicists are very busy with a lot of gabble about preventing 'the unfit' from reproducing their kind. . . . At the present stage in human culture, it would be exceedingly dangerous to allow any group of people to say who shall be allowed to have offspring. I am sure I do not know who is the most unfit, Henry Ford or one of his workers. Should John Sapp, the Ashman who carts away our trash, be castrated while the idiotic Prince of Wales continues to be thrown off horses?") Crookman aligns himself with two other black businessmen to make Black-No-More strategically affordable to African American consumers: the first sanitariums open in black-populated neighborhoods and the procedure costs a reasonable fifty dollars. As the nation's black population disappears, the novel traces the ensuing hysteria over identity brought about by the standard-issue whiteness of the country's complexion and the possibility that every white citizen may have once been black. Against this backdrop, we follow Max Disher, our self-interested black protagonist, the first American consumer of Crookman's product, as he poses as an anthropologist and infiltrates the reigning white supremacist organization of the South, the Knights of Nordica, for personal gain.

Most likely, Schuyler's plot was inspired by Kink-No-More hair straightener, Black-No-More skin cream, and the astonishingly successful cosmetics line started by the African American entrepreneur Madame C. J.

Walker (Mme. Sisseretta Blandish in the novel). Marketed to black consumers, these products promised straighter hair and lighter skin in accordance with hegemonic standards of white beauty (Ferguson, *Sage
of Sugar Hill*, 212–13; Mullen, "Optic White," 76). Ferguson conjectures
that Schuyler built his novel around a joke that circulated in *The Messenger* office: "This joke, which combined implicit commentary on a
range of race-related subjects—including minstrelsy, the cult of progress
surrounding science and the high value placed on light skin by many
blacks—invited playful speculation about what would happen if a scientist invented a formula that would allow blacks to turn white" (212–13).
As the sociologist Guy B. Johnson calculated in an essay from 1925,
"Newspaper Advertisements and Negro Culture," analyzing the advertisements in a range of representative black newspapers, beauty prepara-
tions dominated all other goods and services advertised. Many of these
ads were for hair straighteners and skin lighteners such as the one announcing "NEW DISCOVERY WHITENS SKIN ALMOST OVERNIGHT . . .
Get a jar now—today. Use it for only five nights. Then if you are not
delighted and amazed at the transformation your money will be instantly refunded" (707). A different ad begins with the promise, "TAKES
KINK OUT IN 3 TO 6 DAYS . . . Guaranteed to straighten your hair." A
decade later in 1938, another sociologist would report similar findings:
hair and skin lotions were easily the most common and profitable advertising contracts in the larger, nationally circulating black newspapers
(John Syrjamaki as qtd. in Burma, "Analysis," 179). The prevalence of
such ads would lead Johnson to ask, "Have hair straighteners become
permanent features of the Negro's culture? How can we reconcile the fact
that their most extensive use is found in the class of Negroes who are
most race conscious? Is this a contradiction, or is it merely the same
thing viewed from different angles: namely, the Negro's readiness to do
anything which will contribute to his chances for success?" (709). Similar
questions direct Schuyler's satire.

Black No More exploits the implications of commodities such as lighteners and straighteners: Black-No-More is a black-owned product that
promises whiteness to its black consumers. Yet Dr. Crookman's invention
does Madame C. J. Walker's cosmetic line one better, transforming not
just hair and skin but bodily "features" (13). The scientist's discovery renders Blandish's/Walker's business obsolete. (After undergoing the process, Max rejoices: "Gone was the nappy hair that he had straightened so

meticulously ever since the kink-no-more lotions first wrenched Aframericans from the tyranny and the torture of the comb. There would be no more expenditures for skin whiteners" (18–19).) More fundamentally, Dr. Crookman "subversively fathers whiteness," usurping and eluding the central role of maternal labor in the reproduction of race (Martin, *The White African American Body*, 149). Taking its cue from market culture, then, Dr. Crookman's invention reproduces the singular black body that is able to pass for white on a massive scale. The neon advertisement for Harlem's first Black-No-More sanitarium illustrates this process:

> A large electric sign hung from the roof and the hum of electric motors could be heard low and powerful. . . . First would appear the outline of the arrow; then, BLACK-NO-MORE would flash on and off. Following that the black face would appear at the bottom and beginning at the lower end with its lettering would appear progressively until its tip was reached, when the white face at the top would blazon forth. After that the sign would flash off and on and the process would repeat. (25)

As the lights move from black face to white face, their pattern demonstrates the ways that this product promises nothing less than the mass (re)production of its consumers as white, a kind of "uplift" achieved through technology.[26] It also signals the performative nature of this endeavor: the sign resembles an advertisement for a burlesque club featuring blackface and whiteface acts. The ambiguous nature of the procedure—part-industrial, part-theatrical—is bolstered by the presence of a "crowd of close to four thousand Negroes" who wait outside the building for their chance to become white. The ominous hum of electricity underscores the violence of Black-No-More, the genocide of blackness throughout the nation, an association driven home by Max's comparison of "that horrible machine" to "the electric chair" (18; Ferguson 228). In no uncertain terms, Schuyler suggests that whiteness represents a kind of coercive racial suicide or "social death" for black people.[27]

In this way, the novel pushes the plot of racial passing to its brutal extreme, asking what would happen to U.S. race relations if whiteness could be mechanized, packaged, and sold by black men. In its very premise, *Black No More* merges the black consumer with a standardized white culture of consumption and inquires after the consequences of such an outcome—would "blackness" be lost altogether, would the infusion of black people into the white power structure change the face of politics in the country? Would race disappear as a site of conflict, supplanted by new struggles based upon class inequities?[28]

Through his cynical trickster protagonist, Max, Schuyler provides us with a black character who seizes the means of production for dubious ends.[29] Once Max is equipped with a "pork-colored skin," he masters race relations in the market by deploying two central modes of engagement: observation and contact. He grasps this dialectic in the opening scene of the book, after he has been rebuffed by a white woman from Atlanta whom he meets in a Harlem club and asks for a dance: "[She was] up here trying to get a thrill in the Black Belt but a thrill from *observation* instead of *contact*. Gee, but white folks were funny. They didn't want black folks' game and yet they were always frequenting Negro resorts" (8; emphasis added). If the color line defines race relations by promoting *observation* and prohibiting *contact*, Max's ability to pass will subvert this system entirely.

Max's interaction with the white woman whom we later know as Helen makes him feel excessively embodied, to such a degree that he feels alienated from his body. He first experiences himself as machine-like, then shattered, and finally dismembered. At home that night, he "mechanically" undresses: "His mind was a kaleidoscope: Atlanta, sea-green eyes, slender figure, titian hair, frigid manner. 'I never dance with niggers'" (9). Her refusal splinters his perceptions, including his sense of self. In his musings, he sees a prism of iconic whiteness, an array of racially encoded signs refracting him in their fragments. Later that night, he dreams "of dancing with her, motoring with her, sitting beside her on a golden throne while millions of manacled white slaves prostrated themselves before him. Then there was a nightmare of grim, gray men with shotguns, baying hounds, a heap of gasoline-soaked faggots and a screeching, fanatical mob." What begins as a carnivalesque upheaval of white supremacy ends as a nightmare of lynching, the manacled white slaves rapidly transformed into a "gray" lynch mob. Max's dream depicts Helen as a white femme fatale, as a figure of castration anxiety brutally literalized in the all-too-real threat of lynching (Doane, *Femmes Fatales*, 2). In his dream, Max's hyperembodied demise reinforces the prohibition against miscegenation, the "most intimate violation of the culture of segregation" (Hale, *Making Whiteness*, 196). From the start, the narrative signals an apprehension about the role of white and black women's reproductive sexualities and its instrumentation in racial genealogies of national belonging and exclusion.[30] Though not without trepidation, Max hopes to exploit the possibility of love across the color line ironically in order to claim the exclusive privileges and protections of whiteness.

When Max awakens the next morning after his fantasy-turned-nightmare and hears of Dr. Crookman's recent discovery, he resolves to act upon it at once: "Two objects were uppermost in his mind: To get white and to Atlanta" (13–14). Max's desire for Helen translates into an immediate desire to be white, though, what in fact *defines* whiteness in this novel and also in West's *A Cool Million*, is economic and social privilege, rather than an essential racial identity. Max's plan sheds light on the capitalist underpinnings of racialized gender prescriptions, revealing the degree to which white women are invested with property-in-whiteness and are therefore cast as desirable commodities. As Saidiya Hartman argues, "Masculine mastery entailed the possession of women as the sign of that mastery, and extrapolating from the racialized premises of this logic, the possession of white women was made the ultimate figure of manliness" (190). In Max's estimation, "as a white man he could go anywhere, be anything he wanted to be, do most anything he wanted to do, be a free man at last . . . and probably be able to meet the girl from Atlanta" (10). Whiteness will allow him to exercise fully the masculinist prerogatives of the abstract white citizen-subject. Echoing the injunction to "get out, get white or get along," with the purchase of Black-No-More, Max "gets" whiteness; that is, he understands and possesses whiteness, accruing the material dividends of this newly attained cultural capital. A white wife will potentially provide Max with white progeny, thereby compounding his investment. In this sense, his equation of whiteness with limitless social and economic mobility complicates any simple theory of desire across the color line, the eroticization of difference gleaned from violating social taboo.

Ironically, before a newly whitened Max pursues the titian-haired girl, he tackles Atlanta's leading white supremacist organization, the Knights of Nordica, the institutional approximation of the lynch mob in his dream. He gains contact with them by posing as an anthropologist. Here, Schuyler signifies on the imperialist origins of the discipline of anthropology as well as one of the central paradoxes of modernism's collectionist project, the need to perform in order to collect the "real" thing (Hegeman, *Patterns*, 29). In this case, Max cynically performs as a white man in order to collect money and the girl. Max's pose reveals the absurd assumptions of racial authenticity and purity that so often drove the practice of ethnography—Schuyler would later describe race as "an anthropological fiction"—a critique that would resonate in later work by West, Hurston, Sturges, and others ("The Caucasian Problem," 49).[31] Max parlays his keen skills of observation into a flawless performance of whiteness, ventriloquizing arguments about the purity of whiteness and the sanctity of the country's Anglo-Saxon citizenry. He thus embodies Schuyler's familiar contention in a contemporaneous essay that "while the average Nordic knows nothing of how Negroes actually live and what they think, the Negroes know the Nordic intimately" ("Our White Folks," 74).

In this scene, that passing is a spectatorial transaction rather than an ontological one rings true in a double sense: appropriating the cultural authority of the social sciences, Max sells himself as a professional spectator of the nation's different races, echoing prominent racist scholars such as Madison Grant, a lawyer and eugenicist best known for his book of pro-Nordic theory, *The Passing of the Great Race* (1916), and Ulrich Phillips, the famous historian of the South whose *American Negro Slavery* (1918) was sympathetic to slaveholders. While Max eloquently enumerates his observations (really his observations of white people's "observations"), he is simultaneously observed by the Imperial Wizard of the Knights of Nordica, Rev. Givens: "Rev. Givens *saw* . . . and concluded that this pale, dapper young fellow, with his ready tongue, his sincerity, his scientific training and knowledge of the situation ought to prove a valuable asset to the Knights of Nordica" (48; emphasis added). Even though Max's speech seems to issue a caution to his rapt listener, signaling his own ruse and the instability of race as a meaningful visible or invisible signifier—he says that "already thousands of blacks have passed over into the white race"—the Imperial Wizard proves to be the perfect dupe, believing what he thinks he sees (47).[32] To drive home the bankrupt scopic foundations of the Wizard's racial beliefs, Max ironically asserts at the end of his perfectly executed sales pitch, "I tried to interest some agencies in New York but they are all *blind* to this menace" (48; emphasis added).

This is but one of many hyperbolic scenes that underscore Max's passing as a form of whiteface, at least for the reader, because of the burlesque aspects of his act. Throughout the novel, his performance reflects the grotesque spectacle of whiteness that is naturalized in the

Klonklave proceedings, revealing white supremacy to be a severely contorted logic. When Max plays the white anthropologist, he mirrors his audience's ideas of whiteness back to them. In keeping with this strategy, every scene in which Max lectures to the Klonklave is told from a point of view that overturns the conventional perspective of theater, wherein the audience watches the performer. Instead, alongside our protagonist, we watch the audience. For example, from his position on the dais, Max notes that the audience "was composed of the lower stratum of white working people. . . . The young girls in their cheap finery with circus makeup on their faces; the young men, aged before their time by child labor and a violent environment; the middle-aged folk with their shiny, shabby garb and beaten countenances; all ready and eager to be organized for any purpose except improvement of their intellects and standard of living" (53). Though Max himself would appear to be the spectacle, orating to a rapt crowd, his white audience and their racial formation take center stage in the narrative descriptions much as they will in West's novel and Sturges's *Sullivan's Travels* as well.

Max's performance allows him entry into the Knights of Nordica; he parallels the work of Walter White, civil rights activist and NAACP leader, who used his ability to pass as white to investigate and report on race riots and lynchings in the 1920s. Unlike White, Max aims at personal gain, not social justice: "He had the average Negro's justifiable fear of the poor whites and only planned to use them as a stepladder to the real money" (49). If Dr. Crookman profits from his black consumers' desire to be white, a desire occasioned by their acute experiences of racial oppression and violence, Max builds upon his initial successes preaching fear, scheming to profit from white people's anxieties about the security of their racial privilege in the wake of Black-No-More. Max arrives at his lucrative career when he simultaneously comes to understand that race is not essential ("he found [white people] little different from the Negroes, except that they were uniformly less courteous and less interesting") but that white people will pay a great deal to sustain the belief that there are essential differences between white and black people (43).[33] Max understands that race is a floating sign available for his exploitation once he is in a position of power, an insight which gives him greater flexibility to sell race. In fact, Max's manipulations help us to see more clearly the manner in which race functions as a commodity itself.

While Max realizes that he now has greater geographic and financial mobility as a white man, he also understands that one really profits from whiteness by producing and selling it, not simply owning it. Ironically, he figures out the perfect way to capitalize upon whiteness when he recalls a "Negro street speaker [who argued] . . . that so long as the ignorant white masses could be kept thinking of the menace of the Negro to Caucasian race purity and political control, they would give little thought to labor organization. It suddenly dawned upon Matthew Fisher that this Black-No-More treatment was more of a menace to white business than to white labor" (44). Improvising on the near iconic scene of contact with a persuasive advocate of communism that proliferates in accounts of writers who were attracted to the Communist Party in the thirties, Schuyler all but shows his hand, unmasking the political import of his satire (Wald, *Exiles*, 17).[34] With no more black people to occupy the role of scapegoat and distract white workers from considering their own position as laborers vis-à-vis wealthy white industrialists, they might actually organize around class interests, instead of false notions of racial purity. Accordingly, the white working class's first response to the news of Black-No-More is "a secret feeling akin to relief" because the labor movement will no longer be divided along racial lines (81). (This is not a particularly noble conclusion: now that all workers are white, strikes will not be broken by the threat of cheaper black labor.)

Lest we view this plot development as a confirmation of Orlando Patterson's thesis that without marked racial difference, a new class consciousness would emerge, Schuyler's technological fantasy suggests that race is too flexible to be eradicated with the elimination of heterogeneous phenotype (Mullen, "Optic White," 77). Put differently, racial difference is too enmeshed in the markets, both financial and labor, to be easily effaced, whatever the promise of technology. We see this first in popular culture's swift capitalization upon the loss of black people throughout the nation: "A current popular dance piece 'The Black Man Blues,' was filling the room. The songwriters had been making a fortune recently writing sentimental songs about the passing of the Negro. The plaintive voice of the blues singer rushed out of the loudspeaker: "I wonder where my big black man has gone; / Oh, I wonder where my big black man has gone. / Has he done got faded an' left me all alone?" (107). Commenting upon the minstrel tradition, "The Black Man's Blues" is a literal description of what happens when white immigrant performers black up: the real "black man" is lost, evacuated, replaced by his "faded" interlocutor and a stereotypical, mass-produced image of vernacular blackness. As such, "The Black Man's Blues" parodically riffs on the theme of entertainer Al Jolson's famous "Mammy" in which the blacked-up speaker, "all alone" and "far from home," sings longingly of returning to his lost "Alabammy mammy."

This allusion is made more overt when "America's premier black-faced troubadour," Mr. Jack Albert, performs a live broadcast of his ever popular "Vanishing Mammy," providing the entertainment before the former Klansman Rev. Givens delivers a presidential address to the nation: "I can't help thinkin', Mammy, that you went white. / Of course I can't blame you, Mammy! Mammy! Dear / Because you had so many troubles, Mammy, to bear" (115). In these moments of modernist burlesque, Schuyler deftly sutures together blackface, white supremacy, and American national culture, referring to the Ku Klux Klan's prominence in electoral politics in the presidential races of 1924 and 1928 (Ferguson 236). More specifically, Schuyler signifies on Al Jolson's performance in blackface as Jack Robin, the protagonist in *The Jazz Singer*, the first feature-length talking picture and the first movie musical. In this scene, we see how a Jewish immigrant performer, Jack Albert/Al Jolson, can claim "both whiteness and proximity to the appeal of the exotic and dark" and how "this two-ness, however mythical, could animate highly marketable cultural productions" (Roediger, *Working toward Whiteness*, 125). As Jack Albert broadcasts his voice over the air, we lose the visual embodiment of blackface spectacularized in cinema for the spectral, disembodied but still racialized crooning of his minstrel tune. This elision suggests that an aural blackness is still commodifiable, with or without visible "black" bodies. In "Vanishing Mammy" and the plantation myth it supports—"the old homestead hasn't been the same"—the loss of an agrarian, antebellum South and its supply of happily subservient "black mammys" is superseded by the disappearance of all black people.

Schuyler's plot literalizes a foundational aspect of blackface: as Rogin suggests, "The blackface recovery of a lost essence was promoted by an elite and taken from the folk" and it was predicated on a racialized, temporal vision of the nation, "a black past and a white future," a vision as we shall see that will recur in the Federal Writers' Project's Florida guidebook (49). As Fanon states, "For the black man there is only one destiny. And it is white" (10). Ironically, for both Jack Albert and the nation's formerly black citizenry, their future is white. What Black-No-

More would seem to throw into crisis is the disavowal—"I perform what I am not"—at the heart of the immigrant performer's donning of blackface in a bid for white Americanization (Ferguson 238). For no one is black anymore. Yet, in these instances of "the blackface melting-pot tradition," the blackness each song mourns is a nostalgic projection and production of whiteness (Rogin, *Blackface*, 16). From this angle, African Americans were only incidental to minstrelsy anyway. Daphne Brooks observes, "The genre of melodrama itself . . . ultimately allows for the exposure of the 'truth' of the racialized body—that is, that it is spectacularly inauthentic" (*Bodies*, 30). If the minstrel form was performed by white people to commemorate a blackness and a time that never existed in the first place—Albert claims that his song "carries you back to the good old days that are dead and gone forever"—the loss of the nation's black people to whiteness provides one more occasion for lucrative nostalgia, another opportunity to exploit the profit margins of loss, whether real or imagined (Schuyler 115).

In yet another instance of blackness functioning as fetishized commodity in the wake of Black-No-More, Max suggests to Santop Licorice, Schuyler's caricature of Marcus Garvey, the leader of the Universal Negro Improvement Association and champion of the Back-to-Africa movement, that he might make more money staying black and exhibiting himself in a dime museum as a rarity, a unique figure of black embodiment (90). Each popular manifestation of blackness demonstrates the contradictory circumstances of industrialization that mobilize the popular appeal of the "preindustrial" primitive and the folk, during the Progressive Era through the New Deal. Rogin notes how "modernization produced both the mass-media means for creating new national identities and nostalgia for lost folk worlds" (*Blackface*, 47). The radio transmission of minstrel songs and the curatorial trappings of the freak show foreground the specific technological advances that enable the recovery, even invention, of folk culture in the form of mass commodities ("blues" records and dime museums) for consumers in the interwar period. Put differently, commercial modernity's vanquishing of the folk guarantees a marketable nostalgia for their lost folkways captured just in the nick of time by cutting edge technologies and modes of display.

While these examples play upon consumers' perverse *desire* and nostalgia for blackness once it is "gone," Max devises another way to exploit the disappearance of blackness through an interrelated structure of feeling: *fear*. In Max's capitalist scheme, he reinvents race as an invisible but nonetheless marketable entity. The white workers abandon their initial feelings of relief once Max, now "the Grand Exalted Giraw," orchestrates the notion of the subversive "white Negro" in their midst who "[takes] their jobs and [undermines] their American standard of living" (81). Max uses the impossibility of observing racial difference to spark anxieties about interracial contact: he invokes the invisible specter of "Negro blood," suggesting to his white, working-class following that "one couldn't tell who was who!" (81). With the invention of the "white Negro," the Knights of Nordica switch the emphasis from visible to invisible markers of difference, a discursive move that only crystallizes the crisis of the visible occasioned by standard conceptions of race.

By selling white workers his racist mythology, Max reproduces the laborers' investment in whiteness, over and above considerations of class. He reentrenches class as racially dependent, despite the implications that class is a marker of financial strata. Max explains to Atlanta's leading business men that in contrast to the defunct KKK, his organization works for "the perpetuation of Southern prosperity by the stabilization of industrial relations" (80). Above all, this stabilization depends upon the working class's "possessive investment in whiteness" and their concomitant fear of "black" permeation of the white laboring body.[35] Paradoxically, their very fear of incorporation with a communist, black, Catholic other guarantees their consumption by a pervasive capitalist machine, much in the way that the protagonist of West's *A Cool Million* will meet his catastrophic end.

BIRTH AND BLOOD

In Schuyler's narrative, such ends are reserved not only for ignorant members of the white working class but also for affiliates of the white elite who proudly proclaim their racially pure status as members of the "First Families of Virginia" (122). In an elaborate political subplot, Max strategically combines his organization, the Knights of Nordica, with the exclusive "Anglo-Saxon Association of America," led by Mr. Arthur Snobbcraft, in order to win a national presidential election on the Democratic ticket. Sounding a distinctly eugenicist note, Snobbcraft has hired a statistician, Dr. Samuel Buggerie, to conduct a "nationwide investigation [that] would disclose the various non-Nordic strains in the population. Laws, said he, should then be passed forbidding these strains from mixing or marrying with the pure strains" (122).[36] On the eve of the election, Buggerie's research reveals, in fact, that America has always been "mulatto minded": most of its social leaders "are descendants of colonial stock that came here in bondage" who "intermarried" and "intermixed" with black people. Therefore, the vaunted First Families of Virginia include descendents of African ancestry (141–42). According to the laws of hypodescent sponsored by Snobbcraft, he and his cohort, including Buggerie and Henry Givens from the Knights of Nordica, are technically black. Thus, the scientific method through which they hoped to maintain their "white racial integrity and Anglo-Saxon supremacy" leads to incontrovertible evidence that they and most other Americans hail from miscegenated origins (120). Their genealogies are revealed to be impure according to their own racist dictates.

In the eye-for-an-eye economy of Schuyler's increasingly Juvenalian satire, Snobbcraft and Buggerie proudly hail from families who have disavowed their black relatives, hence, they themselves will be subjected to the most violent and public form of racial disavowal or "exorcism": lynching (Ferguson 243; Harris, *Exorcising Blackness*, xiii). After their research has been stolen by the Republican Party and released to the newspapers nationwide, the two attempt to flee the country but end up in the rural enclave of Happy Hill, Mississippi, instead. Hoping to elude recognition, they blacken their faces only to stumble into a revival meeting for the most fundamentalist Christian sect in the South, the True Faith Christ Lovers' Church, a community known for "its inordinately high illiteracy rate and its lynching record" (164). In fact, the Rev. McPhule and his devout flock have been waiting for a sign from God, a prayer seemingly answered with the appearance of Snobbcraft and Buggerie in blackface. With devastating accuracy, Schuyler points to the ways white Christianity has long served as the handmaiden of white supremacist exploitation and violence.[37] As the lynching progresses, the narration becomes ever more somber and graphic: "The two men, vociferously protesting, were stripped naked, held down by husky and willing farm hands and their ears and genitals cut off with jack knifes amid the fiendish cries of men and women. . . . [T]hey attempted to run down the dusty road, blood streaming down from their bodies. They had only gone a few feet when, at a signal from the militant evangelist, a half-dozen revolvers cracked and the two Virginians pitched forward into the dust amid the uproarious laughter of the congregation" (175). While the scene's setup is grotesque, its violent climax is delivered in the observational voice of documentary.

Schuyler ratchets up the ghastly consequences of America's racial order, sustained through a cruel logic of disavowal. In a general sense, these men have maintained their elite position and stayed out of the fray of quotidian race relations on the factory floor by promoting a psychological wage of whiteness, a wage that enlists working-class whites to conduct white supremacy's most overt and public acts of violence (Du Bois, *Black Reconstruction*, 700). More specifically, Snobbcraft has passed "numerous racial integrity laws," laws that never acknowledge but fully depend upon the extralegal violence of lynching for their force. In a grotesque carnivalesque upheaval of class and race, Snobbcraft and Buggerie become fatally incorporated into the murderous rite of lynching that their efforts have covertly promoted.

One violent, ritualistic, and performative technology of whiteness, minstrelsy, is subsumed by another—lynching, its most lethal counterpart (Brooks, *Bodies*, 28–29). The logic of disavowal that supports minstrelsy and lynching and sustains notions of racial purity is exposed and condemned through the hybridity of Schuyler's modernist burlesque, when his satire becomes documentary by way of the grotesque. The connection between these technologies is made apparent in the grotesque spectacle of two white supremacists lynched in blackface. Schuyler uses irony as a bludgeon. Buggerie and Snobbcraft occupy the role of the subversive "white negroes" Max speaks of in his Klonklave meetings: they adopt blackface, a performative blackness, hoping to be taken as "authentically" black. They do so to avoid being recognized as white people who have black ancestry or, put differently, black people guilty of performative whiteness. Reminiscent of the mechanized, genocidal process of Black-No-More, this scene stages the brutal dimensions, visible and invisible, of racialization in America, the ways that formulations of racial purity are enabled by a concealed structure of passing and performance—Virginia's First Families are all "mixed" but present themselves as racially "pure."

A disfiguring logic of absent-presence pervades the scene, not only in terms of the men's lynched bodies but also in terms of the audience.

Schuyler points to the coerced spectatorship and complicity of the "two or three whitened Negroes, who, remembering what their race had suffered in the past, would fain have gone to the assistance of the two men but fear for their own lives restrained them" (176). This disclosure addresses the readers' position vis-à-vis the lynching, how readers are made to feel their own uneasy incorporation into the scene. On the level of irony and dramatic justice, the novel enlists its readers' desires in its inexorable march toward Snobbcraft's and Buggerie's fate. In desiring this end, we recognize our potential complicity with the Happy Hill community and their abhorrent beliefs in religious fundamentalism, "one-hundred-percent Americanism," and white supremacy. When we distance ourselves from McPhule's flock and feel for the victims, we experience a sorrow incommensurate with the victims' detestable personas and the larger system of white supremacy they have promulgated: in this instance, the victims and victimizers become one and the same (Ferguson 242). In this impossible position, as laughter fades, we confront the absolute horror of whiteness and the rituals and technologies of violence out of which it is constituted.

The lynching scene is one of the most extreme enactments of racial disavowal in the novel. But the novel's final ironic twist on the twinned racialist fear of incorporation and reproduction is reserved for Max, who marries Helen Givens, the daughter of the Imperial Grand Wizard, the femme fatale who initially rebuffed him in the Harlem club. By the end, even Dr. Crookman's invention, an asexual form of racial reproduction, cannot elude the trauma of biological miscegenation at its narrative center (Mullen, "Optic White," 77).[38] If Max acquires his wife as one more way of shoring up his property in whiteness, her reproductive ability potentially maximizes this property for him in the form of white progeny. Alternatively, their offspring may reveal the fact that one parent is not white. In the novel's conclusion, Max and Helen have a mulatto baby. (Max has prevented a previous pregnancy by hiring thugs to burn down the Givenses' ancestral home, thereby giving Helen such a shock that she miscarries.) Schuyler can sustain Max's technological mastery only through an elaborate deus ex machina—the revelation that the South's first families are of mixed racial origin, the nation's consequent embrace of "dusky" skin color, and, in a strange recuperation of biological reproduction and maternal feeling, Helen's sudden open-minded approach to race (178). Conveniently, with the birth of her child, she declares that "all talk of race and color was damned foolishness" (154). Echoing the logic of prior narratives of passing, there are no "white" people in this text, at least according to laws of hypodescent (Weinbaum, *Wayward Reproductions*, 47).

However, we would be mistaken to read this transformation as indicative of a larger shift in attitude toward race on the part of the public. In response to Crookman's latest discovery, as the acting surgeon general, that the black subjects he turned white are a few shades paler than the average Nordic, "the upper-class began to look askance at their very pale complexions. If it were true that extreme whiteness was evidence of the possession of Negro blood, of having once been a member of the pariah class, then surely it were well not to be so white!" (177). Thus begins a new chapter in racial hysteria, marked by the advent of sun-tanning and darkening products, as everyone clamors to become a bit more brown. The narrator comments that "[a] white face became startlingly rare. . . . America was definitely, enthusiastically mulatto-minded" (179). Schuyler sets this final section off in the text with the all-capped words "AND SO ON AND SO ON," so as to underscore the absurdly cyclical pattern at work here: "dusky" may now be a more inclusive skin color, but the capitalist foundation that undergirds America's color-struck society has not changed (176). If passing and miscegenation undermine the viability of discrete races, Schuyler conjoins these forms of interracial contact to subvert white supremacy's claims to racial purity and an essential superiority located in whiteness. Yet, even as the novel wrenches whiteness from its supposedly stable meanings, it insists that the structures of racial oppression consolidated in white supremacy remain. In Schuyler's estimation, America is defined by its shallow mass-consumer culture—miscegenation is only skin deep, a fad that indicates a shift in the market, not a fundamental change in epistemology or ontology.

SHE'S FUNNY THAT WAY

If we recall Max's dream-turned-nightmare about Helen after his first encounter with her at the Harlem club, we see how the narrative is predicated on an apprehension of white and black women's reproductive sexuality and its instrumental role in racial genealogies of national belonging and exclusion. This uneasiness arises, in part, from juridical precedents established during slavery, which stipulated that the racial status and legal condition of a child of a freeborn white man and an enslaved black woman should follow the mother, instead of the father.[39] Given the patriarchal contours of property law, this ruling may seem counterintuitive but therein lies the answer: perpetuating the brutal economics of black subjection and white male prerogative, the law prohibited the interracial child from claiming a monetary or racial inheritance designated by white paternity. In short, the law reproduced the child as property, not progeny.[40] As Hartman observes, "The issue of [slave women's] motherhood concerned the law *only* in regard to the disposition and conveyance of property and the determination and reproduction of subordinate status"; enslaved black mothers received no entitlements or protections within the law (98; emphasis added). The inverse might be said of white women's motherhood. As long as white women behaved in accordance with "racist regulatory norms," foregoing liaisons with black men for white men to stabilize and reproduce white progeny, they qualified for protection under the law. Through the differential allocation and withholding of entitlements, protections, and racial inheritance, the law attempted to make black and white women's bodies relatively fixed racial signifiers, dependable conveyances of racialized progeny and property.

Yet the degree to which antimiscegenation statutes were reinvigorated after emancipation due to increased fears of interracial intimacy and commingling speaks to the palpable anxiety that women's bodies function otherwise, as sites of contamination and impurity (Hartman, *Scenes*, 185, 189; Mullen, "Optic White," 81; Weinbaum 18). In the 1890s and the separate-but-equal era that followed, as Alys Weinbaum suggests, "the legal apparatus attended to the complicated task of investing white blood with value—rendering whiteness a rare inalienable commodity—and then arresting its circulation in the body politic" (20). Schuyler pointedly undermines notions of white purity and genealogy by dedicating his book "to all Caucasians in the great republic who can trace their ancestry back ten generations and confidently assert that there are no Black leaves, twigs, limbs or branches on their family trees." Max pursues love across the color line, becoming another proverbial "black branch" on the tree, ironically, in order to obtain the exclusive privileges of whiteness.

By seizing the means of industrial, cultural, and even biological reproduction for his own gain, Max achieves a kind of masculine racial and economic self-determination. As he purchases whiteness and performs bourgeois manhood, Max inserts himself into the narrative of social mobility that constitutes the American Dream. Given that he appropriates race by means of technology, we might ask, to echo Smith's query, to what degree the consequences of this maneuver are "distributed differentially on the basis of gender"?[41] Significantly, Schuyler's text ends with a spectral return of the protagonist's blackness, in biological form, facilitated by his sexual contact with a white woman. This patriarchal fantasy, which centers on the technological and performative mastery of race as a means of self-determination, attempts to bypass the complex gender dynamics and racialized property relations at the center of reproduction in the United States (Hartman, *Scenes*, 100; Mullen, "Optic White," 77). In Schuyler's story, as technology transforms race into commodity form, it both usurps and effaces the regulated role of black and white maternal labor in (re)producing race as property.

Part of the particular violence of Schuyler's satire is the present-absence of its black women characters. Max explicitly courts white women in his schemes—for two reasons, at least: he gears his machinations toward acquiring the economic privileges that accompany property in whiteness and, significantly, the black women characters in the story, who may or may not be in on the con, are not so easily seduced. By way of several examples, when we first encounter Max, he has been unceremoniously dumped by Minnie, his unsatisfied "high 'yallah' flapper" girlfriend, who, in his estimation, has "grown uppity" and "stuck on her color" (3). (In fact, it is Max who seems especially color-struck.) The successful Madame Blandish is one of the few black characters in the book who wisely express reservations about Black-No-More: "She had lived long enough to have no illusions about the magic of white skin" (40). In response to Max's switch to whiteness, she wryly remarks, "I always said niggers didn't really have any race pride" (28). In accord with Madame Blandish's views, by the end of the novel, Bunny, Max's partner-in-graft, has fallen for Madeleine Scranton, "a sweet Georgia Brown," possibly the "last black gal in the country," a woman who has refused to become white because she is a "race patriot. She's funny that way" (156). Though black women characters play a minor role in the story, their consistent skepticism provides a pivotal template for the reader.

Their dubious perspective informs the reader's relationship with Max and fuels the novel's broader critique. Schuyler renders Max in cartoon strokes. We may shake our heads at his audacious actions with a certain appreciation but also dismay. Schuyler adds to our doubts by employing an omniscient narrator whose interior perspective is limited to Max's thoughts; the narrator telescopes in and out, reporting his protagonist's standpoint and then observing him from afar. Consequently, we experience a doubleness of position: we know what Max thinks and we know a bit more. Schuyler relies on this alternation to emphasize the less appealing aspects of Max's personality. This frustrates our inclination to sympathize, creating a markedly more ambivalent readerly encounter and provoking a degree of self-consciousness about our own reading practice —for example, how are we to feel about Max's happy ending? Schuyler's conclusion raises questions about the reader's own press for standard literary conventions of identification and closure, a challenge echoed in works by West, Hurston, Sturges, and others.

To be sure, *Black No More* makes for uneasy consumption. Far from romanticizing the folk or the masses, Schuyler depicts white workers as pathetic dupes and potential lynchers. The black working class fares somewhat better but is still castigated for the quickness with which it puts aside notions of race pride to purchase Black-No-More. In this damning portrait of the folk, Schuyler rejects appeals to populism in any shape or form and, in the same breath, he predicts the ways that particular racial and ethnic identities would be produced as marketable entities in the service of a nation in crisis. As we shall see in *A Cool Million*, Schuyler's skepticism regarding the folk and the masses in the form of a consuming audience was shared by West. For Schuyler's critique to be effective, readers must separate themselves from the hegemonic majority who "buy into" the ideological system under review. What's more, Schuyler's protagonist offers no beacon of hope either. Readers must distance themselves from Max, who, through his cunning, exploits the system and profits from its cruel absurdity.

Instead, readers must identify with the marginal characters who see the con and the larger system that facilitates it. In other words, the reader must adopt the perspective of the black women characters whose presence hovers on the verge of erasure. By rendering the viewpoint of his black women characters crucial to the reader's understanding of the novel, Schuyler departs from the misogyny prevalent in the male-dominated genre of satire, where women configure the denigrated grounds out of which the text's vitriol emerges (Dickson-Carr, *African*

American Satire, 5; Brooks, "Burnt Sugar," 114). Though Schuyler's portrayal of Helen as the dumb blond femme fatale might seem to conform
to this trend, it teases apart this very dynamic, examining the differential
valuation of women's bodies in the racial formation of the body politic.
He comments specifically on the distinct ways in which black and white
maternal labor has been instrumentalized historically in the reproduction of white patriarchy and racial capitalism. The novel's few black
women characters who refuse the incorporated whiteness of Black-No-
More, yet another technology of racial capitalism, provide instead a
critical perspective with which to comprehend the novel.

As members of the group from which the passer, Max, passes, the
women represent "a community of knowledgeability" and "a certain way
of seeing" (Robinson, "It Takes One," 720, 719). They thus constitute the
book's "in-group clairvoyants," with whom the reader potentially identi-
fies. In this way, we might extend Amy Robinson's concept of a triangular
theater of passing—wherein there is a passer, a dupe, *and* an in-group
clairvoyant—to include the actual reader of the story. The reader is cast as
a literate member of the in-group who is able to comprehend "the apparatus of passing—literally the machinery that enables the performance"
(721). By having access to competing interpretive perspectives, the reader
is equipped to read Max's appearance and actions not as mimetic self-
presentation but as performance. If Max performs particular identities
for personal gain, Schuyler overtly stages these performances in his fiction
for the purpose of examining the human cost of market-driven formulations of identity.[42]

Positioned as members of the in-group who discern Max's graft, we
attain our outsider status in relation to the imbecilic majority in the
novel. The reader's insider position within these triangulated, ideological
theatrics anticipates the performative strategies used by Hughes, West,
Sturges, and many artists of the cultural front to act upon their readers
and viewers. Denning observes in his discussion of Orson Welles's "aesthetics of anti-fascism" in the late 1930s and 1940s that "theatrical metaphors were as ubiquitous in the cultural front as mapping metaphors are
in postmodern discourse" (*Cultural Front*, 375, 366). Denning explains
how Welles "understood fascism as itself a form of showmanship, [and
thus] his exploration of that showmanship became a reflection on fascism" (380). We have only to recall the particular vantage through which
we watch Max orating to the easily conned white masses, the narrative

focus on their gullible and self-defeating acceptance of Max's contradictory white supremacist rhetoric, to understand Schuyler's astute grasp of the uses and abuses of spectacular mass culture for racist and fascist ends. In these scenes and others, Schuyler invites his readers to join him not in the laughter shared by "the great majority" but rather in the laughter of an alienated "civilized minority," a position he enumerated in an essay of the same name that he wrote in 1924 with Theophilus Lewis, the drama critic at *The Messenger* (*Black No More*, 19; Ferguson 66).[43] Schuyler and Lewis described "civilized people," their compatriots in cynicism, as those who "abhor cant, humbug and hypocrisy. As a rule they are never hot to save humanity from any of the thousand and one imbecilities with which the *genus homo* has surrounded itself. To them, life is an interesting spectacle in which they are at times willing and unwilling actors" (Schuyler and Lewis, "Shafts," 288). Though Schuyler would strike this irreverent pose in most of his satirical columns of the 1920s and 1930s, it fails to fully account for the Juvenalian force of his novel. Ultimately, *Black No More*'s culminating spectacle of lynching directs us to resist our own conscription as actors in this national drama.

By way of conclusion, we might recall Max's cynical strategy for subduing the exploited working class: "These people have been raised on the Negro problem, they're used to it, they're trained to react to it. Why should I rack my brain to hunt up something else when I can use a dodge that's always delivered the goods?" (106). Ironically, this provocation might be brought to bear on the critics who fail to grasp fully the connection between race and class articulated in *Black No More*.[44] As I have argued in this chapter, instead of class taking precedence over race or race taking precedence over class, in Schuyler's work, we see a dialectical logic akin to Stuart Hall's contention that "race is . . . the modality in which class is 'lived' " ("Race," 341). The novel persistently reminds us, to paraphrase Hall, that race *conjoined with* gender is the modality through which class is lived, an insight we surely miss by adhering to a rigid dyad of race and class. Even when workers all share the same complexion, thereby eliminating a construction of racial difference according to phenotype, Max is able to divide his working-class employees along racial lines by reproducing blackness as an *invisible* threat. Significantly, Max is accorded this power through his ability to successfully perform white capitalist masculinity. Schuyler may adopt a fantasy of racial standardization as his central plot device, but in the end, his novel underscores our inability to exclude race in its gendered dimensions from a capitalist matrix. Instead of supplanting race as a category, *Black No More* shows that technology augments its commercial viability, its fungible quality in the marketplace. In other words, if new technologies enable new forms of black agency within the market, they are inexorably tied to processes of commodification and hegemony and they are inevitably bounded by gender.

Indeed, in the modernist burlesque of Schuyler and other writers of the Harlem Renaissance as well, we see an engaged exploration of the interplay of race, gender, and the marketplace. This literature emerges within a particular juncture of racial capitalism, when Jim Crow segregation encourages the growth of niche and crossover markets that capitalize upon gendered racial "difference," just as Fordist technologies of mass production usher in the promise of a "democracy of consumers." Limning the depths of these seemingly incongruous conditions, Schuyler takes up the violent manufacture of race in its more hyperbolic forms— passing and blackface—to subvert basic epistemological assumptions about race. He also demonstrates the ease with which race is transformed into a commodity, a transaction dependent, in part, on its visual, performative, and discursive construction. In so doing, Schuyler participates in a central conversation about the African American encounter with the shifting racial and gender coordinates of consumer culture in the interwar period.

Counterintuitive though it may seem in view of his later politics, Schuyler's *Black No More* illuminates an alternative literary genealogy of the New Negro movement, one that centers satirical fiction that explicitly examines class, gender, and the vagaries of race as commodity. In this alternative account, radical class critique is no longer the province of social realism alone; nor is the Harlem Renaissance solely "a cultural nationalism of the parlor" disengaged from "what the hyphenation of class costs" (Lewis, *When Harlem Was in Vogue*, xxviii; Gates, "Harlem," 12). Schuyler's modernist burlesque homes in on the ways that notions of racial authenticity and purity are produced, packaged, and sold for corporate and national interests. In this way, Schuyler and his ilk portend the populist uses of the folk in the cultural efforts of the New Deal and the broader folk revival. They caution against the ways the folk are used to promote the folklore of racial capitalism. Their critique thus frames and forecasts the antifascist, antiracist sentiments of the cultural front, thereby bridging the literary production of the Harlem Renaissance with that of the cultural front in the thirties and beyond. Reiterating the claim he had previously launched so powerfully in *Black No More*, Schuyler wrote in 1936: "Of course, Fascism would be nothing new to American Negroes. As far as they are concerned, it already dominates the overwhelming majority of colored folk. They are everywhere socially ostracized, economically penalized, publically discriminated against and segregated" ("Views and Reviews," 17 October 1936). With the publication of *A Cool Million* in 1934, Nathanael West had already joined Schuyler in making this critique.

Chapter 2.

"Inanimate Hideosities": The Burlesque of Racial Capitalism in Nathanael West's *A Cool Million*

[Epic theater] is less concerned with filling the public with feelings, even seditious ones, than with alienating it in an enduring manner, through thinking, from the conditions in which it lives. It may be noted, by the way, that there is no better start for thinking than laughter.
—WALTER BENJAMIN, "The Author as Producer," address at the Institute for the Study of Fascism, Paris, 27 April 1934

An intelligent man finds it easy to laugh at himself, but his laughter is not sincere if it is thorough. If I could be Hamlet, or even a clown with a breaking heart 'neath his jester's motley, the role would be tolerable. But I always find it necessary to burlesque the mystery of feeling at its source; I must laugh at myself, and if the laugh is "bitter," I must laugh at the laugh. The ritual of feeling demands burlesque and, whether the burlesque is successful or not, a laugh.—NATHANAEL WEST, *The Dream Life of Balso Snell* (1931)

Published three years after *Black No More*, Nathanael West's *A Cool Million, or, The Dismantling of Lemuel Pitkin* (1934) has often been disparaged as his least successful novel. But it, like *Black No More*, should be recognized as a key text of the literary Left for its scathing burlesque of the myth of class mobility and its populist appeal, the underpinning of a pernicious thirties' folklore of racial capitalism. When West first submitted the manuscript to Cap Pearce at Harcourt, Brace for consideration, Pearce rejected it, stating that it failed to "echo" the "brilliant cry" of his prior novel *Miss Lonelyhearts* (Martin, *Nathanael West: The Art*, 241). According to Jay Martin, West's biographer, West would claim that he wrote *A Cool Million* as "a kind of parlor game for his friends" to mask his bitterness over the book's preliminary rejection (242). The book was soon picked up, not only by the New York publisher Covici-Friede but also, curiously, by Hollywood's Columbia Pictures as well. The novel's mixed reception after it was published may have had something to do with its banal and often offensive literary sources—the Horatio Alger stories and Adolf Hitler's *Mein Kampf*, among others (231). Perhaps critics could not accept the book's on-the-nose satire: the novel must be read as a brutal denunciation of the American Dream for it to make any sense at all. In his appraisal "A Particular Kind of Joking," published in 1964, Norman Podhoretz conjectured, "This obvious satire . . . must have come right off the top of West's head. . . . [H]e may have even been trying to satisfy the prevailing left-wing Zeitgeist. . . . [But] what he had to say about fascism he said much better in *The Day of the Locust*, his very unpolitical last novel" (153). Certainly, the novel's politics offended mid-century New York intellectuals such as Podhoretz, who pronounced West an individual genius by separating his fiction from his leftist politics and insisting that his art transcended his times (Veitch, *American Superrealism*, xv).[1] This chapter argues that *A Cool Million* is West's most overtly political effort and no less compelling for it. Read in conjunction with West's actual biography, the book soundly contradicts the claim that West's "achievements . . . were in no way dependent on radical ideas of any kind" (Pells, *Radical Visions*, 194). On the contrary, *A Cool Million* illuminates the radical ideas that drove West's day-to-day activism and his other deeply satirical novels, *The Dream Life of Balso Snell* (1931), *Miss Lonelyhearts* (1933), and *The Day of the Locust* (1939).

In the last decade's wealth of revisionist literary histories of the thirties, scholars have attended to the radical commitments evidenced both in Nathanael West's life and his fiction, including *A Cool Million*. In particular, West's oeuvre has been brilliantly reassessed by critics such as Rita Barnard, Susan Hegeman, Caren Irr, Matthew Roberts, Rachel Rubinstein, and Jonathan Veitch, each of whom rightly emphasizes West's engagement with consumerism, the avant-garde, and nationalism against the backdrop of his personal political orientation.[2] Like George Schuyler and many of the satirists of the thirties, Nathanael West was a self-identified leftist: he socialized and worked with a progressive crowd of fiction writers and screenwriters including the likes of Lester Cole, Lillian Hellman, Josephine Herbst, Mary McCarthy, Horace McCoy, and William Carlos Williams; he attended the Writers' Congress in 1935, signing its manifesto; he spoke on the topic "Makers of Mass Neuroses" at the Western Writers' Congress in 1936; he participated in numerous meetings and strikes and served on a number of executive boards for progressive causes, such as the Motion Picture Guild, "organized for 'the production of liberal and progressive films' " and the Screen Writers' Guild in Hollywood, activism for which his own screenwriting career would suffer in the form of blacklisting; he helped to organize back-lot workers in the CIO (Congress of Industrial Organizations) in the late thirties; and he worked to organize migrant workers in California and the farmers in Buck's County, Pennsylvania (the location of his farm, Erwinna, and the bohemian enclave of leftist writers such as Herbst, Mike Gold, Daniel Fuchs) (Martin, *Nathanael West: The Art*, 344–53).

Though West's political sympathies and activism are no longer ignored, there is disagreement about how exactly to situate his radicalism in relation to his writing. Some critics locate West within the Popular Front, basing their judgment more upon his studio activism than his writing. Other critics look to the iconoclasm of West's novels and his own doubts regarding the political merit of his work and conclude that West was a satellite figure, never entirely attached to one political group or ideology. Michael Denning, for example, positions West as a "studio radical," "part of the Hollywood Popular Front," whereas Jonathan Veitch suggests that West was neither part of the *Partisan Review* crowd, nor was he wholly aligned with "the communist left" or the aesthetic protocols of the Popular Front's populist ideology (Denning, *Cultural Front*, 191, 256; Veitch xi–xvi). Veitch bases this interpretation, in part, on two important pieces of correspondence, the first, a letter West wrote to the modernist literary critic Edmund Wilson in 1939: "The radical press, although I consider myself on their side, doesn't like my 'particular kind of joking,' and think [it] even fascist sometimes, and the literature boys [the *Partisan Review*] whom I detest, detest me in turn. . . . [T]he daily press think me shocking . . . because there is nothing to root for in my books, and what is even worse, no rooters" (qtd. in Veitch xi; qtd. in Martin 334). The second letter, also penned in 1939, was addressed to the Popular Front writer and journalist Malcolm Cowley: "I'm a comic writer and it seems impossible for me to handle any of the 'big things' without seeming to laugh or at least smile. . . . What I mean is that out here we have a strong progressive movement and I devote a great deal of time to it. Yet although this new novel is about Hollywood, I found it impossible to include any of those activities in it. . . . Take the 'mother' in Steinbeck's swell novel—I want to believe in her and yet inside myself, I honestly can't" (qtd. in Martin, *Nathanael West: The Art,* 335–36). On the face of it, two interrelated issues arise in these passages: the inability of West's contemporaneous critics, progressive or conservative, to adequately situate his work within the larger literary landscape of their decade and the apparent gap felt by West himself between his strivings for social justice in his daily life and his cynical assessment of social relations in his fiction.

From another perspective, we can understand the social critique evident in West's literary work as consistent with his political proclivities, if only more skeptical. He and other satirists such as Schuyler were no less occupied than social realists with making truth-claims about the dismal state of the Union from a progressive vantage. But unlike many of their contemporaries, they avoided the mawkish pitfalls of documentary fiction made so popular by Steinbeck and others, opting instead for a destabilizing brew of invective, hyperbole, and incongruity. We might link the particular pathos in West's work to his own sense of internal incongruity: he could not reproduce in earnest the sentimental representations of the folk promoted by the folklore revival and the many populisms of his day, though—and with hindsight, perhaps *because*—he fought passionately for the people not as an abstraction but rather in the real-time formation of disenfranchised studio employees, farmers, migratory workers, and others. Like Schuyler, he refused an obvious politics of empathy so prevalent in the documentary works of the Depression—a strategy of affect that easily served reactionary as well as progressive causes—instead providing the readers of his novels with "nothing to root for" and "no rooters."

West's compulsion to "laugh at the laugh" might be said to reflect his stance toward his own paid work and his sense of complicity: though he allegedly objected to the commodified content of Jewish stage humor exemplified by "Potash and Perlmutter, Fanny Brice and others," as a screenwriter of musicals and comedies in Hollywood, he depended upon the ethnic humor and "commercial spirit" of the largely Jewish entertainment industry (Martin, *Nathanael West: The Art,* 80; Rogin, *Blackface,* 60–64).[3] Certainly, this vein of humor, its vaudeville shenanigans, its crass ethnic jokes, and, most important, its burlesque roots provided rich material for each of his satirical novels. West was self-conscious about these professional and personal "entanglements": he felt internal friction between his artistic aspirations, his desire for financial success and his parents' wish that he would take over the family business in real estate and construction. West's family had emigrated to America from Lithuania in the wake of the Russian pogroms of the 1880s, joining two million Jews who left the Russian Empire between 1880 and 1914. Given the overwhelming German influence in the province of Lithuania, his family regarded themselves as Germans. They followed the path of other German Jews who had recently arrived in the United States, rejecting the shtetl community for Americanization, a process of bourgeois assimilation facilitated by their specific expertise in the building trades, a professional skill that coincided with the boom in building construction in the first decades of the twentieth century (Martin, *Nathanael West: The Art,* 13–27). If West was deeply ambivalent about his Lithuanian immigrant family's desire for a conventionally successful, "assimilated" life, he was also ambivalent about his own Jewishness, defining himself while in college at Brown University in the twenties as a "Jewish outsider," a "Jew and not-Jew at the same time," a liminal position that replays the oscillating distance and proximity of Jewish immigrants to American whiteness at the time (Martin, *Nathanael West: The Art,* 80). Yet West was far from ambivalent about anti-Semitism, the reason behind his family's immigration, immersing himself in its long history (79).[4] He struggled to square his upper-middle-class background with his radical politics and his fiction writing with the conventions of the literary Left of the 1930s. West may have yearned for a way of being that was socially, ethnically, and politically "uncontaminated" but, to his credit, he regarded those very longings as impossible and perhaps even suspect. This understanding allowed him to use these entanglements to great effect in his own fiction.

In *A Cool Million*, West limns the many entanglements of "a pioneer people," drawing upon the frontier and boot-strap myths and their attendant constellations of the folk to consider the rise of fascism in America. Riffing on the Horatio Alger novels of the nineteenth century and their increased popularity in the 1910s and 1920s, West's surreal tale unveils the myth of class mobility and the violent economics of propertied white patriarchy at the heart of the American Dream and Depression-era visions of "a usable past" (Brooks, "On Creating," 219). *A Cool Million* follows the descent—not ascent—of our American boy hero, Lemuel Pitkin, within the world of the marketplace in "the year of our Lord nineteen thirty-four" (117). Lem fails to enact the promise of his "inalienable birthright"—that access to social mobility and self-invention which constitutes his white masculine inheritance (110). Instead, Lem is increasingly acted upon by enterprising capitalists in the most brutal and bodily of ways; he is made to be a stereotype of the Alger folk figure, but one who is continually denied his birthright to the point of death. With this plot, West demonstrates the vexed place of the folk in the Alger stories and the stories' disingenuous populist overtures to "any poor boy who works hard." He also predicts the ways that Alger plot lines would shape some of the populist rhetoric that cohered around the folk in the discourse of national recovery.

Like Schuyler, West in *A Cool Million* adopts a form of modernist burlesque as his modus operandi.[5] Jay Martin recounts how West spoke of burlesque comedy as a classical art form, tracing its literary roots to Greek comedy (*Nathanael West: The Art*, 238). West was a fan of burlesque and vaudeville, part of a generation of writers Edmund Wilson named "The All-Star Literary Vaudeville" (Roza, "American Literary Modernism," 127). Accompanied by his friend, the novelist Robert M. Coates, West often attended burlesque revues, Harlem nightclubs, and the shows of Jimmy Durante (Martin, *Nathanael West: The Art*, 237). He knew all of the standard routines and he even knew some of the performers, introducing friends to the comics backstage after their performances (238). West was also an enormous admirer of the Marx Brothers scripts, written by the humorist and *New Yorker* writer Sid Perelman, his closest friend and his brother-in-law, the person to whom *A Cool Million* is dedicated (238). His deep knowledge of burlesque enabled the ironic distance evident in his work, making it possible for him "to laugh at the laugh" (*The Dream Life*, 27). At the same time, burlesque allowed him to occupy his subject, "to burlesque the ritual of feeling at its source," to mock the narrative production of affect and sentiment from the *inside*. West's burlesque travesties were both distanced and close to their subject, blending high with low, to enact *and* critique the hypocrisies of commercial life in the time of Depression (Glenn, "Taking Burlesque," 93).

Like Schuyler's *Black No More*, West's modernist burlesque created an unruly parody of the popular literary texts and stereotypes that perpetuate America's racial capitalism, imitating and distorting his sources to reveal the grotesque social relations they naturalize and support. In

West's hands, modernist burlesque is nothing less than a form of theorizing. His modernist burlesque confronts the politics of Hollywood theatrics and the theatrics of governmental politics in the age of mass communication, the ideological apparatuses that manufactured the very desire for the folk and other fictions of national belonging. By exposing the inner machinery of such narratives, his novel attempts to disrupt their power upon the reader. This aspect of his work led his friend, the novelist Josephine Herbst, to keenly observe, "The people in West's fiction are not so much looking for something they have lost as for something they *never had* and *never will have*" (15; emphasis added). There is a certain pathos in the recognition of this impossible, double loss, the fabrication of a loss of something never there in the first place. While in West's world, no one can escape this economy of desire, what is available to his readers is a different angle of reception within that economy. As West himself would frame it, we can burlesque "the ritual of feeling," the authenticity and purity that we are supposed to long for, the sentimentality and pity (evacuated of politics) that we are supposed to feel.[6]

When judging West's place within the turbulent decade of the thirties it becomes abundantly clear that his kind of modernist burlesque was distinct from the most recognizable proletarian representations of the day. In contrast to the often sentimental, social realist novels that centered on the plight of the proletariat within a network of capitalist exploitation, West's fiction examined the vagaries of commodity culture and the working-class consumer's role within it. In this way, West's work actually expands our conception of the "fiction of the left" (xiii).[7] As the literary critic Daniel Aaron argues, "There was another kind of writing . . . 'implication literature' tinged with 'just as deep radical dye.' West belonged to that select company of socially committed writers in the Depression Decade who drew revolutionary conclusions in highly idiosyncratic and undoctrinaire ways" ("Late Thoughts," 162).

In his idiosyncratic way, West shifted the lens to look at the role of the masses, not only as exploited workers, but also in their capacity as duped yet avid consumers. From this angle, West provided a fictional narrative of industrial rationalization and its persuasive techniques that would intersect with Antonio Gramsci's nearly simultaneous account of Fordism. Gramsci describes how the American calibration of production with consumption depended upon a "skilful combination of *force* (destruction of working-class trade unionism on a territorial basis) and *persuasion* (high wages, various social benefits, extremely subtle ideological and political propaganda) . . . [and] determined the need to elaborate a new type of man suited to the new type of work and productive process" (*Selections*, 285–86; emphasis added). West elaborates on the incorporation of this "new type of man" into the nation by focusing on the flag-waving clichés that facilitated this process. In his investigations of the desires, dream life, and myths consolidated in the commodities, leisure activities, and national narratives produced and consumed by working people, West evinced a subtle grasp of the hegemonic contours of mass culture in the time of the assembly line.

In his sardonic focus on mass consumer culture and the worker's "implicated" place within it, West was not alone: a range of writers such as Schuyler, Chester Himes, Langston Hughes, Nella Larsen, Sinclair Lewis, Tillie Olsen, and John Dos Passos used satire to explore the consequences of Fordism's bodily, psychic, and economic incorporation. West's *A Cool Million* resonates in particular with Schuyler's *Black No More* on this score, and yet these novels are rarely paired.[8] Each novel responds to the nation's transition from a producer-capitalist economy to a consumption-oriented "culture of abundance," wherein the mass marketplace is increasingly conceived of as "a democracy of consumers" (Barnard, *Great Depression*, 149; Cross, *All-Consuming Century*, 2). As West and Schuyler keenly perceive, the promise of citizenship predicated upon equitable and anonymous buying power is belied by the racialized class structure within the United States and the ways in which spaces of consumption both institute and regulate forms of Jim Crow segregation and anti-Semitism.

Given the Depression's disproportionate impact on people of color and impoverished rural whites who were "not quite white," a penetrating leftist critique of capitalism necessitated a critique of white supremacy (Wray, *Not Quite White*). The burlesques of Schuyler and West offer this account by demonstrating the ways that white supremacist ideology sanctioned an idea of class mobility as a means of shoring up an affiliation of white workers based upon race, rather than class. Cheryl Harris explains the ways whiteness affords white workers "access to a host of public, private, and psychological benefits. . . . It is through the concept of whiteness that class-consciousness among white workers is subordinated and attention is diverted from class oppression" (1760). One of the privileges that accompanies naturalized whiteness is the expectation of class mobility. It is this expectation that West troubles, demonstrating something akin to Gramsci's assessment of the bourgeoisie. Gramsci distinguishes the bourgeois class from previous ruling classes by singling out the claim of class mobility: "The bourgeois class poses itself as an organism . . . capable of absorbing the entire society, assimilating it to its own cultural and economic level. [However] the bourgeois class is 'saturated': it not only does not expand—it starts to disintegrate; not only does it not assimilate new elements, it loses part of itself" (260). In even aspiring to the bourgeoisie, *A Cool Million*'s protagonist embodies this "saturation" as he literally "loses" parts of himself.

Both *A Cool Million* and *Black No More* advance a savvy understanding of domestic racism not only as an articulation of capitalism but also as a form of protofascism, by underscoring the links between lynching and antilabor terror, white supremacist ideology, nativist beliefs, and anti-Semitism, connections consolidated in the activities of the Ku Klux Klan and other related organizations in the 1930s, such as the Black Legion, America First, and the Silver Legion, also known as the Silver Shirts (Kelley, *Hammer*, 120; Veitch 11). In their aesthetics of antifascism, like so many artists of the cultural front later in the decade, West and Schuyler employ theatrical metaphors to investigate the spectacular "attractions" of fascism and implicate their audience, directing us to resist our own conscription as actors in this nationalist drama (Denning 375). Like Schuyler, West suggests that the Jim Crow economy depends upon the violent production of raced bodies as spectacle (or invisible threat) for an audience who pays in more ways than one. To illuminate these productions, they burlesque popular novels of moral instruction and uplift—the novel of racial passing and the Horatio Alger stories—pushing these narratives of self-making to their hyperbolic extremes so as to make legible ideology at work (Wald, *Crossing*, 3). *Black No More* and *A Cool Million* deserve to be read in tandem, then, for their scathing excoriation of a thirties' "folklore of racial capitalism": they are modernist burlesques of racial and class passing that demonstrate how market-driven formulations of the folk shore up capitalism and make fascism possible.[9] In this shared vision of the American scene, fascism and capitalism join together in their mutual logics of racialization and profit motive (Veitch 104).

By centering the oft-overlooked satires of George Schuyler and Nathanael West, new figurations of radical 1930s cultural production and critique come to light (Denning 122). This chapter's reading prioritizes a question not often asked of *A Cool Million*, even in the revisionist scholarship: namely, if West engages with commodity culture through a radically citational writing practice, as Rita Barnard suggests (*Great Depression*, 8), how does this strategy perform a critique of racialized and gendered social relations? In other words, as West burlesques the "folklore of capitalism," how does he make visible not just the operation of class but also the economics of white patriarchy (Veitch 88; Moran and Rogin, "Mr. Capra," 220)? In particular, how does he treat raced, gendered, and classed corporeality and incorporation within Fordist capitalism?

In West's modernist burlesque of a thirties' "folklore of racial capitalism," its literary antecedents and its potentially fascist leanings, he takes a certain risk. As Constance Rourke observes, "to sustain burlesque something more than grotesquerie is needed. Satire enters into its attentions. . . . But pure satire stands aloof, while burlesque wholly possesses its subject and wears the look of friendship" (*American Humor*, 101). West's novel "wholly possesses its subject," to borrow from Rourke (101). It occupies and enacts the literary modes, stereotypes, and power dynamics it sets out to undo: it risks reifying, rather than undermining, the subject of its burlesque. As we shall see, *A Cool Million*'s conclusion poses a conundrum about the possibility of successfully burlesqueing fascism for progressive, antifascist political ends. In short, do the incorporative powers of fascism render this political gesture finally inert? West's "parlor game" of a novel may wear the look of friendship but a subterranean rage seethes through its burlesque, precisely in the moments when the laughter drops out and the book, still wholly in possession of its subject, adopts the aloofness of satire and documentary.

The following reading explores these questions. It investigates West's invocation of the plot lines of the Alger stories and the dime store westerns and their marketing of bootstrap and frontier myths and then turns to West's critique of the culture of collecting and the place of the folk within that project. As West recycles and reverses the plot lines of the dime store novel, he also pilfers other ancillary modes of popular entertainment, such as the Buffalo Bill extravaganzas of the 1880s and 1890s and the dime museum freak shows popular in the first decades of the twentieth century. In exploiting their anarchic, carnivalesque edge, he reveals the fraught historical subtext of these older forms of "authentic" exhibition while at the same time castigating the nostalgia in his own day for these already nostalgic productions. Homing in on the "indexical-excavatory enthusiasm" of the 1930s and its incipient folklore revival, West demonstrates with cruel precision the different ways in which particular racial bodies become fetishized, incorporated, and commodified within a modernist culture of collecting as figures of the folk (Miller, "Inventing," 374). West deploys these spaces of collection and exhibition to expose whiteness as a kind of vaunted commodity within the mass production of racial and ethnic stereotypes, a property marketed to consumers who invest in it at everyone's peril. If the protagonist, Lem, transmogrifies into a series of stereotypes of white masculinity as the Alger folk figure gone awry, the novel's barely present heroine, Betty Prail, is made to be the static stereotype of the collectible and representative—read white—"real American girl." In West's own folklore of racial capitalism, he creates a grotesque fictional burlesque of the documentary collections so popular in the thirties.

THE STORY OF EVERY GREAT AMERICAN

Even the most cursory outline of the novel makes evident West's reliance upon the stereotypes, clichés, and hackneyed plots of the Alger stories, working-girl fiction, and other dime novel formulas produced within the "fiction factories" of the nineteenth century (Denning, *Mechanic Accents*, 18–24). *A Cool Million* begins with the threat of foreclosure on the longtime home of his grandmother and guardian. Lem, ever the dutiful grandson, seeks financial advice from the town's most prominent citizen, the former president and future fascist leader of the United States, Mr. Shagpoke Whipple, a thinly disguised caricature of President Calvin Coolidge, who encourages him to leave his schooling and "go out into the world and win [his] way" (73). Lem repeatedly encounters Whipple, who later forms the fascist National Revolutionary Party, and also Betty, his childhood sweetheart, who is brutalized, exploited, and raped throughout the book. When Lem arrives in New York City with thirty dollars loaned to him by Whipple, his money is stolen, he is falsely accused of stealing, and he is subjected to police brutality, incarceration, and the extraction of all of his teeth by the prison dentist. This sequence of events marks the pattern of Lem's existence in the city. With each transaction, Lem loses another body part—his teeth, an eye, a thumb, a leg, his scalp, and so on. He is literally torn to bits in his efforts to earn "an honest cool million."

The more Lem emulates the fictional model of Horatio Alger and fails, the more his broken body is capitalized upon and the more theatrical he becomes. In other words, Lem's increasing disfigurement enables his stage career as a spectacular freak. At the same time, his public, commodified, and ever malleable embodiment marks him as something less than a proper citizen.[10] In the years following the publication of *A Cool Million*, the Farm Security Administration photographic unit captured and carefully edited pictures of white men visible in the ranks of the unemployed and the relief lines, publicly embodied and fallen from the net of proper citizenship.[11] Such men were given a name—"the little guy" or "the forgotten man"—and they occupied a central role in the rhetorical appeals of politicians, social reformers, activists, and artists on the left and the right. West centers this figure as his duped protagonist, inquiring after the meanings of the white male worker—the nation's most protected class of laborers—who is unable to claim his "inalienable birthright" both in the public sphere and the sphere of labor (110). A story of failed social mobility such as *A Cool Million* reveals the degree to which class boundaries are impenetrable. In West's account, *in spite of* Lem's white, masculine privilege, he cannot overturn the strictures of the American class system.

While Lem is made to be a unique folk exemplar of failed birthright, Betty is made into a desirable collectible, a representative of "genuine native stock" (126). She has no birthright to claim herself in the world of business and her capacity for self-making is never in question—rather, as a white woman, she exists in the novel only to be claimed as a guarantor of whiteness, an accessory to white patriarchy. Put differently, she is the passive avatar, the placeholder, through which enfranchised and disenfranchised men alike hope to claim the privilege of white masculine birthright. As Lem attempts to make his million in New York City, Betty is captured by white slavers and taken to a themed whorehouse nearby, a whorehouse that has become a "one hundred per centum American place," in keeping with the nation's patriotic turn, after its original incarnation as "The House of All Nations." After Betty escapes and meets up with Lem, they head out west by train with Whipple to dig for gold in California to support the growth of his fascist National Revolutionary Party. In California, Lem loses his leg in a bear trap as he tries to prevent a western gold miner from raping Betty. He soon loses his scalp in an Indian uprising against white imperialism. His career path increasingly places him in the public eye. After Lem is rehabilitated with false teeth, glass eye, wig, and prosthetic leg, he joins the "Chamber of American Horrors" as a side-show exhibit. He then becomes a stooge with Riley and Robbins's "15 Minutes of Furious Fun with Belly Laffs Galore" (171). Finally, he ends up assassinated at a convention for Whipple's fascist party, thereby becoming a martyr—an (un)exquisite corpse—for the cause (Veitch 99). Given her supporting role throughout, fittingly, Betty has become Mr. Whipple's secretary.

Lem is made to represent the tragic ending of an all-American boy repeatedly thwarted by "sophisticated aliens" (179). He also becomes a symbol for the triumph of fascism. He is the figure around which the country rallies under the National Revolutionary Party. With this alarming turn of the events, West shows how the American Dream is consolidated through stereotypical figures of success—the conventional Horatio Alger tales—and also *figures of failure*, such as Lem. West thus burlesques the logic of these stereotypes and their deployment within the folklore revival of the 1930s: he reveals the intimate proximity between Alger folk hero and fascist folk martyr, exposing the bankruptcy of racial capitalism and its fascist possibilities. If Lem had succeeded in his bid for social and class mobility, he would be a classic Alger folk hero. In his failure, he becomes a fascist folk martyr instead, for his failure is apparently neither his fault nor the capitalist system's, rather it is the fault of "sophisticated aliens," an external enemy of "the people" (Žižek, "Against the Populist Temptation," 559). In this way, West illuminates a seeming paradox of the Depression—the continued popularity of the American Dream rejuvenated through populist depictions of persevering hard-working folk when those same images might have served as a powerful counterexample of the ways capitalism fails those most vulnerable, the "one third of the nation . . . ill-fed, ill-housed, ill-clothed," who were unemployed or barely managing to eke out a living, no matter how hard they tried. Implicit in this logic is West's suggestion that the iconography and rhetoric of the folk in the period's documentary and ethnography were sometimes shaped by the Alger myth.

Who better to plumb the popular plot lines of American national culture than West, who worked in the "fiction factories" of his own day—the film studios that took over the production of sensationalist stories for the leisure of the working class? Critics have demonstrated that in West's composition of *A Cool Million*, he drew upon his experiences viewing and devising extravagant nationalist collections and displays of America's usable past.[12] Surely another source for West's novel was the fad during the 1920s and 1930s for collecting dime novels, and the Horatio Alger stories' predominance within that realm of circulation and exchange. West was not only troubled by the popular narratives that promoted the American Way of life but the ideological impetus for these stories' collectibility as objects.

West used the sensationalist popular fiction of the nineteenth century and the early twentieth to explore the sustaining myths of the nation and their spectacular racial productions in the form of stereotypes. In particular, West burlesques the myth of upward class mobility by cribbing over one-fifth of his novel from actual Alger texts, in addition to imitating the melodramatic plot lines of working-girl fiction and dime novels of the western frontier (Barnard 142). *A Cool Million* improvises on such popular fiction, rendering visible slippages and aporias, points of productive "contamination."[13] Jeffrey Decker describes how conventional stories of enterprise were constituted through "the separation of gendered spheres, racial segregation and nativism" (*Made in America*, xiv). In West's inversion of the racially coded "moral luck and market pluck" stories, these enabling exclusions come to light (Decker 2). Moreover, as his white protagonist Lem Pitkin repeatedly fails to enact his birthright, we witness what might be described as a performative narrative of unsuccessful class passing. Using the codes and cues of popular fiction, West burlesques the mass production of middle-class formulas for uplift (Decker xiv). Significantly, he not only upends the "values" embedded within popular narratives of success, but he also launches an attack on the nostalgic culture of collecting that imbues the Horatio Alger stories with their retroactively ascribed "purity." Their value as collectibles in the mass-consumer marketplace of his own time issued from their pristine status as the folklore of capitalism; the books were promoted as relics of a "purer" moment of American capitalism, "signs of a lost innocence, unspoiled fragments of an age before mass culture" (Denning, *Mechanic Accents*, 9).

If West's textual appropriation appears straightforward, it is not, given the misappropriation of the Alger stories as *the* representative dime novel series by early literary historiographers and bibliophiles in the first decades of the twentieth century in addition to the Alger stories' own earlier history of appropriations. Though the Alger narratives and the westerns have been canonized in the twentieth century as primary models of the dime novel, Michael Denning, John Cawelti, Jeffrey Decker, and others have shown how this literary historiography obscures the dime novel's working-class commitments and its engagement with "the class conflict of the Gilded Age" and also how this conventional account supplants a wider range of fiction sold under the rubric of sensational fiction—"aristocratic costume romances, detective tales, working-girl stories, tales of the American Revolution, mysteries of the city, outlaw stories" (Denning 15–16; Decker 1–2, 10). Denning observes in *Mechanic Accents* how "Alger's greatest success comes after his death in 1899; not only did he find his largest readership between 1900 and 1915, but beginning in the 1920s his formulaic stories were interpreted as the archetypal narrative of capitalism. . . . Together, the revaluation of the dime novel western and the promotion of Alger as the typical dime novelist allowed an ideological appropriation of the dime novel as the wholesome reading experience of American boys, telling tales of western expansion and inculcating the values of self-made success" (203). In the early 1920s, the first substantial collection of dime novels was bequeathed to the New York Public Library and then acquired by the Huntington Library. This acquisition prompted a spate of commentaries about the genre, including the first book-length consideration, *Dime Novels, or, Following an Old Trail in Popular Literature*, penned by Edmund Pearson, a librarian, and published in 1929 (13–14). According to Denning, much of the commentary about the dime novel beginning in the twenties is marked by a "combination of nostalgia and nationalism" as well as a "disdain for . . . contemporary popular culture, measuring present degeneration against past glory" (14). To this day, the primary periodical about the genre is *Dime Novel Round-Up*, notably published from 1931 onward, an enthusiasts' magazine devoted to "the collecting, preservation and study of old-time dime and nickel novels, popular story papers, series books and pulp magazines." As this surge in collecting activity suggests, in the years preceding West's writing of *A Cool Million*, the dime novels enjoyed renewed interest and the atypical Alger tales came to epitomize the genre.

The story of Alger's (belated) preeminence among nineteenth-century dime novels in the Progressive era represents a number of ironies that

West surely must have found irresistible. The "revaluation" of the dime novel genre occurred just as a broader range of entrepreneurs—white immigrant and African American men and women—attempted to write themselves into the social mobility script, some very successfully. We need only think of Al Jolson's rise to Broadway and cinematic stardom and Madame C. J. Walker's entrepreneurial sweep of the black cosmetics industry in the 1910s, careers not coincidently based upon performances and techniques of self-making—Jolson's famous blackface routine and Walker's specialization in beauty products—for examples of success stories that broadened the scope of the Alger narrative.[14] At the same time, "opportunities for prospective entrepreneurs" declined with the consolidation of large-scale corporations and the move from producer-oriented to consumer-oriented capitalism (Decker xiv, 2). As Alan Trachtenberg and others remind us, the notion of the self-made man as it was sutured to "free-labor" ideology of the mid-nineteenth century was already anachronistic even in the 1870s, given the rise of wage labor (*Incorporation*, 78).

Moreover, the literary historiographers' and bibliophiles' misappropriation of the Alger stories was predicated upon Alger's own appropriations. Denning describes how the "genteel, moralistic" stories of Horatio Alger "attempted to use the dime novel format with varying degrees of success to recapture and reorganize working-class culture" (*Mechanic Accents*, 60–61). In offering a middle-class alternative to working-class dime novels of the period—one that emphasized individual character in the form of "moral luck" available to those whose American birthright was white, masculine, and middle-class—Alger "ventriloquized" the dime novels that preceded his intervention (Decker 2; Denning 83). Much like the plots of the Alger narratives whose protagonists ascend the social ladder through moral strength and a fortunate encounter with a gentleman of means, Alger attempts to elevate the dime novel itself, lifting it from its purportedly cheap and sensationalist origins.

In view of such "ventriloquism," how do we read West's imitation of the form? In a sense, West performs a double burlesque, imitating the Alger narratives and their own middle-class imitation of prior working-class dime-novels. Alger's stories ventriloquize dime novels—one might say, they even "pass" for them in the literary historiography—and, in another register, *A Cool Million* ventriloquizes the Alger formula. Except that it doesn't, not quite: in accordance with the logic of burlesque and satire, West's novel both passes and fails to pass for the source of its derision. Herein lies the novel's performative critique, its self-reflexive citation and dismantling of the nation's myths of economic and occupational advancement. In Alger's formal "success" and West's formal failure, ventriloquism reveals what is at stake in the narrative of social mobility—*performance*. These narratives depend upon performance as a key to class ascension. In West's usage, the rags-to-riches parable of Horatio Alger is a narrative that relies upon an implicit class performance, a class pass, on the part of its protagonist. Much like *Black No More*, his burlesque makes visible the internal performance embedded within the social mobility script, the class pass on the part of the working-class hero upward into the producer-capitalist class.

West's burlesque of the class pass both inverts and ironizes the dynamics of cross-class masquerade so prevalent in 1930s' documentary reportage, wherein the middle- or upper-class ethnographer tried to pass as one of the poor to grasp the real experience of poverty, a strategy evident to varying degrees in texts such as James Agee's and Walker Evan's *Let Us Now Praise Famous Men*, Erskine Caldwell's and Margaret Bourke-White's *You Have Seen Their Faces* (1937), and Preston Sturges's film parody *Sullivan's Travels*. In another sense, *A Cool Million* burlesques the burgeoning genre of 1930s screwball comedy (a genre West himself worked in as a screenwriter), limning their stories of successful cross-class masquerade, social mobility, and self-making achieved through convincing acts of performance, a connection between theater and the marketplace that has a long history. Michael Rogin argues that in the time of Jacksonian democracy, "self-making operated in the marketplace, blackface in the theater. . . . [F]or hundreds of years, the theater and the marketplace were conjoined sites of role-playing exchange" (*Blackface*, 50). Certainly, we can extend and expand this account to include the Alger stories as another "conjoined site" of "role-playing exchange," where consumers bought fictional performances of "marketplace self-making." Though West does not include blackface explicitly in his novel, in his protagonist's spectacular dismantling, he seizes upon its animating energies—its *unmaking* on the way to self-making—to reveal the racialized and gendered performance of class inherent in the formula of the self-made man.

West's ventriloquism of the Alger stories also emphasizes the means of production by which the Alger series and other dime novels were made: the stereotype. In its original usage, the stereotype was a new steam-powered press that used a duplicate impression of an original typographical element for printing. The stereotype revolutionized printing technology in the 1830s and 1840s, making large-scale publishing possible, in terms of efficiency, output, cost, and distribution.[15] In 1922, the journalist Walter Lippman coined the social meaning of the term, describing a stereotype as a "picture in our heads" (*Public Opinion*, 73). It was the mechanical stereotype that fittingly ushered in the dime novel industry, an industry that produced and promoted literary stereotypes, that is, standardized, formulaic, and static representations of people as types, in the commodity form of the book. If the stereotype enabled a new form of commercial culture, metaphorically speaking, the stereotype was its result, too. Traversing the literal and the metaphorical, the invention and the commodity, the term *stereotype* encompasses both the technology that manufactures fictions and the clichéd fictions it reproduces, an excellent example of the enveloping circuit of the marketplace.

A Cool Million comprises a virtual landscape of mass-produced stereotypes and narratives enveloped in this circuit. The proliferation of stereotypes throughout the novel underscores the ways in which they are rampantly produced as commodities and consumed within the arena of mass culture. "Our white hero and heroine" are no less stereotypical, no less wooden and hollow than the novel's supporting characters, a quality that thwarts one type of reader identification with interiority, for another—the stock character. Instead, they are all endlessly reproducible and familiar, products of the narrative machinery of the "fiction factories" (Veitch 101; Denning 17–18). If Lem and Betty eluded West's commodity logic, the novel might appear to reify whiteness through neutrality. Yet, the novel is up to something more complicated. Denning describes how in the dime novels "no narrative formulas were developed that could tell a racial story" other than "conventional, static and negative stereotypes" (210).[16] In West's deft adaptation, an embedded racial story about the production of gendered whiteness emerges by way of the genre's formulaic stereotypes.

As West critiques such narratives of success and their concealed racial story, he shows how the white working class's investment in the rugged individualism of free enterprise assures its incorporation and consumption by a pervasive capitalist machine. Significantly, its incorporation into this economy renders its members duped commodities. Lem is propelled into the marketplace through his naive consumption of clichés of American success, slogans voiced by Mr. Whipple, such as "America is the land of opportunity. . . . She takes care of the honest and industrious and never fails them as long as they are both" (74). West demonstrates the raced, corporeal dimensions of capitalism's capacity for incorporation through his male and female protagonists' besieged embodiment, their status as "authentic," white collectibles, both unique and representative in the commerce of the collection and other modes of exhibition and display. West thus anticipates the ways that the collection of the folk will surface as trope, theme, and plot device in works as varied as Caldwell's and Bourke-White's *You Have Seen Their Faces* (1937), Hurston's *Mules and Men*, the Federal Writers' Project's guidebooks, Agee's and Evans's *Let Us Now Praise Famous Men*, Sherwood Anderson's *Home Town* (1940), Richard Wright's *12 Million Black Voices* (1941), and Preston Sturges's *Sullivan's Travels*.

Through the economy of the collection in *A Cool Million*, profit-seeking opportunists continually reinvent and capitalize upon Lem's and Betty's increasingly desecrated bodies as representative of the American folk. In this way, West's ventriloquism of the Alger stories seizes upon the series' prized status among book collectors in his own time. In West's perverse metaphorical substitution, the body of his Alger wannabe stands in for the corpus of Alger narratives: both are collectible, no matter how broken, no matter how corrupted. With this substitution, West takes aim at the celebration of the Alger stories' "Americanness" by the "cultural arbiters of the middle classes" and their value as relics of the prelapsarian days of producer-oriented capitalism (Denning 204). West actively situates such acts of nostalgic canonization and collection within the "degraded" realm of the mass marketplace that Alger's enthusiasts were so desperate to renounce.

West himself adopts a strategy of collecting, "borrowing" significant portions of the Alger stories along with other popular sources, but he puts this material in the service of a radically different narrative. West's rendering of Lem as a one-man corporeal horror show reveals a profound (im)passe in a mass-produced ideology of class mobility.[17] Consequently, the more Lem acts the dupe and clings to the myth of his entitled birthright—"like [Ford and Rockefeller], you were born poor and on a farm. . . . Like them, by honesty and industry, you cannot fail to succeed"—the more he becomes a deformed spectacle, a product of a bankrupt, nationalist commodity culture (74).

West populates the cardboard landscape of *A Cool Million* with a variety of commercial spaces that traffic in the authentic and the rare—the antique store, the themed whorehouse, and the freak show among them. Such venues of exhibition expose the manufacture of whiteness as a particular kind of commodity within the mass production of racial and ethnic stereotypes. Among the objects on display are people whose differences are produced and capitalized upon in order to sell the nation to itself. Though both Lem and Betty are transformed into types, displayed for the consumption of others, they are each made to represent differently, according to their gender: while Lem's figuration rests on his ever-more distant relationship to his birthright, Betty's figuration rests in her value as a collectible for men who hope to access and achieve the privileges of white masculine birthright. Not coincidently, she is captured and sold into "white slavery" through a vice trust of Chinese and Jewish men, immigrants who are denied access to the promise of social mobility advanced by the Alger stories. As West burlesques the "white slavery" panic of the 1910s, he seizes its raced, classed, and gendered implications and also its implicit story of collection—the victims were coerced and collected against their will by immigrant men who wanted to join the national collective. By attending to the logic of collection, to its producers and consumers as well as the collectibles it promotes—most pointedly, Betty's fetishized and commodified status as "a real American girl"—West's displays reveal the truths that popular modes of display attempt to conceal (Wollen, *Visual Display*, 9–10).

A sign of the "commodification of American Culture," such live exhibitions in *A Cool Million* demonstrate the ease with which people are transformed into types, their bodies made thing-like, the private and the public rendered permeable, all in the expansive realm of commercial culture (Barnard 149). Riffing on a phrase from *Miss Lonelyhearts*, Josephine Herbst once observed that in West's vision, "man's collaboration with things, the paraphernalia of his suffering, is realized in . . . metaphor" ("Nathanael West," 14). In other words, West's use of metaphor, the literary figure that produces sameness between two unlike things, suggests an all-too-intimate relationship between people and things. West's metaphors enact the merging of "man" and thing, perversely animating objects and reifying human characters until they become grotesque. This anxiety about permeability, about the encroachment of commodification onto the body, was fueled by the calibration of mass production with consumption and the period's embrace of Taylorist schemes for scientific management and assembly-line production (Buck-Morss, "Envisioning Capital," 113). But West makes sure to tie this present rationalization in the realm of American business to its violent past, referencing the slave trade, when African Americans were made the objects of commodity exchange, and Native American genocide, when Indians were massacred for land that would feed the United States' expansionist project. The perversely metaphorical exhibits and collections that crowd the pages of *A Cool Million* refer back to this brutal history, suggesting that its meanings radiate into the present.

West shows how the period's zeal for collecting serves not only entrepreneurs, artists, intellectuals, and wealthy elites but also politicians and the nation-state in crisis (Miller, "Inventing," 374). By explicitly exploring the racial stereotypes produced within the period's "folklore of capitalism," West both anticipates and transforms Zora Neale Hurston's formulation of "THE AMERICAN MUSEUM OF UNNATURAL HISTORY."[18] In her famous essay "What White Publishers Won't Print" (1950), Hurston describes a metaphorical museum "dedicated to the convenient 'typical,' " "an intangible built on folk belief": "It is assumed that all non-Anglo-Saxons are uncomplicated stereotypes . . . lay figures mounted in the museum where all may take them in at a glance. In there is the 'typical' Oriental, Jew, Yankee, Westerner, Southerner, Latin, and even out-of-favor Nordics like the German. . . . However, the public willingly accepts the untypical in Nordics, but feels cheated if the untypical is portrayed in others." Calling attention to what becomes naturalized within a hypothetical American Museum of Natural History—the complexity of "Anglo Saxons"—Hurston points to the specular commodification of all other people as folk types whose presumed knowability precedes their visual representation. Notably, Hurston attributes the production of these types to the apparatus of the museum, thereby naming the focal modernist technology of collection within the New Deal's search for a usable past. West constructs several variants of the American Museum of Unnatural History in *A Cool Million*'s numerous collections and exhibits, which either traffic in stereotypes that expose the debased ways of the Nordics, such as the corrupt and fascist Mr. Whipple, or push a variety of racial and ethnic stereotypes to their most shocking extreme to reveal their offensive absurdity, such as the narrator's comment that "the inferior races greatly desire the women of their superiors" (93). In this way his novel showcases the subterranean violence of "the typical." Yet, in addition to all of the book's non-Anglo-Saxon stereotypes, such as the "crafty oriental" Wu Fong, the acquisitive Jewish interior decorator Asa Goldstein, and the "me Injun" Jack Raven, West gives us a white protagonist who aspires to an Anglo-Saxon stereotype of bootstrap success (130, 103, 113).[19] This unnatural history unmasks the "intangible" masculine whiteness bound up in stories of American success.

From the outset, *A Cool Million* frames its plot around several literal and metaphorical variations of the culture of collecting, overlaying an abstract narrative of debt, acquisition, and saving with the crassly material market for antiques. The novel begins with the threat of foreclosure on Lem's grandmother's house. Lem goes to the Rat River National Bank to inquire with Nathan "Shagpoke" Whipple about acquiring a loan. What is significant about this inquiry is not so much the nature of its call, but its location: "[Whipple's] house served as a place of business as well as a residence" (70). The narrator comments that "some people might object to turning a part of their dwelling into a bank. . . . But Shagpoke was . . . of the saving kind" (71). In this instance, the ambit of finance inverts conventional boundaries between private and public. The house-cum-bank echoes the impending fate of Grandmother Pitkin's house. As the narrator describes her "humble" but charming Vermont home, he remarks that "an antique dealer, had one chanced to pass it by, would have been greatly interested in its architecture," only to note parenthetically a page later, "It might interest the reader to know that I was right in my surmise. An interior decorator, on passing the house, had been greatly struck by its appearance. . . . The name of the cause of this tragedy was Asa Goldstein, his business, 'Colonial Exteriors and Interiors.' Mr. Goldstein planned to take the house apart and set it up again in the window of his Fifth Avenue shop" (67–68, 69).

In scenes such as this, West parodies the interwar period's taste for authentic recreations of early American interiors and their furnishings, referencing the living-history museums of Henry Ford's ersatz Greenfield Village (1933), comprising nearly one hundred historical buildings, including Noah Webster's Connecticut home and the Illinois courthouse where Abraham Lincoln practiced law, as well as John D. Rockefeller Jr.'s Colonial Williamsburg home (1932), a "town" replete with appropriately costumed actors (Hegeman, *Patterns*, 151). West signifies on the colonial revival and its attendant antiques craze in the 1920s and 1930s, pointing to the capacious reach of capitalism and the ways that nostalgia for the real thing, for the preindustrial, is galvanized by contemporary mass-consumer culture. There is little coincidence in the fact that Henry Ford's Greenfield Village was financed from the sales of the Model T and the Model A.[20] In 1927, Walter Lippman described a similar circuit of value in his commentary on President Calvin Coolidge and the seeming incongruity of his homespun appeal during the Jazz Age: the public "feel that they are stern, ascetic and devoted to plain living because they vote for a man who is. . . . Thus we have attained a Puritanism de luxe in which it is possible to praise the classic virtues, while continuing to enjoy the modern conveniences" (*Men of Destiny*, 17).

What better example of the desires of Puritanism de luxe than the whorehouse that goes from being a "House of All Nations" to a "one hundred per centum American place"? Through the clichéd moral calculus of prostitution, West critiques the country's invocation of a folk past to bolster a sense of patriotic national identity during the Depression. The brothel where Betty finds herself captive functions like a museum of Americana, a great collection of artifacts, styles, and animate mannequins. Initially, it is designed as a "House of All Nations" boasting "a girl from every country in the known world," with Betty "[rounding] out the collection" (93). But with the Depression, the narrator observes that its proprietor, Wu Fong, "saw that the trend was in the direction of . . . home talent, and when the Hearst papers began their 'Buy American' campaign, he decided to get rid of all of the foreigners in his employ and turn his establishment into an one hundred per centum American place" (126). Wu Fong employs none other than Mr. Asa Goldstein, the interior decorator who purchased Lem's grandmother's house, to redecorate the brothel (103). Goldstein follows the rules of regionalism to the letter, designing "a Pennsylvania Dutch, Old South, Log Cabin Pioneer, Victorian New York, Western Cattle Days, California Monterey, Indian and Modern Girl series of interiors" (West 126). In this way, the whorehouse refers to the historical tourism of Greenfield Village or Colonial Williamsburg, but with a signal difference (Hegeman, *Patterns*, 151–52; Rubinstein, "Nathanael West's Indian," 114–15). West's ersatz whorehouse sells America a nostalgia for no period in particular, rather it sells nostalgia itself. He demonstrates in the crassest terms how retroactive conceptions of the preindustrial past emanate from the corporate capitalist present (Miller, "Inventing," 379). West shows us how the thirties' culture of collecting and its folk artifacts, part of a nostalgia for a precapitalist simplicity, are desires *and* products of the marketplace. Even if the artifacts represent an industrial regime before Fordism, they are still situated within the trajectory of capitalism, not external or prior to it.

In Wu Fong's collaboration with Goldstein and "the Italians" who capture Betty Prail in their white slavery ring, as Rachel Rubinstein observes, West foregrounds the prototypically "American" roles that white ethnics and other immigrants might aspire to play within the creation of a mythical national story: that of the "purveyor," the "appropriator," the profiteer (113). The pairing between Fong and Goldstein is no accident: fueled by nativist fears of "race suicide" and antimonopolist organizational conspiracies, both Chinese and Jewish men were criminalized by vice squads and popular media alike as money-worshiping foreigners who preyed sexually and economically upon unsuspecting, white working-class women in the dangerous environs of the city (Freedman, "Transgressions," 81–85; Diffee, "Sex," 416; Keire, "Vice Trust," 8). In the business partnership between Fong and Goldstein, West burlesques the overlapping stereotypes of what Jonathan Freedman calls "the Jewish Oriental and the Oriental Jew," playing upon their putative avarice, devious industriousness, and their effeminized masculinity as "oriental" pimps (Keire 8).[21] Fong's and Goldstein's access to an even proximal citizenship is predicated upon their ability to ideologically manufacture the nation and a vision of a usable past that historically excludes them. West plays this irony for all it's worth: much to the horror of those who subscribe to the nativist line, both men use nativist rhetoric and concepts to successfully sell their products to those not included in a vision of a "one hundred per centum American place." Fong and Goldstein successfully take a page from the media mogul Hearst and profit from the very Anglo folk types who were created to regulate and police immigrant access to the marketplace and its money-making potential. Yet, by the end of the novel, given the strictures of racial capitalism, it is clear that for Asian and Jewish immigrants such as Fong and Goldstein, buying a place in America is a dangerous game.

Betty supplies the "authentic" folk material for Fong's and Goldstein's business scheme. Significantly, within this story of capital, Betty is the house's first "real American girl" (92). She is dressed in nineteenth-century New England attire and accompanied in her period piece room by "two skillful maids" who help her dress and "an old negro in livery" who serves her breakfast (94, 126). West undercuts the sensationalist, Progressive-era plot line of white female slavery with the historically accurate image of a white mistress with her black slaves. In this way, West suggests that the notion of white slavery gains its power from the fact of African American slavery and its institutionally sanctioned rape and concubinage of laboring black women. The rhetoric of "white slavery" had its origins in the Jacksonian labor movement of the 1830s and 1840s when "chattel slavery provided white workers with a touchstone against which to weigh their fears and a yardstick to measure their reassurance" (Roediger, *Wages*, 66).[22] In the 1910s and 1920s, the story of white slavery was reanimated around the concept of the imperiled, working-class white woman who was sexually coerced by the newly arrived immigrant man, the narrative's purported sexual and moral perversions made legible once more through the haunting presence of what Hortense Spiller has called slavery's "terministic violence" ("Notes," 176). West forces the painful ironies of Betty's role as a "white slave" surrounded by African American "maids" and "livery" within an immigrant-owned brothel, drawing into focus several unacknowledged racial stories that subtend the narrative of America's usable past—the history of slavery and the history of xenophobic anti-Asian, anti-Semitic exclusion.

If the relationship between white domination and black servitude gives white slavery its meaning, it also partially constructs Betty's "authenticity" as a "genuine American," that is, a genuine white American woman (West 93). Susan Hegeman writes, "What is new and startling here is West's suggestions that these regional and national cultural identities are already *false*: at worst, whorehouses, sites of exploitation and degradation; at best, empty categories, the effects of which can be cobbled together—*bought*, rather than inherited—with the right combination of painted pine furniture, spatter and gingham" (*Patterns*, 152). Like the furniture, spatter, and gingham, Betty can be "bought"; she is no more than another material effect of the folk. What *is* inherited, West persistently reminds us, is the brutal history of capitalist exploitation, objectification, and degradation that enabled the regional styles and identities replicated in the whorehouse's interiors. This authenticity augments Betty's popularity: her johns "buy American" in more ways than one. By implication, the novel figures the mania for a folk past as a form of prostitution where the nation exploits its own past and peoples, thereby repeating the exploitation at the core of American history.[23]

The plot line in *A Cool Million* that leads to the whorehouse and its exhibition of American regional culture is derived not only from the public panic over white slavery in the years preceding the First World War but also from the popular working-girl fiction of the nineteenth century. Both of these popular fictions were responses to white, working-class women's shifting encounters with urban, commercial culture as laborers and consumers. While stories of white working women first appeared in the 1840s, the genre of working-girl fiction gained popularity in the years following the Civil War, with the concurrent crisis of the ideology of domesticity, the demise of the sentimental novel, and mounting concern about the plight of needlewomen in sweatshops (Denning 185–86). In composing his female protagonist, West riffs on the stereotypical aspects of the conventional working-girl heroine: orphaned at age twelve because of a fire, from the moment of her parents' death, the comely Betty Prail is repeatedly the victim of sexual assault, abduction, and captivity. Leslie Fiedler bluntly states, West's "Good Good Girl . . . gets her full comeuppance, raped with appalling regularity from the time she is twelve" (327). In the first instance, when the drunken volunteer firemen arrive to put out the blaze, they decide instead to loot her family's farm; a fireman abducts her, whereupon she loses consciousness, remembering nothing of the assault in the morning. Later, in an echo of Cinderella, she is employed as a maid in the evil lawyer Slemp's house, joining his "two ugly daughters and a shrewish wife." As the narrator puts it, "All was not beer and skittles in their household for the poor orphan": the lawyer Slemp (surely a parody of C. Bascom Slemp, the Republican congressman and lawyer from Virginia who worked as President Coolidge's secretary for the duration of his presidency) takes great pleasure in "[beating] her twice a week on her bare behind with his bare hand," for which he pays her a quarter (80). Betty makes her escape from her rural origins of Ottsville, Vermont, and comes to the big city to find work, only to be kidnapped by white slavers and sold to Wu Fong's "House of Nations." Unlike the insistence in working-girl fiction upon its female protagonist's virginity and virtue, the emphasis in West's novel is on Betty's loss of "something which, like her parents, could never be replaced" (79). The narrator begins that chapter with the self-conscious admission, "It is with reluctance that I leave Miss Prail in the lecherous embrace of Tom Baxter to begin a new chapter" and, later, concludes: "The result of this unfortunate encounter we already know" (79, 81). With this invocation of the reader's presumed knowledge, the novel implodes the familiar temporal tensions of melodrama, the pull between a sexual violation "just barely" escaped and one "already" happened (Williams, *Playing*, 32–36).

Given West's citational practice—wherein he *enacts* the threat that the novel of seduction deploys to propel the narrative forward—Betty's serial rapes might be read in comparison with Lem's dismemberment, not only as a sign of the book's potential misogyny, as Fiedler suggests, but also as West's critique of this popular trope in sentimental fiction. (Lem, too, is momentarily captured by Fong and pimped out to a client, but the sexual encounter ends abruptly when Lem's fake teeth and glass eye fall out, much to the horror of his john.) Through Betty's perilous position within the novel, West makes the reader aware of the threat of rape as the central structuring device of popular romance and melodrama and he underscores its violence by acting it out. There is another side to this critique in its seeming hyperbole: in working-girl fiction, the heroine always escapes with her virtue. Yet, in West's version, as Betty's stay at the respected lawyer Slemp's house makes clear, for the working woman, the private, domestic space of the upper-class home provides no safe haven from sexual violence. She is all the more vulnerable there. Her capture into white slavery in the public space of the city is a continuation of this private, sadomasochistic abuse. By extension, while the Fifth Avenue exhibition of Grandmother Pitkin's house seems to violate the sanctity of the home, the reader would be mistaken to ascribe any kind of moral purity to its prior domestic function.

Suturing the short-lived but rampant panic over white slavery to the central tropes of working-girl fiction, West illuminates the disciplinary techniques of the putative "separate spheres" for white working-class women and for men who could not claim the patriarchal privileges of national whiteness. In one of the book's most ironic and jarring lines, the narrator offhandedly observes, "Many of [Fong's] clients were from non-Aryan countries and would appreciate the services of a genuine American. Apropos of this, it is lamentable but a fact, nevertheless, that the inferior races greatly desire the women of their superiors. This is why the Negroes rape so many white women in our southern states" (93). Later, the narrator gratuitously reports that "numbers of orientals, Slavs, Latins, Celts and Semites had visited [Betty]" (125). Burlesquing the anti-immigrant, anti-Semitic, racist arguments of prominent figures like Madison Grant in his *The Passing of the Great Race* (1916) or Lothrop Stoddard in his *Rising Tide of Color against White World-Supremacy* (1920), West goes to great pains to make the raced and gendered contours of the American Dream explicit. These especially offensive remarks along the lines of "forbidden fruit" name one of the more pernicious gender dynamics of racial patriarchy.

What is sold to the brothel's clientele is nothing less than the "usable past" that excludes them (Veitch 93). Wu Fong has discovered a niche market in the Jim Crow economy, offering men excluded from full citizenship the purchase of sex with white women. White women are accorded value due to their instrumental role in reproducing the nation's white citizenry. Thus, Betty's clientele momentarily partake in the trappings of white patriarchal privilege and its American history. Even within the cardboard landscape of the novel, Betty's role is ancillary and exceptionally static—from the beginning, she is only ever the girl to be collected. In the book's crude metaphor, she is a vehicle for masculine entry into the "authentic" body politic. If we witness Lem's spectacular fall throughout the novel, a fluid trajectory in the wrong direction, she remains a flat, stereotypical prop for masculinist, national belonging. In the scene of the "one hundred per centum American" whorehouse and elsewhere, "authentic" America is pointedly equated with racial capitalism and white patriarchal prerogatives.

THE GOLDEN WEST

As West demonstrates the equivalence between "authentic" America and racial capitalism, he introduces fascism as another coordinate in his political critique. This is no more in evidence than in his description of Shagpoke Whipple's efforts to organize a fascist political party against an incongruous cabal of "Jewish international bankers and the Bolshevik labor unions" (111). In Whipple's antagonists, West burlesques the crazed logic of fascist rhetoric in the United States and Germany (Rubinstein 106). Whipple explains to Lem: "The time for a new party with the old American principles was, I realized, overripe. I decided to form it; and so the National Revolutionary Party, popularly known as the 'Leather

Shirts,' was born. The uniform of our 'Storm Troops' is a coonskin cap like the one I am wearing, a deerskin shirt, and a pair of moccasins. Our weapon is the squirrel rifle" (110). His recruiting card reads:

EZRA SILVERBLATT
Official Tailor
to the

NATIONAL REVOLUTIONARY PARTY
Coonskin hats with extra long tails,
deerskin shirts with or without fringes,
blue jeans, moccasins, squirrel rifles,
everything for the American Fascist at
rock bottom prices. 30% off for Cash.

Once more, in the figure of Ezra Silverblatt, we confront a Jewish character who designs and manufactures the paraphernalia of the "American Way of life" and its "imagined national past" (Rubinstein 113). It would seem that Silverblatt is just white enough to function as the National Revolutionary Party's "official tailor." Though he outfits the party, its anti-Semitic ideology militates against his very existence. Veitch demonstrates that Silverblatt was West's fictional incarnation of Milton's Toggery, the Jewish shirt maker's shop that in reality outfitted the Silver Legion, the infamous fascist organization of Dudley Pelley in the early 1930s, as documented in an article by the muckraker John Spivak, published in *New Masses* in 1934 (Veitch 104). Just as the *New Masses* article reproduced the actual advertisement for Milton's Toggery to compound the horrible irony, West includes an advertisement for Silverblatt's services. The Indian chief Jack Raven is another incongruous aid to Whipple in his western exploits, a character who is also based in history. In keeping with the real-life precedent for Silverblatt, as Rachel Rubinstein shows, Raven is the fictional representative of the "redskin" branch of Pelley's fascist organization intended to eliminate communism on the reservations (Rubinstein 113). As we soon see in the novel's penultimate (lynching) scene, there are limits to this attempt at capitalist assimilation into the nation's economy by its minoritized subjects: Silverblatt and Raven may indirectly profit from fascism, but the paraphernalia that they sell inescapably exacts a cost of suffering from Jews and Native Americans like themselves, alongside African Americans, Catholics, Quakers, and other immigrants.

With the help of Silverblatt and Chief Jack Raven, Whipple nostalgically draws upon a ludicrous Daniel Boone iconography in order to promote his political aims. The frontiersman-like particulars of the costume allude to the legacy of westward expansionism—the United States' central imperialist project of the nineteenth century—and predict Lem's and Betty's sojourn west, to mine gold in California to finance the party.[24] This passage reveals the fascist desires behind a deployment of authenticity. West suggests that fascism and capitalism exist in a mutually beneficial relationship: in simple terms, the more the accouterments of fascism sell, the more money Whipple makes to put back into the party. In West's account, it is difficult to ascertain which goal takes precedence: is Whipple selling fascism to make money or making money to further the fascist party? What *is* clear is that fascism depends upon a discourse of authenticity—here frontier Americana—and that nothing sells in the marketplace quite like the "authentic." What's more, notions of the "authentic" neither precede nor contradict the marketplace, rather they issue *from* the marketplace.

While the example of the whorehouse illustrates Betty's commodification—her reduction to a representative artifact—the example of the fascist uniforms illustrates the construction and marketing of purportedly American paraphernalia. In both examples, person and thing are transformed into "authentic" commodities in the service of old American principles: white supremacy and expansionism, in particular. Every time we encounter an invocation of nationalist rhetoric that attempts to pass as "natural" and neutral, West points up the historical atrocities it means to repress. In so doing, he allows us to witness the process of commodification as a double movement of repression and articulation, the attempt to sever style from politics and any meaningful historical context.

Lem himself is increasingly caught up in this movement as a commodified bearer of history. His fate is sealed in the West when he attempts to save Betty from the lecherous embrace of "a man . . . who might have sat for the photograph of a Western bad man without any alteration in his countenance or apparel" (147). In the ensuing scuffle with this cartoon simulacrum of a simulacrum emanating from the nineteenth-century dime novel, Lem's leg is caught in a bear trap, and his friend, Jack Raven, is thought to be killed. Raven's people are encamped at the nearby "California Indian Reservation," and they come to avenge his death but confuse Lem with the western bad man. In the mix-up, Lem loses his scalp, along with his "store teeth and glass eye" (158). His mutilation leads to his next job under the direction of Mr. Whipple as an "exhibit . . . as the last man to have been scalped by the Indians and the sole survivor of the Yuba River massacre" (159). A relic of westward expansion, its "last" white casualty, Lem can be marketed as a nostalgic spectacle of the passing frontier. He is a broken icon befitting the Wild West Shows, the widely popular vaudeville-cum-circus styled extravaganzas that toured the nation around the start of the twentieth century. Several months later, Lem and Whipple join a larger pageant, the aptly named "Chamber of American Horrors, Inanimate and Animate Hideosities": "Although it appeared to be a museum, [it] was in reality a bureau for disseminating propaganda of the most subversive nature" (162). It is run by a failed poet and secret member of the Third International, West's doppelganger, Sylvanus Snodgrasse. In a moment that reads as an ironic articulation of West's own self-loathing regarding his lack of commercial success and his ambivalent desire for it, the narrator reports that "having lost faith in himself, [Snodgrasse] thought it his duty to undermine the nation's faith in itself." He is yet another false prophet (Hegeman, *Patterns*, 150).

The exhibits in the "Chamber of American Horrors" double and make overt the content of the other exhibits in *A Cool Million*, naming the subtext of West's burlesque. The "inanimates" consist of kitschy "manufactured articles": "a Venus de Milo with a clock in her abdomen. . . . collections of objects whose distinction lay in the great skills with which their materials had been disguised. Paper had been made to look like wood, wood like rubber, rubber like steel, steel like cheese . . . instruments whose purposes were dual and sometimes triple . . . pencil sharpeners that could also be used as earpicks, can openers as hair brushes. . . . Then, too, there was a large variety of objects whose real uses had been cleverly camouflaged. The visitor saw flower pots that were really victrolas, revolvers that held candy." (162, 163). In this antithesis of the World's Fair and its Century of Progress, art objects are reproduced as appliances; manufactured goods are made to look like raw materials and vice versa; use value is exponentially and perversely multiplied and disguised (Barnard, *Great Depression*, 151).

The illustrious, Harvard-educated Chief Israel Satinpenny declares in his screed against "the palefaces" when he rouses his tribe to avenge Jack

Raven's injury: "When the paleface controlled the things he manufactured, we red men could only wonder at and praise his ability to hide his vomit. But now all the secret places of the earth are full. Now even the Grand Canyon will no longer hold razor blades. . . . [H]e is up to his neck in the articles of his manufacture . . . he is dying in a surfeit of shoddy" (157). Placed within the context of American Horrors, the paraphernalia and debris of mass-consumer culture is shown to be nothing more than a "surfeit of shoddy." Yet, are we really to believe in the authentic and the pastoral—"this was a fair, sweet land"—for which West's Jewish Indian chief Satinpenny so eloquently advocates (Rubinstein 113)? As Rubinstein argues, in the novel "the critique of the commercial in favor of the 'authentic' becomes increasingly and troublingly articulated through racial and ethnic typologies" (111). Yet such "authentic" racial typologies that West shows again and again to be commercial products *of* the marketplace, not antidotes to the market.

It is the human cost of this "surfeit of shoddy"—including these racial and ethnic typologies and their place in the history of capitalist exploitation—that gives Satinpenny's (and West's) denunciation its weight. For the "inanimate hideosities" are accompanied by "animate hideosities." A spectacle entitled "The Pageant of America or a Curse on Columbus" consists of "short sketches in which Quakers were shown being branded, Indians brutalized and cheated, Negroes sold, children sweated to death" (163). These short sketches foreshadow the fascist riot that will take place in *A Cool Million*'s own plot, the moment when the novel's burlesque wears the look of rage, not friendship. The ease with which such obscene inanimate objects are manipulated and the ensuing "confusion of form and function" simultaneously illustrate and conceal the ease with which particular bodies have been violently turned into "things" (Veitch 102–3). The incongruous use of a pencil sharpener for an earpick and the incongruous appearance of rubber that looks like steel alludes to a more horrifying history of commodification, the incongruous conversion of people into chattel and their treatment as objects, branded and brutalized (Veitch 167n18).

To drive this point home, the sketches are accompanied by an agit-prop "playlet" depicting a sweet old grandmother swindled out of all of her Liberty Bonds by the "Indefatigable Investment Company of Wall Street," who ends up dying in the gutter surrounded by her three grandchildren already dead of starvation. Two millionaires trip over them laughing about the Investment Company's successful scam. In this scene, West signals the reformist documentary version of the story he both tells and burlesques through his novel's grotesqueries. Arguably, he both recuperates and disavows this style of social realism. He shows how easily such populist representations of sweet old grandmothers and dying children can be used by charlatans such as Snodgrasse, the curator and producer of the "Chamber of American Horrors," for profit. This critique is complicated by the narrator's comment that Snodgrasse's arguments "were not very convincing" (164). Similarly, Whipple explains to a questioning Lem, "The grandmother didn't have to buy the bonds unless she wanted to. Secondly, the whole piece is made ridiculous by the fact that no one can die in the streets. The authorities won't stand for it" (166). If West can't tell the story straight, he cautions against those who would dismiss such accounts as "unconvincing" or "ridiculous" by providing those responses in the mouths of the exceedingly unreliable narrator and the novel's resident fascist.

West's readers most likely distance themselves from Lem the dupe and his fascist counsel. Nevertheless, within the novel, Whipple's opinions hold sway over the townspeople of Beulah, Mississippi (surely not far from *Black No More*'s Happy Hill, Mississippi): "All the inhabitants of Beulah who were not colored, Jewish or Catholic assembled under a famous tree from whose every branch a Negro had dangled at one time or other. They stood together, almost a thousand strong, drinking Coca-Colas and joking with their friends. . . . [E]very third citizen carried either a rope or a gun" (167–68). In a speech, Whipple warns them that they are at risk of becoming "the slaves of Socialists and Bolsheviks" at the hands of Sylvanus Snodgrasse, inciting a lynch mob that rapidly becomes convinced that "the South had again seceded from the Union" (169). Cokes and ropes in hand, American history repeats itself and West's chatty narration goes flat, switching to the characteristically graphic and passive voice of documentary: "The heads of Negroes were paraded on poles. A Jewish drummer was nailed to the door of his hotel room. The housekeeper of the local Catholic priest was raped" (170). Akin to the horrifying climax of *Black No More*, when the white supremacists are lynched in blackface, in this scene the humor drops away as if to say, a year before Sinclair Lewis, "It *has* happened here and it can and will happen here again."

ALL HAIL, THE AMERICAN BOY!

A Cool Million has often been dismissed as one of West's lesser works, in part because of its persistently tasteless quality and its cartoonish depictions, which evoke little pathos or sympathy. By the end of the novel, Lem is nothing more than a "dysfunctional automaton" (Solomon, *Literature*, 143). This depersonalized effect is precisely the point; it inhibits a liberal politics of empathy. Recall how West described his own fiction: "There is nothing to root for in my books, and what is even worse, no rooters" (Martin, *Nathanael West: The Art*, 334). In West's burlesque, he denounces liberal capitalism under the guise of recuperating it in all of its Alger glory (Veitch 101). As he repeatedly shows us, populist appeals around a figure like Lem work more often than not to promote elite interests (Moran and Rogin 218). In response to a prevalent romanticization of "the little guy," that folksy variant who would materialize in later works such as Steinbeck's *The Grapes of Wrath* (1939), Frank Capra's "little man cycle," *Mr. Deeds Goes to Town* (1936), *Mr. Smith Goes to Washington* (1939), and *Meet John Doe* (1941), or the most widely circulated Farm Security Administration images, West's novel suggests that these modes of representation are at risk of enacting the very thing they mean to rectify, the reifying effects of mass production (227).

West takes a different tack, demonstrating the process of reification and revealing the ideological apparatus that mobilizes depictions of white masculine suffering in various manifestations of the "little guy," much in the way that Sturges will in *Sullivan's Travels*. If there is no way to get outside of the appropriating force of the market, then he shows us how it works and the historical "hideosities" that it means to conceal. An excellent illustration of this occurs in the scene when Lem joins the comedy team of Robbins and Riley, "the opportunity of a lifetime" (171). Not surprisingly, he plays the "stooge." In the act, "both actors turned on Lem and beat him violently over the head and body with their rolled up newspapers. Their object was to knock off his toupee or to knock out his teeth and eye. When they had accomplished one or all of these goals, they stopped clubbing him. Then Lem, whose part it was not to move while he was being hit, bent over and with sober dignity took from the box at his feet, which contained a large assortment of false hair, teeth and eyes, whatever he needed to replace the things that had been knocked off or out" (173–74). To add insult to injury, Lem purchases the newspapers each day for his performance that night, "[fashioning] the clubs used to beat him" (174). He saves the papers for his own reading pleasure after the performance: "They formed his only relaxation, for his meager salary made more complicated amusements impossible." Lem is thus ritualistically dismantled in front of a live audience: the very repetition of his dismembering renders him a spectacle composed of fake body parts and feeble mind. Moreover, he invests in the literary materials used to beat him, an echo of his investment in slogans of American success emanating from the Alger stories that lead to his own exploitation.

The Riley and Robbins Act metatextually condenses the action of the novel. In the show's finale, "[Riley and Robbins] brought out an enormous wooden mallet labeled 'The Works' and with it completely demolished our hero. His toupee flew off, his eye and teeth popped out, and his wooden leg was knocked into the audience. . . . [T]he spectators were convulsed with joy" (174). In this passage, West interpellates the reader as audience member, as consumer, and it is a profoundly uncomfortable role to play. This set-up recalls Amy Robinson's designation of passing as a "triangular theater" that includes the passer, the hegemonic dupe, and the "literate member of [the passer's] in-group community," one who can recognize the passer's performance (723, 728). In this paradigm, what happens if the (unsuccessful) class passer happens also to be the "hegemonic dupe"? By staging Lem as dupe, as stooge, throughout his own tale, West hopes to transform his readers into more "literate" members of Lem's in-group community. To the end, Lem "refuses to be discouraged or grow bitter and become a carping critic of things as they are" (171). It is up to West's readers to adopt this critical stance.

When the fascist revolution occurs in *A Cool Million*, it coheres around Lem's somatic breakdown. In the final chapter of the novel, Lem is asked by Mr. Whipple to speak out at a rally for the National Revolutionary Party in New York City. Just as Lem utters his first sentences—" 'I am a clown . . . but there are times when even clowns must grow serious. This is such a time. I . . . .' "—he is shot dead, at the hands, no less, of one of Mr. Whipple's associates (177). Lem's birthday becomes a national holiday inspiring youth marches across the land to the tune of "The Lemuel Pitkin Song": "A million hearts for Pitkin, oh! / To do and die with Pitkin, oh!" (178). Once more, the enterprising fascists are able to produce a coherent metaphoric and synecdochic spectacle of white masculine suffering out of Lem's uniquely damaged body: as Mr. Whipple declares, "Although dead, yet he speaks. Of what is it that he speaks? Of the right of every American boy to go into the world and there receive fair play and a chance to make his fortune by industry and probity without being laughed at or conspired against by sophisticated aliens" (179). Even in death, Lem's wrecked and now inert body is conscripted to represent "the American Boy." As in every other performance, his suffering is read not as a sign of the nation's potentially false promise of upward class mobility; rather, his injured body is read as evidence of a national masculine whiteness on the brink of violation by racial, religious, and foreign others. In the party's postrevolutionary commemoration, the new dictator, Mr. Whipple, victoriously declaims: "Through his martyrdom the National Revolutionary Party triumphed . . . this country was delivered from sophistication, Marxism and International Capitalism. Through the National Revolution its people were purged of alien diseases and America became again American." Lem is finally made into a fascist folk figure, the last stereotype in a seemingly endless string: "Our young hero"; the single white survivor of the Yuba Massacre; freakish stooge in the Riley and Robbins's burlesque; martyr to the National Revolutionary Party (Solomon 143; West 74). When Lem becomes the standard bearer for the fascist party, this concluding irony shows the cannibalistic, self-perpetuating underpinnings of racial patriarchy and its Gospel of Success (Veitch 94).

Lest West's counterparable appear nostalgic for the "olden days" when a character such as Lem could perform a "class pass" successfully, West insists that this nostalgia for a "pure" account of American self-making is yet another ideological product of the nationalist marketplace easily harnessed for fascist yearnings. *A Cool Million* foregrounds the production of the folklore of racial capitalism for profit, showing the ways that cultural forms such as the Horatio Alger stories sustain a hard-working labor force through the promise of class ascension that ever recedes into the distance (Veitch 98). As we witness in Whipple's relentless sales pitches regarding Henry Ford, "the land of opportunity," and "the old American principles," the failure of whiteness to deliver economic success is often repressed through the repeated insistence that the promise of class mobility will be realized in the future (West 73, 110). The rags-to-riches formula works financially for those like Whipple and, to a lesser degree, those like Wu Fong, Asa Goldstein, and Ezra Silverblatt, who are willing to sell it and other forms of American exceptionalism; not for those who try to follow its prescriptions. In the end, Mr. Whipple is right about only one thing, his contention that the "inalienable birthright" of American citizens is "the right to sell their labor and their children's labor without restrictions as to either price or hours"—the right to be exploited (110). The more battered Lem becomes, ironically, the better his body can be used as a sign of American "progress"—the last white survivor of the frontier that is now "settled," the last American boy to be victimized by "sophisticated aliens," who have now all been "purged" from the body politic (179). As Slavoj Žižek observes, "An ideology really succeeds when even the facts which at first sight contradict it start to function as arguments in its favor"; in this way the malleable and broken figure of Lem exemplifies the smooth workings of capitalist and fascist ideology (*Sublime Object*, 49). Lem is thoroughly incorporated within exploitative capitalist relations.

With the folk figure of Lem, West lambasts the populist rhetoric rapidly taking hold of the nation in the wake of the Depression, a populist rhetoric that would shape many of the era's documentary and ethnographic productions of the folk, including the Federal Writers' Project's Florida guidebook, discussed in part 2 of this book. He investigates the brutal, material consequences of "buying in" ideologically to particular narratives of purity and success. He demonstrates the ways that fascism and Jim Crow capitalism facilitate each other through their mutual logic of racialization. What he anticipates, finally, is the way that Hitler's rant of the Volk would shadow the debates around the meaning of "the people" in the political culture of the 1930s (Moran and Rogin 224, 223). In this way, *A Cool Million* sustains an incisive critique of American exceptionalism, the country's founding mythology of meritocracy and upward mobility, by foregrounding its dependence upon codified nationalist slogans and the protofascist production of "authentic" raced and gendered American bodies and narratives. Literally "caught in the act" of attempting to pass into the business class—to rise above his class origins—Lem becomes all too embodied and subsequently dismembered. In order to make a living, Lem continuously performs the impossibility of his class pass for an audience, including the reader. In a metatextual sleight of hand, West accomplishes his critique by staging his novel as a failed "pass" for a Horatio Alger tale. In sum, Lem becomes a perverse icon, undermining the conventional representation of the "authentic" bootstrap hero and revealing it to be yet another one of the mass-produced racial and gender stereotypes that proliferate within the pages of *A Cool Million*. In the words of the narrator, "Alas, to such a sorry pass had [Lem] come" (116).

A Cool Million's conclusion raises several questions: Does an invocation of the folk *without* burlesque lead to fascism? Is it possible to successfully burlesque fascism for progressive, antifascist political ends? Or do the incorporative powers of fascism render this political gesture finally inert? In a cantankerous essay, Jonathan Raban criticized West's novels for being "as much symptoms as they are diagnoses of the disease" of mass commodity culture, a critique that might be extended to West's replication of the reifying processes of fascism (Raban, "A Surfeit of Commodities," 229–31). Following Constance Rourke's definition of burlesque, West's novel "wholly possesses its subject," dismantling American formulas of success and their fascist possibilities before the reader's very eyes. Yet if, by the end, the dismantled, now dead Alger folk figure can still be turned into a folk martyr for fascism, what are we left with? West's modernist burlesque might finally fail in the face of fascism's incorporative powers, its totalitarian ability to turn the best counter-example into supporting evidence for its own ideology. But this is West's point. As he stages the mechanics of this failure, we see just how the folk are incorporated within fascist narratives and how the audience is set up as potential dupes like Lem. In their probable alienation from the "convulsing audience" in attendance at the Riley and Robbins smack-down and the flag-waving youths in Whipple's parade, West's audience must develop a resistant reading practice and become the "sophisticated aliens" the fascists so revile (179). The didactic implication of these theatrical scenes, the self-reflexive transformation of the reader into a "sophisticated alien," thus literalizes Brechtian alienation effects, effects "which prevent the audience from losing itself passively and completely in the character created by the actor [in this case, West the writer], and which consequently lead the audience to be a consciously critical observer" (Brecht, "Alienation Effects," 91). It is finally up to *A Cool Million*'s audience to refuse Whipple's imperative: "All Hail the American Boy!"

A screenwriter in the modern "fiction factories" of the thirties, West was able to tell a different story about and through the lens of the dime novels, one that engages with the fraught dimensions of "the culture of the new masses" (Denning, *Mechanic Accents*, 16). West demonstrated the limits of racial capitalism and its exclusive American Dream in *A*

Cool Million. At the same time, much like his novel's immigrant entrepreneurs who work as "cultural middlemen," he also wrote scripts for Hollywood that promoted the rags-to-riches formula—a formula that more often included Jews as its external purveyors, rather than its internal protagonists (Rogin, *Blackface*, 64). Even the legendary (and Jewish) Al Jolson wrote himself into the social mobility script through his self-conscious staging of the rags-to-riches formula—by exposing the manufacture of his self-making into American whiteness through his popular blackface routine (66). Given West's own ambivalent position as a worker inside the emerging culture industries, it is fitting that *A Cool Million*'s final twist concerns its afterlife as a screenplay.[25] Columbia Studios bought the film rights to the novel in 1934, its pitch: "Honesty will buy you pain and disgrace" (Martin, *Nathanael West: The Art*, 245; Veitch 105). After the novel moldered in the studio files for six years, West and his screenwriting partner Boris Ingster wrote a short adaptation of the novel in 1940, framing it as a screwball comedy. Columbia then assigned the adaptation to one of their most valued screenwriters, Sidney Buchman, who had just written the populist blockbuster *Mr. Deeds* directed by Frank Capra. This last contorted product proved unfilmable.

Yet, as this book's concluding chapter shows, the novel's grotesque exploration of the limits of class passing and the American creed would animate the plot of another movie, Preston Sturges's *Sullivan's Travels*, in 1941. More immediately, *A Cool Million*'s burlesque of the folk would pose a challenge to the populist folk revival of the mid-thirties evidenced in New Deal cultural projects such as the Federal Writers' Project Guidebook Series and other ethnographic endeavors. And in Zora Neale Hurston's work, we see the imprint of *A Cool Million*'s performative dismantling of authenticity, its parsing of the patriotic contours of the folk in the marketplace, though with radically different results.

PART II
Performing the Folk

But even in life the Negro was not wholly primitive;
his satire was often conscious; and the everyday comedy
of the Yankee and the backwoodsman almost invariably
wore the air of contrivance. Occasionally in practical jokes
their humor seemed only gross and physical; yet at best even
these contained a deliberate fantasy. As the three figures were
projected in stories or on the stage the effect of consciousness
was greatly heightened. With all their rude poetry it was
about a mind that these myths centered, a conscious,
indeed an acutely self-conscious mind.

—CONSTANCE ROURKE, *American Humor:*
A Study of the National Character (1931)

2. Zora Neale Hurston, half-length portrait, standing, facing front, looking at book, *American Stuff*, at New York Times Book Fair, November 1937. Library of Congress, Prints and Photographs Division, LC-USZ62-126945.

Chapter 3.

"The Last American Frontier":
Mapping the Folk in the Federal Writers' Project's
Florida: A Guide to the Southernmost State

I shall want a guidebook that can stifle its passion for statistics and arrow-heads long enough to leave some room to write about American people. But I'm afraid I'll be disappointed, and that guidebooks will continue to treat people as they always have—as ethnological wax groups frozen behind the glass exhibit-cases of a natural history museum.
—ROBERT LITTELL, "Putting America on Paper,"
Today 5 (30 November 1935)

Though the Federal Writers' Project (FWP) state guidebooks are now sold in the antiquarian marketplace, back in their day, they served as a conduit for selling something much larger: the nation itself. As predicted by the satires of Nathanael West and George Schuyler, the folk con-stituted a major populist component of the New Deal's cultural cam-paign. The American Guide Series' detailed chronicling of America, its efforts to uncover the "real" United States through an officially sanc-tioned cultural geography, fit into the New Deal's larger documentary project of recollecting and representing the country to its citizens for the purpose of rebuilding the nation, both ideologically and economically.[1] As Grace Overmyer put it, each guidebook provided "a sort of road map for the cultural rediscovery of America from within" (qtd. in Stott, *Documentary Expression*, 110).

   This chapter demonstrates how the American Guide Series effectively set out to manage the space and time of the nation, reorganizing it for popular consumption. In this effort, it provided its readers with a layper-son's ethnography of the country's folk types, at once inviting them to identify with the "common man" figure of the tourist who travels through its pages and also to participate as amateur anthropologists in the study of each state's own native others. As one wpa poster promised, the American Guide Series aimed to "illustrate a national way of life" while at the same time "portray variants in local patterns of living."[2] The Guide Series negotiated its dual purpose by deploying a narrative strategy of populist synecdoche wherein the contemporary "common man" tourist stood in for the modern nation and the folk stood in for its agrarian-capitalist past.[3] As the Guide Series seized upon the folk as figural points of origin in its narrative of New Deal progress, it partook in a modernist culture of collecting. Paradoxically, the folk types featured in the series were simultaneously included and excluded within its temporal and spatial mapping of the nation (Carbado, "Racial Naturalization," 698).[4]

Perpetuating an already robust nostalgia for "authentic" culture in the thirties, many of the guides derived specificity from segregation and other forms of federal and state-mandated exclusions to create a marketable dichotomy centered on the modern white collective and its "colored" and colorful folk past. The guides' epistemology of folk types encompassed each group's particularities within its inclusive, democratic pretext, versing the traveler in their various traits and behaviors. In this way, the tourist gaze within the series was constructed through a taxonomy of "types": above all, the folk were designated as the locus of the real, coordinates on the New Deal's map of American culture, the urtext upon which its narrative of American progress and nationhood was built. With slogans such as "Be your own gypsy," "Abandon all rules and directions and . . . make up your own tours," the American Guide Series capitalized upon cultural and racial difference as a means of promoting "exotic" adventure in the United States, encouraging its potential travelers not only to observe their "picturesque" neighbors but also to adopt the purportedly "wandering spirit" of the transient folk-laborers who populated the regions of the nation (Brown, *Inventing New England*, 206).

Such a state-sponsored mandate for wanderlust was made possible by the increasingly affordable automobile, the endgame of Henry Ford's quest for a mass-produced "people's car," realized first in the Model T of 1908 and, by the 1920s, in a range of makes and more reliable, faster models pitched to middle-class consumers (Jakle and Sculle, *Motoring*, 19–20; Cross, *All-Consuming Century*, 49–50). The Depression notwithstanding, half of American families owned automobiles; passenger car registration jumped from eight million vehicles in 1920 to twenty-three million vehicles by the end of the 1930s (Young and Young, *Great Depression*, 36, 559). Automobiles thus became the principal mode of leisure travel, superseding rail travel and accounting for 90 percent of all travel (in miles) by 1940 (Zimring, " 'Neon,' " 96; Young and Young 559). The American Guide Series' advocacy for travel was also enabled by "the golden age of highway building," from 1921 to 1936, when motorists and industry successfully lobbied for expanding an interconnected system of interstate highways with the support of federal and state governments (Jakle and Sculle 73–75). Gary Cross observes that such improvements "let thousands of easterners tour picturesque New England towns in the summers and journey to the Florida seashore in winter" (53). The New Deal's Public Works Administration's focus on road construction projects worked synergistically, then, with the American Guide Series' efforts to encourage Americans to take to the open road.[5] A modern sense of automotive freedom and access led to new and capacious articulations of the nation, mapped out in a multiplicity of scenic tours.

The sheer size of the project—over a thousand books and pamphlets—poses a conundrum for a specific accounting of the actual guides' content, tone, and narrative construction. Perhaps for this reason, with the exception of a few significant interventions such as Christine Bold's *The wpa Guides: Mapping America* (1999), Marguerite Shaffer's *See America First* (2001), and Michael Szalay's *New Deal Modernism: American Literature and the Invention of the Welfare State* (2000), literary critics and historians have tended to focus on the *fact* of the project rather than the content of its actual writing or the ideological implications of its existence.[6] To make broader arguments about the series as a whole, inevitably, the critic must extend her analysis of a particular guidebook to encompass a synecdochic relation to the rest of the series. Such generalizations are tentative at best. Although the central office of the fwp in Washington, D.C., attempted to exert editorial control, the project was too large to fully monitor and, as a result, its quality is inconsistent, both within and between individual guide books. Moreover, the political standpoint of the guidebooks shifted from state to state. Some of the books, such as *The wpa Guide to New York City* (1939), delivered extraordinarily nuanced accounts of racialized economic and social conditions in America, while others did not (Bold 92). In a broad assessment of the project, it is easy to overlook the radical energies that animated some of the state guides (Denning, *Cultural Front*, 86). As this chapter argues, the guides' polyvocal production and hybrid composition—their collective authorship by many different writers—led to internal inconsistencies which may be, in some cases, their most compelling attributes.

In order to investigate the American Guide Series beyond its directives and the structure of its operation, this chapter repeats the synecdochic logic of the project but reads it against the grain. I turn to a specific example, *Florida: A Guide to the Southernmost State* (1939). This particular guide functions as a rich case study for several reasons: by the 1930s, Florida occupied a pivotal spot in the nation's incipient tourist economy (Mormino, "Sunbelt Dreams," 4). Tourism is fundamental to our understanding of the construction of the folk in the Depression because it represents one of the industries most overtly engaged in marketing the folk and their nostalgic temporalities to the American public. In 1930, tourism comprised over 20 percent of Florida's total economic base, a percentage that would only increase in the decades to come (Stronge, *Sunshine Economy*, 115). In 1935, tourists spent double the value of all of the products manufactured in the state (Florida State [guide] 87). More roadside attractions were opened in Florida during the 1930s than any other decade in the state's history (142). It is not surprising, then, that Florida's early economic recovery during the Depression—from a contraction that originated not with the nation's stock market collapse but the collapse of the state's real estate boom in 1926—was achieved largely through the turnaround of the state's tourism industry (Stronge 140). Mary Woods argues that at this time, in tourist spots around the nation, there were "glimpses of an emerging service economy supplanting a traditional industry and agriculture," yet south Florida constituted "the first and most developed example of the postindustrial economy of the late twentieth and early twenty-first centuries" (Woods, *Beyond the Architect's Eye*, 216).[7] Florida was thus the vanguard of a new kind of tourism incipient in the thirties. Given the region's growing reputation as a modern tourist empire, the Florida guide thus enacts an especially revealing metacommentary about the state's tourist draw.

As a more democratized, "mass rather than class" tourism took hold of the nation in the 1930s and 1940s, one inclusive of middle-class and even working-class tourists, not for the first time, history was cast as heritage (Woods 215; Shaffer 218).[8] Florida's modeling of a thoroughly modern

service economy was dependent, in part, on a carefully calibrated reinvention of its past: just as its growing cities switched architectural styles
from the Mediterranean revival so popular in the 1920s to futuristic
streamline modern in the 1930s, the state's adjoining rural areas were
advertised as "the last American frontier," a temporal and spatial periphery which gave new meanings to Old South and New South, quaint and
modern, folk and cosmopolite (Woods 175–77; Florida State, foreword).
As Woods suggests and the Florida guide bears out, the narration of
temporal slippages and spatial displacements was crucial to the state's
tourist appeal.

The Florida guide sold prospective visitors a particular relation to the
"other," in this case an array of folk types who occupied the nostalgic
temporality of "the last frontier," free from the homogenizing influence
of mass culture yet somehow visible and accessible to the modern automobile traveler. The volume navigates Florida's multiethnic population
of native inhabitants as well as its complex history of four centuries of
colonization and conquest by deploying the thrill of anthropological
discovery on the frontier in order to captivate its readers. Echoing earlier
travel writing about Florida after the Civil War, the Florida guidebook
tells a story of regional diversity and national unity—it composes a narrative of northern and southern reconciliation in the era of Jim Crow,
treating the rural folk both as a problem and a resource within "uneven
modernity" (Hegeman, *Patterns*, 4). In this way, the folk are central
players in a story meant to reunite the nation by binding together ever
more tightly the economic ties between the North and South through
tourism. The Florida guide's concentrated emphasis on tourism and
ethnography provides unique insights into the ways the guidebooks incorporated racial, cultural, and regional difference into a story of New
Deal progress. Hailed as "the first indigenous guidebooks" of America,
the American Guide Series, in the words of Marguerite Shaffer, positioned "America as a modern folk nation" (Bold 9; Shaffer 203). If the
folk were a construct of the modern nation, they were pointedly located
as its past and precursor. The Florida guide played a vital role in this
modern folk construction.

This chapter's investigation of the Florida guide also works in tandem
with my reading of Zora Neale Hurston's *Mules and Men* (1935), another
ethnographically minded collection devoted to Florida, in my next chapter. Arguably, the Florida guide is the least satirical text in my study—the

text that constructs the folk in earnest—and therefore my archive's proverbial straight man. However, as we shall see, the guide often adopts a
double voice about its own promotion of Florida's tourist sites, establishing its ethnographic authority against the superficial slogans of the travel
industry. Moreover, it includes voices such as Hurston's that signify on the
construction of the folk elsewhere within its pages. My research might be
said to enact one more "search for Zora" story, though not so grand as
Alice Walker's and the biographers who have followed in her footsteps.
Under the employ of the Federal Writers' Project from 1938 to 1939,
Hurston wrote for the Florida guide and for a later-published work entitled *The Florida Negro: A Federal Writers' Project Legacy* (ed. McDonogh,
1993). Hurston's prose nearly jumps off the page when compared to the
"federalese" that comprises much of the guide's text (Kennedy, "Working," 65). Her contributions to *Florida: A Guide to the Southernmost State*
by contrast theorize and expose in bold relief the guidebook's distinct
strategies of mapping race, labor, and nationhood within a climate of New
Deal liberalism. By limning the depths of this fissure, this chapter demonstrates the Guide Series' deployment of documentary aesthetics and ethnographic pleasures in its construction of a laboring folk tableau vivant
meant to provide a usable past for a region and nation in crisis.

DEMOCRATIC MIMESIS AND POPULIST SYNECDOCHE

If the notion of a Federal Writers' Project is thrilling, there is something
perverse about its chief creation, the American Guide Series. In spite of
its prodigious output, the Federal Writers' Project was legally prohibited
from making a profit from the series (Szalay 63). In keeping with this
ethos, the writers were salaried workers, their "craftsman's wage" derived
from the hours they worked, not the particular pieces of writing they
produced (27–28). In this way, Michael Szalay suggests, "the Federal
Writers' Project assimilated working-class politics, wage labor and a performative aesthetic" (28). In spite of its nonprofit status, considerations
of the marketplace were never entirely outside of the series' purview. By
securing the interest of potential travelers, the series not only aimed to
increase the amount of money spent on tourism in the United States but
also to invigorate employment in the service industry. The national
director of the Federal Writers' Project, Harry Alsberg, explained, "If the

guides keep some of the American millions, normally spent abroad, right here and add to them some of the European millions . . . they will do much to alleviate financial conditions in this country and reduce unemployment" (qtd. in Weigle, "Finding," 63). As an ideological and fiscal remedy to the crisis tendencies of capitalism, so evident in the Depression economy, the encyclopedic scope and the documentary method of the guidebooks fit into a larger program of rationalized state planning on a massive scale.

The internal structure of the organization was top-down, at least in concept. Riven with internal bureaucratic and ideological conflicts, the central office of the Federal Writers' Project in Washington attempted to consolidate its authority over its state offices and unify their product by establishing parameters that would dictate the form and content of each guidebook. Alsberg sent out a handbook of instructions, "The American Guide Manual," to every state editor at the beginning of the project in 1935.[9] In the end, eighteen revised drafts of this manual circulated among the state offices, a number that illustrates the difficulties of large-scale textual standardization (Bold 30). The national editor who first conceived of the guidebook series, Katherine Kellock, "insisted that the guides satisfy all travelers, whether drivers on interstate highways or hardy trail explorers"—though, in the end, no doubt in part due to their 600-page heft, the guides were mainly written for drivers (Weigle 63). While Kellock preferred a volume primarily devoted to actual tourist routes, the project's director, Alsberg, and the associate director, George Cronyn, wanted to develop a detailed encyclopedia of each state for armchair travelers and historians (Penkower, *Federal Writers' Project*, 31; Weigle 62). In keeping with their vision, the instruction manual asserted that "for the average citizen who cannot afford to travel extensively, yet is interested in all the resources of his country, the guide will provide in simple language a medium to acquaint him with every section of this vast country" (supplement 7771-1). An eventual editorial compromise resulted in the standard format found in all of the state guides, a three-part structure composed of essays regarding local history, culture, and economics; city profiles; and actual automobile routes. This form impelled the guidebooks to cover a good deal of ground and incorporate a range of discourses emanating from the social sciences.

Intended to capitalize on an increasingly mobile middle class,[10] the guidebooks linked together a discourse of progressive ethnography with an economics of tourism to produce a comprehensive and potentially lucrative vision of America.[11] Due to this marriage of multiple aims, each guide is heterogeneous, simultaneously drawing upon several different epistemological domains in its approach. The guide's historical sections rewrote the nation's origins and substantiated its present progress, while geographical data marked the country spatially. Its ethnographic sections documented America's "folk" populations and its cultural and physical descriptions outlined the architectural, artistic, and literary attributes of each region. Its often whimsical prefatory remarks situated the prospective tourist—most often white, male, and economically mobile, perhaps with a family in tow—as a traveling citizen of the nation. Its financial statistics provided this potential consumer with a "business report" for his future speculations (Behdad, *Belated Travelers*, 39). In order to accurately incorporate information from these various fields of knowledge, "The American Guide Manual" instructed each state director to take into consideration the multiple specializations required of his or her writers. In its "Division of Task" section, for example, the manual suggests: "Each state director would have to keep in touch with the editorial staff to determine who among them has a specialized training in some specific field so that he can be entrusted with special sections of the work. Thus, for instance, if one of the workers has had special training in *sociology* or *anthropology*, he may be assigned to check on the material of sociological interests, and racial groups and their cultural contributions" (supplement 8077-3; emphasis added). The assignment of labor according to specialty quite literally manifests the text's polyvocal authorship, an authorship rendered all the more complicated by the often contentious relationships that developed between state and federal editors.

The manual's examples of professional expertise, anthropology and sociology, speak to the American Guide Series' explicitly ethnographic purpose. The project's implicit definitions of who counted as "authentic" —the racialized folk in the figure of the Indian, "the Negro," and other groups—demonstrate the extent to which the contemporaneous "scientific" practices of anthropology, folklore, and documentary informed the fwp's primary aims. While Popular Front intellectuals such as B. A. Botkin, the national fwp folklore editor, advocated a pluralist approach to America's folk cultures, one that included the urban in its fieldwork, the guidebooks most often privileged seemingly timeless, rural lore. Driven by an aestheticized notion of the ordinary, the everyday, the "common man," and the folk, the guide writers were encouraged to suss out the "real" thing in their travels and subsequent writings: one press release from the central office claimed "material has actually been collected locally, on the spot, by Guide workers who are native to the location and can catch its real spirit" (qtd. in Shaffer 205). As a result, the writers often represented their subjects—the community's residents—as exotic bearers of the real, to be viewed by tourists from other states. Given the fact that the FWP workers were all hired to work in the regions in which they lived, these depictions might include the writers themselves, rendering them, simultaneously, writing observers and subjects of their own gaze, much in the way that Zora Neale Hurston situated herself in *Mules and Men* and her other ethnographic projects of the same decade (Bold 21; Wald, *Constituting*, 106). Christine Bold notes that "Alsberg and others seem initially to have read the heterogeneity of employees mimetically, expecting them to demonstrate America's rich democratic diversity by delivering their indigenous beliefs, habits and knowledges in their localized voices" (29). They were hired according to region on the presumption that as inhabitants, as cultural and geographic "insiders," they would lend the project an authenticity and familiarity absent from previous guidebooks.

On a conceptual level, then, the guides were governed by an ethos of democratic mimesis—that is, a mode of representation characterized by a seemingly all-encompassing approach to its subject wherein the leveling force of democracy renders every historical moment and nuance of commensurate value. The guides depended upon a putatively one-to-one correspondence between the writers, their social and ethnic backgrounds, and their regions. If the writers and their taxonomies of "real" types were supposed to represent the diversity of each state, then so, too, was each guidebook's exhaustive itemization of facts, a documentary method of excessive factuality that a writer like James Agee would push into overdrive in his collaboration with Walker Evans, *Let Us Now Praise Famous Men*. The series' documentary aesthetics went hand in hand with the New Deal's vision of an orderly and harmonious national collective, its present comprising ordinary citizens and its past comprising often overlooked marginalized communities and indigenous regional cultures, a variant of what Michael Rogin describes as "a black past and a white present" (Filene, *Romancing*, 134; Rogin, *Blackface*, 49).

Like the guides' writers, the guides' readers were also, on occasion, its subjects. Depending upon the reader's interests and home state, the guides might simultaneously feature him as a tourist in one guide and a native "type" in another. Hypothetically, then, the guide's exhaustive coverage placed the reader in multiple roles in relation to its content—armchair traveler, prospective tourist, native subject, editor. Although the FWP central office aimed to introduce a new travel-writing style in America, one "restrained and dignified"—more documentary-inspired than the typical chamber of commerce "ballyhoo"—the guides' capacious collection of "useless" facts often makes for monotonous reading (Penkower 75).[12] Readers must judiciously scan the text according to their own interests. In this way, the process of reading a guidebook literally informed and figuratively mirrored the process of traveling. A traveler might consult sections from a state guidebook to make decisions about where to visit and how to get there. Alternatively, when an armchair traveler browsed a guide, the process of reading became a performative act of navigation and narration, a continuous process of avoiding monotony by choosing more engaging passages.

While it is nearly impossible to account for actual patterns of reading, it is not so difficult to trace the ways that the guide editors situated an ideal reader within each text. By examining the reader's inscription within the guides, we see how the act of reading not only constitutes a kind of narrative traveling but also enacts a process of citizenship whereby the reader enters the imagined collective through his or her own selective narration of the collection of facts. And here, the guides' purported quality of inclusiveness becomes quite discriminating, for their envisaged reader is constructed as a privileged traveling and seeing subject. The guides' anticipated audience has everything to do with its visions of nation, its fantasies of a unified, democratic, and implicitly white collective and the incursion of a contradictory United States, replete with its inequitably divided communities and constituents.

The scope of the guidebooks' national vision was perpetually in question, dependent upon an individual state guide's practices of inclusion and exclusion, practices largely dependent upon the editors' political inclinations and the anticipated readership. Unequal power relations along racial, class, gender, and regional lines were often masked in textual elisions and a language of "equivalent" facts. As Monty Penkower describes in his historical account *The Federal Writers' Project* (1977), the Guide Series was troubled by internal and public conflicts with regard to its readers about the reportage of various politically charged events in United States history: "When it became apparent that the Civil War was still being fought in some states, the Washington office decided that 'War between the States' could be substituted for that term in Dixie guidebooks" (Penkower 76).[13] The phrase "War between the States" frames the Civil War in more conciliatory terms, as a regional dispute over states' rights and the southern "way of life" rather than a mortal conflict over the preservation of chattel slavery or the overtly white supremacist imperatives that would sustain the color line into the thirties and beyond, implications that might have offended the books' southern, white readership. The "Dixie" guides participated in a larger project of sectional reconciliation between the North and the South by redirecting their focus away from white and black racial strife and all but eclipsing the region's equally fraught conflict over white people's federally sanctioned land grab from indigenous peoples who lived in the territory first. Ironically, reconciliation meant using different terminology for different regional audiences, the more euphemistic phrase eliding questions of racism and social justice, all toward invigorating a robust federal collective grounded in what the historians Grace Elizabeth Hale and Ed Blum describe as a white ethnic nationalism (Hale, *Making Whiteness*, 66, 67–74; Blum, *Reforging*, 7–17). Regional debates aside, the guides were edited to be as inoffensive as possible to the readership deemed most valuable.

Given the impossibility of actually achieving democratic mimesis in the guide series' sweep—an inventory so vast that every last fact, place, and person would be represented—the guidebooks adopted instead a populist synecdochic strategy.[14] Outlining the project's mission, "The American Guide Manual" stated: "It is absolutely essential to make the [series] the complete, standard, authoritative work on the United States *as a whole and of every part of it*" (17; emphasis added). According to B. A. Botkin, the project was to support an inclusive nationalism that would relate "the part to the whole" (qtd. in Hirsch, "Cultural Pluralism," 51). This strategy emanated from the very conception of the New Deal itself: Franklin Roosevelt claimed in 1933, for example, that his legislation had "not just been a collection of haphazard schemes, but rather the orderly component *parts* of a connected and logical *whole*" ("Fireside Chat," 61; emphasis added). In keeping with Roosevelt's state rationalization, every locale depicted in the guides is measured by an implicit national standard. When a state falls short of this criterion, the New Deal is poised to intervene and ameliorate its infrastructural failures, thereby reincorporating it into the nation.[15] Given the series' realist aims, its populist synecdochic strategy was not meant to appear to be a strategy at all, and certainly not ideological. Rather, the guides were represented as a natural unearthing of a national story both past and present, a documentary that shape-shifts, conforming to the interests of its individual citizen-readers and the contours of the country as a whole.[16]

Within the Guide Series' populist synecdochic strategy, the tourist-reader most often stood in for the nation's modern "common man." In an adjacent set of populist synecdochic representations compatible with the series' reclamation of American folkways, certain folk types stood in for each region's past inhabitants and certain facts stood in for each region's past history. In the specific case of *Florida: A Guide to the Southernmost State*, the guide set out to attract visitors to the state by representing the region's folk types as simultaneously anomalous and typical, exotic and familiar. The guide drew upon four populist types—the outsider Yankee "common man" and the native folk comprising the "cracker," the Indian, and the Negro—a constellation that dovetailed with the archetypal folk trio of the Yankee, the backwoodsman, and the blackface minstrel advanced eight years earlier in Constance Rourke's *American Humor: A Study of National Character*. As George Schuyler and Nathanael West so skillfully prophesied, the patriotic representations of the folk promoted by the New Deal cultural programs in many ways had their antecedents in minstrelsy's frenetic types, the anti-aristocratic popular theater of P. T. Barnum and the Jacksonian era out of which minstrelsy emerged (Toll, *Blacking Up*, 6–21).[17]

In the Florida guide's populist types, the Yankee was positioned as the tourist "common man" who interacted with the state's native folk trio, a designation consistent with the Yankee's initial appearance in the regional humor of the 1820s. Robert Toll describes how "the Yankee possessed the good traits of Europeans stripped of their decadence, pretension and corruption. He represented the American Everyman, arisen and triumphant. . . . [H]e provided a symbol ordinary Americans could identify with and believe in" (14). As we shall see, in their tourist transactions, the Yankee is bound to his folksy southern antecedent, the cracker. Within the guide, their droll encounters enact a drama of sectional reconciliation based upon a presumed common whiteness—the cracker's liminal "not quite white" status sutured to the stable whiteness of the Yankee—that ultimately works in the service of a modern white national collective (Wray, *Not Quite White*, 17).

The Florida guide offered conflicting definitions of the state's observable folk types, definitions that fluctuated due to specific histories of racial exclusion. In particular, it would vacillate about the status of "Latin-Americans" (in its expansive usage, people originally "from Cuba, Spain and Italy") as a fourth, native folk type. Like the guide's other nonwhite native folk types—African Americans and Native Americans—"Latin-Americans" are featured as a source of trouble for the state. Foreshadowed in the guide's glowing commentary about missionary efforts to control and "civilize" Indians, the book recounts in rapid succession a litany of problems posed by the state's nonwhite inhabitants: "The Seminole Indians were the first great *problem* of American settlers who moved to Florida"; "On November 5, 1865, the convention ratified the Thirteenth Amendment and gave the governor power to appoint a commission to make recommendations, chiefly on the *problem* of assimilating the Negro into the new government"; finally, "Cuban immigrants brought their *political troubles* along with their cigar business to Florida" (56, 58, 60; emphasis added). The state's Seminoles, African Americans, and Cuban immigrants all pose distinct "problems" in the United States' colonization of the Florida territory: as such, they necessitate a policy of management to enable their quasi-incorporation into the nation. In contrast with these pejorative representations, the "Folklore" chapter designates these same groups, with the addition of Florida's "cracker," as the state's authentic producers of "real" folk culture, an excellent source for ethnographic study, formative of its populist synecdoches of the folk.

Though the Florida guide mentions Latin Americans in its "Folklore" chapter, beyond a curtailed discussion of the state's folk heritage it largely excludes them elsewhere in its depictions of the state's past (128, 133). This exclusion suggests that within the guide, Florida's Latin Americans undergo, in the words of Devon Carbado, "a kind of national identity displacement or racial extraterritorialization"; still perceived as foreigners, they had not yet been conscripted into the role of domestic other in the state's regional identity, an "inclusionary form of exclusion" extended to poor whites, African Americans, and Native Americans (698). This elision is deeply ironic for it actively forgets the presence of people of

Spanish descent who colonized the territory well before its Anglo settlers. Committing what could be described as racialized historical amnesia, the Florida guide's most prevalent populist synecdoches thus cohere around two categories: that of the native folk (poor whites, African Americans, and Indians) and that of the Yankee "common man."

In the Florida guide, the anticipated Yankee reader-tourist is incorporated into the state's tourist economy as a visitor-turned-resident, no longer just a consumer but a producer, too. Even the state's folk populations become small-time producers in this economy—the state's Seminoles and "crackers" conscripted to perform the primitive in order to partake in a cottage industry of roadside attractions. African American labor, past and present, inadvertently becomes another tourist site in this travel circuit. Whether or not the state's folk overtly participate in the tourist industries, the guide suggests that they all hope to make enough money to become tourists one day. Amateur producers. Aspiring tourists. "Local color" laborers. These roles aside, it is the folk's ethnographic intrigue, the way they are made to stand in for an agrarian-capitalist past on the brink of forgotten, that decisively incorporates them into the New Deal story of the modern state and nation.

THE NATIVE FOLK VERSUS THE COMMON MAN

The Florida guide draws a distinction between the native folk populations it documents and the common-man Yankee reader-tourist for whom it is ostensibly written. In part, this separation depends upon the temporal dimensions of the guide's strategy of populist synecdoche, wherein the Yankee common man stands in for the modern white American collective and Florida's native folk are subject to a temporal and spatial "inclusive exclusion," relegated to the past and to the geographic margins of society—segregated urban spaces, reservations, rural enclaves, and the backwoods (Carbado 639). Given the legal doctrine of "separate but equal," African Americans could not be represented in a facile synecdochic relation to the entire nation, "a part for a whole." Instead, the guide consistently juxtaposes Florida's African American population with the more privileged white population of the state, asserting that the federal government and its New Deal programs, in particular, the WPA (the FWP's parent agency), are making significant improvements in the lives of black people. In a candid assessment of Florida's segregated education system, the guide notes: "The constitution of 1885 contains the provision: 'White and colored children shall not be taught in the same school but impartial provision shall be made for both.' The principle of segregation has been carried out, but educational facilities for Negro and white children are far from equal" (103). The guide's critique centers on the fact that the state has not carried out the law in an *impartial* manner; its educational facilities serve white children far more adequately than black children.

In every chapter, African Americans are depicted as the recipients of Jim Crow hostility and exploitation. In a certain sense, even as the guide critiques the effects of segregation, it maintains a separate but equal stance toward its black subjects in its textual arrangement, discussing the state's white population first, then moving to an analysis of the state's black population and finally concluding with a summary of the federal government's programs designed to improve living conditions for its African American constituents. Where the state fails in delivering "equal" services, the New Deal attempts to make up for its inadequacies, building new hospitals, establishing day nurseries, expanding public programming in sports and recreation for black children and teens. As if to rectify a ruptured synecdochic relation between state and nation, then, the federal government allegedly steps in to fix the malfunctioning segments of regional jurisdiction.

When the Florida guide addresses Jim Crow, it asserts that *local* living and working conditions are not equal between blacks and whites. In a kind of bait and switch, the inequities of Jim Crow are thus seen to stem from the state, not federal law. Rather than addressing the system of segregation itself—as did some of the Farm Security Administration photographers who documented the daily impact of segregation upon people of color—the guide's solutions usually entail government intervention in the form of welfare programs to bring the most conspicuously racist state regions up to the "national standard."[18] But, of course, the national standard *is* segregation, the very social, economic, and political system that grounds the guide's fetishization of cultural difference and its marketing of a commodified relation to the racialized folk. As Carbado suggests, "Blackness has often been included in the juridical order solely in the form of its exclusion (that is, its capacity to be subordinated). This inclusive exclusion historically has positioned black people both inside and outside America's national imagination—as a matter of law, politics and social life" (639). In a variation of this "inclusive exclusion," given Jim Crow's official status, Florida's African American citizens are never imagined as the guide's "common men," even when they are portrayed as "folk."[19]

The guide's ambivalent figuration of African Americans exemplifies the particular ways in which the New Deal's designated folk populations were bound by a "modern racial regime" wrought out of "legal codes of segregation, exclusion, reservations and anti-miscegenation" (Denning, *Cultural Front*, 33). In different ways then, black people, Indians, and poor whites occupied a liminal relationship to the nation in the 1930s, even as the New Deal sought to rectify, with greater and lesser degrees of commitment, the poverty and despair disproportionately shouldered by these groups (Sullivan, *Days of Hope*, 60). Here, we might recall the New Deal's Indian Reorganization Act (IRA) of 1934, which launched a policy granting *partial* sovereignty to tribes—what some critics describe as a technique of indirect colonial domination—wherein Native Americans might establish governments recognized as legitimate by the United States. Though the IRA represented a liberal turn away from the infamous Dawes Act of 1887, which authorized the president to survey and divide tribal lands into allotments for individual Indian families, leading to an eventual loss of over ninety million acres of treaty land, nonetheless, Congress opposed and eliminated the IRA's more radical measures, "grandfathering in" the previous land deeds from the Dawes Act (Carlson, "Federal Policy," 33; Pfister, *Individuality*, 201). The Florida guide describes this recent governmental shift in terms rank with benevolent paternalism: "The Florida legislature has concerned itself with the Seminole only to the extent of setting aside reservations for his use. He is tried in civil courts but shown the utmost leniency in his transgressions. There is a tacit understanding with Federal authorities that Indian tribal law shall prevail on the reservation" (46–47).

As Joel Pfister shows, many critics would describe "New Deal 'self-governing' as tantamount to No Deal governing" (*Individuality*, 207–8). Pfister argues that the IRA reflected the romantic and homogeneous conception of the "Indian" held by the Bureau of Indian Affairs commissioner, John Collier, by emphasizing the entity of the tribe as the primary legal, social, and political formation for organizing native life (203–4).

The IRA's focus on the tribe overlooked the diversity of actual native communities, ignoring factionalism within tribes, issues of clan autonomy, and the more complex working communities in which many traditional and assimilated Indians actually lived (199–211). Significantly, the incorporation of Indian tribes allowed them to exist as financial entities—"tribal corporations"—a transformation the Florida guide reflects in its jokey portrayal of the entrepreneurial Seminole with his highway-accessible "palm-thatched village" (Florida State 5).

The New Deal's efforts to ameliorate the impoverished living conditions of poor rural whites, its other liminally situated folk, took shape largely through its economic policies directed at the South. Despite Roosevelt's declaration that the South represented "the nation's number one economic problem" and the New Deal's sustained efforts to improve the region through the work of the Rural Electrification Administration, the Farm Security Administration, and the Works Progress Administration, among other agencies, the South's widespread feudal system continued to oppress its least well-off residents, hurting African Americans most acutely (Sullivan 65). Due to the seasonal and migratory nature of employment for skilled and unskilled laborers in Florida's industries such as "naval-stores production, lumbering, fishing, fruit packing, mining, cigar making and sponge fishing," as well as the tourist industry, labor organization in the state was all the more difficult (Florida State 87). The Florida guide ambivalently credits and blames Cuban émigrés ("Latin-Americans") who worked in the state's cigar industry for creating Florida's first labor union. In spite of such efforts, Florida's average hourly wage fell well under the South's average wage and was much less than the national average wage: the guide quotes the U.S. Department of Labor's figures for July 1936 in which common laborers in Florida made twenty-three cents an hour, compared to thirty-three cents an hour in the entire South and forty-three cents for the nation as a whole (94).

Many of Florida's agricultural workers were subject to the vagaries of exploitive industrialized farming, rather than the more typical problems of farm tenancy and debt peonage in the South: in addition to negligible wages, these itinerant workers were often homeless. A pernicious politics of disenfranchisement further increased the South's gulf between rich and poor: poll taxes and other restrictions blocked most people of color and a majority of low-income white people ("crackers" in the parlance of the guide) from voting (Sullivan 66). Given these regional dynamics, the New Deal's efforts to improve the lives of poor white people among its other marginalized constituents were often frustrated. The Florida guide's native trio of folk—black people, Indians, and poor whites—were subject to varying degrees and forms of disenfranchisement. It is worth noting that class matters most in the representations of Florida's white folk, a sign of the guide's bootstrap nostalgia for the originary (white) little guy, both lauded and potentially saved by capitalism. In the guide's narrative of liberal progress, the very fact of the folk's disenfranchisement effectively locates them as harbingers of the past and its previous regimes of oppression, with the implied promise that it is only a matter of time before the welfare state improves their living conditions. However, those changes have not yet occurred and, for this reason, the guide excludes them from its populist synecdoche of the common man.

Instead, the guide's folk subjects figure prominently in an adjacent populist synecdochic relation that is temporal: deemed representative of Florida's folklife, they stand in for the folk cultures of greater America, located principally in the past. In its brief ethnographic descriptions, "the 'cracker,' the Negro, the Latin-American, and the Seminole" are markedly local populations, their existence presented as spatially and temporally static. For the exotic yet quaint appeal of the state, these groups are seen either as rural relics or as colorful, urban imports worthy of the tourist's anthropological observation. The guide condenses its sections on "Latin Americans" presumably in accord with the nativist view at the time that Florida's Cuban population were immigrants who had not yet fully assimilated to the United States.[20] The guide denies the coevalness—the shared contemporary modern time—of the pioneering "cracker, the Negro . . . and the Seminole": the cracker functions as a backwoods antecedent to the (white Yankee) common man of the thirties; the African American functions as "primitive" domestic other; and the Seminole functions as a "vanishing" predecessor of the nation (128).[21] Conforming to the nostalgic prototype of the heritage industry, each represents a previous part for a present-day whole. By setting Florida's folk in a timeless past, the guide shores up the series' claims to an American indigenousness, where Native Americans coexist with other folk types, their long, complex histories on the North American continent merely fascinating archaeological precursor to the inexorable sweep of nation building. Shaffer observes that the standard chronological sequence of essays in all of the guidebooks evidenced "an evolutionary trajectory from colonization and settlement to the emergence of a native folk culture, culminating in the developments of modern capitalism" (212).

In addition to providing a plinth for America's claims of folk nation-hood, a sign of where the country had been and where it might go—Recovery! Progress!—the folk, as drawn in the Florida guide and else-where, provided middle-class travelers with a vision of time before the industrialism of Ford and Taylor. As tourists sought "time off" in the cities of south Florida, for example—a break from "the regulation and mechanization of everyday life"—their modern sense of leisure was an-chored by the nostalgic temporalities of the folk, whom they might see or encounter on a scenic tour or day trip (Woods 175). The ironies are abundant. Ever apparent is the degree to which modern, capitalist technologies and infrastructure such as advertising, media, automobiles, motels, and highways delivered the folk to touristic consumers by fo-menting a sense of disjuncture between the tourist's contemporary mod-ern time and the folk's pastoral time. As Woods adds, the same roads and railways that brought tourists to the state in the winter served migrants looking for seasonal work and transported the agricultural products of their labor out of the state (177). Moreover, the factory farms where one might find the guide's folk engaged in "stoop labor" were some of the nation's leading agribusiness ventures (179–80). Interestingly, the guide acknowledges the Seminoles and the cracker as active participants in the state's tourist economy, but primarily as roadside merchants; their busi-ness practices are antiquated, reminiscent of cottage industries, in com-parison to industrial production that predominates commerce in the country's urban centers. A literal illustration of tourism's tension be-tween stasis and movement, the stationary roadside business depends upon the fluid capital and constant movement of tourists driving by in their cars.

Constitutive of an altogether different narrative of migration, the common man in the form of the Yankee travels through the state in order to enjoy its pleasant climate and view its folk populations and its subtropical flora and fauna. As part of the guidebook's romantic view of Florida, it suggests that without the visitor's regulating gaze and, more important, his improving tourist dollar, Florida's frontier would revert back to its lush, tropical languor, inhabited by only "unrefined" clans.

Paradoxically, these highly marketable "exotic" qualities are endangered by tourism, the very industry that most centrally profits from their existence. Expanding upon these incongruities, the guide reinvents Florida's appeal by ascribing these same organic primordial tendencies to the state's diverse native populations, even as it documents their increased participation in the modern tourist trade. Culture is correlated with landscape, in keeping with the conventions of regionalism (Shaffer 212). In this way, then, the guide locates Florida's exotic appeal not only in its flora and fauna but in its native folk as well.

A SOUTHERNMOST EXAMPLE

The 1939 Florida guidebook was not the first piece of Florida travel writing to feature the state's native folk as part of the region's appeal. Though the American Guide Series was inspired by the popular Baedeker series of travel books, its state guides often followed the precedent of prior individuated, regional guides before them (Findlay and Bing, "Touring Florida," 290). The Florida guide adopted the iconography, rhetorical enticements, and conciliatory sectional politics first articulated in Florida's earliest tourist guides, such as Harriet Beecher Stowe's literary sketches of the state collected in *Palmetto Leaves* (1873), Thomas Bangs Thorpe's essays in *Picturesque America* (1872), Edward King's extensive "tour of observation" recorded originally for *Scribner's Monthly* and collected in *The Great South* (1875), and Silvia Sunshine's *Petals Plucked from Sunny Climes* (1880). Each of these tourist guides was published during Florida's first significant tourist boom after the Civil War, when the South had recovered enough to attract tourists and travel writers from the North in the 1870s (Burnett, *Florida's Past*, 52; McIntyre, "Promoting," 47; Winders, "Imperfectly Imperial," 400–403). These promotional tracts were written for northerners, advertising the state of Florida as a strange, feminized semitropical land of swamps and other grotesque flora and fauna, populated by equally sleepy and primitive enclaves of black and white folk who lived close to the land: if Florida was alluring in its untamed, exotic excess, it was also capable of being brought to order through northern modes of industriousness. Partaking in a politics of sectional reconciliation, these texts advanced a romantic reunion between the hard-working, industrial North and the domestic, "premodern" South. The travel literature of the day thus ousted the Civil War and Reconstruction period's political divisions over slavery and African American emancipation with a narrative of a healthy white republic, united and revived by a foray into the "leisure, relaxation and romance" of the South and its ruins of antebellum aristocracy (Silber, *Romance*, 66–67, 69, 76–77).

In the post-Reconstruction period, Florida became the center of southern tourism. As Stowe would enumerate in her idyllic sketches, "Florida [had] two sides to it,—one side all tag-rag and thrums, without order or position; and the other side showing flowers and arabesques and brilliant coloring" (26). Hovering between verdant disarray, on the one hand, and radiant harmony, on the other, the state offered "a sort of tumble-down, wild, picnicky kind of life" (36). Throughout her account, Stowe emphasized how "the disadvantages of [Florida's] burning climate [might], to a degree, be evaded and overcome by the application of the same patient industry and ingenuity which rendered fruitful the iron soil and freezing climate of the New England States" (246). She transforms the acrimonious sectional battle of the Civil War into an affable contest between untouched, rebellious southern nature and northern civilization. Blum observes how quickly Stowe "took up the banners of sectional reconciliation and abandoned calls for racial justice" (103). Counter to her prior condemnation of the enslavement of African Americans in her famous *Uncle Tom's Cabin*, here Stowe scripts the state's newly freed black laborers as content and compliant; they exemplify the "general happy-go-luckiness which Florida inculcates" (36). To the immediate question on every prospective northern buyer's mind, "Who shall do the work for us?" Stowe would point to this exploitable class of laborers as the answer (279). In her rendering, as in much of the travel literature of the period, the state's freedpeople were an extension of Florida's uncultivated flora and fauna: "The black laborers whom we leave in the field pursue their toil, if anything, more actively, more cheerfully, than during the cooler months. The sun awakes their vigor and all their boundless jollity" (280). For this reason, "one [might] be pardoned for thinking the negro . . . the natural laborer of the tropical regions" (283). Though the Florida guide was published some seventy-six years later, in the era of Jim Crow, it too would promote the state's untamed appeal, both in plant life and folk population, in the service of North-South reconciliation and a harmonious national collective.

Much like its predecessors, the Florida guide attempts to hook its readers by presenting the state as the "last American frontier," a border upon which a drama of highlife exclusivity and hardscrabble simplicity is staged (foreword). This allows the guide to figuratively play out both sides of the frontier: it deploys and then critiques conventional tourist discourse, which focuses on the allure of Florida's resort culture, counterbalancing that "superficial" account with an appraisal of the state's "real" folk inhabitants. This oscillation, in part, depends upon the guide's anticipated ideal reader-tourist, one entitled enough to gain entry, at least momentarily, into a range of social spaces from the elite to the impoverished. Pitched to Floridians as well as the million or so tourists who visit the state every year, the guide pledges to escort its readers through "four centuries of varying culture under five flags . . . from quaint old St. Augustine to metropolitan Miami, or from the exclusiveness of antebellum Tallahassee to the exclusiveness of modern Palm Beach." Distinct markers of race, class, and gender are embedded within its general invitation to travel through the state: the promise to take the reader through "the exclusiveness of ante-bellum Tallahassee" nostalgically invokes the state's history of slavery and white supremacy, echoed in the Jim Crow laws of the thirties. Just who wants to visit this exclusive terrain? Who can afford to? Presumably, the guide's ideal traveler has enough money and leisure time to own an automobile and travel. Presumably, he has access to racially segregated environments like Palm Beach because he is white. In spite of objections raised by Sterling Brown, the poet and national "Negro Affairs" editor of the series, about the guides' failure to include realistic travel options for African American travelers and his contention that their coverage of African American life was scant and often offensive, the Florida guide catered its content to its "ideal" conception of the tourist-citizen who happened to be white, moneyed, and male (Hurston, *Go Gator*, 19).

In the guide's theatrics of the frontier, those who would usually remain hidden in the wings come to occupy center stage for the guide's tourists, constituting a kind of laboring folk tableau vivant. The narrator coyly explains that "Florida is at once a continuation of the Deep South and the beginning of a new realm in which the system of two-party politics reasserts itself. . . . Politically and socially, Florida has its own North and South, but its northern area is strictly southern and its southern area definitely northern" (3).[22] With these light-hearted mergings and reversals of the state's own North and South, areas at once representative of a "Deep Southern" past and a forward moving (implicitly northern) future, Florida stands as a microcosm of sectional reunion within the macrocosm of the nation. The state's symbolic temporal and spatial dimensions all but flatten out into a balanced present, presumably palatable to residents and visitors of either "northern" or "southern" inclination. While at times the chapter evinces a nuanced understanding of the state's history, the guide's official gaze fixes this North-South division, eliding its vexed racial past and its current implications for the color line. Consider the following excerpt:

> To the visitor, Florida is at once a pageant of extravagance and a land of pastoral simplicity, a flood-lighted stage of frivolity and a behind-the-scenes struggle for existence. For the person with a house car it is a succession of trailer camps and a vagabond social life. For the Palm Beach patron, it is a wintertime Newport made up of the same society, servants and pastimes. For migratory agricultural labor it means several months of winter employment in the open under pleasant skies; and for the Negro turpentine worker, an unvarying job in the pine woods. (4)

In its depiction of a complex web of social and economic relations, a slippage occurs in the passage's reliance upon artifice and reality. For the traveler with a trailer, Florida is a circuitry of roads and camps, a social network built around touring. For the mobile, white bourgeois visitor-resident, Florida is a state equipped with elite luxuries fit for the vacationer who can afford them. For the migratory or immobile black worker, Florida is a state of agrarian hardship and alienated labor. In spite of this passage's attention to class and racial difference, its euphemistic tone reduces its description to nothing more than an account of Floridian types, equating whiteness and class privilege with movement and play and blackness and the migratory working class with an "unvarying" bucolic innocence. Florida's African American laborers and its multiracial working class may struggle, but they do so under relatively "pleasant" circumstances.

This excerpt offers a condensed example of a peculiar double movement that occurs throughout the book. The guide has it both ways, deploying the myth of Florida's "glamour and superficiality," even as it distances itself from this kind of romanticized, commercial perspective.[23] Thus, the passage astutely suggests that the laborers who undergird Florida's state economy remain "behind-the-scenes" but central to the inner workings of the region's extravagant tourist productions. With this observation, the guide brings invisible labor into focus, in keeping with the proletarian culture of the 1930s but it naturalizes this workforce in the process: "Attempts to romanticize Florida's playground features have resulted in an elaborate painting of the lily. . . . This superimposed glitter diverts attention from Florida's more characteristic native life" (4). By juxtaposing popular provincialisms with a grittier reality, it thereby distinguishes its own comprehensive, realist emphasis from previous tourist accounts. Designated as authentic examples of Florida's "native life"—part of the guide's democratic sweep—the laborers' poverty makes them all the more vulnerable to the guide's gaze: they become a central spectacle within the text. Yet, while the passage renders their struggle momentarily visible, it quickly forecloses the possibility of a more thorough analysis of social and economic exploitation.[24]

The highway provides the means for viewing the offstage doings of the state; it is a purveyor of modern progress as it grants access to Florida's folk populations—African Americans, crackers, and Indians. With the help of WPA-improved roads, the "land of pastoral simplicity" populated by the state's folk becomes another kind of pageant for the tourist. There is no more explicit example of this gaze than the guide's blithe description of the turpentine still roadside attraction: "The first-time viewer is primarily a sightseer. He is a principal customer for the admission places along the road. He learns very soon how far Florida is supposed to project from the Old South by the discovery that the turpentine still with its Negro quarters has been turned into a tourist attraction and advertised as a survival of bygone plantation days" (6). The turpentine still is one more example of the 1930s' penchant for "living" history monuments such as Ford's Greenfield Village and Rockefeller's Colonial Williamsburg—or, for that matter, Nathanael West's fictional "one hundred per centum American" whorehouse in *A Cool Million*. Yet the guide's description might be considered a survival itself—of the plantation mythology advanced by the travel literature of Florida's first tourist boom in the 1870s and its present circulation within narratives of sectional reconciliation and the culture of segregation in the 1930s (Silber 74–84; Hale 43–84). As Hale elucidates, relics of the Lost Cause of the Confederacy such as the guide's "turpentine still with its Negro quarters," "widened into a narration of the sectional and racial dynamics of the nation. . . . Reimagining the recent past, southern whites celebrated a plantation pastoral of racial harmony and a noble war of principle and valor, while making Reconstruction the fall that made segregation the only possible future" (48). Viewed by white Yankee tourists, the turpentine still renders slavery and its legacy of segregated labor imminently consumable, a narrative the guide supports with its flippant tone.

There is an acute irony here, for if this particular still has been turned into a tourist site, perhaps due to the exhaustion of the immediate area's resin supply, we know from the work of Stetson Kennedy, a folklorist—for the Florida Federal Writers' Project no less—that in 1939 there were plenty of other turpentine camps in full operation, camps that offered a modern example of debt peonage, extraordinarily dangerous and exploitive working conditions, and segregated living quarters for black and white workers (Kennedy, *Palmetto*, 257–68). At the time, Florida produced 20 percent of the turpentine consumed in the global market. In a sense, by situating the turpentine still safely in the past as a relic of the "bygone plantation days"—in Hale's words, part of the state's "plantation pastoral"—the guide avoids the far more contentious topic of racialized, forced labor in its modern present (Hale, *Making*, 48).[25]

It comes as no surprise, then, that the active African American labor force that supports Florida's agricultural economy is reduced to another roadside attraction, viewed from a distanced white gaze. The omniscient narrator recounts all of the sights the newcomer will see as he makes a "clockwise and counter-clockwise circuit of the state," including circus animals, art museums, scrub cypress, and "Negro workers harvesting thousands of carloads of beans and other fresh food supplies." As John Jakle and Keith Sculle suggest, "The highway sequences the motorist's experience as sightseer. . . . Life is experienced rather like a sequence of pictures rapidly emerging but also rapidly occluding" (3). For the touring motorist, black laborers are transformed into static place markers—tourist sites, "local color," as it were—commodified as folk coordinates in the guide's mapping of the region.[26] Such roadside attractions recall Guy Debord's formulation of the spectacle: the spectacle is not so much a collection of images; rather, images mediate a social relation among people (*Society*, 1). Both the roving gaze of the guide and its tourist rely upon control over mobility, a mobility that reflects and reinforces their relative power. In this way, the mobile travelers represent roaming capital, while the laborers, in spite of their migratory status, are fixed as remnants of an older form of agrarian-based capitalism.

In the case of the Seminoles, the highway converts them to the business of tourism in another way: they are compelled to perform primitivism for passing motorists. "Where the United States Army and a hundred years of persuasion failed, a highway has succeeded. The Seminole Indians surrendered to the Tamiami Trail. From the Everglades the remnants of this race emerged, soon after the trail was built, to set up their palm-thatched villages along the road and to hoist tribal flags as a lure to passing motorists. Like their white brethren [the crackers], they sell articles of handicraft and for a nominal fee will pose for photographs" (5). No longer able to resist the imperialist policies of the government, the Seminoles "surrender" to "persuasive" capitalism, finally selling their cultural difference instead of deploying it against the United States' annihilating conquest policies. As tribal members become entrepreneurs who perform primitivism for material gain—producers and consumers "like their white brethren"—for the first time, the federal government regards them as quasi-citizens, proximal participants in a "democracy of consumers." Once more, the "frontier" in the figure of the Seminole has been conquered in the name of monetary gain.

The highway and its business of tourism correspondingly convert the native cracker. To clarify its purportedly nonpejorative use of the term, the guide asserts: "The cracker, a pioneer backwoods settler of Georgia and Florida, has come to be known as a gaunt, shiftless person, but originally the term meant simply a native, regardless of his circumstances" (128).[27] When the British took control of Florida in the 1760s, they recruited white settlers to come colonize the territory; the term *cracker* refers to these frontiersmen and their descendents. As Matt Wray demonstrates, the term *cracker* eclipsed the mid-eighteenth-century term *lubber*, a name for poor whites that implied cultural backwardness, laziness, and deficient hygiene (31–33). Crackers were portrayed as outcasts who did not respect the legal, moral, or racial codes of the dominant social order (Wray 34–39). The guide both draws upon and dilutes these various historical meanings in its elucidation of cracker life: "The cracker's wants are simple. . . . Fish is an important item of diet, and when the cracker is satiated with it he has been heard to say: 'I done et so free o' fish, my stommick rises and falls with the tide.' " A literal interpretation of living close to the land, the metaphor merges the cracker with his backwoods surroundings, the two entities interchangeable. In a further illustration of the cracker's putatively primitive ways, the guide claims that "superstition rules the life of the cracker" (129). The native cracker is poor and provincial, an exemplar of Florida's preindustrial white "folk."

In keeping with this portrait, the cracker "knew little of life beyond his own small clearing," until the highways exposed him to "many persons in motorcars" (4–5). In this contact narrative, the increased traffic "arouses his instinct for profit" and soon, the enterprising pioneer sets up "gasoline pumps" and "overnight cabins." With that, the guide concludes, "he was in the tourist business." By way of a warning, the guide explains the difficulty of reading the cracker's countenance in tourist transactions: "Generations of contact with hardship and poverty have made him undemonstrative, and he seldom displays any but the strongest emotions. He has appropriated the defensive guile of the Negro and turned it to good account in his dealings. Consequently, he drives a hard bargain with soft words" (129). Playing up the stereotype of the wily native, the guide suggests that the cracker's duplicity is not innate, rather it is a "trait" borrowed from African Americans. In this instance, then, the passage intimates that the cracker's (and the African American's) "defensive guile" is a sign not only of class but also of the cracker's "not quite white" racial status (Wray 17).[28]

The guide further throws into question the cracker's racial status while at the same time demonstrating its own knowledge about the intricate dynamics of tourist commerce: for the cracker, "the Yankee is his special prey and to best a Yankee by any device is legitimate. 'In the winter,' the cracker boasts, 'we live on Yankee, and in the summer on fish' " (129).[29] The cracker's boast acknowledges the potentially cannibalistic economy of tourism: in this example, the cracker is the predator and the Yankee the unsuspecting prey, at least at first glance.[30] The guide amends this assertion by pointing out that this model of capitalist advantage potentially works both ways—"with all of [the cracker's] bargaining craft, he is often cheated" (129). In making these observations, the guide distances itself from the crass side of the tourist business, providing a user-friendly ethnography of tourism and its possible traps: in these roadside exchanges, the guide will not be fooled, nor will its readers. In spite of the imminent possibility of deceit in tourist transactions, the incorporation of Florida's laboring folk into the commerce of the state ultimately renders their frontier ways manageable.

OF CRACKERS AND YANKEES

As we have seen, even the laborers who work in rural industries detached from Florida's tourist centers are not altogether separate from the state's tourist economy. The laboring folk lend the guide its most "authentic" material, erecting a necessary frontier to be crossed between the glitz of Florida's resorts and the state's "more characteristic native life" (4). These laborers are part of the folk tableau vivant to which the guide directs its readers' scrutiny. Although the actual labor of the folk may form the invisible edifice that supports the tourist trade, their folkways and even their embodied labor are incorporated into the industry in a highly visible manner. In the specific examples of the Seminole and the cracker, the state's native inhabitants are "civilized" through their participation as producers and consumers in the tourist economy, their heretofore troubling difference rendered exotic and marketable.

A related process of acclimation transforms tourists—cultural outsiders—into insiders, as they move from consumers to producers in the state's economy. It is the billboard, the quintessential sign of tourism and consumption, that initiates this process. The signboard "introduces the Yankee to the cracker and quickly establishes the fact that the two have much in *common* though their customs differ" (6; emphasis added). This example suggests that the Yankee's and the cracker's most obvious common ground is advertising and its economy of exchange. Though "the native Floridian [aka the cracker] . . . is likely to be puzzled at the abysmal ignorance that causes the Yankee to refer to orange groves as 'orchards,' sandspurs as 'sandburs,' and sandflies as 'sandfleas,'" their natural frame of reference is essentially the same. Florida's flora and fauna is comfortingly familiar to the Yankee, even if he knows it by another name. The minor distinctions in terminology serve as a metaphor for understanding these two "types": just as one kind of plant is referred to by two names, the guide suggests that these two types of men are fundamentally similar, only different according to their regional backgrounds. As Constance Rourke observed in her study of the nation's folklore: "It was always possible to see where the Yankee left off and the backwoodsman began" in the folklore that mixed the two characters (68). While the Yankee-cum-tourist is the "common man" in the text, he also has something in common with the cracker: they are both white, in spite of the cracker's provocatively liminal racial status.[31] By locating a common whiteness in these two figures, the guide metaphorically reconciles northerners with southerners, paving the way for a collective national identity grounded in an "ethnic nationalism of whiteness" retroactively constructed as continuous from the past to the present (Blum 237).

The differences and similarities between the northerner and the Floridian point to a pivotal dramatic tension within the guidebook: Florida must appear unusual enough in its down-home way to merit a visit from the outsider Yankee, yet not so radically unique that the state poses a threat to the New Deal's vision of collective national identity. Not only do the signboards introduce the Yankee to the cracker in a familiar commercial context but, in a metatextual sense, they shed light on the guide's method of marketing these "types" to the reader. In the guide's lexicon of types, it depicts "the 'cracker,' the Negro . . . the Seminole," and also the Yankee, much in the manner of Zora Neale Hurston's American Museum of Unnatural History (128).[32] Its portrayal of the Yankee conforms to its putatively democratic stance toward all people: no type escapes the guide's jocular tone. However, because the guide imagines the Yankee as Florida's ideal tourist, its depictions of the northerner are intended to make him laugh in self-recognition, while the state's other types function primarily as local color for outsiders, even if the guide self-consciously claims to reject this mode. In the examples of the Seminoles, the crackers, and the ubiquitous and anachronistic signboards, the guide implies that Florida is unified by industry, its native dissidents now a vital part of its tourist trade. In this fashion, Florida, the final frontier, is rendered altogether familiar by its central position in a nationwide consumer economy.

The socioeconomic link between state and nation is fortified by the outsiders from other states who eventually become residents. Echoing the pull between exoticism and familiarity in the guide's depiction of Florida's native inhabitants, the guide's readers are situated within the text as tourists-who-become-residents, an ambivalent position defined by a tension between distance and proximity. The knowing narrator of the introduction describes a chronology of displacement, recounting the evolution of a tourist as he buys a home "and becomes by slow degrees a citizen and a critic" (8). Like the Seminole and the cracker, his citizenship is predicated upon the fusion of his roles as consumer and producer (Szalay 267). In "the agonies of transition," moving from tourist to resident, "his visits to Florida thereafter shift to visits back home, and these latter become less frequent; but 'back home' has left an indelible imprint, which he proposes to stamp on Florida." In a certain sense, this ambivalence determines the preferable role for the tourist-turned-resident: "He becomes an incurable nonconformist, vigorously defending his adopted State and indignantly decrying it by turns. . . . He comes here to play and to relax but at the slightest provocation he resumes his business or profession if for no other reason than to demonstrate that the sound economic practices of his home state will pull Florida out of the doldrums he perceives it to be in" (Florida State 8). As a recent convert to the state, the northern newcomer is zealous, a perfect candidate for the masculine job of managing Florida's feminized, vast empty space.[33] In this description, we hear an echo of Horatio Alger. The tourist-turned-resident is an example of a successful Alger hero, who magnanimously uses his Yankee ingenuity to fix the problem of Florida's distinctly southern inactivity.

Ironically, the fantasy of tropical and primeval excess, simultaneously threatening and alluring, is Florida's primary draw; the guidebook must manipulate the fantasy to make the state appear accessible, but not so much that the state loses its mystique altogether. Ending on a positive but cautionary note, the chapter suggests that "one desire seems to be common to all—the desire to improve Florida. . . . [I]f [man's subduing] efforts were relaxed for a generation, much of Florida would become primeval territory again. In combating nature and in trying to reconcile divergent ideas, the citizen performs a public service" (9). The tourist-citizen sustains Florida as a proper state, instead of letting it revert back to a territory where citizenship and civility are no longer operative categories. In this way, the tourist-consumer becomes the resident-producer. The term "tourist economy" becomes synonymous with all economy, but in particular with a program of national commerce and rationalized state planning upheld by the tourist, the guidebook, the FWP, and the New Deal. The tourist is integral to the settling of the state's perpetual frontier.

Figuring European colonizers as precursors to the modern-day tourist,

the guide playfully insists that there is no position, geographical or social, outside of a totalizing tourist equation of consumption: "Throughout more than four centuries, from Ponce de Leon in his caravels to the
latest Pennsylvanian in his Buick, Florida has been invaded by seekers of
gold or of sunshine; yet it has retained an identity and a character distinctive to itself" (3). In keeping with this logic, the guide deftly situates
the detritus of older forms of tourism as important historical sites: "Although signboards ruin beautiful stretches of country, they are, in fact, a
significant part of the Florida scene. . . . A great deal of early history is
presented on roadside signs, and farther south the flora and fauna are
similarly publicized for commercial purposes" (6). If the anachronistic
signs visibly alter the very flora and fauna they promote, they have also
decayed into an organic part of that antediluvian scene. They maintain
and preserve Florida's history by attesting to an earlier moment of the
state's tourist past. By linking tourist production and consumption to
citizenship, in the example of the once wayward, now entrepreneurial
Seminole and cracker, and by situating tourism's economic imperatives
within the state's long history of colonization, in the example of the
Pennsylvanian with his Buick, the guide implies that the creation and
production of tourism in turn created and produced the modern state of
Florida. And though the book's account of this process partakes in a
good deal of mythmaking, it is difficult not to agree with this contention.

UNEARTHING "ARCHAEOLOGY AND INDIANS"

If in the guide's representation, tourism, indeed, created the modern
state of Florida, that creation depended upon the manufacture of the
state's primitive and primordial appeal to outsiders: the state becomes
modern through the management and promotion of its primeval past.
For the travel guide attempting to provide a compelling picture of the
state without resorting to the "ballyhoo" of typical tourist fare, the social
sciences' rational romance of data collection and fieldwork proved in-
valuable. When the narrative turns to the highly diverse population of
Florida natives—to people who occupied the state far before the arrival
of conquesting Europeans—the guide bolsters and enlivens its realist
claims by deploying an anthropological gaze.[34] The state's Native American communities and "their lore" occupy a pivotal place in the guide's

excavatory appeal to its readers. As Rourke observed about white people's obsession in the nineteenth century with the figure of the Indian:
"About his figure the American seemed to wrap a desire to return to the
primitive life of the wilderness" (98). In a sense, the Depression's cautionary tale about the ravages of capitalism reinvigorated this narrative's
appeal. It is no accident that the chapters that organize the guidebook's
first section, "Florida's Background," are arranged in an implicitly retro-
spective order: "Contemporary Scene," "Natural Setting and Conservation," "Archaeology and Indians," "History," and so on. In contrast to the
contemporary scene, the state's Indians exist as remnants of the region's
natural environment and its deep past. Situated as amateur anthropologists, the prospective reader-tourist was invited to unearth the precapitalist past of the Indians by way of a set of contact stories between natives
and encroaching European colonizers.[35] In a metadiscursive way, these
stories from the past frame the present encounter between the modern
tourist and the "primitive" native.

In "Archaeology and Indians," the guide narrates Florida's colonization as a series of contact stories, either between Florida's native inhabitants and invading European countries, or between archaeologists and
excavation mounds that contain artifacts predating "contact with the
whites" (37). In fact, the American Guide Series as a whole adopts its
information and approach from a body of literature that includes archaeology and anthropology as well as the early travelogues written by
colonial explorers.[36] Borrowing from these particular discourses, the
Florida guide invites its readers and travelers to view Florida's indigenous population from the perspective of the anthropologists, the archaeologists, and the explorers who have visited the state for the last five
hundred years. By emplotting the reader-traveler in this way, the guide
illustrates one of the central enticements of tourism in the twentieth
century: tourist travel gains its appeal from a paradoxical pleasure in the
recognition of the unfamiliar, a practice of prescriptive matching. As
John Frow asserts, "For the tourist gaze, things are read as signs of
themselves. A place, a gesture, a use of language are understood not as
given bits of the real but as suffused with ideality, giving onto the *type*
of the beautiful, the extraordinary or the culturally authentic" ("Tourism," 125). The *type* as an epistemological category gains its authority
from claims of representativeness. It becomes the ideal standard through
which the tourist encounter is evaluated as authentic or inauthentic, as

real or unreal: in this way, the fantasy of type not only precedes reality but designates what is taken for reality (Frow, "Tourism," 124).

This fantasy of type is bolstered by the guide's source material: it collates previous accounts of the Indians written by archaeologists, ethnologists, and naturalists in an earlier era. Consequently, the Florida guide performs an archaeology of all previous archaeological accounts of Florida and the state's native populations.[37] For example, the guide debunks an early theory of the west Florida tribes' supposed cannibalism, explaining "the absence of some bones in many of the skeletons tends to support the theory that these Indians removed the flesh from the bodies before interment. . . . [T]his was done by exposure to the weather or by cooking. This custom may have given rise to the early belief, *now doubted by most authorities*, that the Florida Indians were cannibals" (36–37; emphasis added). In this instance, the guide has it both ways: it introduces the thrilling urtext of anthropology, the trope of cannibalism, and then retreats from this possibility by invoking the consensus of most authorities. In contrast with the introduction's depiction of present-day Seminoles who participate in Florida's current tourist economy, the guide nostalgically invokes this story of burial-cum-cannibalism in order to recall a less "assimilated" time when the relationship of traveler to "native" produced greater cultural difference (Curtis and Pajackowska, " 'Getting There,' " 202).

The Florida guide is torn between acknowledging the Seminoles' co-evalness and trying to reinforce their status as a particular type—the state's mythic "primitives." The Seminoles present the guide with a problem because their community is felt as a tangible presence in the modern Florida scene of the thirties, even though they are often described in anachronistic terms. In but one of many examples, the guide teeters between an exotic vision of colorful, hand-crafted, "authentic" costuming only to later self-consciously retreat from this claim, insisting that, in truth, the most notable aspects of this dress (leather leggings and turbans) are worn primarily for commercial tourist purposes in the present day.

The section concludes with a stereotypical joke at the expense of Native Americans ("Injun" humor in the vein of many Hollywood westerns) that tells the truth of the Seminoles' function within the guide. The guide reports: "A truce between the Seminole and the United States Government was signed in 1934, publicized as bringing to a close the longest war in history. Another such treaty was signed in 1937. A story has it that one of the Indians present on this occasion kept muttering a word that no one understood until an interpreter translated it: "He say 'lotta bull' " (47). The Indian's skepticism needs to be restated in English for the Anglo representatives' comprehension and, ironically, "lotta bull" indicates that there is no understanding, even in translation. This joke emphasizes a fundamental disjuncture between the Seminoles and the United States: the truce does not translate. By suggesting that the Seminoles are predictably hostile, the joke attempts to justify its punch line, the actual truth of the "truce," the continuation of the government's discriminatory policies. The chapter's final anecdote suggests that the Seminoles are enigmatic as usual. A common joke about cultural difference, it depicts the Indians as recognizably inscrutable—in their use of the English language, in their attitude toward the truce, and in their oppositional stance toward the United States' imperialist policies.

Even as each section emphasizes difference, this mode of specificity is eventually reduced to a homogenizing discourse of American types. As the guide attempts to transform and inscribe Florida's folk "types" into an organically unified narrative of the state and finally of the nation, it invites its readers to participate in the drama. Tourists act as "civilizing" agents who order and categorize the "primal" folk types they observe. In spite of the guide's excessive factuality, the folk can never be adequately apprehended; their very ambiguity perpetuates the guide's numerous taxonomies. In providing such taxonomies of the folk, the Florida guide enacts Michel de Certeau's paradox of travel (by way of Claude Lévi-Strauss): "What does travel ultimately produce if it is not, by a sort of reversal, an 'exploration of the deserted places of my memory,' the return to nearby exoticism by way of a detour through distant places, and the 'discovery' of relics and legends" (de Certeau, *Practice*, 107). This formulation of the great detour to a nearby exoticism (seemingly of the mind) is literalized in the Florida guide by its promise of the exotic, in the form of the region's folk populations, to relatively nearby northern states.

AN INSIDE THING TO LIVE BY:
MAPPING THE IMAGINARY

In the Florida guide's preface, the state director, Carita Doggett Corse, refers to the guide's polyvocality, describing the FWP's thoroughly heterogeneous staff: "So many individuals and agencies have contributed to this State guide for Florida that it may properly be described as a co-operative product. . . . After extensive and adequate files of Floridiana had been accumulated, our work became that of selecting, compiling, writing and editing the book. More than 400 experts on special topics served as consultants." Aside from demonstrating the collective nature of the project, this passage simultaneously underscores the anonymity and expert status of its contributors as well as its narrative strategy of accumulation—its excessive factuality. The editors of the Florida guide-book construct a seemingly neutral and "expert" gaze that examines and visualizes the state for the reader and the tourist. The specialists are listed in a bibliography and a three-page list of consultants, followed by a lengthy index. Thus, the encyclopedic function and format of the guides extends to its aggregation of all-star contributors, their own names serving to reinforce the authoritative scope of the guide. In this way, the guide was promoted as a serious alternative to typically superficial tourist fare.

If the Florida guide achieves a particular authority from its collective authorship, that collective composition also leads to its most provocative fissures, contradictions, and hybridities, the moments when the literary ruptures its reference book assuredness. In spite of the guide's pervasive hegemonic mapping of racial difference, it is a polyvocal text, a composite of many writers' labors and voices. This structure opens up the possibility of reversals of tone and perspective. The literary critic Mary Wainwright vividly recalls coming across one such reversal in the guide, instantly recognizing its anonymous author to be Zora Neale Hurston: "Inserted into the otherwise dry prosaic writing style that typifies this volume is this paragraph: 'A Negro field worker who passed unscathed through several hurricanes has graphically described the velocity of a tropical gale: "One day the wind blowed so hard, it blowed a well up out the ground; blowed so hard, it blowed a crooked road straight.'" Even when she was responsible for simply accumulating and recording data and statistics, Hurston, it seems, could not resist spicing up her prose with a bit of 'lying'" (62). The shift from dull federalese to lively narrative accomplishes more than just rousing the reader. In Hurston's capable hands, literary modes of folktelling do nothing less than overturn the fixed folk typologies promoted elsewhere in the guide. Emblematic of her signifying ethnography in *Mules and Men* (1935), published four years earlier, Hurston's contributions to the guide effectively resist its incorporation of African Americans into its all-consuming tourist economy.

Hurston's actual role in the creation of the Florida guide and a second work, *The Florida Negro*, was curtailed by the racist labor practices of the FWP headquarters in town, as the historian Pam Bordelon has amply demonstrated in her recovery of Hurston's work for the Florida FWP. A case in point: the few black writers employed by the Florida unit of the FWP were relegated to an office in the black section of Jacksonville, apart from this central office. According to Bordelon, "Hurston was given the lowliest position, 'relief worker,' despite the fact that she was the most published writer in the unit. She bore the added humiliation of seeing less qualified white writers given editorial positions at double her relief salary" (Hurston, *Go Gator*, ix). Even after Alsberg demanded that Hurston be made the editor of *The Florida Negro*, a position in which she would have supervised a staff of white and black writers, the state supervisors flouted his directives. Instead, they paid Hurston an additional sum of money in "travel allowance" that made her overall salary nearly commensurate with the state editor's but without the official cachet or presence of a formal editorial position. What is so ironic about this story is that the Florida guide's publication was held up for months because of the federal editor's concern over its poor writing and its "lack of editorial support." We can only imagine how different the end result might have been had Hurston been given the editorial control Alsberg and others requested. Stetson Kennedy, the Florida FWP folklore editor who traveled with Hurston on several collecting expeditions, lamented: "There we were, doing our very best to see to it that everything that went into the guide was couched not only in staid Federalese but also in the specific guidebook jargon set forth in the FWP Style Manual; and there was Zora, turning in these veritable prose poems of African eloquence and imagery! What to do? Inevitably, the inferior triumphed over the superior, and not much of Zora, beyond her inimitable folksongs and tales, got into the guide. We rationalized this tragedy by reminding ourselves that, after all, the guides were meant to be exemplars of the merits of collective authorship" (Kennedy, "Working with Zora," 65). Although Hurston had a hand only in the last several months of the Florida guide's production—she worked for the FWP for one year—her imprint, if scant, is still unmistakable.

Herein lie some of text's most dynamic moments of contradiction, moments that counter the state's production and management of racial and ethnic difference (coincidentally, moments that describe the region's black turpentiners, once again).[38] By way of example, in the final section of the Florida guide devoted to automobile tours, "Tour #7," from Jacksonville to Pensacola, includes Hurston's account of four mythical places popular in the folklore of the black turpentiners in that part of the state. The tour is introduced with the caveat that "the people, architecture, and economic conditions of this region, first in the State to be settled and the first to have a railroad, remain largely untouched by the seasonal tourist influence, standing in sharp contrast to the Florida pictured in resort literature" (428). In other words, this region relies on turpentine camps as one of its main sources of commerce.

In a profoundly divergent description of a turpentine plantation from the one viewed from the window of a speeding car, Hurston discusses the turpentiners' circulation of a series of stories about "mythical cities and countries" (431). Her account is introduced with the tour marker: "A large turpentine still, 32 miles [into the tour], is surrounded by cabins of Negro workers. Many are painted and neatly kept, their gardens bright with flowers." Moving away from this fixed geographical site, the text next describes the turpentiners' folkways, their "typical songs and chants," and then their folklore: "Negroes have their mythical cities and countries which are discussed and referred to in everyday conversation as if they actually existed. Among them are Diddy-Wah-Diddy, Beluthahatchie [*sic*], Heaven and West Hell." The first place, "Diddy-Wah-Diddy" is "a place of no work and no worry for man or beast. . . . All curbstones are chairs and the food is already cooked. Baked chickens and sweet potato pies, with convenient knives and forks, drift along crying "Eat me! Eat me!" Everything is on a gigantic scale. . . . Everybody would live in Diddy-Wah-Diddy if it were not so hard to find and so difficult to get to, even if one knew the way." The next mythical place, Beluthahatchee, is "a country where all unpleasant doings and sayings are forgotten, a land of forgiveness and forgetfulness."

The final mythical place in Hurston's account is a dystopia called "West Hell." It is "the toughest and hottest part of that notorious resort" and Big John de Conqueror resides there before he elopes with the Devil's daughter. As Hurston documented in *Mules and Men*, Big John de Conqueror was "the great human culture hero in Negro folklore . . . the wish-fulfillment hero of the race. The one, who nevertheless, or in spite of laughter, usually defeats Ole Massa, God and the Devil. Even when Massa seems to have him in a hopeless dilemma he wins out by a trick" (247). In her equally brilliant treatise "Characteristics of Negro Expression," she further explored the monumental power of Big John: "First off, he was a whisper, a will to hope, a wish to find something worthy of laughter and song. . . . The sign of this man was a laugh, and his singing-symbol was a drum-beat. . . . It was an inside thing to live by. . . . It helped the slaves endure. . . . It is no accident that High John de Conqueror has evaded the ears of white people. They were not supposed to know" (69–70). In the story recounted in the Florida guide, Big John, an avatar of High John, successfully battles for freedom, tearing off the Devil's arm and almost beating him to death with it. As Big John leaves hell with his bride, he "passes out ice water" and "turns down the dampers" because he expects to visit his wife's family soon and he "doesn't like the house kept so hot" (432). This story serves as an allegory of rebellion and liberation in which the hero beats the (white) man in power, running away with his daughter and transforming the abysmal living conditions of those he leaves behind. As Bordelon claims, these stories provide a kind of catharsis for black workers subjected to the brutal conditions of the turpentine labor camps. Hurston's contribution of Big John's battle with the Devil signifies on the guide's generally complimentary representations of Florida: "that notorious resort" "West Hell" is perhaps not so far from that state's playground of whites-only resorts that prosper with the support of a severely exploited African American workforce.

Within the context of the Florida guide itself, these stories have yet another function: they point to the unmappable—a subversive space of imagination, desire, and agency—a space that resists the fixing gaze of the tourist and the state. For even as Hurston situates these stories within the geographical landscape of Interstate 90, the stories describe places whose liberatory promise rests on the fact that they *cannot be* plotted on a map. Hurston's folktales speak an important truth: they illustrate the limits of a seemingly impartial strategy of excessive factuality that is bereft of an account of power. They signify on the realist imperatives of so much of the guide and the American Guide Series, pointing instead to a realm of African American life that actively defies this form of racial management, a mode she used to great effect, as we shall see in the next chapter, in her ethnographic masterpiece, *Mules and Men*.

The American Guide Series was remarkable in scope. As numerous commentators have suggested, at first glance it seems counterintuitive that the government and its New Deal cultural programs would seize upon "the depression-era vogue for marginalized Americans" as a means of reimagining the nation (Filene 133). Yet, the folk proved to be a pivotal point of origin in the New Deal's vision of the nation. For all of the series' attention to America's disenfranchised, as we see in the example of *Florida: A Guide to the Southernmost State*, those communities were made to stand for more and less than their contemporary existence implied: a tableau vivant of laboring folk, a pageant of the past, at best folksy precursors (as in the case of the crackers), they were never interpellated as coeval "common men," the series' most prominent constituency. That designation was reserved for the white Yankee, who would provide the basis for the modern white national collective. In spite of the overall "middlebrow" regionalism of the project, some of the series' own writers and editors worked toward radical representations of the nation and its (dis)contents. That tenor of critique would find powerful expression in other works of the period. With razor-sharp acuity, George Schuyler and Nathanael West enacted in their modernist burlesques the ways in which the folk would serve the period's more racist populisms. An iconoclastic group of writers and filmmakers—Zora Neale Hurston and Preston Sturges, among them—would adopt sightlines similar to those of Schuyler and West in their radically incongruous visions of the nation's folk to reveal the skew of the official populisms of the New Deal. As we shall see in the next chapter, Zora Neale Hurston, in particular, would revel in the performativity underlying the folk's most putatively "authentic" traits. In her extraordinary signifying ethnography *Mules and Men*, Hurston would preempt the New Deal's populist synecdoches of the folk in the past. By mapping Florida's black "folk" into the space and time of the modern nation, not simply as precedent, Hurston would trouble the ways in which such synecdoches whitewashed a concept of the national collective.

Chapter 4.
"Ah Gives Myself de Privilege to Go": Navigating the Field and the Folk in Zora Neale Hurston's *Mules and Men*

Folklore is not something far away and long ago, but real and living among us.—B. A. BOTKIN, *Fighting Words* (1940)

Mules and Men subverts the very project of a guidebook altogether, upending its static depictions of place and people. Though *Florida: A Guide to the Southernmost State* listed Zora Neale Hurston simply as "a widely read contemporary Negro writer" in its literature section, the impact of her writing on Florida and the South would far surpass the guidebook's own contributions, especially in comprehending the region's nuances of race, gender, and labor and the lives of its African American residents. In every storied version of her life as an anthropologist, a folklorist, a dramatist, a performer, and a novelist, Zora Neale Hurston declared her close connection to the South. By all accounts, her childhood in the all-black township of Eatonville, Florida, served as a vital source for her charisma and her creativity. In her memoir *Dust Tracks on the Road* (1942), she wrote: "I was a Southerner, and had the map of Dixie on my tongue" (98). With characteristic lyricism and wit, Hurston reverses the spatial coordinates of standard autobiographies: rather than inhabiting a static place on the map, she has her external geography figuratively inscribed within her. Hurston cites the South at the same time as her voice imaginatively articulates its contours. As she represents herself and her region in dialectical terms, significantly, she reveals identity and place to be discursive products of language, of embodied speaking.

At once the cartographer and the map, Hurston was always a consummate insider and outsider. Among other things, she was a rural

southerner who migrated up north to the city for an Ivy League education and the luminous artistry of the Harlem Renaissance; an anthropologist who, at the urging of the discipline's most eminent practitioner,
Franz Boas, returned down south for fieldwork; a folklorist who brought
fictional modes of storytelling to the practice of ethnography; a writer
who relied upon ethnographic details for the local texture of her novels.
Each of these regional, professional, and methodological crossings was
animated by a tension between her insider and outsider status. This is
certainly true of the figure of "Zora," her fictional self-presentation, who
appears not only in *Dust Tracks* but, before that, in her first book of
folklore, *Mules and Men*, a collection of seventy southern African American folktales, together with hoodoo rites, folksongs, and other folkways,
published in 1935. That volume represented the fruits of Hurston's expeditions to the South during the late twenties, to Florida, her hometown
of Eatonville, and neighboring Polk County, as well as Mobile Bay, Alabama, and New Orleans, Louisiana.

In her introduction to *Mules and Men*, Hurston elaborated on her
unique qualifications for researching and authoring the project, invoking her authenticity as both a scholarly folklorist and woman born of
the "folk."

> I didn't go back [to my birthplace first] so that the home folks could make
> admiration over me because I had been up North to college and come
> back with a diploma and a Chevrolet. I knew that they were not going to
> pay either one of these items too much mind. I was just Lucy Hurston's
> daughter, and even if I had—to use one of our down-home expressions—
> had a Kaiser baby, and that's something that hasn't been done in this
> Country yet, I'd still be just Zora to the neighbors. (2)

Hurston downplays her college degree but she manages to make note of
it in her introduction all the same. While her neighbors may not pay
attention to her successes up north, her readers most likely will.[1] However,
even as she alludes to her schooling in New York, she positions herself as
"Lucy Hurston's daughter," an authentic, native informant (Humphries,
Different Dispatches, 130). As an Eatonville mother's daughter *and* a
skilled Columbia-trained ethnographer, she is able to offer up down-
home sayings like "a Kaiser baby," and then provide an explanatory foot-
note that translates the idiom to a broader audience of readers comprising
community insiders and intrigued outsiders.

Hurston adopts a deeply performative style of presentation throughout *Mules and Men*, a mode that I refer to as signifying ethnography: her insider and outsider claims loop together like a Möbius strip to stretch the very limits of participant observation methodology heralded by the period's most renowned cultural anthropologists, Franz Boas, Ruth Benedict, Margaret Mead, and Branislaw Malinowski.[2] Fatimah Tobing Rony observes, "Instead of participant observation, Hurston's methods may be characterized as observing participation" (*Third Eye*, 206). In this regard, Hurston enacted and critiqued modernist anthropology not from beyond its confines, as a postmodernist before her time, but rather from *within* (Carr and Cooper, "Zora Neale Hurston," 303–6; Hegeman, *Patterns*, 27–31; Walters, " 'He Can Read,' " 365). The more striking aspects of her practice reflect larger transformations afoot within the discipline of anthropology as described by Susan Hegeman in her *Patterns for America*: "Between 1900 and 1940 . . . anthropology would be consolidated as a professional academic discipline, no longer tied to the ethnological museum, the field practice of 'salvage' ethnography, or the ideological function of documenting American 'progress.' . . . [T]here was a significant, and often troubled, transition to be made from the institutional spaces of the museum and the university, from 'amateur' to 'professional' identities and practices, from artifact collection to participant-observer fieldwork" (29–30). Never one to shirk contradiction, Hurston made this troubled transition her own, shuttling between "amateur" and "professional," between a mode of "salvage" ethnography and an ever incomplete account of "Negro folk-lore . . . still in the making" (Boyd, *Wrapped*, 167). Indeed, the practice of shuttling is part of her signifying ethnography; it allows her to create a radically hybrid text that traverses the space between informant and ethnographer and fiction and nonfiction.

By returning home to conduct fieldwork, Hurston not only complicated anthropology's insider/outsider paradigm but also its founding metaphors of space and time, such as subject/object, traveler/native, and contemporary/primitive. While many anthropologists of her day emphasized dwelling in the field, they elided their travels to and from that location. In contrast, Hurston made this aspect of ethnographic practice visible, recounting significant moments of travel and reconfiguring the spatial and temporal contours of the field as flexible (Duck, " 'Go there,' " 275).[3] Her approach called into question the anonymous rhetoric of the New Deal's major ethnographic effort, the Federal Writers' Project

Guide Series, a project for which she herself later wrote. Counter to the Florida Guide's register of static black agricultural laborers visible from a moving automobile is Hurston's account, which emerged out of research conducted *within* her Chevrolet. On several occasions her informants not only initiated but navigated her car trips to nearby towns to collect more folklore (Humphries, 152; Retman, " 'Real' Collective," 162). As her subjects occupied a seat in Hurston's car, the reader is positioned as a listener along for the ride as well. We all share something with her: the time and space of modernity. Dependent upon overlapping sites for her material, she constructed her ethnographic field around a complex set of social relations, contingent upon active subjects who narrated mutable and multiple stories. *Mules and Men*'s folktales, secrets, and spells emerge from gatherings on the porch, trips to neighboring towns, get-togethers in jook-joints, and an extended stay in New Orleans studying with the city's most celebrated practitioners of hoodoo.

The radical spatial and temporal aspects of Hurston's practice extend to the tales themselves, for the tales not only reflect but also *produce* space.[4] As Mary Pat Brady observes: "Viewing space as produced, productive and producing means viewing it as interanimating and dependent in part on its productive effects . . . rather than inert or transparent" (*Extinct Land*, 7). The collection of tales animates the itinerant dimensions of Hurston's collecting practice. In her deft narration, the tales become adaptable agents of their tellers. They "refuse a too rigid binary between the material and the discursive"; as such, the tales make for particularly unruly ethnographic objects (Brady 6; Carr and Cooper 298). Their performative function in the collection forecasts Hurston's ingenious mapping of made-up folkloric places in the actual automobile tour section of the Federal Writers' Project Florida guidebook in 1939, encapsulating the "imaginative mobility" that the critic Philip Joseph finds more generally in her work after the publication of *Their Eyes Were Watching God* in 1937 ("Verdict," 476). By designating fictional tales as the real artifacts of her ethnography, Hurston asserts the centrality of the imaginary to any true understanding of place, a perspective that challenges the encyclopedic factuality of the guidebooks.

In the case of *Mules and Men*, Hurston ties the mythic inexorably to modernity, delineating the bounds of rationalization and commodification intrinsic to modernism itself. In this way, she illuminates the production of the folk and the primitive crucial not only to anthropological practice but also to the cultural capital of high modernism, the Harlem Renaissance, and the New Deal. A black woman of limited means, Hurston was acutely vulnerable to the commodity logic of the literary and intellectual marketplace. She deployed contradictory ethnographic strategies as a way of navigating the competing demands of her patron, the wealthy primitivist Charlotte Osgood Mason, who "owned" everything she collected; her academic mentor, Franz Boas, upon whom she depended for academic advice and institutional support; and the fickle publishing industry, which required a major revision of her work for popular consumption. After being rejected by several publishers, Lippincott finally agreed to put out the collection on the condition that Hurston rewrite the manuscript "so that it would not be too technical for the average reader" (qtd. in Hemenway, *Zora Neale Hurston*, 163). To meet this stipulation, she included the frame story for which the book is now so famous. In this manner, she positioned herself as "market mediator," the folklorist who packages the tales for exchange in a "paying market" (Sanchez-Eppler, "Telling Anthropology," 476–77). Given the circumstances of the volume's production and its insider/outsider dynamics, it is no wonder, then, that Hurston uses the frame story in conversation with its collection of tales as a vehicle for producing a self-reflexive "complicity critique" regarding her own role in "the commodification of the primitive" and the folk (Pfister, "Complicity," 610, 620–23; Carr and Cooper 290, 287–93; Miller, "Inventing," 375). In so doing, she joined George Schuyler, Langston Hughes, Nathanael West, and others in foregrounding a central paradox of the period: that although the primitive and the folk were defined as entities outside of the commerce of the modern nation, they were nevertheless situated thoroughly within it. Each of these writers reveals the primitive and the folk to be nothing less but sometimes more than nationally vested, market-driven formations of authentic identity.

By reading *Mules and Men* in the context of the populist rhetoric of New Deal documentary and the practice of modernist anthropology, we see how Hurston's unique production of the folk is compelled by the imperatives of commodification yet also challenges the objectification inherent in that process. In its signifying ethnography, Hurston's collection self-consciously "lies up" a particular vision of identity and community, one that dismantles the pastoral, preindustrial portrait of the folk so popular in the 1930s.[5] The coordinates of this vision become apparent in Hurston's contradictory theories of African American cultural production, especially in her claims regarding the authentically dramatic nature of "negro expression." This ironic conceit—the performative authenticity of blackness—at once inflects Hurston's formulation of her own subjectivity, as she establishes the insider and outsider authority of her narrative voice, and also extends to her conception of the space, time, and labor of fieldwork and folklore. The text's key moments of gathering and transition reveal the radically flexible gendered and geographical contours of Hurston's collection. Chapter by chapter, her signifying ethnography builds a narrative arc, beginning with apparent disclosure and intimacy and concluding with secrets and questions, a collection perpetually incomplete and inexhaustible. In the mobile space of her book, the temporal flux of her participant observation, and her radically performative narration and self-presentation, Hurston maps the unmappable, "lying up a nation" from the many perspectives of a group of people of which she herself was a part.

THE EXCHANGE AND REEXCHANGE OF IDEAS

Hurston drew upon her experiences as both a storyteller and an anthropologist to define cultural production in terms of dynamic participation and transmission. Her representations of region invoke a similarly processual sense of place and identity (Carr and Cooper 301; Retman 164). Told mostly in the vernacular of Eatonville, Hurston constructs an autobiographical frame for the folktales collected in part 1 of *Mules and Men*. The interstitial narrative enacts a subtle analysis of the tales that the collection seems to lack upon a first read. This formulation collapses the distinction defined by Cheryl Wall between a "presentational" methodology and an "analytical" one: instead of locating the analysis in a separate passage of dry observation like the other ethnographic works of her day, Hurston situates her critique in the "presentation" ("*Mules and Men*," 671).[6] Specifically, the tales and the between-stories action function as paired metaphoric reflections; the tales are linked together in contiguous series to represent a complex vision of community.

The radical narrative structure of *Mules and Men* reflects Hurston's understanding of folklore as a contemporary, flexible form. Every topic fits within the scope of these folkways, no one is too grand to be a character in a folktale; religious hierarchies of good and evil are not sacred, and neither are America's white, wealthy elite. In an essay entitled "Characteristics of Negro Expression," first published in Nancy Cunard's *Negro: An Anthology* (1934), Hurston wrote: "Negro folklore is not a thing of the past. It is still in the making. Its great variety shows the adaptability of the black man: nothing is too old or too new, domestic or foreign, high or low, for his use. God and the Devil are paired, and are treated no more reverently than Rockefeller and Ford. Both of these men are prominent in folklore . . . and they talk and act like good-natured stevedores or mill-hands" (Hurston, "Characteristics," 56). Hurston evokes the Federal Writers' Project's strategy of democratic mimesis, a comprehensive approach in which the leveling force of democracy renders each historical moment and nuance of commensurate value. The famed capitalist Henry Ford "works" in the tales, just like any adept millhand. There can be no question that in this formulation, the tales are produced within the time of modernity, of Fordism (Duck 272–77).

Elsewhere in the essay, Hurston describes a notion of culture as an ongoing translation of forms back and forth between groups of people. While still maintaining distinct racial categories of white and black, she defines art and ideas as heterogeneous and fluid. Under the subheading "Originality" she states:

> The Negro is a very original being. While he lives and moves in the midst of a white civilization, everything that he touches is re-interpreted for his own use. . . . Everyone is familiar with the Negro's modifications of the whites' musical instruments, so that his interpretation has been adopted by the white man himself and then re-interpreted. . . . Thus has arisen a new art in the civilized world, and thus has our so-called civilization come. The exchange and re-exchange of ideas between people. ("Characteristics," 58)

This philosophy resonates with the argument offered by the anthropologist James Clifford in his book *Routes*, that "human location [is] constituted by displacement as much as stasis . . . [and] human difference [is] articulated in displacement, tangled cultural experiences, structures and possibilities of an increasingly connected but not homogenous world" (2). Hurston's prescient idea of exchange and proliferation is particularly relevant to the transmission of stories in *Mules and Men*: many of the tales revise previously told tales and incorporate different renditions passed on from other regions.

Yet, as Hazel Carby points out, Hurston's ideas about African American culture were not always consistent ("Politics," 76–77). In *Mules and Men*, Hurston mentions only her own travels "up North," thus relegating the fact of the massive African American migration northward to the subtext of her work on folklore. There can be little doubt that the migration's attendant associations of diffusion and assimilation fueled her sometimes romanticization of the South as an isolated locus of pristine folklore (76). She shares this impulse with the Federal Writers' Project Guide Series and other projects of cultural recovery in the 1930s. All of these endeavors upheld a nostalgic view of the "folk" and the nation's rural regions in response to a range of technological and social changes: the mechanization and corporate consolidation of farming, urban industrialization, the massive exodus of people to northern and western urban centers, as well as a thriving national popular culture. This sentiment was augmented by the fact of "geographic differences [within the United States] in the experiences of modernity" and the feeling that modernization would inevitably usher in national standardization (Hegeman 23). Giving voice to this anxiety, after Hurston went on her first collecting trip to Florida in 1927, she complained that "the bulk of the population now spends its leisure in the motion picture theaters or with the phonograph and its blues," echoing a common assumption among folklorists of the time that "race records" were a commercial appropriation of traditional music (Hemenway 92).[7]

In the spirit of salvage anthropology—the practice of rescuing what is left of a culture before it purportedly disappears—Hurston worried about the sanctity of a specifically African American folk tradition.[8] Boas affirmed and expanded upon this concern in his *Anthropology and Modern Life* (1928), noting in particular Hurston's findings:

> Even more striking is the rapidity of change of culture among the Negroes of the United States. Since their introduction as slaves their language, their ancient customs and beliefs, have disappeared apace with their absorption in the economic life of America. Dr. Parsons, Dr. Herskovits, and Miss Zora Hurston have shown that, as we proceed from south to north . . . the survivals of Negro culture become less and less. The Negro districts of

the South retain some African elements, while the northern Negro city dweller is to all intents and purposes like his White neighbor. (132–36)

Both Boas and Hurston affirm a model of "stable" cultural output based upon "isolation" (Boas's terms) and racial and regional difference. In this view, all cultures change, but these transformations occur more rapidly when groups come in contact with their neighbors, especially Europeans, and "accidents of a geographical or social nature" befall them (Boas 212).[9]

In his explanation of cultural stability and modification, Boas measures the authenticity of "Negro culture" by the quantity of African elements—the aura of the "primitive"—still evident in its various collective forms. He suggests that "negro" folk culture is derived from primitive origins. His account of modernization in the United States provides a temporal narrative of progress that is mapped spatially according to place: African Americans who reside in the rural South uphold African retentions of the past, whereas African Americans in northern urban centers conform to the protocols of white standardization in the present. Boas's model is founded—like the Florida guide—on the notion of "a black past and a white present" (Rogin, *Blackface*, 49). Boas promotes salvage ethnography as a means of sustaining African retentions before they are entirely "absorbed," yet this very paradigm exudes the logic of commodity it purportedly resists. These "vanishing" objects, peoples, and places gained currency within commercial modernity (Carr and Cooper 294). Within this marketplace, such artifacts were retroactively designated as worthy based upon a sense of their imminent loss (Miller 374–79).

Hurston's views vacillate between situating vernacular culture within modernity and before it. On the one hand, Hurston endorses a theory of folklore that views the cultural exchanges between groups as a highly creative and contemporary process. On the other hand, she embraces a perspective that sees these exchanges as detrimental to the preservation of "authentic," culturally specific forms. Her preservationist theory overlooks the ways that cultures have always materialized out of exchanges and reinterpretations made at various, shifting contact zones with the other/outsider.[10] The tensions between these two positions are perfectly illustrated in the ambiguous logic of Hurston's description of drama and "Negro expression": "Every phase of Negro life is highly dramatized. No matter how joyful or sad the case there is sufficient poise for drama. Everything is acted out. Unconsciously for the most part of course. There is an impromptu ceremony always ready for every hour of life. No little moment passes unadorned" ("Characteristics," 49). The central paradox of this passage condenses an implicit dialectic in *Mules and Men*, between hereditary and cultural definitions of identity and artistic production. In Hurston's estimation, what is essential about "Negro expression" is a profound performativity: every moment is acted, constructed, embellished, and ritualized. In a sense, she has it both ways: the only organic quality of this expression is its essentially inorganic nature. In this theory, performance and its practice encompass the locus of authenticity. It provides the basis for her modus operandi, her signifying ethnography. By blurring the lines between "real" life and artifice, the authentic and the inauthentic, she disrupts foundational categories of identity and expression so integral to the practice of ethnography and the project of the documentary collection that she herself pursues.[11]

Hurston's informants deploy a similarly cryptic discourse of authenticity when they describe the folktales they tell and she collects. In the second chapter of *Mules and Men*, George Thomas, one of the local Eatonville porch-sitters, exclaims: "Zora, you come to de right place if lies is what you want. Ah'm gointer lie up a nation" (19).[12] Thomas affirms Hurston's instinct for locating folktales, and, at the same time, he renames them "lies," cleverly signifying on the notion of a "pure," cultural artifact and unadulterated ethnographic evidence. As his metaphor suggests, he will give her a proverbial country of folklore: his lies are so big that they supersede and, in fact, create "place." Leigh Anne Duck remarks that *Mules and Men* "represent(s) a chronotope, or time-space, present in the larger US" (277). In the savvy words of Thomas, not only do the tales exist within the nation, but they fundamentally create the nation, a point not lost on the architects who designed the New Deal's cultural recovery.

Folktales were the perfect slippery ethnographic subject for Hurston's contradictory theories about authentic African American cultural production and her practice of signifying ethnography. As her book amply demonstrates, folklore constituted a particularly performative kind of authentic fiction with bonafide truth-claims and truth-effects that shaped the communities in which it was produced and circulated. At once boldly imaginary and deeply real, readily recorded but always incomplete, easily imported yet context-bound, the tales form the terrain out of which place and identity emerge. It is this fluid, local, and communal rendering of place and identity that the Florida guidebook largely misses. With Thomas's vow, then, he outlines both the premise and promise of the collection: as *Mules and Men* details Eatonville's folktales —its lies—it subverts hegemonic models of ethnographic writing in order to explore various locations of knowledge and knowledges of locale within the "intersubjective" time-space of the nation (Duck 275).

I SING 'EM BACK TO THE PEOPLE UNTIL THEY TELL ME I CAN SING 'EM JUST LIKE THEM

Under Franz Boas's tutelage, Hurston was encouraged to use her insider status as a means of gaining access to material that white collectors could not obtain. In the end, Hurston's choice of narrative strategy would determine the nature of this insider material as much as her actual collecting activities. In response to Hurston's field notes from her collecting trip to Jacksonville in 1927, Boas wrote: "What you obtained is very largely a repetition of the kind of material that has been collected so much. . . . You remember that when we talked about this matter I asked you particularly to pay attention, not so much to content, but rather to the form of diction, movements and so on" (qtd. in Hemenway 91). He believed that Hurston would be allowed to observe "habitual movements in telling tales, or in ordinary conversation," rather than feigned performances staged for white anthropologists. In this way, Hurston's project could move beyond a recording of the folktale to a chronicling of folk style. In keeping with these directives, she explained in a later letter that the collection consisted of "folktales with background so that they are in atmosphere and not just stuck out in cold space. I want the reader to see why Negroes tell such glorious tales" (163). Yet, in her request to Boas that he write the preface to the book, she somewhat apologetically attempted to explain her inclusion of "between-story conversation": "[Mr. Lippincott] wants a very readable book that the average reader can understand, at the same time one that will have value as a reference book. I have inserted the between-story conversation and business because when I offered it without every publisher said it was too monotonous" (163). In a sense, her justifications seem unnecessary. *Mules and Men* satisfies Boas's summons for an account of folk style and bests the famed Polish-born British anthropologist Branislaw Malinowski's dictate that the ethnographer must learn the native vernacular while in the field.[13] To appeal to a broad readership and create an engaging adventure of collecting, Hurston uses her advantage as an investigator back home in the field, narrating her tales in the style and manner of her informants, instead of writing them in "carefully accented Barnardese," the formal diction of her college education (*Dust Tracks*, 175).

Although some of Hurston's contemporaries may have scoffed at the unorthodoxy of her approach to questions of audience and context, they were not above these concerns.[14] For example, in his celebrated account of the inhabitants of the Trobriand Islands, *Argonauts of the Western Pacific*,[15] Malinowski attempts to engage the reader in two ways, by invoking an ethnographic present and using an active voice. He entreats the reader to picture with him the scene he is about to describe ("Let us imagine that we are sailing . . ." [33]) and he narrates a present-tense movement from place to place and sight to sight, guiding the reader to travel with him ("In order to visit one of the typical, large settlements of these natives . . . it would be best to go ashore. . . . We enter a clear, lofty grove. . . . When we approach the natives closer and scan their personal appearance, we are struck. . . . On the whole, they give at first approach not so much the impression of wild savages as of smug and self-satisfied bourgeois" [35–36]).[16] Malinowski remarks on the natives' surprising familiarity; in the words of his fellow Polish-born British writer, Joseph Conrad, in his novel *Lord Jim*, any among them might have been "one of us" (100).

While Hurston collapses the distance between ethnographer-observer and native informant, eschewing Malinowski's "scientific" tone and rendering her account in vernacular, both she and Malinowski attempt to engage the reader as an invisible companion in the escapades of the ethnographer out in the field. Indeed, as Henry Lee Moon stated in his review in the *New Republic* at the time of *Mules and Men*'s publication: "The intimacy [Hurston] established with her subjects, she reproduces on the printed page, enabling the reader to feel himself a part of that circle" (10). Moon suggests that the book invites its readers to join the boasters and the listeners on the porch. Given the complexity of Hurston's reader address, that invitation is provisional at best.

Unlike the single-voiced observations on the part of the anthropologist found in the traditional account, in Hurston's ethnography, while there exists a unifying narrator, "Zora," the collection is filled with a multiplicity of storytellers. As other commentators have suggested, the volume is polyvocal, a structural aspect it shares with the Federal Writers' Project's guidebooks (Carr and Cooper 301; Gordon, "Politics," 162; Sanchez-Eppler 477). In a sense, the narrator's voice is divided between ethnographic commentary, personal reflections, and participatory banter with the town informants. To further complicate matters, the narrator's personal reflections about her own identity and position reveal internal bifurcations as well. In a frequently quoted passage from her introduction, Hurston claims:

> When I pitched headforemost into the world I landed in the crib of negroism. From the earliest rocking of my cradle, I had known about the capers Brer Rabbit is apt to cut and what the Squinch Owl says from the house top. But it was fitting me like a tight chemise. I couldn't see it for wearing it. It was only when I was off in college, away from my native surroundings, that I could see myself like somebody else and stand off and look at my garment. Then I had to have the spy-glass of Anthropology to look through at that. (1)

In her justification of her intent to collect "Negro" folklore with the tools of anthropology, the speaking "I" in her formulation precedes even her myth of origins, "the crib of negroism" she landed in upon entering the world. That cradle provides her with an immediate understanding of southern African American folklore, a narrative of place and people, as part of its "negroist" designation. (Her choice of the word "crib" also suggests, in its verb form, the ways that her claims to these authentic origins inherently involve a kind of copying, stealing, or borrowing, a kind of signifying practice.) Changing the metaphor from a crib to clothing, Hurston speaks of her identity as a garment that fits too close to the skin, something like a second skin. College is implicitly coded as a place of foreign whiteness. As it takes her away from her birthplace, it provides her with the possibility of self-inspection (as she puts it, she is able to see herself "like somebody else"). The "spy-glass" of anthropology aids her investigation of the garment, her own African American identity.

Hurston's explanation of her identity is constructed through a revealing slippage of metaphors: first figured as location (the crib and also her "native surroundings"), then as stories (Brer Rabbit), and finally, as clothes (the garment), the "self" she constructs is mutable. Depending upon her spatial location and her ontological tools, she can "put on," reexamine, and renegotiate various identities. In other words, her concept of subjectivity is dependent upon both the construction of place and a notion of articulation (in this case, storytelling). If places, in Hurston's terms, seem to construct the subjects within them—and subjects, in turn, actively define place (by "landing" and "looking")—then, to borrow from Doreen Massey, the identity of place is a "double articulation" (*Space*, 8). Place, narrative, and identity are inextricably related: one term constitutes the other. Before Hurston embarks upon the project of collecting Eatonville's folklore, she instructs the reader about this linkage that so informs her own dialectical position. Her readers see how she self-consciously constructs herself as folk insider and anthropologist outsider, and in the process, they confront their own place within the narrative as listeners who press for this hybrid form of authenticity.

In the final image of this passage, she delineates her multiple perspectives again when she stands off from her "garment" and views it with the "spy-glass of anthropology." Riffing on W. E. B. Du Bois's "double-consciousness, this sense of always looking at one's self through the eyes of others," Hurston's "spy-glass of anthropology" imbues her with an objective authority that allows her to "stand off" and view herself and her community from a distance (*Souls*, 2). The spyglass metaphor thus reveals the potential for a specular violence within the practice of anthropology (Hernandez, "Multiple Mediations," 353–54). The spyglass is able to "render that which is far into sharp and *static* focus," in turn transforming its subjects into "objects" and others. As Hurston ambiguously traverses her roles as insider and outsider, she essentially turns the spyglass's gaze onto the discipline of anthropology itself. Evident in the metaphoric slippages describing her own identity formation, it is altogether unclear where to locate the "real" and unified Hurston.

It is no easier to detect her position in the pages that follow. As she analyzes the difficulties of collecting folklore, she occupies several different speaking positions all in the course of a paragraph:

> Folklore is not as easy to collect as it sounds. The best source is where there are the least outside influences and these people, being usually underprivileged, are the shyest. They are most reluctant at times to reveal that

which the soul lives by. . . . The Negro offers a feather-bed resistance. That is, we let the probe enter, but it never comes out. . . . The theory behind our tactics: "The white man is always trying to know into somebody else's business. All right, I'll set something outside the door of my mind for him to play with and handle. He can read my writing but he sho' can't read my mind. I'll put this play toy in his hand, and he will seize it and go away. Then I'll say my say and sing my song." (2–3)

In this rich account, Hurston's pronoun designations shift from "these people" to "the Negro" to a distinction between "we" and the "white man" (Carr and Cooper 296–97; Johnson, "Thresholds," 286–87; Retman 175–76; Walters 349–50). By placing her theory of evasive tactics in quotation marks, she adopts a speaking voice for all African American informants.[17] Signifying on the discipline of anthropology and the commercial market for folklore, she points out that the white man is always trying to "know *into* somebody else's business"; the associative rhyme and substitution implies that "knowing" is often as invasive as "going" into somebody else's business. Hurston is complicit herself as a collector. The reader who wants to know and figuratively go is implicated as well. At the same time, this connection also links knowledge production to travel and mobility, a relationship that is literalized in the figure of her car as a vehicle for her collecting practice.

As Hurston riffs on "knowing" and "going," she deploys several complex spatial metaphors that foreground the implicit issue of social access in this equation. When she speaks of "setting something outside the door of my mind for him to play with and handle," the figure of the door represents the liminal space between public and private identities, foreshadowing the threshold of the porch, the place where stories are told and retold for an eager audience. In both scenarios, the white anthropologist, expecting full access, never knows that he has been duped; his informants strategically give him something "to know" and elude his inspection (Johnson 286–87). Either case underscores the severe limitations of the spyglass, which in view of this passage seems as ineffectual as the "probe" that never comes out. Furthermore, Hurston's tactical theory implicitly equates "writing" with the "play toy" that reveals so little ("he can read my writing but he sure can't read my mind"). This equation opens up an interesting quandary for Hurston's readers: foremost among them, how do we know when we are being given a "play toy"?

What do we make of her writing when she professes to let us read her inner thoughts? Last, where do we locate Hurston when, after her long meditation on the (white) collector's difficult job, she observes, "I knew that even *I* was going to have some hindrance among strangers" (3). This perpetual ambiguity resists a facile reading either of the collection of tales or Hurston's own multiple roles as an African American woman anthropologist returning to her birthplace to do research. Moreover, it undercuts any easy understanding of the reader's own location within the text—is the reader her accomplice? The "white man"? Somebody else?

The final paragraph of her introduction echoes the ambiguity of her position and ours as well. Her narration switches to an apparent blow-by-blow account of her journey in her Chevrolet to Eatonville. As she drives, she recalls the tales she heard as a child: in particular, she recounts a story of origins about God's creation of souls for people: "When I was rounding Lily Lake I was remembering how God had made the world and the elements and people" (3). In the story, God creates souls but decides to wait before handing them out because "folks ain't ready for souls yet. . . . [I]t's de strongest thing Ah ever made"; he waits thousands of years for men to grow strong enough to bear their souls and "all de time de soul-piece, it was setting 'round covered up wid God's loose raiment." (This reference to "raiment" mirrors her earlier invocation of "negroism" as a chemise and a garment; in both scenarios, a soul implicitly or explicitly lies underneath the clothing.) When God's vestments blow aside, accidentally revealing the soul-piece, it causes meteorological disturbances, thereby inspiring awe and caution in the "white man," "the Indian and the Negro" as they pass by it. In an anti-Semitic turn, the Jew cannot resist the soul-piece, and so he snatches it and runs away. It burns and tosses him about, carrying him over a mountain top and all the while, little chips and pieces fall to the earth. God gathers together the fragments, mixes them with feelings and parcels them out: "Way after while when He ketch dat Jew, He's goin' to 'vide things up more ekal" (4). Somewhat ambiguously (perhaps a strange Christian spin on the fact that Jesus was a Jew), the stereotyped avarice of the Jew is also the source of his generous sacrifice for humankind within the tale: if he had resisted the tempting soul-piece like the others, no one would have souls today.

The tale falters between a particular and a universalizing mode of representation: every ethnic and cultural group has a soul, though the

Jew apparently has more soul than his fair share, a situation God intends to amend if he ever catches him. Significantly, each group remains distinctly named and depicted. Thus, the first tale told in the collection functions as an allegory of beginnings, the story that begets all other stories. As such, it implicitly designates the recovery of lost origins as a central subject in the collection and it overtly raises questions about hierarchies of racial and cultural difference in relation to narrative (Walters 361–62). Hurston tells this inaugural story and she tells it in vernacular (Johnson 286; Retman 178; Walters 355). Hurston establishes her knowledge of Eatonville's particular dialect *before* she sets foot in the town, thus reinforcing her role as an authoritative insider and revealing her potential capacity to serve as an erudite subject of her own study. Contrary to Robert Hemenway's assessment that Hurston "deliberately [underplays] her knowledge of Eatonville so that the reader will not feel alienated," Hurston subtly situates herself as a representative of the "folk" as well as an objective folklorist (167).

After Hurston recounts the tale, she approaches the outer district of her hometown: "I rounded Park Lake and came speeding down the straight stretch into Eatonville, the city of five lakes, three croquet courts, three hundred brown skins, three hundred good swimmers, plenty guavas, two schools and no jail-house" (4). At this point she pauses: "Before I enter the township, I wish to make acknowledgments to Mrs. R. Osgood Mason of New York City." Just as she proves her familiarity with the community she means to observe by briefly outlining its salient features, she halts, as if to emphasize the transitional space between the township and Maitland as well as the textual gap between the actual collection of tales and the introduction which precedes it. Before she enters her southern "native surroundings," she pays her respects to her patron, seeming to rid herself of her last obligation to her benefactor and, at the same time, signal her own commodified relation to white capital (Baker 303; Carr and Cooper 290; Johnson 286; Retman 179; Walters 345, 356–63).[18] (This ambivalent gesture suggests that while Mason may "own" Hurston's research, she entirely depends upon Hurston for its implementation and delivery.) If Hurston marks her complicity here as a mediator who will deliver the folk, she signals her readers' complicity as well. Mason sponsored her initial research of the folk and the reader has invested in this project, too. As Hurston "crosses the line" into this southern space, she brings her readers along with her. Her pause emphatically underscores her privileged access as a collector and, by extension, ours as readers of her collection. In so doing, it demarcates the difference race and region make when decoding the "lies" she collects.

THE TOWN HAD NOT CHANGED

As readers, we approach the first chapter with increasing anticipation, relying on textual clues to map out our transitory position in the narrative. Hurston accomplishes this effect by providing detailed and increasingly local geographical coordinates: below Palatka, she begins to feel eager; as she rounds Lily Lake, she remembers various folk figures; as she circles Park Lake, she describes Eatonville: "As I crossed the Maitland-Eatonville township line I could see a group on the store porch. I was delighted. The town had not changed. Same love of talk and song" (7).[19] She glimpses her final destination—the store porch, the town's primary meeting place.[20] Its centrality is emphasized by the narrative's particular command of our gaze, an effect which also serves to reinforce Hurston's position as the reader's geographical and cultural guide. She is in the driver's seat, both figuratively and metaphorically. Accordingly, when she states, "I hailed [the men on the porch] as I went into neutral," her meaning is double. Hurston's access to her material depends, in part, upon the nature of this homecoming: she must appear nonchalant, all the while actively and objectively reading the people around her.

This first scene enacts the ethnographic trope of the arrival story, but with a difference (Boxwell, "Sis Cat," 611; Clifford, *Predicaments*, 23–27). The arrival anecdote is a narrative device meant to convince readers that the facts put before them were objectively acquired, not subjectively created (Clifford 29). For example, Malinowski writes in his account: "The natives . . . immediately surround the visitor in large groups. . . . It is difficult to convey the feelings of intense interest and suspense with which the Ethnographer enters for the first time the district that is to be the future scene of his fieldwork" (51). The double sighting in this textual moment is crucial: Malinowski must witness the natives apprehending him for the first time; their encircling of him serves as a validation of his authority; he was actually there, living among the natives. The suspense (predictably) lies in the unpredictable contact between observer and native.

In contrast to Malinowski's precarious arrival, Hurston is casually received. Immediately, she explains the purpose of her visit (something she does not do on her arrival in Polk County, which I discuss later). The mayor says to her, "We heard all about you up North. You back home for good, I hope," and she replies: "Nope, Ah come to collect some old stories and tales and Ah know y'all know a plenty of 'em and that's why Ah headed straight for home" (7–8). Invoking the archetypal trope of the return of the small-town hero made good, this scene illustrates Hurston's difference via geography (she has been up north) while also indicating her comfortable reentry and assimilation back into the town of Eatonville. While the mayor symbolically officiates at her arrival and verifies her presence as a local luminary, her intention to collect stories is still met by the townspeople with disbelief. George Thomas exclaims, "Aw shucks Zora, don't you come here and tell de biggest lie first thing. Who you reckon want to read all them old-time tales about Brer Rabbit and Brer Bear?" She answers with a standard argument of salvage ethnography: "Plenty of people, George. They are a lot more valuable than you might think. We want to set them down before it's too late" (8). In this instance, it is unclear who the "we" is in the preservation effort: is it the community of Eatonville or the community of anthropologists up north? Furthermore, the teacherly tone of the scene, ostensibly concerning the edification of the "provincial" inhabitants, feels overtly staged for the reader's enlightenment.[21]

Before any stories are told, Hurston establishes the scene, describing a ritualized space of exchange: after warning Calvin Daniels to let Hurston get settled, George Thomas suggests that later "we'll all go down and tell lies and eat ginger bread. Dat's de way to do" (8). In a reversal of the usual fieldwork paradigm, in which the ethnographer must seek out his or her informants, they come to her, so anxious to begin telling tales that they must be restrained from starting right in. Equally striking is the way that this scene frames the activity of collecting as a customary transaction between collector and informant through consumption and orality. As the porch-sitters gather together in Armetta Jones's house to provide Hurston with their oral narratives, she and Armetta provide them with gingerbread. While this scene reinforces traditional gender roles—the men talk and the women cook—it breaks down the typical mode of barter found in other field accounts. In the second chapter, people gather together again for a second night of telling "lies": "It was a hilarious night with a pinch of everything social mixed in with the storytelling. Everybody ate ginger bread; some drank the buttermilk provided and some provided coon dick for themselves. Nobody guzzled it—just took it in social sips. But they told stories enough for a volume by itself" (19). Hurston's offering of gingerbread and buttermilk facilitates the "pinch of everything social." She is more than compensated for her offering: they take "social sips" and share the food and, in return, they provide her with a volume of tales.[22] Hurston depicts her fieldwork activities as friendly exchanges, a familiar dimension of the town's usual social rituals.

In a further recuperation of the purportedly organic nature of Hurston's field activities, she records the storytelling as if she were transcribing it at that moment, in "real time" as it were, disruptions and all. In the first chapter, James impatiently interrupts Calvin, the first storyteller, who is in the midst of a dull rendition of "John and the Frog." Accordingly, James's tale, entitled "Witness of the Johnstown Flood in Heaven," is a folkloric allegory about the pitfalls of not taking the audience into proper account. John, the protagonist, is drowned in a flood caused by a flurry of activities in Heaven (in the tale's cosmology of weather, "when it lightenings, de angels is peepin' in de lookin' glass; when it thunders, they's rollin' out do rain barrel; and when it rains, somebody done dropped a barrel or two and bust it" [11]). When John goes to heaven, he repeatedly tries to tell the angels the story of his death but, because they caused the flood, they are familiar with the narrative already. They grow weary of him. In turn, John becomes increasingly aggravated by their rude retreat; finally, he starts to tell his tale to an old, bearded man who curtly replies "Shucks! You ain't seen no water!" The punch line of the joke is that John unwittingly chooses Noah as his listener.

This story establishes "the evaluative criteria used by insiders for judging 'big, old lies' " (Walters 352). John looks foolish, telling people tales they already know, because he fails to take into account the knowledge, experience, and authority of others. He makes his mistake because he misunderstands the exchange between author and audience as a relation of power, position, and access. Some stories are more important than others: the joke of the Johnstown tale turns on Noah's flood as the urtext, the biblical allegory that upstages all others. Every flood story refers back to this narrative in one way or another. Thus, John's myopic yarn serves as a cautionary tale for all storytellers, including Hurston's informants and Hurston herself.[23] By telling an allegory about monotonous storytelling, James signifies on Calvin, suggesting that "John and the Frog" is too mundane for Hurston's discerning ear. (Much like the angels in the story, Hurston is familiar with many of Eatonville's tales; thus, her expertise must be taken into account before embarking on just any tale.) James's folktale is one of a series of narratives within the collection that partake in a critique of ethnography itself. In this instance, the tale outlines a central problematic for any ethnography of folktales: a successful collection must respectfully represent and contextualize a particular lineage of stories, not only interesting to outsiders but satisfying to an audience of insiders as well.[24] A successful collection assumes a diversity of readers.

MY TOE WENT ON THE LINE WITH THE REST

As the tale of "John and the Frog" suggests, *Mules and Men* is aimed at both "modern" outsiders as well as "folk" insiders, a conception of multiple audiences which refuses the different temporal frames—the modern and the primitive—that structure many other ethnographic accounts of the period, including the Florida guide.[25] Hurston shares the same time with her informants in that most modern of conveyances, her Chevrolet, and by implication, so do her readers. By suggesting that her broadly conceived audience experiences the stories contemporaneously, she negates the supposed gap between the two groups. Even as she does this, she continues to emphasize the "exotic" aspects of her findings for those not in "the know." Chapter 1 ends with an account of a "toe-party," a scene that not only foregrounds Hurston's own subjectivity as a central narrative concern but also demonstrates the way that she represents her relationship with her informants as coeval (Duck 275; Retman 185).

When Hurston explains the toe-party, she plays to her audience in a number of ways: Calvin tells her that he has decided to go to a toe-party and she exclaims in a virtual stage whisper, "A toe-party! What on earth is that?" (9). Her declared ignorance reinforces the toe-party's potential value for folklorists; if she is unfamiliar with this social ritual, it must be a unique custom indeed.[26] Calvin urges her to come with him and see, leaving her (and the reader) in a state of narrative suspense. As she goes to the party to answer her question, we are drawn into a palpable ethnographic present.[27] Each discovery for Hurston is a discovery for the reader. Once she is behind the curtain about to sell her toes, she asks one of the other women, "Say, what *is* this toe-party business?" to which the woman replies, "Good gracious, Zora! Ain't you never been to a toe-party before?" (14). Hurston explains: "They don't have 'em up North where Ah been and Ah just got back today." Her friend describes the meaning of the ritual. The party is a fund-raising event for the Wood Bridge lodge: women line up behind a curtain and take off their shoes to display their toes. Men buy "the toes" they want for a dime and with this purchase, they are obliged to treat the woman to everything she wants (15). While Hurston may not be familiar with the ritual because she has been a temporary outsider, she finds out by participating as an insider, by putting her "toe on the line with the rest" (her toe is sold five times during the party). In a discursive move similar to the Federal Writers' Project's Guide Series, Hurston sustains the exotic otherness of the social event to draw the reader in, by simultaneously depicting herself as an outsider and an insider in her fieldwork.

Yet Hurston's mobility literally and figuratively extends from her car in a manner entirely unlike the Guide Series' use of the car for touristic surveillance. Whereas in the Guide Series, the car provides a privileged space from which to view a stationary folk tableau vivant, Hurston uses her car as another place of interaction with her informants. In so doing, she reworks the traditional conception of the field by detailing her travels to and from Wood Bridge. The Eatonville faction drives to the party in a fleet of five cars, including Hurston's Chevrolet. She loads her car up with "neighbors." In her description, "We were the tail end of the line and as we turned off the highway we could hear the boys in the first car doing what Ellis Jones called bookooing before they even hit the ground. Charlie Jones was woofing louder than anybody else" (13). The text includes footnotes that define "bookooing" and "woofing" as "loud talking, bullying, woofing. . . . From French *beaucoup*" (13n4). Though seemingly insignificant, this scene expands the theory of participant observation in new directions: as Hurston drives with her informants to collect new material, she also gathers it on the way; the field for collecting becomes respatialized to include transitory moments of travel as well as fixed spaces of dwelling.[28] In scenes like these, we "see the temporality of the 'folk' mapped onto that of the highway—the simultaneous, cross-space time in which Hurston 'speeds' from New York to Eatonville" and, in a more obvious sense, we see Hurston and her informants driving cars, achieving the mobile promise of modernity in its most iconic form, the automobile (Duck 275).

Hurston distinguishes Wood Bridge, their destination, as "a Negro community . . . lacking in Eatonville's feeling of unity. In fact, a white woman lives there" (13). As she and her neighbors cross into the next town in her Chevrolet, preparing to mingle with "folks from Altamonte, Longwood and Winter Park," she draws a distinction between Eatonville and the neighboring town: Eatonville's regional unity is reinforced by racial solidarity and the "enterprising souls" who built the town. While seeming to fit naturally within the plot of the chapter, her passing comment provides ethnographic data that differentiates between various African American communities, breaking with a monolithic conception of rural southern African American communities. A few paragraphs later, Hurston writes, "They had the carcass of a party lying around up until the minute Eatonville burst in on it. Then it woke up" (14). Her group arrives to liven things up. Hurston sets out to provide a typical example of a toe-party but manages to avoid the language of stasis found in the standard discourse of thirties' anthropological and travel writing. In so doing, she implicitly critiques the lifeless "natural history museum" approach to observing informants as nothing more than specimens.

Additionally, this scene suggests the ways in which contact between groups—in this case Eatonville's, Wood Bridge's, and Altamonte's inhabitants—enables a vital process of interactive cultural production. The Eatonville group gets the party going, enabling Hurston to participate in "this toe-party business" and collect primary material. Later in the scene, this process is compounded yet again: "Eatonville began to move back home right then. Nearly everybody was packed in one of the five cars when the delegation from Altamonte arrived. . . . Everybody piled out again" (16). Johnny Barton of the Altamonte crowd brings a guitar with him, so Hurston is able to collect songs as well. The cultural exchange and reinterpretation continues and symbolically the regions mingle: Barton passes his guitar around so that eventually Eatonville's George Thomas, together with Altamonte's Georgia Burke, gets to sing a song about Polk County, "where the water tastes like wine." When the party is really over, the communities consolidate once again into their little coteries. Hurston describes: "I staggered sleepily forth to the little Chevrolet for Eatonville. The car was overflowing with passengers but I was so dull from lack of sleep that I didn't know who they were. All I knew is they

belonged in Eatonville" (17). During the singing, individuals stand synecdochically for their community, a part for a whole; in the end, there are
only distinct townships. Eatonville is unified once again, defined not by
its individuals, but by a tautological notion of belonging: the passengers
in the car are rendered familiar solely by their concurrent desire to
return there. If the narrative enacts "Zora's" identity as a series of inter-
pellations dependent upon her social context—from Franz Boas's student, to the "crib of negroism," to Lucy Hurston's daughter to bootlegger's girlfriend—here, the process extends to her informants and possibly
to the reader who figuratively accompanies the rest of the group on the
way back to Eatonville.

Hurston's first chapter refuses a monolithic, primitive portrait of the
folk. Instead, we experience the field and its folkways in action. Pointing
to the structural and atmospheric disparities between communities that
might otherwise be lumped together, Hurston demonstrates how the
momentary convergence of regional differences transforms culture, how
new songs and stories are created. As she drives, talks, and sings with
her informants, she shares contemporary time with them. By proxy, so
do we.

YOU DON'T KNOW POLK COUNTY LIKE I DO

Hurston's own identity—in particular, the social dimensions of her labor
as a black woman ethnographer—comes under scrutiny when she leaves
the familiarity of her hometown of Eatonville for the enticing songs of
the sawmill workers in Polk County. In a move reminiscent of the textual
break between the introduction and part 1 that marks her crossing into
Eatonville, Hurston heads south to Loughman, Polk County, in the conclusion of chapter 3 and arrives at its Everglades Cypress Lumber Company in the beginning of chapter 4. The Chevy synecdochically stands in
for Hurston and her journey: "A hasty good-bye to Eatonville's oaks and
oleanders and the wheels of the Chevvie split Orlando wide open—
headed south-west for corn (likker) and song" (57). As she narrates her
travels, her car becomes her wary companion. The Chevy's alleged cir-
cumspection portends a vexed arrival scene far different from Hurston's
comfortable return to Eatonville: "We had meant to keep on to Bartow
or Lakeland and we debated the subject between us until we reached the

opening, then I won. We went in. The little Chevrolet was all against it. The thirty odd miles that we had come, it argued, was nothing but an appetizer. Lakeland was still thirty miles away and no telling what the road held. But it sauntered on down the bark-covered road and into the quarters just as if it had wanted to come" (59). She transforms her own internal split into a dispute between herself and her car. By personifying the Chevy, imbuing it with a sense of foreboding and then an air of nonchalance, Hurston maintains her jaunty, comic narration. She manages to express her own anxiety, through the synecdoche of her car, and simultaneously distance herself from the potentially disempowering effects of that disclosure. This textual maneuver foreshadows the final harrowing jook scene of part 1 and underscores the potential danger she confronts as a single woman, traveling by herself into an unfamiliar and reputedly violent community. Without a companion, she has only her ability to perform, to feign a saunter and swagger.

For the first time in the narrative, Hurston suffers from a profound sense of displacement, the dominant sentiment in the "exotic" field accounts of researchers like Malinowski and others.[29] That first night, she receives a less than warm welcome as the men from the quarters come "to look over the new addition" (60). So begins her awkward initiation into the community as an outsider: "Very little was said directly to me and when I tried to be friendly there was a noticeable disposition to *fend* me off. This worried me because I saw at once that this group of several hundred Negroes from all over the South was a rich field for folk-lore, but here was I figuratively starving to death in the midst of plenty." Unlike Eatonville's familiar mode of mutual consumption—amicable exchanges of gingerbread, buttermilk, and tales—Polk County's inhabitants leave Hurston's hunger for tales unsatiated. She is unaccustomed to the mores of Polk County, and, as a result, she has not figured out an appropriate mode of interacting with her potential informants. Finally, after being the recipient of "feather-bed tactics" for a time ("The men would crowd in and buy soft drinks and woof at me, the stranger, but I knew I wasn't getting on"), she drives down to Lakeland with one of the locals, Cliffert Ulmer. He trusts her enough to tell her that the shiny Chevrolet is her biggest obstacle: "The car made me look too preposterous. . . . [S]ince most of them were fugitives from justice or had done plenty time, a detective was just the last thing they felt they needed" (61). The car ride facilitates Cliffert's trust and, ironically, the car is also the crux of the problem.

In fact, the problem of the car for the migrant camp workers illuminates an aspect of folklife often neglected in the scholarship surrounding *Mules and Men*—the place of the "folk" within modernity.[30] The first image of the Everglades Cypress Lumber Company is one of the most industrial in the book: "The asphalt curved deeply and when it straightened out we saw a huge smoke-stack blowing smut against the sky" (59). In apparent contrast, the work and living conditions inside "the quarters" are in many ways reminiscent of slavery—a fact emphasized by the concentration of stories that focus on "slavery time talk" contained within this section of the book (*Mules and Men*, 80; Meisenhelder, "Conflict," 271). Yet, these internal capitalist conditions are not indicative of migrant workers' delayed entrance into modernity or, as Hazel Carby suggests, Hurston's "romantic and . . . colonial imagination" (Carby 80). Rather, in accordance with the notion of "intranational colonialism," formulated by Eva Cherniavsky, these conditions demonstrate the "differential incorporation" of a rural, migrant African American labor force *within* modernity (xix). As the smokestack indicates, this is a modern workplace in that it is "marked at once by the time-space relations of the metropolitan culture (increased spatial mobility, spurred by centralized systems of agricultural production and resource extraction, and by the creation/expansion of administrative centers) and the 'feudal' relations of production along the periphery (indentured/conscripted rather than 'free' wage labor)" (xvii). In *Mules and Men*, the "time-space relations of the metropolitan culture" are evidenced in the log train that carries the company's product nationwide, the rationalized time and production of the work day, and the creation of the satellite company town, while "the feudal relations . . . along the periphery" are evidenced in the exploitive and segregated labor conditions under which black migrants labor in the Jim Crow South. Hurston's car quite literally traverses these "heterogeneous regimes" (xvii). The car is not only a symbol of modernity's mass consumer culture; it is the transport of a detective, a sign of the law that polices and sustains these unequal labor relations.

Given the Chevrolet's symbolic freight, Hurston ends up employing it as a crucial prop: "I took occasion that night to impress the job with the fact that I was also a fugitive from justice, 'bootlegging.' They were hot behind me in Jacksonville and they wanted me in Miami. I was hiding out. That sounded reasonable. Bootleggers always have cars. I was taken in" (61). If the car is the vehicle of the law, of detectives come to investigate the lumber camps incognito, she reverses this association, turning it into a badge of her break with the law. The ruse is still insufficient. Later that night she discovers from a potential woofer, Mr. Pitts, that " 'uh heap uf dese hard heads wants to woof at you but dey skeered. . . . [D]ey say youse rich and dey ain't got de nerve to open dey mouf" (63). Hurston mentally curses the $12.74 dress from Macy's that she wears among all of the $1.98 mail-order dresses and embellishes her bootleg lie: "Oh, Ah ain't got doodley squat. . . . Mah man bought me dis dress de las' time he went to Jacksonville. We wuz sellin' plenty stuff den and makin' good money. Wisht Ah had dat money now" (64). Her awkward dress in this scene recalls her statements in the introduction about the too-tight-chemise of her "negroist" identity (1). Initially, she required the distancing techniques of anthropology to view her own identity, to "stand off and look at [her] garment"; this time, paradoxically, she must shed her identity as an ethnographer with a stipend and Macy dresses in order to deploy the spyglass of anthropology and view another community. To examine Eatonville's folklore and her own insider status, she becomes an outsider up north; to examine Polk County's folklore and gain an outsider perspective, she becomes a community insider.

Hurston is finally initiated into the community through her collaborative efforts with other established members of the group: it is through this process of cultural transmission and invention that she gains entry into the inner circle. After her "laughing acceptance of Pitts' woofing had put everyone at ease," she asks James Preseley to play "John Henry" on his guitar. He agrees to, on the condition that she sing to his accompaniment:

> I started to sing the verses I knew. They put me on the table and everybody urged me to spread my jenk [have a good time], so I did the best I could. Joe Willard knew two verses and sang them. Eugene Oliver knew one; Big Sweet knew one. . . . By the time the song was over . . . I knew that I was in the inner circle. I had first to convince the "job" that I was not an enemy in the person of the law; and, second, I had to prove that I was their kind. "John Henry" got me over my second hurdle. After that, my car was everybody's car. James Preseley, Slim and I teamed up and we had to do "John Henry" wherever we appeared. . . . We went to Mulberry, Pierce, and Lakeland. (65)

As David Nicholls demonstrates, by singing "John Henry," the famous work song that pits the powerful black spike driver against the steam drill that will eventually replace him, Hurston establishes her fluency with "the cultural language of the workers on the job" (471). Significantly, the song itself sounds anachronistic here; the men don't sing it as they work but rather to celebrate at a pay-day party. What we see in the between-story moments, then, is a form of resistance achieved not by besting the machine but by performing the nonalienated labor of storytelling, of singing the song about "the worker's alienation under capitalism and . . . the ever-present threat of replacement by machines" (Nicholls, "Migrant Labor," 471). Notably, "John Henry" is one of the last songs Hurston learned from Charlie back in Eatonville. In a teleological narrative move-ment, she has learned just enough from her fieldwork in her hometown to negotiate the difficulties of Polk County. This development emerges from the basic material she has collected as well as her shifting perspec-tive of anthropology based on her experience in the field. Thus, Hurston redefines the labor of ethnographer to consist not only of collecting and observing folklore but also of circulating and inventing folklore with her informants. She tours together with James Preseley and Slim in her travels to collect more folklore. Once again, her car becomes everybody's car in the production of a multilocale ethnography and field.

At the same time that her initiation would seem to support a theory of flexible culture based on transmission, translation, and reinvention (everyone transforms the song by adding a verse not known by the others), Hurston implicitly suggests that her informants discover in her singing an essential folk quality that they share—she is "their kind." This assumption is complicated by the fact that in Polk County, for Hurston to collect "lies," she has to exchange them. As she lies to her informants about her social position, pretending she is a bootlegger's woman, she adopts the social values of Polk County. When she assumes the persona of a fugitive, in a meta-ethnographic way, her lie makes her an outlaw within the received ethics of anthropology and it also signifies on the ways in which performance is always already a part of the fieldworker's voca-tion. Recalling her formulation of the essential performativity of African American expression and once more illuminating the central role of per-formative authenticity in her ethnographic self-presentation, her forged identity reinforces the dialectic inherent in that belief: through a multiple set of lies, she establishes that she is their "kind." Her artifice establishes her realness.[31] When she later discloses her actual intentions, "at first they couldn't conceive of anybody wanting to put down 'lies,' " but once they get over their astonishment, they all participate in her lying contest and it is "a huge success in every way" (65). As she tells it, the potentially damaging import of her initial lies is outweighed by her ability to perform. Hurston's readers benefit from her ability to lie—as our protagonist, "Zora" is safe; as our ethnographer, she has gained access to new material; and as our informant, the story of her lies and how she came to tell them is perhaps the most riveting tale of all.

Hurston's faltering entry into the camp quarters illuminates a complex set of class relations that rest, in part, on labor and region. Ultimately, what haunts the text in this section is the uneasy truth of the workers' initial misrecognition of Hurston—for, in a sense, she *is* a detective, performing the work of the middle-class observer, the documentarian, the anthropologist who will collect evidence, construct a narrative, and eventually produce her transcriptions as cultural commodities (Sanchez-Eppler 477). This vocational truth is subtly expressed in Hurston's shift from first to third person once she gains entry into the camp community (Nicholls 471). While she initially renders her own labor as an ethnographer apparent, in this section, her narration is soon subsumed by the workers' tales when she joins the swamp crew on the job. When the men wait that early morning for the white swamp-boss to show up, they tell tales that express their anger over the myriad abuses of white bosses. As it turns out, their logging duties have been suspended that day, but the foreman, instead of granting them a day off, instructs them to check with the mill for work.

The men saunter to the mill, effectively creating a work slow-down, and they amplify this act of resistance by narrating two stories about the origins of work that each end with the inequitable share of labor falling on black women and men.[32] In the first story, after God finishes making the world, he sets down a hefty bundle in the middle of the road which remains there for thousands of years until Ole Missus tells Ole Massa to pick it up. Ole Massa demands that his black slave pick it up, and he, in turn, asks his wife to pick it up. Thinking it is a gift, she grabs the box, only to discover that it is "full of hard work" (74). The tale concludes: "Dat's de reason the sister in black works harder than anyone else in de world." The second tale revises the first, beginning again with bundles set down by God. This time a white and black man must race to see who can pick up the biggest bundle first. The black man outruns the white man only to find that the bundle he grabbed contains "a pick and shovel and hoe and a plow and a chop-axe" (75). The white man's bundle contains "a writin'-pen and ink." Ever since then, while the black man performs manual labor with his tools, "de white man been sittin' up figgerin', ought's a ought, figger's a figger; all for de white man, none for de nigger."

In these moments, Hurston's presence all but vanishes so that she can seemingly perform the labor of "putting down lies" (65; Nicholls 471). Michael Elliot writes, "Hurston's narrative disappearance during these scenes suggests a gold standard of ethnography—a moment when the scientist renders herself invisible and simply records the words around her" (*Culture Concept*, 174). Arguably, though, her absence is made present in this ethnographic transcription. As the men's tales confront the unjust conditions of the logging camp, they subtly signify on the conventional racial and gender dynamics of Hurston's own profession, anthropology, depicted in the white man who writes for a living. If Hurston is potentially scripted as "the sister in black who works hardest" in the first story (at the behest of her patrons, Mrs. Meyer, Mrs. Mason, and her readers), she has appropriated the white man's pen and ink and the undeniable power of "figgerin' " in the second story to give voice to the laborers' folkloric protest (Nicholls 471–75). Her labor as a middle-class observer is not so invisible after all.

As Hurston figuratively defies white masculine authority here, her actions match the behavior of many of the women who reside in the camp. While everyone in the quarters is a fugitive from justice, the women garner special mention in Hurston's narrative. She herself breaks the law when she enters the quarters (recall the signs prohibiting entry without permission from the company). Moreover, the first person she describes at any length is "Babe" Hill, who shot and killed her husband. "Babe" ran from the law but the authorities apprehended her and sent her to jail; after a few months time, she was allowed to go home. Hurston dryly concludes: "Negro women are punished in these parts for killing men, but only if they exceed the quota. I don't remember what the quota is. . . . One woman had killed five when I left the turpentine still where she lived. The sheriff was thinking of calling on her and scolding her severely" (60). In Polk County, women flout the law as much as the men do and, often, they take just as active a role in mapping the social space of the quarters.

There is no better example of this than when Big Sweet, one of the most powerful women of Polk County, refuses to hand over her weapon to the quarter's boss after he breaks up a fight between her and her rivals, Lucy and Ella Wall. After he demands the knife, she replies: "Naw suh! Nobody gits *mah* knife. . . . Ah'll kill her, law or no law. Don't you touch me white folks!" (152). The boss kicks Lucy and Ella Wall out of the jook and feebly answers Big Sweet: "Now you behave yo'self. . . . Ah don't wanna hafta jail yuh!" After the altercation, her current man, Joe Willard, congratulates her: "You wuz a whole woman and half uh man. You made dat cracker stand off a *you*." By fiercely refusing to comply with white, male authority, Big Sweet reconfigures the spatial dynamics of the jook, both in terms of race and gender. Through a negotiation of space much more dramatic than the gender debate in chapter 2, she empowers herself to speak and to act.[33]

The final scene of part 1 violently encapsulates the women's contest over power in the jook. Aiming to kill Hurston, Lucy enters the jook declaring, "Ah means to turn dis place out right now. Ah got do law in my mouf" (179). Big Sweet comes to Hurston's rescue and in the ensuing brawl, Jim Preseley urges her to run. The potential reification that haunts Hurston's own position as both "a subject and an object of her discipline" ruptures her study, further blurring the lines between the material and the discursive (Elliot 171; Brady, *Extinct Land*, 6). As the field becomes deadly, as the collection's potentially objectified subjects threaten to extinguish their collector—in a sense, to reverse the relation and render her a lifeless object—Hurston makes her solo escape to an altogether new collecting ground, New Orleans, to gather material among its underground hoodoo community. Even though the conflict with Lucy is literally about a man's affections, the fallout suggests something more: her informant's refusal to have her labor objectified and turned into a commodity, even, or perhaps especially, when it is storytelling, a form of nonmaterial production. Graciela Hernandez observes the demise of Hurston's authority in this scene: "The power to define the terms upon which an ethnographer works, records, and leaves the field lies not with the interlocutor, but with the informants" (360). Certainly here, more than ever, her "informants are active narrators" rather than "passive repositories of information" (Elliot 174). Yet this reading neglects the literal and discursive valence of Hurston's mobility and the fact that the narration does not end; rather, it shifts to her collection of hoodoo in part 2.

In simple terms, while the aggressor Lucy's mobility is severely limited, Hurston's class position and vocation, symbolized in her car, enables her to drive away, abandoning her transgressive participant observation in exchange for the more traditional posture of the distanced ethnographer. Hurston recounts, "Jim and Slim helped me throw my bags into the car and I saw the sun rising as I approached Crescent City" (179). The narrator "Zora" wins the fight with Lucy in another sense as well: through her retroactive narration, Hurston takes the law in her mouth, and the jook joint scrape becomes another adventure (albeit bloody) in the day of the life of an ethnographer. In the beginning of part 2, Hurston recollects her experience with a pastoral reserve: "Winter passed and caterpillars began to cross the road again. I had spent a year in gathering and culling over folk-tales. I loved it" (183). Once she leaves the field of Polk County, that moment becomes more a lyrical memory than a vivid brush with death. As in her initial, nostalgic portrayal of Eatonville, she deploys an allochronic discourse when she describes her year of collecting. Thus, she conveniently leaves Lucy in the past, constructing an ethnographic present in a city far, far away.

NOTHING WORTH PUTTING ON PAPER

Hurston leaves that suddenly allochronic Polk County for the coeval city of New Orleans: her sites may change, but the transient nature of her collecting practice and its objects remains with her. Part 2 of *Mules and Men*, a section possibly tacked on at the request of her publisher, documents Hurston's foray into "the hoodoo capital of America . . . [where] it is burning with a flame . . . with all the intensity of a suppressed religion" (183).[34] She introduces her subject through another story of origins harkening back to the acquisition by Moses and the Ethiopian Queen of Sheba of hoodoo or "gold-making words": "Belief in magic is older than writing. So nobody knows how it started. The way we tell it, hoodoo started way back there before everything" (183). Positioning herself unequivocally as an insider and a believer, Hurston suggests that hoodoo somewhat mysteriously preceded and initiated representation, describing the way it will function in her own text throughout: she portrays her own acquisition of hoodoo but not many of its actual rites, curses, or spells in their entirety. Put differently, the hoodoo she collects remains fundamentally a secret. In this way, she respects the dictates of the religion itself, maintaining, for the most part, the "profound silence of the initiated" (185).

Not coincidentally, in the section that documents a set of African diasporic cultural practices most likely to be commodified as "primitive," Hurston insists upon their fundamentally elusive and inaccessible nature. Turner, one of the city's foremost "two-headed doctors," recounts how white people attended what they thought were hoodoo dances in Congo Square led by the famous priestess Marie Leveau: "But Marie Leveau never hold no hoodoo dance. That was a pleasure dance. . . . Hoodoo is private. . . . The white people come look on, and think they see all, when they only see a dance" (193). If hoodoo is by definition always private, it resists the reach of public, commodity culture. Rather, it functions as a vast underground economy of spiritual and material exchange.[35] Like the feather-bed resistance of the introduction, "mouths don't empty themselves unless the ears are sympathetic and knowing" (185). Anticipating that her readers' ears may not be either, Hurston provides us with a model for interpreting hoodoo straight away, in the figures of Mrs. Rachel Silas from Sanford, Florida, and her neighbor, Mrs. Viney White, both of whom express initial dismay at Hurston's inquiry into "dat ole fogeyism" (186). Mrs. Silas exclaims, "Ah don't believe nobody kin do me no harm lessen they git somthin' in mah mouth," only to dissemble moments later, after Hurston challenges her: "Well, well, well! Maybe things *kin* be done tuh harm yuh, cause Ah done heard *good* folks—folks dat ought to know—say dat it sho is a fact. Anyhow Ah figger it pays tuh be keerful." Mrs. White agrees, helping Mrs. Silas tell the story of woman overcome by "uh gopher in her belly." After this, they direct Hurston to her first teacher, Eulalia, who specializes in "man-and-woman cases." Hurston can only gain access to these stories and Eulalia by insisting on the veracity of hoodoo (Humphries, *Different Dispatches*, 149). Her informants test her belief before disclosing their own knowledge. At the same time, they allow that even if they don't believe in it entirely, they respect its power enough "tuh be keerful," a provision that potentially includes Hurston's doubting readers and her own careful text.

The New Orleans segment of the collection frustrates any reader's wish for a specific, detailed account of hoodoo, instead documenting Hurston's slow path to knowledge as she successively petitions the city's conjurers to gain entry into the next phase of mystical practice (Carr and Cooper 302). In other words, the narrative is animated by her *desire to know* but few of her actual findings. About this evasiveness, she reminds us that "it is the meaning, not the material that counts"; "the details do not matter" (198). Summing up her first major initiation ceremony, she writes: "For sixty-nine hours I lay there. I had five psychic experiences and awoke at last with no feeling of hunger, only one of exaltation" (199). Leigh Ann Duck describes this moment as "an incommensurable inter-section of temporalities—the modern social scientist in a hoodoo trance" (275). Hurston increasingly embodies the peculiar transient space and time of her investigation, literally registering the experience in her body, but that turn to materiality is interior and private. It is certainly no guar-antee of legibility for the reader (Humphries 150; Boxwell, "Sis Cat," 612).

To extend this claim, there is something incommensurable about Hurs-ton's object of study itself: if hoodoo has preceded writing, it is also finally its limit—as the initiated she cannot or will not represent it, thereby confounding the apparent goals of her own collection (Duck 275; Carr and Cooper 302). This is especially clear in her tutelage with the charis-matic Father Watson, under whose mentorship she obtains the vaunted Black Cat Bone, which allows her to "be able to walk invisible. . . . [when] things must be done in deep secret" (220). The initiation rite is the "most terrible of experiences. . . . Indescribable noises, sights, feelings. Death was at hand! Seemed unavoidable! I don't know. Many times I have thought and felt, and I always have to say the same thing. I don't know, I don't know" (221–22). Once again, we find Hurston in a near-death experience that pushes the limits of her own comprehension and threat-ens to destabilize her authority. At the same, this scene enacts a kind of textual invisibility or opacity that the rite promises. There will be no "knowing into somebody else's business" here (3).

How do we assess an ethnographic collection of secrets that remain secrets? A narrative quest where we are led to the shape of the secret but not the secret itself? We are left with a collection that is perpetually incomplete, dependent upon ethnographic objects that refuse to reveal themselves. If, in part 1, we have seen how the tales revise and upend each other, in part 2, we bear partial witness to the generative power of secrets. In both cases, the verbal artifact undercuts the presumed stasis of its position within the collection. Throughout *Mules and Men*, Hurston uses collecting as both a narrative strategy and focus, as do many of the classic documentaries and ethnographies of her day, yet in this work she rarely falls into the fixed typologies of the folk and the primitive that seemed to spring so readily from this approach.

THE SIS CAT REPRISE

The oft-cited epilogue of *Mules and Men*—the Sis Cat tale—offers a compelling addendum to Hurston's revision of the folklorist's role.[36] The epilogue designates the ethnographic method as an act of consumption shaped by lessons drawn from experience. In the first part of the story, Sis Cat catches herself a rat, and, just as she is about to eat him, he chides her for her bad manners. Worried about seeming rude, she starts to wash her hands and face and the rat makes his escape. The second half of the story is a repetition of the first with a significant difference:

> So de cat caught herself a rat again and set down to eat. So de Rat said, "Where's yo' manners at, Sis Cat? You going to eat 'thout washing yo' face and hands?"
>
> "Oh, Ah got plenty manners," de cat told 'im. "But Ah eats mah dinner and washes mah face and uses mah manners afterwards." So she et right on 'im and washed her face and hands. And cat's washin' after eatin' ever since. (245–46)

Sis Cat learns from her previous disappointment. The first time around, in exchange for her niceties, she gets nothing in return, so she revises her method: she eats first and cleans up later. If the tale functions as an allegory for Hurston's own fieldwork, it suggests that the niceties of ethnographic etiquette are better used for tidying up, after the collecting is done. As she discovered in her first course of fieldwork, "Barnardese" will leave you "figuratively starving in the midst of plenty" (60). Hurston enhances the metatextual significance of the tale by explicitly representing herself as Sis Cat: "I'm sitting here like Sis Cat, washing my face and usin' my manners" (246). Sis Cat's unorthodox style of eating reflects Hurston's unconventional method of ethnography: out in the field, she uses a practical strategy that may appear coarse to "proper" folklorists but it guarantees results; she refines her presentation later.

In Hurston's best storytelling voice, she once again introduces the question of authenticity in relation to her self-presentation, suggesting that the reader has been deceived, swallowed like the rat: given the book's mode of signifying ethnography, where does one locate the "real" Zora Hurston throughout the narrative, the one who performs her version of an essential "folk" identity to gain access to material or the one who mediates this folk material via academic discourse and rural vernacular for a range of readers? Which tales have been given to the reader "straight" and which have been tidied up? The key quality that she shares with her informants—her ability to tell a tale—also happens to be an indispensable asset for her professional aims as an ethnographer. Finally, it seems that the quintessential Zora Neale Hurston showcases her own "poise for drama," adopting a range of insider and outsider identities, in order to stage the production of racialized "authenticity." In so doing, Hurston destabilizes her readers' assumptions about their own access to the book's subjects, about the fundamental knowability of Hurston's informants and Hurston herself. The folk's tales—their negotiations of identity and community—finally suggest a method for understanding the stories we tell about the folk. From this angle, the ruse of authenticity is endlessly generative of more tales, more performances, and more questions. It is no wonder, then, that she concludes the collection on a note of confident, self-congratulatory pleasure: she is the cat who swallowed the rat and her readers are still left speculating.

Having blurred the borders of anthropological representation, Hurston forces her audience to reformulate standard conceptions of the folklorist and her informants alongside conventions of the space and time of fieldwork. At times, she charts and traverses the mobile contours of her field with her informants in her car, an inclusive gesture that overtly situates her folk subjects within modernity, coeval with herself and her other readers. The tales and secrets that emerge out of these encounters are shown to be central mediums through which social space is produced and contested: the volume's storytellers and hoodoo doctors deploy the tales, spells, and rites not only to narrate stories of origins but also to shape the present and the future, disputing gender roles, critiquing Jim Crow labor relations, querying inter- and intraracial divisions of class, and rectifying matters of the heart. In spite of Hurston's claims regarding the tales' imminently salvageable status as rare and fixed repositories of culture, *Mules and Men* demonstrates that folklore and hoodoo are complex living practices, inexhaustible and always in flux.

As Hurston adheres to an ethic of performance and mobility, her approach frustrates the phenomenon of "The American Museum of Unnatural History," she would dispute some twenty-five years later in her essay "What White Publishers Won't Print" (1950). This perverse museum "is dedicated to the convenient 'typical.' In there is the 'typical' Oriental, Jew, Yankee, Western, Southerner, Latin, and even out-of-favor Nordics like the German" (169). "Amazed by the Anglo-Saxon's lack of curiosity about the internal lives and emotions of the Negroes," Hurston castigates the easy commodification and consumption of racial and ethnic stereotypes, stereotypes long perpetuated by the authority of natural history museums, ethnological practice, and tourist manuals like the future Florida guidebook. Trading on her professional credentials yet refusing the most stultifying and reductive racist practices of her disciplinary training, Hurston's participant observation grappled with the "internal lives and emotions" of her subjects yet self-consciously eluded the appropriative "probing" of her white readership, publishers, patrons, and mentors.

Neither a straightforward social document nor a conventional collection of folklore but, rather, a work of signifying ethnography, *Mules and Men* provided an ingeniously textured answer to the query of where and how the folk—Hurston's folk—fit into the modern nation. She charted a map of Dixie and its rural and urban black inhabitants that took into account complexities of race, gender, labor, and region. The ambiguity of her folklore collection and her later novels would elicit criticisms such as Alain Locke's rhetorical lament in his 1937 review of *Their Eyes Were Watching God*: "When will the Negro novelist of maturity, who knows how to tell a story convincingly—which is Miss Hurston's cradle gift, come to grips with motive fiction and *social document fiction*?" (Locke 18; emphasis added). In a sense, though, by centering her collection on tales that emerged from the domestic, leisure, and work spaces of her informants' lives—by documenting their fluid social fiction—Hurston had already met the complaints of her future critics head-on.

PART III
Populist Masquerade

While the people of the county found a new evening of
pleasure in their New World, I strolled along wrapped in my
envelope of Anglo-Saxon shyness and superiority. We had
grabbed off everything, I thought, we owned it all—money,
land, factories, shiny cars, nice houses—yet these people,
confined to their shacks and their slums, really possessed
America; they alone, of the pioneers who cleared the land,
had learned how to enjoy themselves in this big, lonesome
continent; they were the only full-blown Americans.

—ALAN LOMAX,
The Land Where the Blues Began (1993)

3. The director Preston Sturges on set with Veronica Lake (as "the Girl") as he adjusts her hobo drag. *Sullivan's Travels*, dir. Preston Sturges (Paramount, 1941). Courtesy of Photofest.

(below) 4. Sullivan as he dresses up as a hobo assisted by his butler. *Sullivan's Travels*, dir. Preston Sturges (Paramount, 1941). Courtesy of Photofest.

Chapter 5.

"Am I Laughing?":
Burlesque Incongruities of Genre, Gender,
and Audience in Preston Sturges's
Sullivan's Travels

People say that it is terrible to hear a man cry. I think it worse to hear a man laugh.—NATHANAEL WEST, *The Dream Life of Balso Snell* (1931)

Play the age as comedy if you want to get away with murder.
—JAMES AGEE, "Review of *The Miracle of Morgan's Creek*,"
The Nation, 5 February 1944

In the many anecdotes about directors who would one day be great is the story of Willie Wyler and John Huston. In the early thirties, they wanted to make a film called *The Forgotten Boys* about the multitude of children and teens riding the rails (Herman, *Talent for Trouble*, 109).[1] Though the movie was never made, the filmmakers performed research for their script by traveling as hobos through the train yards of Los Angeles and the skid rows of Fresno and Bakersfield (Huston, *Open Book*, 60; Jacobs, *Christmas*, 248). Allegedly, they spent several nights in a flophouse and they were accompanied by a friend, a charismatic and talented screen-writer by the name of Preston Sturges, who had recently joined the Universal lot where Wyler worked.

While all three men would later have illustrious careers in film, Wyler making *The Little Foxes* (1941) and *Ben Hur* (1959) and Huston making *The Maltese Falcon* (1941) and *The African Queen* (1951), in the end, it was Sturges who would parlay their research into his extraordinary *Sullivan's Travels* (1941), though not in the way it was originally intended. He based the plot of *Sullivan's Travels* not on the findings of Wyler's and Huston's expedition but rather on the process through which the men obtained it, their populist impersonation of hobo life. Like Zora Neale Hurston before him, Sturges adopted the frame story of Wyler's and Huston's efforts to collect and document ethnographic detail as his film's point of departure: its protagonist, a famous director of movie musicals, John L. Sullivan (Joel McCrea), suffers a pang of conscience and wants to make a serious film about the "poor and needy" for "the poor and needy," so he dons tramp garb and goes out on the road to learn about being poor (Henderson, *Five Screenplays*, 552–53). Somehow, Sullivan always ends up back in Hollywood. Capitalizing on the promise of authenticity and romance that initially led Wyler and Huston on their slumming mission, Sturges's film investigates, among other things, the belief that experience is the truest basis for knowledge; the notion that poverty guarantees a moral purity ironically available to those who can successfully pretend to be poor; and the identification with a fugitive masculinity beyond the reach of feminized consumer culture summed up in the phrase "hobohemia," a term made popular by Nels Anderson, of the Chicago School of Sociology, in the 1920s (DePastino, *Citizen Hobo*, 61). These assumptions fit within the larger populist imaginary that fueled the 1930s mania for classifying "authentic" groups and regions through the technology of the collection.

If much of the ethnography and documentary asked where and how the folk fit into the nation, from the official New Deal collecting endeavors to the work of Dorothea Lange and Richard Wright, Sturges like Hurston turned the camera lens onto the spectator and asked just *who* it was who wanted to *see* the folk in the form of the tramp and *why*. In order to arrive at an answer, Sturges used his movie camera in the same way that Hurston deployed her spyglass of anthropology, viewing the spectator from both outside and inside. In a further echo of Hurston's tactics, Sturges adopted masquerade: as his protagonist Sullivan impersonates a tramp, he inadvertently transforms himself from a director into an audience member. Sturges hung his inquiry into spectatorship on the question of genre: did the average moviegoer want to watch romantic comedy, cartoons, Keystone chasers, melodrama, or social realism? To frame it in the dichotomous terms through which the director Sullivan, our protagonist, understands this dilemma, did audiences want to see the slapstick antics of "the Tramp," played by Charlie Chaplin, or down-and-out dramatizations of the tramp in newsreels and films like

Wild Boys of the Road (1933) and *Girls of the Road* (1940)?[2] As we see by the film's conclusion, there are no simple answers.

Sturges drew upon a motley array of cinematic genres in *Sullivan's Travels* to stage this inquiry, reveling in the anarchic possibilities of a spectacular modernist hybridity. By the time he began to work on the film for Paramount, he was well known for his play with madcap plots and disparate storytelling modes and tones (Henderson 518). His previous films were all idiosyncratic screwball comedies, an already eclectic genre born of the Depression "based upon the 'boy meets girl' formula— gone 'topsy turvy' ": Sturges's *Christmas in July* (1940) spoofs American consumer culture; *The Great McGinty* (1940) condemns political corruption; and *The Lady Eve* (1941) satirizes social class (Gehring, *Handbook*, 105). On the heels of these successful comedies, Sturges could afford to take a partial detour into the somber realm of thirties' social realism. Yet he also understood the risk he took in combining "deep-dish" drama with farce, an unwieldy hybrid if ever there was one. During the editing of *Sullivan's Travels*, he reportedly told his fellow director Ernst Lubitsch, "It's a combination of smart comedy, slapstick and serious drama with a message. If it doesn't jell correctly, it's likely to be a big flop" (Spoto, *Madcap*, 173). In spite of his fears, the film did not flop, at least in terms of its critical reception: while early trade paper reviews ran from negative to positive, the response to the film's official debut at the New York Paramount Theater was "overwhelmingly favorable" (Jacobs 260). Sturges's gambit more or less paid off with the popular press and the moviegoing public. The reviews were generally good and the film set a sales record during its first week at the Paramount, and it stayed a *Motion Picture Herald* box office champion for a month (262). As James Agee would write a few years later in a 1944 film review of Sturges's *The Miracle of Morgan's Creek* for *Time* magazine: "Sturges . . . has always understood the liberating power of blending comedy with realism, wild farce with cool intellect" (*Agee on Film*, 328).

In the decades since its release, *Sullivan's Travels* has become something of a critic's darling, regularly appearing on various "top 100" lists of American cinema.[3] Yet popularity has not made the film a text of much scholarly analysis. This may be due, in Sturges's own admittance, to the film's uneven tone, its jumble of genres, or its apparently ham-and-eggs message about the universality of laughter. Only in the last three decades have historians and political scientists such as Lawrence Levine, Kathleen Moran and Michael Rogin, and Warren Susman argued for the film's significance within the context of the Depression.[4] They have demonstrated its trenchant commentary on the aesthetic and political concerns of the Popular Front, "the [alliance] of antifascist, pro–New Deal, pro-labor . . . mental and manual workers, liberals, Socialists, and Communists" that emerged in the mid-1930s (Moran and Rogin, "What's the Matter," 106). The film announces its satirical engagement with the Popular Front at the outset, when Sullivan claims that he wants to make a serious film as an "answer to communists," to show that " 'we're not ducking our head in the sand.'" Out of all of the texts in my study, given its filmic medium and its Hollywood origins, setting, and subject matter, *Sullivan's Travels* constitutes the most direct negotiation—and meta-negotiation—of the pivotal role of the culture industry in the "cultural front," Michael Denning's term for the broad affiliation of cultural workers on the left who aligned themselves in their art and activism against fascism (xiii–xx).

Taking up the metasubject of *Sullivan's Travels*—a comedy director's frustrated desire to make meaningful films for his audience—scholars have rightly suggested that the plot has implications not only for the actual audience's self-conscious experience as viewers but also for an understanding of "audience" as a concept within the thirties.[5] Though Sullivan thinks he already knows his audience, Sturges inquires after their desire through his protagonist's encounters with "the people," not only on the road but diegetically in the movie theater. This question implies several others: which audiences constitute "the people"? Do "the people" want to see realist films about the folk in the form of the hobo? In positing a viewing relationship between "the people" and the folk, Sturges aligns himself with ethnographic projects such as the Federal Writers' Project's American Guide Series and even more specific endeavors like Hurston's *Mules and Men*. As federal folklorists and writers marshaled together images, songs, and stories of the folk in the Guide Series and other archives to ennoble "the people" and their sense of the past, Sturges's film would use vaudeville, burlesque, and silent-era slapstick comedy, humor associated with working-class audiences, for similar ends. In parsing the very subject formation of "the people" and the folk as well as their purported desires, Sturges joins the satire of George

Schuyler and Nathanael West. Sturges thus enters a key debate of the period: Denning writes, "The question of 'representing the people'—to depict and speak for the people—lies at the center of the artistic and intellectual works of the cultural front" (125).[6] Given the film's engagement with this debate, Moran and Rogin persuasively argue for *Sullivan's Travel*'s eminence as "the last 1930s social protest film," instead of Frank Capra's trilogy, *Mr. Deeds Goes to Town* (1936), *Mr. Smith Goes to Washington* (1939), and *Meet John Doe* (1941), films that "shared none of [the Popular Front's] political positions save the populism and founding-father patriotism that would later sustain [Ronald] Reagan" ("What's the Matter," 111–12). By situating *Sullivan's Travels* as a reigning classic of the Popular Front, Moran and Rogin introduce a convincing if counterintuitive criterion through which to evaluate this exceedingly slippery film.

Building upon this criterion, I explore how *Sullivan's Travels* works within the vein of modernist burlesque to reflect upon the central populist concerns and dominant folk iconographies of the cultural front and the New Deal. As I have suggested in previous chapters, modernist burlesque was an aesthetic strategy often used by the literary Left to unmask the authentic aura surrounding the nation's most sacrosanct narratives and protagonists, such as the bootstrap myth, the folk, and the self-made man. When we understand the ways these "authentic" identities enact particular gendered, raced, and classed scripts, we grasp their performative and ideological dimensions. For all that *Sullivan's Travels'* burlesque overtly depends upon masquerade and performativity, critics have not sufficiently considered the film's logic of impersonation, nor have they attended to the particular gendered, raced, and classed contours of the genres, identities, and audiences the film "puts on." This chapter intervenes by examining the ways the film's burlesque contrasts competing configurations of genre and gender, "popular desire," and spectatorship through masquerade (Moran and Rogin 107). Masquerade is the vehicle for the film's burlesque. As the film cites rival populist arguments for "serious" and "escapist" films, as it transmogrifies from one genre to another, as it quotes dominant folk iconographies in its visual field, and as it invokes different moviegoing audiences, it pushes these narrative and cinematic elements into spectacular excess. The film's masquerade thus capitalizes on the hyperbolic energies of cross-dressing, one of burlesque's and vaudeville's most popular routines, paying tribute to the entertainments Sturges sees as precursors to Hollywood's best cinematic farces, including his own (Rogin, *Blackface*, 29).

Every turn of the plot ushers in a change of genre, requiring first the sartorial and then the social transformation of the film's main characters. Put differently, within the film's burlesque, as genre goes, so goes gender, in concert with shifting formations of sexuality, race, and class. As the film's genres proliferate and hybridize, these formations are jumbled, yet their corresponding gender performances seem to exert a gravitational pull toward heterosexual coupling.[7] The film swings from romantic comedy to gritty realism and back again, and Sullivan quite literally follows suit, along with his sidekick, "the Girl" (Veronica Lake), an unsuccessful Hollywood extra who accompanies him on his journey dressed as a teenage boy in similar hobo attire. As Sullivan travels through different Hollywood genres masquerading in various guises, he undergoes a masculine transformation that also entails his education in the ways of "proper" heterosexuality. His quest is supported by the Girl's overtly performative femininity. The Girl embodies the romantic comedy plot in contradistinction with the (homo)social realist, "go to jail" plot in which Sullivan finally attains "authentic" manhood—ironically, a masculinity that renders him a suitable heterosexual companion for the Girl and the film's flimsy screwball ending. Indeed, the film radically conflates performances of genre and gender, to the degree that one cannot talk about one aspect of the film's identity without signaling the other.

The film's incessant masquerade both invokes and undermines the "authenticity" claims of its various genres and genders. It advances its burlesque through an oscillation between masquerade and its failure: more often than not, the film's impersonations self-consciously fail, a practice that results in "spectacular incongruities" instead (Brooks, *Bodies*, 25).[8] The film fails to pass entirely as a romantic comedy or as a work of social realism (a documentary, a social problem film, or a prison exposé); the Girl fails to pass as a boy, in spite of her hobo drag; and Sullivan may pass as a tramp within the film, but not with the actual audience, until he suffers amnesia and the plot takes a turn for the worse. If neither the director, Sullivan, nor the actor, the Girl, can fully pass as someone else, what "real" identities do they default to? How much of their performance transforms their "true" identity? When Sullivan's and the Girl's disguises fail to work, their "true selves" are putatively revealed. Yet, as we see time and again, in keeping with Hurston's performative authenticity, that "true" self is just as performed.

The film draws upon the incongruities of failed impersonation to launch its commentary on popular desire and spectatorship as well. In a general sense, the film "puts on" different genres to explore their claims of authenticity and prospective audiences. More specifically, in order for Sullivan to develop a better understanding of his audience—both their desires *and* their reality—he must impersonate them, finally becoming a spectator himself. Filmed in the era in which Gallup polls were invented and when talk of middlebrow and lowbrow tastes dominated discussions of mass consumer culture among intellectuals and investors alike, Sturges was more than familiar with the film industry's fulminations about its product in terms of distinct and overlapping audiences. In Sturges's representations of people attending the movies, he posits many different audiences for different types of films: the people who flock to melodramas are not necessarily the same people who clamor for cartoons. This difference extends to *Sullivan's Travels* itself. In order to distinguish between the audiences Sturges depicts within the film and the film's actual audiences, I alternate between third-person descriptions of the diegetic audience and the first-person plural, "we," to indicate the implied viewing audience. If the moviegoers shown in the film somehow impersonate or stand in for us, the actual audience, there are limits to this performance.

Given the film's failed impersonations and its critique of authenticity, how do we determine the film's genre by the end—is it really a screwball comedy, a social protest film, or something else? As the film stages and critiques each genre, it self-consciously rejects the popular iconography of white suffering prevalent in the most lauded populist films of the late thirties and early forties, such as John Ford's *The Grapes of Wrath* (1940) and Capra's populist trilogy, a move that should establish its importance in contemporary discussions of cultural front cinema. Through the transport of masquerade, *Sullivan's Travels* instead invokes a more radical iconography of interracial populism, especially in its envisioning of the collective parameters of spectatorship. Of course, given the film's relentless burlesque and its potential cynicism, it is difficult to know if we are supposed to take this seriously. Sturges's own politics were hardly progressive. His biographer, Diane Jacobs, asserts that he "joined nothing and sided with no one," not only declining membership in the Screen Writers Guild and the Screen Directors Guild, to which most of his friends belonged, but also the more conservative union, Screen Playwrights (183, 245).

Nevertheless, Sturges's film takes up the "impious rebellion" of the Hollywood cultural front, shaped by screenwriters such as West, Dalton Trumbo, John Lawson, and Horace McCoy (Burke, *Philosophy*, 62; Denning, *Cultural Front*, 255–56).[9] In its modernist burlesque, *Sullivan's Travels* harnesses the force of hybridity made spectacular. At times, the film's hybrid mergings resemble what Denning calls the "proletarian grotesque," a central trope of the cultural front. The proletarian grotesque deploys the logic of the oxymoron and its "contradictory fusions" in an attempt "to wrench us out of the repose and distance of the 'aesthetic'" (118, 122–23). Denning draws upon the literary critic Kenneth Burke's theorization of the grotesque as the expressive form most appropriate to times of crisis and transformation, a powerful figuration of the period's contradictions wherein "the perception of discordancies is perceived without smile or laughter" (qtd. in *Cultural Front*, 122). The proletarian grotesque obviates the refuge of aesthetic distance for its audience by directing the anti-aesthetic energies of Dada and surrealism toward plebeian subjects most often associated with social realism.

The structural hybridity of *Sullivan's Travels* conforms to the logic of the oxymoron, yet the tenor of its contradictions fall along a spectrum, from the proletarian grotesque's "contradictory fusions" to modernist burlesque's "extravagant incongruities," to borrow another term from Burke. Often, the film's modernist burlesque creates a relation of "extravagant incongruities," one that elicits a self-conscious stance of critical distance *and* political commitment, instead of "aesthetic distance" or its seeming opposite, a liberal politics of sentimental empathy (Burke, *Philosophy*, 352).[10] With regard to *Sullivan's Travels'* use of opposing genres, its staging of failed masquerade, and its discordant depictions of audiences who may or may not approximate the film's actual audience, the film does not "jell," as Sturges wanted it to. Rather, it "flops," but in the most provocative of ways, creating an extravagantly incongruous viewing experience for the audience, one at times diametrically opposed to the audiences depicted on screen, one at times "wholly grim" (Burke 352). Following West's assertion that it is "terrible to hear a man cry" but "worse to hear a man laugh," Sturges opens up the possibility that laughter may not signify humor but its opposite.

Sullivan's Travels galvanizes a riotous dialectic between humor and the grotesque, the conservative and the revolutionary. On one level, in the vein of the proletarian grotesque, the film invokes contradictory fusions in its merging of Sullivan with his fellow convicts in the celebrated "laughter scene," in its marrying of its ex-con hero to a romantic comedy heroine, and in its blending of the middlebrow audience with the masses in its conclusion. On another level, in the vein of modernist burlesque, the film is a dizzying spiral of incongruous hybrids: it throws melodrama against farce, documentary against slapstick, romance against the prison exposé; it contrasts the audience's responses on screen with those of its actual audience; and, perhaps least surprisingly, it flanks comedy with tragedy (Denning 123). By the film's conclusion, Sturges has ironically resuscitated screwball comedy through its deployment of the cultural front's aesthetic strategies, its iconography of working-class masculinity and its vision of interracial populism.

IF EVER A PLOT NEEDED A TWIST

The structure of *Sullivan's Travels* imitates that of Jonathan Swift's famous *Gulliver's Travels* (1726): like that classic work of satire, the film traces four journeys; in each, Sturges invokes a different set of genres that further Sullivan's pending transformation (Moran and Rogin 118). What becomes clear in a summary of the film's convoluted and episodic plot is the degree to which Sturges both adopts and then jettisons the most popular genres of the era and the way he limns the vaudeville tradition for his ethos of burlesque masquerade throughout.[11] A strategy of impersonation, both in terms of narrative- and self-presentation, facilitates the film's performative antics but also, paradoxically, guarantees the life experience—the "reality"—for which Sullivan so desperately searches (Butler, "Performative Acts," 278). By virtue of Sullivan's own self-conscious impersonation or by the film's contortions of plot, his experiences on the road are "real only to the extent that [they] are performed" (278). As we shall see, Sullivan's journeys are initiated by his personal quest to attain the "authentic" masculinity of the fugitive hobo, an endeavor that only illustrates by the film's end that all masculinities are profoundly performative.

The first journey is comprised of slapstick set pieces and the beginnings of the screwball plot. Of course, it reverses the usual class trajectory of the form. Instead of the common man being propelled into wealth through intentional disguise or a case of mistaken identity—as in Ernst Lubitsch's *Trouble in Paradise* (1932); Mitchell Leisen's *Easy Living* (1937), for which Sturges wrote the screenplay; and some of Sturges's other films, such as *The Lady Eve* (1941) and *The Palm Beach Story* (1942)— Sullivan camouflages himself to purposefully enter a lower social class. Sullivan is tailed by a large studio-sponsored land yacht that he tries to elude by hitching a ride with a zany youngster. A lengthy car chase ensues. After agreeing to meet up with his handlers in Las Vegas in two weeks' time, he shacks up with a widow and her prudish spinster sister in exchange for manual labor. He escapes their flirtatious attentions in the back of a truck only to discover that it is bound for Hollywood. It drops him off at a diner, where he first encounters the Girl. By way of a false arrest, Sullivan and the Girl end up at his Hollywood manse.[12]

In the second journey, he sets out again, this time with the Girl in tow. Her presence consolidates the romantic comedy plot and introduces a bit of melodrama as well. Just as important, her outrageously performative self-presentation props up his unstable masculinity, making it appear more secure. They ride the rails to Las Vegas, where they meet up with the waiting land yacht. Sullivan contracts the flu and, once more, they return to Hollywood. The third journey consists of a silent montage, the closest the film ever actually comes to deploying the visual codes of documentary. This segment merges comedy, melodrama, romance, and realism as we watch Sullivan and the Girl wait in bread lines, sleep in a flophouse, attend a Salvation Army mission service, and contemplate eating food from a garbage can (Harvey, *Romantic Comedy*, 592). Emboldened by his adventures, Sullivan dresses up one more time in his bedraggled costume and distributes five-dollar bills to the poor to thank them for his education. But the film's school of hard knocks has saved the sucker punch for last. A tramp knocks Sullivan unconscious, taking his money. The tramp runs away, only to be struck and killed by an oncoming train. He is deemed to be Sullivan, tragically killed in his high moment of philanthropy. The real Sullivan awakens the next day with a mild case of amnesia and gets into a fight with the Yard Bull, a railroad police officer, at the rail yard. Unrecognizable to the law and himself, Sullivan is sentenced to six years of hard labor somewhere in the South.

So begins his fourth and final journey, as the film becomes a quasi-realist exposé of grim prison life in the vein of *I Am a Fugitive from a Chain Gang* (1932). Sullivan labors on the chain gang and joins the other prisoners for their weekly privilege of attending a screening of cartoons at a nearby black Baptist church. In the film's most famous scene, Sullivan finds himself overcome by riotous laughter alongside his convulsed fellow convicts. This life-changing experience paves the way for Sullivan to join the Girl, a character who in many ways represents the desires of an audience he courts by the film's end. Eventually, Sullivan schemes his way to freedom by claiming to be the murderer of the famous director John L. Sullivan, a confession that lands his picture on the front page of national newspapers, where the studio executives discover him. While all of these journeys eventually lead back to Hollywood, the last finally accomplishes the edification necessary for Sullivan's masculine, heterosexual transformation.

NO MATTER WHERE I START OUT FOR, I ALWAYS END UP RIGHT BACK HERE IN HOLLYWOOD

The first scenes of *Sullivan's Travels* frame the film's investigation of genre and audience in relation to notions of authenticity. As the film introduces its main players, it asks its primary questions: Which genres and which subjects appeal to which audiences—does the middlebrow movie-going public really prefer musicals, and do the communists in the music halls really prefer social problem films? Do people who have suffered economic deprivation want to see suffering on the screen, or do they desire escapist fantasy instead? Which genres and which audiences are the most "authentic" within the populist rhetoric of the period? And who can make these films—do you have to have experienced trouble to accurately depict it? Each of these questions turns on prevailing ideas of audience desire, authentic experience, and realist depiction. In particular, these questions dovetail with many of the arguments and assumptions of the New Deal's cultural projects in their attempts to represent the folk through a practice of documentary.

Predictably, the film begins with the Paramount logo. The camera

5. The film *Sullivan's Travels* masquerades as a book. *Sullivan's Travels*, dir. Preston Sturges (Paramount, 1941).

slowly pans back, revealing the logo to be, in actuality, a seal that fastens a white wrapped package. A manicured woman's hand opens the parcel to reveal the cover of a picture book bearing the film's title alongside an illustration of a hobo couple (in the likeness of Joel McCrea and Veronica Lake), the man walking with a bindle stick in tow, his arm resting on the shoulders of his female companion as they look past us into the distance. They are surrounded by tiny, ankle-high figures of people dressed in similarly tattered clothes, an obvious allusion to Swift's Lilliputians in *Gulliver's Travels*. The credits roll with each turn of the book's pages, ending with a dedication: "To the memory of those who made us laugh: the motley mountebanks, the clowns, the buffoons, in all times and in all nations, whose efforts have lightened our burden a little, this picture is affectionately dedicated." The film's visual reference to the book form in its title sequence self-consciously heightens the audience's awareness of the fact that this is a mediated representation—we are watching a film masquerading as a book. The sequence also locates the film's origins within two significant comic traditions, Swiftian satire and the more recent conventions of burlesque, vaudeville, and slapstick, from which Sturges adopts his method of masquerade. Given Sturges's reputation as Hollywood's next comic genius in line with Ernst Lubitsch, this opening rings more than a little self-congratulatory. At the very least, it justifies the value of escapist comedy over other popular filmic genres, an opinion that will become more explicit by the movie's conclusion.

After the credits, the film commences with the image of a train as it ominously barrels into the frame from left to right in a reference to the Lumière brothers' *Arrival of a Train at the Station* (1895), an "actuality" film, one of the first films screened in public and one of the first primitive documentaries.[13] The film then cuts to a prolonged chase scene involving two men—one wearing a ripped sweater (Labor), the other, a suit (Capital)—on the top of a moving freight car in pitch black night. As the train passes over a bridge, the well-dressed man shoots the other man and they stagger about, finally plunging into the water below, gripped in a death lock. "The End" floats up to the water's surface with a tragic swell of the film score. Until this moment, we've been unaware that we are watching a film-within-the-film. Cut to a screening room in Hollywood, where three men argue about the film they have just viewed. Sullivan has shown this film to his producers, Mr. Hadrian (Porter Hall) and Mr. Lebrand (Robert Warwick), in hopes of persuading them to support a like-minded project of his own to be called *O Brother, Where Art Thou?* authored by one Sinclair Beckstein, a name that is obviously an amalgamation of the famed social realists Upton Sinclair, Sinclair Lewis, and John Steinbeck.

SULLIVAN: You see? You see the symbolism of it? Capital and labor destroy each other. It teaches a lesson, a moral lesson. It has social significance. I want this picture to be a commentary on modern conditions, stark realism, the problems that confront the average man. . . .

LEBRAND: But with a little sex in it. . . .

SULLIVAN: A little, but I don't want to stress it. . . . I want this picture to be a document. I want to hold a mirror up to life. I want this to be a picture of dignity, a true canvass of the suffering of humanity.

Sullivan expresses his desire to make a serious film by invoking clichés about documentary. By suggesting that realism is the most expedient form for depicting the fight between "capital and labor," he emphasizes the progressive and reformist aims most often associated the genre. When he points to the film's symbolic characterizations, the drama of capitalism demonstrated through a physical confrontation between a rich man and a poor man, he ensures that we grasp a tension within the genre between its often didactic narrative types and its more complex "real" subjects. Throughout the scene, Sullivan insists that "socially significant" art must realistically depict the average man's plight within capitalism through visual mimesis.

By 1941, the iconography of the social problem film is so familiar that Sturges can burlesque it by citing its central attributes and claims through his protagonist, Sullivan. The humor of the scene depends upon the audience's ability to discern the difference between genres, between ludicrous action sequences and sentimental documentary depictions. Sullivan rants about the weightiness of this kind of fictional documentary: he wants his picture to "realize the potentialities of film as the sociological and artistic medium that it is." From the short clip we have witnessed alongside his producers, Sullivan's exemplar hardly resembles the realist portrait he describes. With the first shot of the train, we think we are watching the real movie, (not a film-within-a-film) and it is . . . a high-wire thriller. It is a set up. In its very failure to meet the conventions of documentary though, the film-within-the-film unmasks that genre's foundational paradox, its bid to represent reality *as if* it was unmediated. This scene shows documentary to be a narrative construction with familiar tropes and images, much like comedy or melodrama. What we have just seen does not conform to documentary convention. In a more subtle sense, the artifice of the film-within-the-film establishes the surrounding scenes between Sullivan and his producers as relatively "real." What we are seeing, then, is an insider's view of behind-the-scenes Hollywood, similar to the back lot musical plot, nothing less than a satirical "document" of the motion picture industry itself.

The debate between the producers and Sullivan about the value of social realism turns on the question of the audience's desires (and, for the studio, their money). After the screening, the producers urge him to make "nice musicals" because the moviegoing public "might like to forget" the troubled state of the world. Disgusted by the film Sullivan has screened, Hadrian implores, "Who wants to see that kind of stuff? It gives me the creeps." Sullivan insists the film was held over a fifth week in the music halls, to which Hadrian replies, "Who goes to the music halls? Communists!" After the producers mention that the film flopped in Pittsburgh (not coincidentally, the capital of steel production), Sullivan quips, "If they knew what they liked, they wouldn't live in Pittsburgh. If you pander to the public, we'd still be in the horse age. . . . We'd still be making Keystone chasers, bathing beauties, custard pie." Lebrand, the other producer, mutters, "And a fortune." In this absurd battle between capital (the executive producers) and labor (the film director), a faint echo of the fight on the train, the irony is laid on thick.

A drama of capital and labor haunts *Sullivan's Travels* throughout.[14] In a meta sense, it's difficult not to view Sullivan as a stand-in for Sturges, given the fact that Sturges made the film on the heels of his runaway hit in the previous year, *The Lady Eve*, a romantic comedy no less (Jacobs, *Christmas*, 165; Harvey 583). More to the point, when Sturges was shooting *Sullivan's Travels*, he increasingly wrangled with the new head of production at Paramount, Buddy DeSylva, a producer with little feel for satire and even less tolerance for film as an artistic medium (Jacobs 245–61). These biographical factors in combination with the film's insistence that there is no outside beyond Hollywood—masquerade is all there is—may be read as a sign of Sturges's criticism of the insularity of the studio system, even though he thrived within it. Before its conclusion, Sturges's film will deliver us key elements of all of the filmic genres Sullivan dismisses by name in this exchange: slapstick set pieces such as a protracted car chase, a pratfall into a swimming pool, a pie in the black cook's face (custard-pie shtick meets whiteface), among others. Perhaps the most interesting aspect of this volley is its delineation of several distinct moviegoing audiences, the "nice musical" crowd versus the commies at the music hall. These distinct conceptions of "the people" illuminate the tension between contrary populist rhetorics that comprised the New Deal era (Denning 263).

Of course, we must ask how the actual audience is interpellated into the scene, for as the film theorist Christopher Ames aptly suggests, the film-within-the-film "makes us the audience and then ironically pulls back to reveal an insider's argument about what audiences want" (91). It is difficult to know how to locate ourselves in this debate among film industry insiders—given the typical narrative contract between protagonist and viewer, the viewer's sympathies may lie with Sullivan, even if he seems naive.[15] However, this is complicated by Sullivan's flouting of his public, and by implication, his audience. As for the desires of the audience, described in this scene, it is either the mainstream, middlebrow public who doesn't know what it wants or an apparently minority communist faction interested only in socially conscious films.[16] In the spirit of Hurston's performative ethnographies and Schuyler's and West's incendiary burlesques, each of which implicates their readers, the film has put its audience on notice, making us aware, once again, of our own habits of consumption, particularly our press for certain generic conventions.

The film makes us self-conscious about our spectatorship in tandem with Sullivan's increasing self-scrutiny regarding his own social position vis-à-vis the "trouble" he means to capture in his next film. For, if his

cinematic exemplar of labor and capital hardly meets the narrative criterion for social realism, his producers point out that he himself is lacking
authentic knowledge about the human suffering of the "average man."
As they fabricate hardscrabble stories of their youth, they badger him
with questions—"What do you know about trouble? . . . You want to
make a picture about garbage cans. What do you know about garbage
cans? When did you eat your last meal out of one? You want to grind
10,000 feet of hard luck and all I'm asking you is, what do you know
about hard luck?"[17] Sullivan grudgingly concedes that he has grown up
with a "silver spoon" and "doesn't have any idea what [trouble] is." On
the spot, he devises a plan to make up for this deficit: he will take a leave
of absence and go undercover as a tramp to investigate trouble: "It may
take one week, one month or one year. I don't know where I'm going but
I'm not coming back until I know what trouble is." Sullivan thus plays
out a particular "model of class relations"—cross-class impersonation—
to rectify his "crisis of cultural authority" (Schocket, "Undercover," 121;
Lears, *No Place*, 1). Eric Schocket writes, "Working-class impersonation . . . [offered a means by which] a middle-class 'lack' [was] fulfilled
through lower-class 'experience,' bourgeois ennui cured by way of proletarian pain" (121). In the case of *Sullivan's Travels*, it is not just the
protagonist's "cultural authority" at stake here but his *masculine* authority. He is uninitiated in the hard-boiled ways of the world compared
to his producers, with their fictitious stories of Alger-like escapades in
moral luck and pluck. In his producers' parlance, Sullivan is by turns a
"gentleman," a "genius," and a "bonehead." Whichever the designation,
he doesn't "know about trouble." By insisting that he must "find out for
himself," Sullivan upholds a timeworn romantic notion about the creative process, that artists only produce powerful, "authentic" work when
it is based upon their lived experiences.

This belief is immediately sent up by the introduction of the first
woman in the film, who interrupts the telos of social realism in the plot,
bringing it back to romantic comedy or, more accurately, comedy about
the failure of romance. It is no accident that at this juncture, right as
Sullivan's masculinity has been called into question, just as he carefully
selects his hobo outfit from clothes taken from the studio's wardrobe
department, he is disrupted by a phone call from his estranged wife,
referred to as "Mrs. Sullivan" (Jan Buckingham) or, alternately, "the
Panther Woman," who inquires after the regular monthly check that

6. Surrounded by his producers, Sullivan admits he knows nothing of "hard luck."

funds her lavish lifestyle.[18] From what we witness of Sullivan's rancorous matrimonial situation, he is hardly experienced in the ways of love, yet in spite of this lack of personal knowledge, he is a successful director of romantic comedies. (In his personal life, he knows the rancor without the resolution of happy union guaranteed within the genre.) Thus, the premise of his journey, the insistence upon a direct correlation between ontology and epistemology summed up in the edict that "you write what you know"—that one must experience trouble (or romance) to be able to represent it authentically—is already rendered ridiculous. At the same time, this scene absurdly enacts the producer's mandate that stark realism be made seductive by including "a little sex in it." In broader terms, the Panther Woman's interruption signals the incursion of screwball comedy and heterosexual (dis)union into the unfolding plot of social realism and it solidifies Sullivan's identification with the fugitive masculinity of the tramp, unencumbered by the world of feminized consumption.

This scene makes explicit the masculine and heterosexual contours of Sullivan's quest. Paula Rabinowitz observes, "During the 1930s, class struggle in the United States was metaphorically engendered through a discourse that re-presented class conflict through the language of sexual difference. The prevailing verbal and visual imagery reveled in an excessively masculine and virile proletariat poised to struggle against the effeminate and decadent bourgeoisie. Thus the potentially revolutionary struggles of the working class were recontained within the framework of the eternal battle between the sexes found in domestic fiction" (*Labor*, 8). *Sullivan's Travels* overtly stages this gendered and classed imagery against the backdrop of the battle of the sexes: the very scene of Sullivan's working-class transformation is momentarily stymied by the demands of his spoiled and estranged bourgeois wife.

Sullivan's interaction with the hyperbolic Panther Woman, while momentarily deflecting the focus from him, calls attention to the gendered performances already under way in the film. The entire opening exchange between Sullivan and the producers is shot in one take (Jacobs 256–57). The effect of this camera work is to create a manic, hot-house energy between the men as they wrangle, pacing back and forth in the studio office. In the next scene, Sullivan is again surrounded, but this time by his two butlers in close proximity as they help him dress up as a hobo in his swank bedroom. Soon they are joined by three handlers from the studio. Sullivan is constantly encircled by male caretakers making a fuss over him, a fact that lends him a certain vulnerability. Sullivan remarks, "You'd think I was a child." While he isn't exactly depicted as an effete mollycoddle, when his producers describe him as a precocious genius and a "gentleman," they underscore his heretofore sheltered existence. Through the support of social and economic institutions such as his well-to-do family, boarding school, college, and the studio, Sullivan has always prospered: he has never had to be self-reliant. As Brian Henderson observes, "No matter how unlikely Joel McCrea may be as a director of comedy, the stolidity and smugness he brings to the role effectively project that freedom from anxiety and fear of failure that Sturges sees in Sullivan" (522). According to a masculinist narrative of bootstrap success, he suffers from a naive sense of the world and his privileged place within it.

For Sullivan, then, the journey he undertakes ultimately promises to be life-altering regarding the intertwined categories of vocation and masculinity; he "[goes] forth . . . in search of a deferred masculinity, which is dressed in the guise of experiential authority and Arcadian authenticity" (Schocket, "Undercover," 122). He adopts the iconic, itinerant white masculinity of the hobo, the manly, wandering worker bereft of permanent employment and uninterested in accumulation and acquisition, a figure whose very presence agitates for social change (DePastino, *Citizen Hobo*, 68–69).[19] *Sullivan's Travels* merges the hobo and the tramp as one, appropriating the wayward qualities that these "populist outsider" types seem to share (211). According to Ben Reitman, the preeminent historian and hobo, who was connected to the Chicago School of Sociology in the 1920s and 1930s: "There are three types of the genus vagrant, the hobo, the tramp and the bum. The hobo works and wanders, the tramp dreams and wanders and the bum drinks and wanders" (qtd. in McCallum, "The Tramp," para. 5). The hobo, who occupies "the top of a homeless hierarchy," is seemingly emasculated by capitalism, at once a sign of its ostensible failure and its true inner workings, its need for a "cheap and flexible labor force" (DePastino 65, 58). However, in his self-sufficiency, in the brotherhood of the road, and in the counterculture and folkways of "the jungle" romanticized in dime novels, blues songs, and films, the hobo gains a compensatory atavistic masculinity seemingly outside of the bourgeois, feminized strictures of commercial capitalism (81). With his class "pass" downward, Sullivan aims to acquire the masculinity of hobohemia. At the same time, he enacts one of the central anxieties of the Depression for those in power, that they might descend the ladder of social class (Moran and Rogin 121).[20] Given the comedic tone of the film thus far, alongside the familiar "slumming" pretense for Sullivan's hobo drag, we have fair reason to expect that his privilege will be restored in the end.

WHERE'S THE GIRL FIT INTO THE PICTURE?

Notably, in commentary about the film, Lake's performance comes in for criticism and the Girl is often dismissed as a superfluous character. The film historian James Harvey suggests that "in the logic of the material [the Girl] seems dispensable. . . . [H]er extraneousness may have something to do with the fact that she is rather half-heartedly executed, less interestingly written and played than most of Sturges's other heroines" (584–85). In a similar vein, Moran and Rogin describe how "the romance that drives this film is Sully's with the people, not with the (unnamed) Girl" (119).[21] Yet there is a sense in which the Girl stands in for the people, a point to which my argument will return. She is certainly pivotal to the film's construction of Sullivan's masculinity and heterosexuality. Indeed, the Girl is only superfluous in an appraisal that ignores the masquerade, masculine quest, and marriage plot that organizes *Sullivan's Travels*.

The plot of *Sullivan's Travels* is fueled by a logic of masquerade embraced at an ironic distance, self-consciously performed as a burlesque of social realism, like Schuyler's burlesque of racial passing and West's burlesque of the myth of upward class mobility. Sturges's protagonists, male and female, are never far from masquerade. As many critics have remarked, if the concept of masquerade frees us from essentializing discourses of sexuality, it does not provide an altogether liberating mode of free play for its subjects. Rather, it is the mechanism by which power and its real material effects are produced (Doane, *Femmes*, 38). With this caveat in mind, when Sullivan puts on the clothes of a tramp, in this cross-class impersonation, he "puts on" a visibly marginalized, white, working-class masculinity. Within this guise, he is more vulnerable to the overtures of the middle-class women he encounters. In a more abstract sense, the very fact of his tramp drag threatens to render him less "authentically" masculine—he is a pretender. However, he is protected by the Girl. As the screwball comedienne, her outrageous performances of femininity compensate for his performative masculinity. She appears to be the far more theatrical of the two. Her performance comments upon the authenticity that Sullivan so doggedly pursues. The failure of her masquerade either consolidates a prior authentic identity—she can't pass as a boy because she is really girl—*or* masquerade is all there is, constituting a kind of radically performative authenticity. In the latter interpretation, there is no "real" prior, beyond or external to masquerade—she cannot pass as a boy only because she passes so well as a girl. In either case, the Girl most actively shores up normative gender and sexual identity in the film. The armature of the film rests on the Girl's capacity to endlessly play different supporting roles that prop up Sullivan's hetero-masculinity-in-flux.

Two scenes in Sullivan's initial journey illustrate his newly vulnerable social status as a working-class man vis-à-vis women. The first scene occurs when he seeks work from two middle-aged sisters in exchange for room and board. It begins with an aerial shot of Sullivan, shirtless and sweaty, chopping wood, surrounded by clucking hens. Gazing upon him from her second-story bedroom window, the widow Miz Zeffie (Esther Howard) coyly interrupts—"Yoo-hoo! Don't get too tired!"—to which he vigorously swings his axe and replies testily, "Yes, Ma'am." The establishing shot eroticizes his laboring body, as we momentarily share the widow's perspective. The humor lies in Sullivan's compromised position, emphasized by the cinematography: in order to pass as a tramp, he is beholden to the peeping widow. She pointedly asks her spinster sister Ursula (Almira Sessions), "Did you notice his torso?"[22] As revealed in his

7. The widow, Miz Zeffie, coyly interrupts Sullivan's labor: "Yoo-hoo! Don't get too tired!"

profound discomfort, up until this point he has been shielded from the processes of commodification and public embodiment to which minoritized subjects are vulnerable.[23] (As a film director, he has been the disembodied agent of commodification, but never its object.) And yet, in another sense, the shot of Sullivan's bare chest reinforces his masculinity as relatively natural and nonperformative, inexorably tied to his male body, recalling the populist imagery of the autonomous, muscle-bound worker promoted in the New Deal wpa murals and the Farm Security Administration photographic archive (Halberstam, *Female Masculinity*, 234). This situation echoes Sullivan's earlier communication with his wife, suggesting that counter to Sullivan's visions of manly freedom on the road, he remains hemmed in by economically and sexually avaricious women. Once more, a woman gets in the way of his work.

This pattern repeats itself with a crucial difference in his first run-in with the Girl, whom Sullivan meets in a Hollywood diner after escaping the overly solicitous widow. With his entrance into the diner, the musical score turns sweet, announcing the official arrival of the romantic comedy plot via the Girl. He sits and orders a cup of coffee and donut, to which a woman says in a sultry command, her back to the camera, "Give him some ham and eggs." He protests, "That's very kind of you, sister . . . a sinker and a cup of coffee will fix me up fine," but she turns to him and insists, "Don't be a sucker. Give him some ham and eggs. The way I'm fixed, thirty-five cents isn't going to make a difference." She is glamorous, dressed in evening clothes, looking every inch the star, in marked contrast to Sullivan's torn attire and gruff facade. She offers him a cigarette. In spite of their disparate appearances, their common use of street slang unites them. (We assume that Sullivan has taken a lesson from the movies.) But when Sullivan starts to expound upon these "troublous times," she quips, "Drink your coffee," and, when he takes too personal an interest in her Hollywood hardships, she retorts, "Say, who's being sorry for whom? Am I buying you the eggs or are you buying me the eggs?" She explains, "You know the nice thing about buying a man food is you don't have to laugh at his jokes. Just think, if you were a big casting director or something, I'd be staring into your bridgework saying 'Yes, Mr. Smearkase. No, Mr. Smearkase. Not really, Mr. Smearkase. Oh, Mr. Smearkase . . . that's my knee!'" Like the prior scene with the sister pair, we witness a reversal of bourgeois gender roles due to the fact that the Girl apparently has more money than Sullivan, though in this case, crucially, she asks for little in return other than taking pleasure in this (momentary) reversal. Because of her relative economic privilege and the power she gains from her charity, she doesn't have to put on an act for him. In fact, she can tell him what to do, even direct him to be quiet. This scene playfully illuminates the fact that empathy is always about relational power: it skirts a fragile line between caring and condescension. Echoing West's denunciation of a liberal politics of empathy and foreshadowing the film's own critique, this scene implicates its viewers and their attitudes toward the nation's folk, its poor and dispossessed, the primary subjects of the era's documentary.

In her self-conscious "Mr. Smearkase" routine, the Girl burlesques conventional modes of femininity, showing them to be calculated performances produced within the Hollywood culture industry. And, much like the effect of the film-within-the-film at the outset of *Sullivan's Travels*, her overt quotation of the complicit ingénue-act establishes the relative authenticity of her actions. The Girl's theatrical performance of an aspiring starlet sustains the *fiction* that there is, indeed, a prior, genuine womanliness "masked by [such] masquerade."[24] Yet, in her response to Sullivan's question "Can you act?," she alludes to her real life as a kind of performance as well, sarcastically replying, "My next act will be an impersonation of a young lady going home . . . on the thumb." We know from the trajectory of the plot that the Girl, if a failed extra now, will become a star; she accomplishes this, in part, by joining in Sullivan's impersonation, dressing as his male hobo companion. Hence, she is an actor through and through, versed in a variety of gender performances, including queer male companion and heterosexual fiancée. Echoing

8. The Girl and Sullivan encounter each other in the diner: "Give him some ham and eggs."

Hurston's claims regarding the authentically dramatic nature of "negro expression," what is most authentic about the Girl is her ability and propensity to perform—her performative authenticity.

In contrast with the Girl's stagey self-presentation, Sullivan sustains the role of tramp, pulling off his "class pass" throughout their meeting in the diner.[25] In comparison with the Girl's gag about how she would behave if he were a man of power and connections, a joke that demonstrates her usual subservient and inauthentic position in such encounters, his performance is a show of privilege. He elects to play the part for the purpose of research rather than material need, proving his butler's point, "The poor know all about poverty and only the morbid rich would find the topic glamorous." This is why she justifiably pushes Sullivan into his enormous swimming pool after she discovers his real persona. (To her chagrin, she has bought breakfast for a man in a social position akin not to the fictional Mr. Smearkase, but rather to Mr. Smearkase's *boss*.) If the diner scene establishes the authentically performative appeal of the Girl, it also demonstrates the fact that Sullivan passes as a tramp diegetically—both the sisters and the Girl, at least initially, are unsuspecting of his guise. The incongruity between their perspective and those who are in the know—both his Hollywood entourage and the viewing audience—suggests that while Sullivan's masculinity and the tenor of his sexual attachments may be under revision, they are not up for radical interpretation.

In other words, Sullivan's plausible tramp act naturalizes his masculinity and heterosexuality as a somewhat continuous aspect of his persona, whether he is dressed as his millionaire self or a hobo, in spite of the fact that these aspects of his identity will be crucially transformed by the fourth journey. Sturges's casting of Joel McCrea is particularly savvy in this regard. Given McCrea's reputation as the "other Gary Cooper," the "regular guy romantic hero," he seems a counterintuitive choice for playing the wealthy John L. Sullivan, at least at first glance (Studlar, *This Mad Masquerade*, 251).[26] In fact, though, while McCrea rarely played the millionaire raised with a silver spoon, his performance as the tramp would have struck viewers as not too far afield from his previous roles. For Sturges as a director, it would be more difficult to get a male actor such as Cary Grant, known for playing the suave, affluent socialite, to do a credible turn at playing a tramp, given the star text of his performance. As McCrea performs Sullivan's masculinity in transition, he leaves the more overtly campy gendered performances to his costar, Veronica Lake.

This is where the Girl fits into the picture. In one of the most unabashedly metamoments of the film, Sturges anticipates the critics' objections to the Girl and her seeming superfluousness, slyly framing their critique as a question. After Sullivan and the Girl are arrested in his sports car because the police misrecognize him in his hobo get-up, they ask "Where's the girl fit into this picture?" Sullivan dryly replies, "There's always a girl in the picture. Haven't you been to the movies?" Though this throwaway line implies that the Girl's presence complies with the obligatory protocols of genre, the Girl fits into the picture in several ways: without her, Sturges has no screwball comedy with which to counter the competing genre of social realism, the homosocial prison exposé, in the plot (Ames, *Movies*, 92). In a more subtle sense, the film narrates a transformative journey for Sullivan, which is primarily dependent upon his impersonation of the hobo, a folksy variant of the cultural front's imagery of "authentic" working-class masculinity. This theatrical process renders gender legible. Sullivan's performance is meant to fix his own alienated, bourgeois masculinity; instead, it demonstrates the degree to which all masculinities are performed and therefore inauthentic. As in the case of the Girl, his "real" life is no less a performance: first the boy wonder director of comedies, then the concerned director who wants to make serious fare for the people, the director in hobo drag, the despairing convict, the laughing spectator, and finally, the romantic hetero-hero.

The Girl provides a paradoxical foil for Sullivan's performance: from the outset, her "authenticity" is established by her overt performance of hyperbolic femininity, her acknowledgment that femininity is fundamentally performed. Her presentation is incongruous: though her glamorous, expensive-looking clothes suggest otherwise, she is an "extra girl," a failed actress whose lack of success in Hollywood forces her to go back home. In comparison to Sullivan, even though he plays tramp to her "real girl" blues in their first scene together, the Girl's gender identity is the more *visibly* performative of the two. Sullivan *passes*, asserting a masculine continuity from his millionaire self to his working-class impersonation, suggesting "This is what I am, regardless of class," while the Girl wears her theatrical capacity as a woman and an actress on her sleeve, announcing at every turn that she is performing. It is no accident that the Girl overtly performs and destabilizes "femininity" in her first meeting with Sullivan, who has only just begun his journey, the initial outing in his quest for "authentic" masculinity and heterosexual union. These gender performances announce the different genres each protagonist represents and inhabits. The Girl's presence and the love plot that unfolds in the film's first three journeys consistently naturalizes Sullivan's "masculinity," making it appear more stable.

This is no more evident than in the second and third journeys of the film, when the Girl accompanies Sullivan on his vagabond adventure dressed as an adolescent boy. As they are about to jump aboard a train dressed up as hobos, Sullivan remarks to the Girl that she looks "as much like a boy as Mae West," to which she answers, "All right, they'll think I'm your frail"—his girl in the hobo-argot of the film. This exchange sets up a prism through which to read the Girl's less-than-successful attempt at masculine drag. Sullivan's reference to Mae West raises the issue of gender parody and camp, specifically, the fact that West routed her performance of femininity through New York's drag queen subculture, and, at times, also played herself as masculine according to this same theatrical ethos. In this comparison, Sullivan suggests either that the Girl, even dressed as a boy, resembles more West's hyperbolic femininity, or that the Girl fails to pass in the same ways that West failed to pass on the occasions when she (West) performed masculinity. The Girl counters that if her performance isn't plausible, no matter, she will simply be seen as his girl.

We have to wonder why Sturges chooses to dress Lake in this manner

9. Sullivan remarks to the Girl that she looks "as much like a boy as Mae West," to which she answers, "All right, they'll think I'm your frail [your girl]."

at all rather than as an impoverished woman of the Hoovervilles, the shanty towns inhabited by people left unemployed and homeless by the Depression. There was a precedent for Sturges's decision. For the women transients who rode the rails in the thirties, Todd McCallum suggests, their mobility "distinguished them from 'lady travellers,' prostitutes and *les flâneuses. . . .* [T]he road meant cross-dressing and other signs of 'ambiguous gender and sexual identities,' including stories of a 'secretive lesbian subculture'" (para. 12.) To provide the Girl with the mobility of hobo life, Sturges cloaks her in male masquerade, a choice that opens up the possibility that she is either Sully's younger male lover or his butch companion. This choice reflects the history of gender reversal in the theater, about which Judith Halberstam observes, "If boys can play girls and women but women can play only boys, mature masculinity once again remains an authentic property of adult male bodies while all other gender roles are available for interpretation" (233). Here, they appear as a queer couple, yet the Girl may play a boy, but her performance is far from convincing. In line with her general characterization, this failing performance consolidates her "authentic" femininity once again. A "femme pretender" rather than a drag king, Lake's disguise as a boy, her overtly feminine gestures and appearance, signal the "disjuncture between biological sex and gender" in a campy way (Halberstam 248). At the same time, it consolidates her heterosexual connection to Sullivan and constructs Sullivan's tramp masculinity as relatively "authentic" by comparison. While Sullivan has not attained mature hetero-masculinity at this point in the film, the Girl's boyish, femme performance cordons off that future identity as entirely his province.

SIX ACTS OF VAUDEVILLE ON MY TAIL

Along with the Girl's supporting act, Sullivan's hetero-masculine trans-formation is propped up and superseded by other highly visible, marginal characters in the film as well, characters who expose the racial dimensions of Sullivan's performance and the many genres invoked throughout the film. In the car chase scene when the Hollywood land yacht pursues Sullivan, who has hitched a ride with a maniacal boy behind the wheel of a roadster, the sight gags gratuitously establish the carnivalesque implica-tions of Sullivan's undertaking: as the land yacht collides with a row of hay bales, the black cook's face is covered with white batter, the white motor-cycle cop's face is splashed with mud, just as the secretary in the front seat is tossed on her back, her skirt falling over her face to reveal her shapely legs. The cook's proverbial whiteface, the cop's blackface, and the secre-tary's topsy turvy skin show at once reiterate and displace the joke of disguise and reversal that constitutes much of Sullivan's adventure. More-over, these classic slapstick moments refer back to the genres of vaudeville and burlesque from whence they came, the comic forms Sturges seems to want to recuperate. By the film's conclusion, while traces of vaudeville's racial masquerade remain, Sturges will reference and ultimately reject many of the iconic representations of whiteness found in screwball com-edy's stories of cross-class interaction and social realism's spectacles of impoverished white suffering.

Of particular importance is Sturges's allusion not only to blackface but also to whiteface. While it fits his signature propensity for the extreme reversals found in all of his screwball comedies—"I'll take this conven-tion, turn it on its head and then overturn it again"—it suggests some-thing more, the fact that whiteness is similarly put on, performed, and constructed. Certainly, Sully's hobo drag performs a particular version of white masculinity. As Todd DePastino writes in his book *Citizen Hobo*, "In the parlance of the road, the term 'white man' was synonymous with 'hobo' "; hobohemia was a "preserve of working-class whiteness" (81). One might argue that the cook's whiteface, a retrograde moment of a piece with the blackface cinema of the 1920s and 1930s, offers a key to the way race functions in the movie and in many of the screwball films of the period. The spectacle of whiteface disables whiteness's pretense of neu-trality, instead rendering it visible. In the film's first three journeys, the cast is white, white, white, whether in the studio, on the highway, or riding the rails. Questions of realism aside, this casting brings attention to the racial formations at work here and their connections to genre and the film's larger critique of a white-washed "racial populism" (Denning 265). The stereotypical cook (played by Charles R. Moore) is an exception in Sturges's white cast at this point in the film, but the exception that proves the rule: if screwball comedy is almost always about an exploration of gender bending and the traversal of social class, it is carefully bound by the whiteness of its main players. So many of the screwball plots of the 1930s hinge on gaining (illicit) access to a world of millionaires defined in cinematic terms as the domain of white privilege. These films enact a fantasy of assimilation and the class pass via disguise and masquerade particularly available to white ethnics.

Sturges signals the hyperbolic whiteness of the genre in *Sullivan's Travels* by the strategic placement of his black characters. The inclusion of the black cook sheds light intentionally or unintentionally on the exaggerated yet naturalized whiteness of screwball that prevails in the first three journeys. With the shift to the prison exposé in the fourth journey, the film's racial composition changes altogether: Sullivan undergoes his transformation within the confines of an interracial chain gang and a black church.[27] Part of the governing "reality principle" of the prison exposé is its interracial makeup, at least in Sturges's handling. Sturges makes a deliberate choice here, one in keeping with the historical fact of interracial chain gangs but one that significantly departs from the racial iconography of many of the most popular documents of social realism from the 1930s. As Denning argues, part of the mythic status of John Steinbeck's novel *The Grapes of Wrath* (1939) and John Ford's Oscar-winning film based upon the book has to do with its "racial populism"—a consolidation of the narrative of dispossessed white Okies predicated on a willful forgetting of the concurrent, massive migration of African Americans or the agricultural battles of Mexican, Filipino, Chinese, and Japanese farmworkers in the state of California (260–62, 267). Sturges refuses this narrative, opting instead for an interracial populism by his film's conclusion. This reading of the film heeds Denning's warning that the "gallery of allegorical icons of victimization, innocence and resilience, ranging from Franklin Roosevelt's 'forgotten man' to Steinbeck's Ma Joad, from Dorothea Lange's Migrant Mother to Frank Capra's Mr. Smith . . . should not be lumped together into an undifferentiated 'populism'; the apparent consensus of the 'thirties'—the shared rhetoric of the people—obscures deeper divisions and conflicts" (126). Sturges's recuperation of an interracial populist raison d'être distinctly contrasts with John Ford's and Frank Capra's sentimental populisms centered on "the white, ethnically unmarked, forgotten [man]" (128). At the same time, given the film's ethos of modernist burlesque, Sturges's deployment of interracial populism should be qualified with quotation marks, like every other reference in the film.

NOW LET'S JUST SIT HERE AND TRY TO FEEL LIKE A COUPLE OF TRAMPS

Sullivan's Travels sets the stage for Sullivan's transformation via a vision of interracial populism in the fourth journey by first invoking and exhausting the period's most popular icons of white suffering in Sullivan's and the Girl's third journey out. The film's first three journeys pointedly ask the audience to identify with the stars who traipse through this mediated landscape, rather than the impoverished white subjects captured in these scenes. In perhaps the most memorable monologue in the movie, Sullivan's butler (Eric Grieg) offers his negative opinion of Sullivan's "noble experiment," warning him that "people are always fascinated by that which they don't know." Of course, the film trades on the audience's potential fascination with the Hollywood high life that Sullivan so assiduously wishes to elude in his expedition. Half of the intrigue of *Sullivan's Travels* is the film's tongue-in-cheek exposure of the inner machinery of the motion picture industry and Sturges knows this.

Accordingly, once Sullivan and the Girl venture into the world of hobo jungles, Hoovervilles, and missions, he situates them as incongruous, visible interlopers, especially in their initial outing together (Sullivan's second journey), which solidifies their courtship. With Lake's glowing complexion and her cap set at the rakish angle of her peek-a-boo hairstyle underneath, she still resembles a glamour girl. Like the illustration in the opening credits that depicts Sullivan and the Girl looming over tiny, knee-high human figures, the couple is lit from below to stand out in the frame in contrast with the rest of the people they encounter (Ames 89). Their star power renders the others Lilliputians in comparison. If we identify with them as we are asked to do, by proxy, we distinguish ourselves from the crowds through which Sullivan and the Girl move. No matter the audience's actual economic circumstances, we are positioned as viewers who gain access to this other world through Sullivan and the Girl. They are our interclass mediators. Part of the fantasy and pleasure

10. Sullivan and the Girl
are interlopers in a
Hooverville.

the film offers its viewers, then, is to occupy the position of bourgeois insiders in the Hollywood culture industry, as opposed to the down-and-out folk for whom Sullivan and the Girl pass in the film, even if they are dismissed by real tramps as "amateurs."

We are asked to identify with the stars while they witness the poor. From this alienated position, we become acutely aware of our own spectatorship, particularly once the film shifts to the serious subject matter of realist genres such as documentary and the prison exposé in the film's third and fourth journeys. While in the movie's opening Sullivan's cinematic exemplar of "Labor and Capital" may fall far short of the documentary of the day, in these later scenes Sturges himself proves to be a master of the form, especially in the extraordinary montage that sums up the film's third journey, Sullivan's and the Girl's foray into the mostly white, unemployed underclass. In Moran and Rogin's estimation, "the hobo jungle and prison farm that take over Sturges's movie mark it as the last 1930s social protest film" (111). Last and possibly the strangest, the montage sequence is one of the more anomalous moments in the film. Sturges draws a connection between the slapstick characters of the silent film era and the folk grotesques pictured in a work like the bestselling documentary book, *You Have Seen Their Faces* (1937), by the writer Erskine Caldwell and the photographer Margaret Bourke-White.

In this segment, with a few exceptions, poor people are represented as overwhelmingly white. Here we see depictions of the folk as suffering and in need of government intervention. Sturges self-consciously invokes the white racial populism of Ford's classic film *The Grapes of Wrath* (1940), a narrative mode that he will reject in the prison exposé of the fourth journey. The entire six-minute sequence is silent but for the overbearing orchestral score: dolorous strings force the pathos of the scene. To mark shifts in tone, the melody is occasionally interrupted by the sprightly trill of woodwinds as Sully and the Girl are attacked by bed bugs and fall into a fit of laughter, or by overly dramatic horns that mark the fire and brimstone pitch of the preacher's sermon in counterpoint with the resigned faces of his parishioners. Like silent films of the past, but without dialogue cards, the montage relies only on the score and the protagonists' physical actions to direct the audience's emotions. Lake comes the closest she ever gets to looking destitute: her face is grimy, she wears no lipstick, and her outfit is disheveled. The camera follows the couple as they walk through a homeless encampment from right to left as if it were a wax museum; all of its occupants go about their private domestic rituals, shaving, eating, and sleeping with only a despondent glance at Sullivan and the Girl. As our interlocutors peruse their faces, the shot perspective issues from Sullivan's and the Girl's gaze, their shadows falling on the figures they size up.

As we the audience "notice [Sullivan and the Girl] noticing," a photographer literally snaps a picture of our stand-in spectators while they wait in a bread line, suggesting that the montage is not so much about the folk they see but their own bourgeois gaze, and by proxy, the audience's gaze.[28] Though the photographer is most likely from one of the Hollywood media who track the story of Sullivan's incredible journey for studio publicity, his surveying presence recalls the work of the photographic unit in the New Deal's Farm Security Administration. In referencing these central image-producing sources of the 1930s, the segment's cinematography echoes the populist iconography of the New Deal and underlines Ford's quotation of these images in *The Grapes of Wrath*, released the year before in 1940. Sturges thus blurs the lines between fiction (the Hollywood dream machine) and purported reality (the Depression era's photojournalistic representations of the folk).

The montage returns us back to Sturges's central question—just *who* wants to *see* the folk in the form of the tramp and the dispossessed white occupants of the Hoovervilles and *why*? This metamoment not only brings to mind the incessant documentation of poverty during the thirties but overtly reminds us that we are witnesses of Sullivan's and the Girl's witnessing, much in the way that Zora Neale Hurston's ethnography goes to great lengths to remind the audience of its own mediated spectatorship. Thus, we occupy the position of many viewers of 1930s documentary, summed up in the title of Caldwell's and Bourke-White's *You Have Seen Their Faces*. In this way, the montage marks the limits of documentary's empathic liberal project by making us feel the awkwardness of our passive position, encapsulated in Sullivan's rebuke to the Girl in an earlier scene, "Now let's just sit here and try to feel like a couple of tramps." What are the limits of "trying to feel like" someone else? Around which bodies does such sentimental populism cohere? Who is left out of the picture? Like Nathanael West in his novel *A Cool Million*, Sturges suggests that a liberal politics of empathy and its solution of personal charity potentially prevents a more progressive, collective response to the systemic poverty of the Depression and the economic injustices of racial capitalism. Moreover, there is something disturbingly self-referential about this kind of politics—an emphasis on how much the viewer *feels* for the documentary subject paradoxically occludes the very personhood of the subject in question.[29]

Sullivan and the Girl reiterate the ambivalence of their position as spectators in their responses to the film's Hooverville: following a classic shot-reverse shot pattern, each vignette is anchored by a full frontal framing of the couple as they earnestly survey their surroundings or by their simultaneously amused and disgusted reactions to the grotesques in their midst (the man who sits across from them at the mission, chewing with no teeth, or the man who snores, mouth agape, in Sullivan's face on the mission floor as they all try to sleep). When Sullivan and the Girl begin to search for food in a garbage can, their repulsion overwhelms them; with this image—one that recalls the studio producers' goading question, "When did you last eat from a garbage can?"—Sullivan and the Girl run out of the frame, back to Hollywood. Blending pathos with comedy, documentary images with silent film, Sturges's montage offers us social realism and racial populism in quotation marks as it ironically enacts and burlesques Sullivan's noble experiment and intensifies the romance between Sully and the Girl.[30]

AM I LAUGHING?

If the montage ends up promoting the romantic comedy plot, the fourth journey consolidates Sullivan's "authentic" masculinity wrought out of physical self-defense, hard labor, incarceration, and interracial contact, paradoxically making him over into a fit romantic partner for the Girl by the movie's conclusion. In order for this transformation to take place, the Girl drops out of the picture and the film switches genres once again, to the realist prison exposé, a brutal world of men. This is the sequence upon which all critics base their interpretations of the film—Sullivan's conversion as he shares in the uproarious laughter of his fellow prisoners, a moment which causes him to favorably view his own work as a director of comedy. If the viewer laughs with the laugh on screen, she may feel satisfied with Sullivan's return to his original vocation by the film's conclusion. The film is about the importance of laughter as a cathartic mode of escape for "the people," for the masses, for the folk. But what of the viewer who experiences the laugh not as funny, but as grotesquely incongruous, and perhaps even "wholly grim," to borrow from Kenneth Burke? From that perspective, how does the film's conclusion square with the pivotal laughter scene?

Significantly, in this section, Sullivan's play acting is literalized. He is no longer acting within the plot of the film: at first due to his own amnesia and then due to the inequities of the justice system, he is stuck in the lowest rung of society, the prison. With this turn of circumstances, ostensibly he no longer performs masculinity (Moran and Rogin 121). This shift is no more evident than in the first scene depicting the laboring chain gang, when the camera slowly sweeps from right to left, taking in the countless sweaty backs of white and black men as they work the line along a river bank, until it finally rests on Sullivan working among them. Here the light-hearted pastoral musical score plays with and against the mise-en-scène: an appropriate if dismaying accompaniment to the warden's leisurely boating as he oversees the prisoners, it jarringly contrasts with the incarcerated men's hard labor, an ironic disjuncture that may prepare the audience for reading against the grain in later scenes.[31] Seemingly, Sullivan has lost all salient facets of his identity but one—his masculinity, which the film signifies and naturalizes through a shot of his naked torso, literally chained to the other white and black bodies of the toiling inmates. Free of women, from his wife's manipulations to the Girl's ministrations, Sullivan's masculinity is put to the test in the company of an interracial group of men. When Sullivan spies a headline "Strange Death of Hollywood Director" on the trusty's folded newspaper and impulsively grabs the paper to read it, the warden, Mr. Carson (Alan

Bridge), sentences him to time in the sweatbox in the woods as punishment. In one of the film's more wrenching scenes, after Sullivan is finally let out in the cover of night, he falls to his knees, mumbling incoherently, his arms around the sympathetic trusty (Jimmy Conlin), a man half his size: Sullivan is nearly broken. In an effort to raise his spirits, the trusty speaks of the prospect of attending the picture show that Saturday night. Foretold in this setup, Sullivan's dark night of the soul is the necessary precursor to his discovery in the church of his true calling.

Sullivan appears to undergo an epiphany regarding his life's work in what is surely the most memorable and perplexing moment in the film, when he and his fellow inmates watch a Disney cartoon at a nearby African American Baptist church. The scene opens with a shot of the old church shrouded in mist and bordered by ominous, primordial swamps. An organ plays in the background as the benevolent black preacher (Jess Lee Brooks) instructs one of his parishioners, Charlie, to let the projection sheet "down easy"; as it hastily unfurls, he jokes, "Charlie's a little anxious," to which his congregation laughs a bit too readily and loudly. Next, he introduces the night's film and sermonizes: "And once again, brothers and sisters, we're gonna share our entertainment with some neighbors less fortunate than ourselves. . . . And when they get here, I'm gonna ask you once more, neither by word, nor by action, nor by look . . . are we to make our guests feel unwelcome for we's all equal in the sight of God." To a solemn chorus of "Go Down Moses," the convicts enter the church, the camera focused on the chains around their feet, which clang in time with the music.

In a familiar cinematic move, Sturges exploits what Michael Rogin describes as "the surplus symbolic value of blacks, the power to make African Americans represent something besides themselves" in American popular culture (*Blackface*, 14). The film's depiction of black people as prayerful folk, the flipside of the earlier whiteface/blackface minstrelsy of the car chase sequence, advances a corrective Hollywood characterization, progressive for its time in 1941 (though on its way to becoming a cliché itself) (Ames 94). Diane Jacobs, Sturges's biographer, reports that an NAACP executive officer wrote to Sturges to commend him for the "decent treatment of Negroes" in the church scene: "I was in Hollywood recently and am to return there soon for conferences with production head writers, directors, and actors and actresses in an effort to induce broader and more decent picturization of the Negro instead of limiting

11. The chain gang enters the church.

him to menial or comic roles. The sequence in *Sullivan's Travels* is a step in that direction and I want you to know how grateful we are" (262). As the film puts forth a more dignified representation of black people, it simultaneously foregrounds the continuation of slavery in the form of the chain gang. That Sullivan, now one of the downtrodden prisoners, is taken in by a poor, rural black church emphasizes the degree to which he has descended the social and economic ladder.

When shooting this section of the film, Sturges concerned himself with accuracy to varying degrees. We know that he borrowed and screened a copy of *I Am a Fugitive from a Chain Gang* (1932) as a reference for his own representations (Harvey, *Romantic Comedy*, 592; Moran and Rogin 121). Yet Thomas Cripps rightly views this scene of entry as a moment of "supreme irony" when the plea for freedom in "Go Down Moses" is extended to incarcerated white men (*Slow Fade*, 366). It is an irony wrought out of a peculiar history: chain gangs were one of the few state-sanctioned, integrated institutions visible in the interwar period. (If chain gangs were integrated, they were overwhelmingly African American, though one would never glean this from the film, judging from its majority of white convicts.) Part of the zeitgeist, *Sullivan's Travels* limned this terrain around the same time that several blues artists of the cultural front released theme albums on major labels also illustrating the mistreatment of the chain gang: Lawrence Gellert's collection of chain gang songs called *"Me and My Captain" (Chain Gang)* (1939), Josh White's *Chain Gang* (1940) and *Southern Exposure* (1941), and Leadbelly's *The Midnight Special and Other Prison Songs* (1940) (Denning 355). There is another historical irony here as well. The scene ignores the entrenched racial segregation of churches in the era of Jim Crow, summed up in the phrase "Sunday morning is the most segregated hour of the week" (Emerson and Blum, "Dreams," 5). Most white people refused to attend church with black people because it would undermine the "spiritual wage of whiteness" proffered and sanctified by white Christian congregations (Blum, *W. E. B. DuBois*, 15-6).[32]

While this congregation departs from reality—comprising as it does the racially integrated convicts *and* the black parishioners—it constitutes one prevailing populist formation of "the people" and the "folk" around which concepts of the authentic accrued in the iconography and rhetoric of the cultural front.[33] As Denning describes, within the leftist aesthetic ideologies of the period that favored a "pan-ethnic Americanism," "African American culture [anchored in the spiritual] often became the touchstone for [a] new 'American' culture" (130, 132). This formation was animated by a linkage between conceptions of the "black folk" and the proletarian masses.[34] *Sullivan's Travels* invokes a facet of the cultural front's "pan-ethnic Americanism" as part of its "social surrealism" (Denning 121). In so doing, it departs from many of the social problem films of the 1930s that centered exclusively on the image of white suffering, from King Vidor's *Our Daily Bread* (1934) and Frank Capra's small-town trilogy to *The Grapes of Wrath*.

By understanding this segment not just in terms of the social problem film but also as the film's one nod to the musical with its inclusion of "Go Down Moses," we see how Sturges correspondingly tweaks that form's conventional racial dynamics as well. During the early forties, the generically integrated musical was coming into vogue, a form that overtly linked musical numbers to the film's storyline and character development: "In [generically] *integrated* musicals, characters break into song when they should be talking, instead of only when they are 'putting on a show' (as in the 'backstager' subgenre)" (Griffin, "The Gang's All Here," 21; emphasis added). Sean Griffin observes that generically integrated musicals were racially segregated, whereas the "nonintegrated" musicals of the period—films that relied on a variety show structure inherited from vaudeville—showcased "specialty" acts not directly connected to the storyline of the film and often featured "minority performers" in those spots. Thus, the "nonintegrated" musicals were more racially integrated than the generically integrated musicals.

In Sturges's own version of a "backstager,"[35] just as his protagonist descends into the terrain of realism seemingly beyond the reach of the motion picture industry, he provides us with a generically *and* racially integrated musical scene. Sturges's departure from the generic and racial conventions of the musical at that time underscores the narrative choices he makes in order to ground Sullivan's transformation in a particular vision of interracial populism. It is telling that along with urging Sturges to eliminate some "gruesome characters," Buddy DeSylva, the new head of Paramount, also suggested he cut the "shot of preacher, then panning shot of people; or drop the preacher altogether" (qtd. in Jacobs 259–60). While the irony of the chained convicts entering the church to the song "Go Down Moses" would have remained, the continuity of that scene equally depends upon the preacher's words of democratic compassion and the black congregation's assent. DeSylva's cuts would have undermined one of the more progressive aspects of the film. If the montage of the Hooverville depicts a racial populism in the style of *The Grapes of Wrath*, this scene rejects that imagery in favor of an interracial constellation of the folk, wrought out of the faithful, the poor, and the oppressed, a constellation that conforms to the radical racial politics of the cultural front. At the same time, this scene of "pan-ethnic Americanism" also stages one of the film's most disquieting and "extravagant incongruities" —Sullivan's and the prisoners' frenzied response to the movie they are shown—raising questions about the film's stance with regard to those politics.

Once the song is over, the film-within-the-film, *Playful Pluto* (1934), begins: a cartoon about the frustrations of being stuck, it features Pluto, who is violently ensnared first within a chest of drawers, then by fly paper, and finally by a window shade which rolls up around him (Ames 94). The cartoon isn't necessarily funny. Yet the inmates laugh uproariously, literally convulsed with joy, and they are soon joined by the churchgoers. An unsmiling Sullivan surveys the crowd in horror. And then he laughs himself. He turns to the trusty and asks "Am I laughing?," at which point he becomes one of them, abandoning himself to laughter. In this interracial public, we see the purported democracy of consumption in action: black and white, men and women, old and young, free and incarcerated, they all share in the laugh.

However, for anyone who has seen the film, this is its most unforgettable moment because the audience's frenzied laughter is potentially deeply unsettling. It is surreal. We may not share in their laughter. Given

12.1–12.4.
Sullivan asks, "Am I laughing?,"
at which point he becomes one
of them, abandoning himself to
laughter. The audience becomes
grotesque.

that this scene delivers Sullivan's primary object lesson, all critics grapple with it as a pivotal point in their reading. The standard interpretation accepts Sullivan's conversion at face value. By way of example, Jacobs claims, "Laughter is infectious and undiscriminating—available to all humanity. The comic experience, as Sturges portrays it, is—like religion for the faithful—a profound, if temporary release from suffering. It won't change the world but it will make life more tolerable. It's no coincidence that the cartoon scene, the film's emotional climax, takes place in a church" (251).[36] Thus, this scene fits harmoniously with the film's dedication "to the memory of those who made us laugh." Sullivan now grasps his producers' initial point: mirrored in the scene's swampy, primal surroundings, folks who are down on their luck have basic needs and desires—they just want to laugh. Partaking in the laughter, Sullivan understands his audience and their urgent need for fantasy; this strengthens his conviction to make the light fare for which he is famous.

What this conventional reading ignores is the way that the audience's laughter renders them grotesque: the contorted faces of individual viewers are shot in close-up, much like the hobos Sullivan and the Girl encounter at the mission and the flophouse in the montage sequence of the third journey. This time around, instead of laughing at them, Sullivan momentarily joins the gallery of grotesques.[37] As he merges with his fellow prisoners, the scene exemplifies a "contradictory fusion," an instance of Denning's proletarian grotesque (Denning 122). This is an enormous departure from Sullivan's earlier revulsion at the moviegoing public when he attends a quadruple feature with the cloying sisters in his first journey. The violence of the cartoon is replicated in the convicts' furious laughter. This discordant moment tells a particular truth about the audience depicted on screen. In Sturges's caricature of the audience's responses to the cartoon on the screen, their abject mania becomes the spectacle, demonstrating a collective madness rent out of acute suffering that drives their frenetic consumption of images. Moran and Rogin persuasively suggest that if we identify with the audience—if we momentarily fuse with them as the proletarian grotesque asks us to do—we confront "our faces, reflected back in the disturbing, needy laughter of the prisoners, that drive the fantasies on screen. . . . [Much like] the laughter of another late 1930s document . . . [Nathanael West's] *The Day of the Locust* . . . [i]t is the laughter at the death of innocent laughter, the laughter that comes after and with the chain gang which it cannot wipe away" (126–27). As Sullivan crosses over, he is our proxy, a stark reminder of how closely we merge with or skirt the void ourselves. We watch this drama unfold and we are implicated. Our laughter—or failure to laugh—is no longer innocent.

This is a brilliant reading of this enigmatic scene, though it depends to some degree upon the actual audience's laughter with the audiences depicted onscreen. What happens if we fail to identify, to fuse, with Sullivan and his fellow audience members in this moment? By showing us the film-within-the-film, Sturges raises the stakes of the scene. As we watch the audience watch the cartoon, and as we watch the cartoon ourselves, we witness from one angle a profound incongruity between the violent action in the cartoon and their heightened response. Like the scenes in West's *A Cool Million* when his protagonist is beaten up in a vaudeville routine to the uproar of the crowd, the cartoon is not all that funny, nor is their laughter. This scene offers the most direct evidence for Sullivan's thesis that people want escape in the movies, yet ironically the scene is not necessarily pleasurable for its viewers.

If we fail to share in the laugh "available to all humanity"—if we ask ourselves, "Am I laughing?" and the answer is no—we occupy an oddly ambivalent and alienated position. We experience the proximate difference of our position, a "there but for the grace of God, go I" with an acknowledgment that we're not quite there yet. That difference of position is equally as disconcerting as laughing *with* the laugh. Those in the actual audience who don't laugh may constitute a self-conscious, counteraudience. Importantly, though, Sturges's burlesque never allows anyone outside of the circuit of spectatorship—as we watch *Sullivan's Travels* and its cartoon-within-the-film, alienated or not, we are self-reflexively constructed as the audience. In this sense, we remain profoundly (dis)located *within* the circuit of spectatorship. Unlike Sullivan, whose initial response to the moviegoing public when he attends a film with the sisters is one of revulsion, we are not permitted that distance. For those who don't laugh with the laugh, this scene is both painful and unsentimental. In Agee's words, "The fun is painfully unfunny" (*Agee on Film*, 329). In this scene, we confront an instance of the proletarian grotesque—Sullivan momentarily fuses with the prisoners and together they constitute a gallery of grotesques—a moment that is potentially far more disturbing than conventional documentary renderings of despair. In another register of meaning delivered by way of burlesque, we confront the potential incongruity of our own position vis-à-vis the diegetic audience. The film no longer revels in the play between serious highbrow aims and lowbrow slapstick: arguably, this is its most sobering moment.

If the laugh, the movie's climax, exemplifies both the proletarian grotesque's fusions and the modernist burlesque's incongruities, two related radical instantiations of cultural front aesthetics, Sturges owes a great deal, then, to the very modes of politically motivated, (sur)realist art he appears to want to shirk. While the scene may seem to prove his position regarding comedy and escapism, it is also the moment in the film that most closely enacts a cultural front strategy of modernist burlesque: the laugh constitutes the heart of his satire, the moment when the comedy drops out, when the laugh itself no longer necessarily signifies humor. In this way, the laugh not only points to the limits of realism but it also demarcates the limits of comedy, a self-reflexive implication that has led many film historians to proclaim Sturges as the last director of screwball comedies. The French film critic André Bazin describes how Sturges at once revived and did away with the screwball genre by introducing irony to its humor. As West would put it, Sturges introduced "a laugh at the laugh" (*Dream Life*, 27). With the "death of innocent laughter" so evident in this film and the films that preceded and followed it, *The Lady Eve* (1941) and *The Palm Beach Story* (1942), Sturges razes the conventions of comedy to which he is beholden (Moran and Rogin 127).

MEN MUST WORK AND WOMEN MUST WEEP,
OR HOWEVER IT GOES

The possibility that we may not laugh with the audience in the church calls attention to the film's depiction of several different audiences throughout. The film's numerous "congregation scenes" change considerably between Sullivan's first and final journey (Jacobs 251). Who are these different audiences and how are they represented? How does the Girl stand in for the people? If actual viewers of the film fail to laugh with the convicts in the church, how might this reaction comment upon Sullivan's (and Sturges's) roles as producers of fantasies that are never quite sufficient for their audiences? In the fourth journey, we witness the moviegoers' "authentic," existential despair, whereas prior scenes portray an audience characterized by feminized, middlebrow, white consumer desire.

Throughout *Sullivan's Travels*, one of the more disconcerting aspects of making movies, a form of commercial leisure, is having to accommodate consumer desire, a pressure increasingly felt in the shift from producer to consumer culture in the 1930s (Cohen, *Consumer's Republic*, 22–28).[38] Certainly, the opening argument between Sullivan and his producers centers on this issue. In addition to this scene, the beginning of the film finds Sullivan connected to an array of women with whom he is uncomfortably, contractually bound. These relationships implicate him in a corrupt world of feminized consumption.[39] The women in the film are always interrupting Sullivan's work; however, it is all of a piece for, in some sense, they are his work. Kathy Peiss suggests that during the 1920s and 1930s, "consumption [was] coded as a female pursuit, frivolous and even wasteful, a form of leisure rather than productive work" ("American Women," para. 1). Or, as Kenon Breazeale bluntly puts it, "Men produce and women shop" ("In Spite," 226). Recall the entrance of the first woman in the film, Sullivan's legal wife, the so-called Panther Woman: married to make money in an IRS scam, each will benefit from a fiscal deduction of $12,000, but Sullivan accrues no such savings because she needs the full amount ($24,000) to satisfy her requirements as a consumer. The next pair of women he encounters are the widow and her sister: in exchange for room and board, he not only chops their wood but is obliged to accompany them to the movies. As they take in a seemingly interminable quadruple feature of maudlin titles—*Beyond These Tears, The Valley of Shadow, The Buzzard of Berlin*, and *Swingo*—children fidget, one toots a whistle, a baby cries, and an unkempt man obliviously crunches his popcorn, all of these annoyances compounded by the flirtatious widow's stealth attempt to clasp Sullivan's hand. This first comic manifestation of the white moviegoing public and its uncouth viewing habits and pleasures repels Sullivan.[40] Interestingly, we never see the films they are watching; we never join them in their spectatorship and therefore, we are never asked to identify with their position, as in the case of the pivotal cartoon scene in the fourth journey (Ames 91). Though there are a few men visible in the audience, the crowd is feminized, its "inarticulate longings" and "dormant desires" run amok, in spite of middle-class protocols of respectability (Peiss para. 9). This gendered representation is aptly summed up in the lyrics the coy widow sings as she turns down Sullivan's bed, "Men must work and women must weep, or however it goes."

13. Sullivan is repulsed by the audience (note the boy tooting his whistle in the top right corner of the image and the girl and the man obliviously munching popcorn to the left side of the image).

In connection with this initially feminized audience, as Jay Rozgonyi proposes, we might understand the Girl as a more palatable representative of an everywoman moviegoer, a middlebrow, Midwestern one at that (she jokingly asks Sullivan to drop her off in Chicago when he offers her a ride home in their first meeting) (*Preston Sturges's Vision*, 85–86). From this vantage, Moran's and Rogin's contention that "the romance that drives this film is Sully's with the people, not with the (unnamed) Girl" might be reworked: "the romance that drives the film is Sully's with the people in the guise of the Girl" (119). Part of Sullivan's quest, then, is to reconcile himself with "the people" by way of the Girl. In her first acquaintance with Sullivan, when she is still unaware of his true profession, the Girl mentions her love of *Hey, Hey in the Hayloft*, one of his directorial efforts. She describes an absurd incident from the film involving a couple, a kissing pig, and a sneezing horse, concluding "that was a wonderful scene. Of course, it was stupid but it was wonderful." Sullivan replies, "Don't you think with the world in its present condition, with death snarling at you from every street corner, people are a little allergic to comedies?" Foreshadowing Sullivan's discovery in the church contained within the grim prison segment of the film, the Girl warns, "There's nothing like a deep-dish movie to drive you out in the open." In this moment, the Girl becomes Sturges's mouthpiece, anticipating his later explanation of the film to reviewers, "*Sullivan's Travels* is the result of an urge, an urge to tell some of my fellow filmwrights that they were getting a little deep-dish and to leave the preaching to the preachers" (qtd. in Jacobs 263). Given the broad strokes of the Girl's representational function, denoted in the generality of her title, it is no wonder that her role seems somewhat unrealized in plot and execution: in addition to carrying the weight of the romantic comedy genre, she stands in for "the people," in their most honest, uncomplicated, and alluring guise, and also for the director.

The Girl signifies an alternative to the reprehensible feminized consumer Sullivan confronts at the beginning of the film by eschewing a position of acquisitive manipulation for the possibility of acting. In this way, she both conforms to the film's characterization of consumption as a feminine realm in contrast with the masculine realm of production and also challenges that conventional dichotomy as well. Not content with the role of mere spectator, she aspires to be an actor and thereby gain full entry into the world of work and leisure. Once again, there is no getting outside of Hollywood and its "direct entanglements": the Girl's consumption of popular film motivates her drive to become an actor; simultaneously, her employment in Hollywood would guarantee her ability to consume (Denning 140). Of course, if acting provides her with a greater degree of agency, it is still severely circumscribed by the paternalistic studio system. When we finally glimpse her at work on a Hollywood lot, the moment she sees Sullivan's face on the front page of the newspapers as a confessed murderer, she is wearing a ludicrous hoop skirt, the proverbial armature of nineteenth-century, white southern hyperfemininity, which knocks everyone out of her path as she runs to alert the producers of her discovery. As in the Mr. Smearkase routine in the diner, once again Sturges demonstrates the constrained power of these feminine performances: the skirt that confines her clears a path at the same time.

In a parallel but reverse pattern, Sullivan must come to terms with his work as a director; he must reaffirm his touch for "the people" by briefly becoming a consumer. If this threatens to irreparably "feminize" him, he is rescued by the "realness" of the interracial proletariat that enables this consumption—primarily, the immanently authentic, incarcerated men of the chain gang as well as the black parishioners. Moreover, his consumption is a reward for his satisfactory physical labor, his hard time on the line, a form of homosocial masculine production to which he has had little exposure until now. In accordance with these circumstances, Sullivan cannot simply stage his consumption. He must lose his characteristic distance altogether. The plotting suggests that it is only when he no longer impersonates someone else, when he is shorn of his privilege and profession and forced to contend with arbitrary and menial authority, that he can acquire truly life-changing experience.

To drive this point home, Sullivan gains his freedom by claiming to be the murderer of John L. Sullivan, the famous movie director: symbolically, he must murder himself to get back his former identity. As he reclaims this past self, he is no longer the same man for he has now suffered deprivation and despair. At the same time, those very experiences make him more comfortable with the films he has made in the past and, in this sense, he is more himself than ever. Changed man or no, the method through which he frees himself establishes his fundamental difference from the other underprivileged convicts. Relying upon his directorial talent, Sullivan strikes upon his plan with the heavy-handed line "If ever a plot needed a twist, this one does." This remark condenses the film's strategy in bringing about Sullivan's final journey, the section of the film that comes closest to enacting the social problem genre. Ironically, in order to both thrust his protagonist into this "real" predicament and later pull him out of it, Sturges must twist the plot in the most fictional of ways. Yet this fictional twist tells a certain truth. Sullivan's false claim to have murdered himself suggests what would happen to him were he either to remain stuck within the genre of social realism (the prison plot) or to adopt this genre as a director: it would be the professional "death" of John L. Sullivan, as we know him.

In a larger sense, the prison exposé of the fourth journey functions as a necessary incursion of 1930s social realism, shoring up its protagonist's "authentic" hetero-masculinity and thereby making him an appropriate suitor within the plot of the romantic comedy that is restored in the film's conclusion. Moran and Rogin show how the film invokes the road movie, notably "three great road movies of the end of the decade, *The Wizard of Oz* (1939), *Stagecoach* (1939), and *The Grapes of Wrath* (1940). . . . But Sully's adventures authorize neither class reconciliation nor social transformation" (118). This assessment holds true when we consider the film's function as a "real" look at Hollywood by way of self-conscious filmic enactments of its various genres. We are always aware that we are watching a film. Sturges is bent on demonstrating that social realism and its related filmic expressions (documentary, the social problem film, the prison exposé) are no less mediated than melodrama. In Sullivan's final journey, Sturges rejects mainstream populist depictions of white suffering for a more radical interracial populism of the cultural front. As he invokes these progressive aesthetics, their modified "realisms," he demonstrates how they are just as mediated as more overtly fictional genres (Denning 121).

Nevertheless, even as Sturges burlesques the conventions of social realism and its more radical configurations, still some residue of the reality principle stays with the film's characterizations, transforming both Sullivan and its conception of audiences. Sturges may dispense with the genre—marking its failure, seemingly in accord with the lesson Sullivan has learned about laughter; nonetheless, its codes of authentic masculinity have made a "real" man out his protagonist. Moreover, its cultural front iconography reconfigures the audience—a poor, incarcerated lot of white and black men alongside the church's black parishioners—as a more "authentic" and therefore more *worthy* constellation of "the people," the changed Sully in their midst, in comparison with the white, feminized, superficial audiences and consumers of the film's beginning. If this more "authentic" and deserving audience constitutes the "real" demographic for Sullivan's comedies, he can continue in good conscience to make the light and cheerful fare for which he is known. It is no accident that the montage of laughing audience members at the film's conclusion includes the convicts, the parishioners, female nurses and male patients in a hospital ward, and children, with nary a widow or spinster in sight. Through the proletarian grotesque's contradictory mergings and modernist burlesque's extravagant incongruities, the film has aligned the suffering, proletarian masses with the feminized middle-brow as recuperated by the Girl. In addition, the film has resuscitated the screwball comedy, if only for a moment, by way of the cultural front's representations of "authentic" working-class masculinity and its vision of interracial populism.

IT'S BETTER THAN NOTHING

According to the account of the thirties offered within *Sullivan's Travels*, it may have been a decade of social problem films in the style of Capra, but it was also a decade of romantic comedies in the style of Lubitsch and, at least superficially, romance wins out. When the Girl reenters the picture, we find ourselves in this realm once again. Sullivan can fulfill the promise of that genre, marrying the Girl in a cross-class alliance while embracing his work as a successful director of lowbrow, escapist film. In addition to abetting his hetero-masculine transformation, his disappearance has led to his estranged wife's marriage to his business manager, making her a bigamist and an easy divorce. The Girl and Sullivan gleefully ruminate on his impending liberty: as Sullivan puts it, "Then I'll be free." Sullivan's staging of his own death not only frees him from jail but also from the prison house of domesticity ruled by his wife's voracious habits of consumption.

By shedding himself of the Panther Woman and marrying the Girl, an altogether different kind of female consumer, one who also wants to be a producer, Sullivan will make comedies (romantic?) based on his actual happy experience, presumably for the first time. To his producers' collective horror, he explains that he cannot make *O Brother, Where Art Thou?*: "In the first place, I'm too happy to make 'O Brother, Where Art Thou' and in the second place, I haven't suffered enough to make 'O Brother, Where Art Thou.'" After Sturges has trotted out the absurdities of the realist dictate, to make art based upon what you know, Sullivan reiterates that logic once again. At this point, it is an inane maxim that justifies nothing so much as the status quo: boy gets girl, makes romantic comedies. After all that we've seen, are we really expected to take this seriously?

The film's ending provides us with an ironic lens through which to evaluate the fictions of authenticity that Hollywood proves so adept at producing, including *Sullivan's Travels'* own deployment of "authentic" masculinity by way of white "hobohemia" or a proletariat interracial homosociality. In this way, Sturges lampoons the popularity of "tramp ethnography" and the larger, late thirties' folk revival of which it was a part, showing us how the film industry, that most commercial of enterprises, manufactures the folk, calibrating "realness" for maximum audience draw (DePastino 210–11). At its best, Sturges's film edifies the viewer: it reveals Hollywood's inner machinery to produce a critique of its sentimental populist iconography, the ways it recuperated racial capitalism through images of white suffering under the guise of criticizing it (Veitch, *American Superrealism*, 101). Like West's fiction, the film skeptically evaluates a politics of empathy and its inevitably individualist parameters. Given its burlesque tactics, *Sullivan's Travels* potentially encourages a disidentification with its own sappy message, asking its audience to regard critically the media's rampant populist posturing in the

1930s, to take a hard look at the ways "the people" and the folk function in a variety of self-serving, capitalist narratives authored by the studio executives and Sullivan himself.

In his often perceptive review of *Sullivan's Travels*, André Bazin contends that the film "leaves us unsatisfied" because it fails to fully realize its ironic potential: "The tragic interlude does not, for directorial reasons, contain sufficient violence and authenticity. . . . Since Hollywood has to be contrasted with reality, the script should not have contained anything from Hollywood. . . . [R]eality should have overwhelmed the film. . . . Only then would the final return to Hollywood have had the ironic character it needed and which would have made the viewer question Sullivan's final wisdom" (*Cinema of Cruelty*, 37). Of course, to suggest that the social realism of the film's "tragic interlude" lies outside the realm of Hollywood convention is to fall into Sullivan's flawed premise. Sturges revels in those realist conventions as much as the slapstick of earlier scenes. In fact, the film "overwhelms" us with a violent truth in its fleeting but unforgettable depiction of the laugh, the film's pivotal incongruity. That moment undermines Sullivan's final pat line, "There's a lot to be said for making people laugh. Did you know that's all some people have? It isn't much but it's better than nothing in this cockeyed caravan! Boy!" To understand the anguished truth of the laugh, the way it simultaneously dismantles and shores up Sullivan's claim, revealing it to be a point about the abject state of "the people" rather than simply a sentimental cop-out about escapism, we must see how it deconstructs the conventional opposition between comedy and tragedy. As the convicts laugh, and perhaps as we laugh, too, we see how the escapist cartoon returns us to comedy by way of suffering and suffering by way of comedy. In turn, this perspective potentially renders legible a perverse kind of "social realism," or at the very least, a "truth-claim," at the heart of the best screwball comedies in their performative critique of class and gender and their fantasies of self-invention, which so often begin with the failure of the bootstrap myth to actually deliver the goods.

In the end, through its modernist burlesque, *Sullivan's Travels* stages a radical dialectic between genres—putting pressure on certain generic codes so that they not only reveal themselves but also their opposite mode. As Sturges surveys the popular genres of the 1930s, particularly as they intersect with cultural front concerns, he demonstrates how all genres are constructed by focusing on the conventions that render them so recognizable that they cease to be apparent to us. In this way, his film adopts the animus of masquerade both in the realm of genre and the realm of identity, pursuing an ostensibly endless oscillation between the real and the fake. Sturges foregrounds the ways particular genres construct and sustain an array of gendered, raced, and classed identities, from the Girl on top in the diner scene, a staple of the romantic comedy, to the display of Sullivan's "authentic masculinity" in the prison exposé. If he naturalizes these performances in his film, we watch that process unfold before our very own eyes. As the film repeatedly situates us as spectators in the "know," it makes us acutely aware of our own press for particular plot twists and endings, especially if we want Sully to escape the chain gang and end up with the Girl. Thus, Sturges forces us to confront not only the mechanics of the performance but also our own potential desire for such artifice. Though he never throws out the category of truth altogether, Sturges suggests that we glean truth both when realism seamlessly succeeds and sometimes also when it fails, when we can glimpse the apparatus of representation itself along with our own investments in particular narrative outcomes.

Sturges delivers this point through his invocation of the proletarian grotesque's contradictory fusions and modernist burlesque's extravagant incongruities, deploying the most provocative aesthetic strategies of the cultural front. If the film leaves us unsatisfied, perhaps it is because we've been dragged out of our complacency, forced to confront our own conflicting desires: we may want the Girl and Sully to hook up, but it is difficult to wholly subscribe to Sullivan's hokey conclusion, that laughter "isn't much but it's better than nothing," because Sturges has asked us to think too much along the way (Denning 123). Moreover, Sturges's own film has violated that dictate: it has gained as much power from its moments of melodrama and social surrealism as its slapstick. After the film was released, Sturges himself referred to the problem of the ending in a letter to Bosley Crowther, the film reviewer for the *New York Times*: "I know it wasn't right, but I didn't know how to solve the problem which was not only to show what Sullivan found out but also to tie up the love story. It would have been very easy to make a big finish either way, but one would have defeated the other" (Jacobs 263). His genre and identity crossings allow for a kind of trespass and incongruity bordering on delirium. Though Sturges gestures toward order with Sully's misty-eyed testimonial, in the wake of such radical indeterminacy such tidiness appears to me to be the least satisfying alternative. We can accept his conclusion at face value and contend with its facile sentimentality or we can understand it as purposefully shallow, as burlesquing Hollywood's smug self-satisfaction, and we might be tempted to conclude that, indeed, Hollywood "isn't much," just barely "better than nothing."

And yet, we'd miss the point that it is Sturges's inability or unwillingness to solve this concluding dilemma—this extravagant incongruity—that opens up the space for this very query (Ames 95). This is the work of modernist burlesque in *Sullivan's Travels*. As Denning writes, "Nothing characterizes the works of the cultural front so much as the inability to imagine a completed narrative" (119). In the end, the genres that anchor this debate, social realism and screwball comedy, are associated with two distinct "golden age" stories of the 1930s: in the narrative and ideological crisis of the Depression, people either wanted the "real thing" or they wanted grand fictions (Stott, *Documentary*, xi). Sturges gives us an oxymoronic, self-referential mix of realist and escapist cinematic modes that never quite fuse, with their attendant pains and pleasures made overt. In so doing, he pays ironic homage to the inadequacy of such golden age accounts, creating a certain success out of their failures. In a perversely funny way, then, as *Sullivan's Travels* saves screwball comedy by way of the Left's aesthetic strategies, it testifies not to the death of the cultural front and its satirical energies but rather to its animating power and future legacy in the postwar decades.

Afterpiece

The Coen Brothers' Ol'-Timey Blues
in *O Brother, Where Art Thou?*

Not minstrelsy; this-here's just a dodge.
—EVERETT ULYSSES MCGILL, in Joel Coen, dir.,
O Brother, Where Art Thou? (2000)

If Sullivan felt incapable of making *O Brother, Where Art Thou?* because
he was "too happy" and he hadn't "suffered enough," Joel and Ethan
Coen demonstrated no such compunction. *O Brother, Where Art Thou?*
is the namesake for their insane Depression-era lark released in 2000.
The self-designated legatees of Sullivan's abandoned script and Sturges's
madcap style and scorch-and-burn satirical approach, the Coen brothers
put into motion a postmodernist burlesque in *O Brother* wrought out of
the cinematic genres, popular musical forms, regional myths, and populist iconography that anchored thirties' debates about the folk.[1] Based
loosely on Homer's *The Odyssey*, the film's parodic picaresque follows
three white convicts, Ulysses Everett McGill (George Clooney), Pete
Hogwallop (John Turturro), and Delmar O'Donnell (Tim Blake Nelson), just escaped from Parchman Farm, the notorious, almost all-black
prison camp in Mississippi. Moving through a spare, ochre-washed
South, the men search for buried treasure, their quest punctuated by
several run-ins with Mississippi's (extra-) legal forces of law and order,
including the police, the Devil, the KKK, and the state's crooked guber-
natorial candidates. Along the way, they join up with a black bluesman,
Tommy Johnson (a riff on the influential Mississippi blues guitarists
Tommy Johnson and Robert Johnson, played by Chris Thomas King).
When they hear a rumor that you can make easy money "for singing into
a can," they call themselves the Soggy Bottom Boys and record what will

14. *O Brother, Where Art Thou?* by Sinclair Beckstein is the book Sullivan will not make into a movie by the conclusion of *Sullivan's Travels*. *Sullivan's Travels*, dir. Preston Sturges (Paramount, 1941).

soon become a hit song, "Man of Constant Sorrow," produced by a blind engineer at a local radio station who doesn't see the interracial makeup of the band. During the film's climax, at a political rally, the Soggy Bottom Boys reprise their song, unaware of its popularity. They win over their white audience, ensuring that the slightly less corrupt candidate for governor will succeed and that they themselves will be pardoned and ultimately saved from their nemesis, the sheriff-cum-Satan. In the end, our protagonist, Everett McGill, reestablishes his good standing in the eyes of his estranged ex-wife, Penelope (Holly Hunter), and he reunites with her and their seven daughters.

Though the narrative and cinematic parallels between *O Brother* and *Sullivan's Travels* are many, one of the most striking echoes in the Coen brothers' film is its iteration of masquerade in the form of racial passing and performance. If *Sullivan's Travels* uses masquerade as a way of invoking and querying populist assumptions about the authenticity of different cinematic genres, identities, and audiences, *O Brother* uses masquerade as a means of exploring those assumptions about authenticity and their legacy manifested in Depression-era and contemporary conceptions of "ol'-timey" music. By way of masquerade, the film plays conventional notions of white and black musical genres against visual and sonic representations of racialized bodies and voices who pass (Knight, *Disintegrating*, 237).

These juxtapositions emerge overtly in the exchange between the soon-to-be-named Soggy Bottom Boys and the blind station engineer as they try to interest him in recording their ad-hoc group. The engineer asks "You boys do Negro songs?" and Everett gamely answers, "Sir, we are

15. The three white convicts escape. *O Brother, Where Art Thou?* dir. Joel Coen (Universal, 2000).

Negroes. All except . . . the fella that plays the gui-tar." The engineer asserts, "Well, I don't record Negro songs. I'm lookin' for some ol'-timey material. Why people just can't get enough of it," to which Everett replies, "Sir, the Soggy Bottom Boys been steeped in ol'-timey material. Heck, you're silly with it, aintcha boys?" Delmar retorts, "We ain't really Negroes!" Pete adds, "All except fer our a-cump-uh-nust!" To understand the full irony of this exchange, it helps to know that the term *ol'-timey* or *old-time music* was first used by Okeh Records in 1923 to market Georgia Fiddlin' John Carson's record and by the following year, the tag *old-time tune music* held, only to be superseded by the term *hillbilly music* (Green, *Torching,* 19; Malone, *Country,* 38). In this scene, we see how *O Brother* nostalgically burlesques an earlier period's nostalgia by reviving the folk revival of the thirties (Middleton, "O Brother," 56). The Soggy Bottom Boys record their song certainly for money, not necessarily for art, and they just happen to be good. The men are literally interpellated by the market. Nowhere does the film suggest that the song's production and distribution within the commercial circuit of radio render the music inauthentic. Rather, the film illuminates the way the song emerges in a market that both mobilizes and capitalizes upon anxieties about authenticity in the promotion of the music as "ol'-timey." The scene skillfully exposes the ways that the music being "revived" is a modern invention of the market for populism, its putatively discrete racial contours part of its value.

O Brother slyly signifies on the construction, production, and fetishization of racially distinct musical genres—Negro songs versus "ol'-timey material"—and the ways that such notions of racial purity inevitably depend upon masquerade. As Sean Chadwell suggests, the film demonstrates how "authenticity is invoked by cultures actively engaged in erasing or avoiding their actual roots. . . . in this case, it is African American music and culture" ("Inventing," 4). Making themselves over into whatever the blind engineer, and by extension, the market wants, Everett, Delmar, and Pete potentially pass for black and Tommy for white. In terms of their vocal stylings and musicianship, the men appear to have little concern about being able to sing or play capably in either genre.[2] And in both configurations of the band, in the passing version and the "real" version, it is interracial. Yet the power dynamics are not equal: Everett's bid for putting on popular musical blackness smacks of the appropriations of the minstrel tradition, a tradition from which white men profited materially and psychically. Moreover, the engineer wants "ol'-timey material," a genre coded as white. Whiteness is thus secured in the scene's oscillation between logics of racial purity and performance.

At the same time, the presumption of whiteness is also called into question. The Coen brothers not only expose the commercial invention and revival of ol'-timey music but they also upend the notion that ol'-timey material is "white," what with Tommy Johnson's "mighty fine pickin' " on "Man of Constant Sorrow"—the way his guitar playing both sonically and visually anchors the song—and the engineer's later remark that the sought-after Soggy Bottom Boys are "colored boys, I believe."[3] On the liner notes for the film's Grammy Award–winning soundtrack, Ethan Coen explains that "the mountain music, the delta blues and gospel, the chain-gang chants, related to field chants, would individually and in combination with each other, later evolve into bluegrass, commercial country music and rock-and-roll" (qtd. in Oermann, "*O Brother*"). Notably Coen describes these musical genres in terms of their site-specific associations and he points to the music's hybridity in creating new, vital forms. Benjamin Filene shows how Coen's perspective is beholden to some of the more radical thinking about folklore from the thirties, evidenced, for example, in B. A. Botkin's assessment that " 'hillbilly' has its place in the hierarchy of American folk styles. . . . [It] is not a pure but hybrid activity" (qtd. in Filene, "O Brother," 54). If Sturges restores screwball comedy by way of social realism, the Coen brothers revive ol'-timey music by way of the blues. Indeed, these musical genres converge in their mournful lament for what was lost and what might be found in the sweet hereafter and, as many critics have shown, their roots

16. The impromptu Soggy Bottom Boys record "ol'-timey" music for the blind recording engineer.

are inseparable, emblematic of what J. M. Mancini describes as "the interracial modernity of the circulating market" ("Messin'," 212). The film's plotting and soundtrack thus argue for a celebration of the populist miscegenated roots of "roots" music.

The film, in an oversimplified split, establishes the commercial, vernacular music of the thirties as authentic populism as opposed to the period's populist political rhetoric. The political workings of populism are represented by the familiar white southern demagogue, Pappy O'Daniel (Charles Durning), based on Huey Long and other historical figures, and the populist "reform" candidate, "Friend of the Little Man," Homer Stokes (Wayne Duvall), who is the grand wizard of the Ku Klux Klan, as we soon discover.[4] Both candidates harness ol'-timey music as a means of "mass communicatin'" with their constituencies, whether at the political rally or the Klan meeting. (One can only wonder how Ralph Stanley felt about his a cappella version of "O Death" being sung by the Grand Dragon as he officiates the lynching ceremony for the bluesman Tommy Johnson.) In the Coen brothers' plotting, as the politicians claim vacuous racial populisms from the left and the right in the service of varying degrees of white supremacy, the music constitutes a meaningful interracial populism whose power exceeds the politics to which it is sutured. In a pivotal scene, at a political rally, the audience of constituents becomes enraptured by the music, much in the way the convicts are bowled over with laughter at the Pluto cartoon in Sullivan's Travels (Harries, "Coen Brothers' New Film," B14). Unlike Sullivan's Travels, which deliberately reconfigures the film audience as interracial, poor, and oppressed, the audience the Soggy Bottom Boys win over is white, thus

17. The white audience goes wild for the Soggy Bottom Boys.

raising the question, what kind of populism does the music advance when the audience is so clearly segregated? As Stokes, the "reform" candidate, tries to shout down the band—"You's miscegenated! All you boys! Miscegenated!" and "These boys is not white! Hell, they ain't even ol'-timey!"—he is greeted by jeers and rotten tomatoes until he is literally run out on a rail. What the music achieves then is not so much the "embrace of a universal brotherhood that transcends race," as some critics have suggested, but a consolidation of "good" white populism versus "bad" (Content, Kreider, and White, "*O Brother*," 42).

Such simplistic designations follow Joel Coen's own assessment of the film's cartoonish politics: "The political undercurrent of the movie functions primarily for dramatic purposes, because the politics are frankly pretty primitive. The bad guys are racial bigots and KKK Grand Dragons, and the good guys are the heroes of the movie" (240, qtd. in Knight). "Good" white populism is consolidated through the white audience's (momentary) acceptance of integration in a manner consistent with the ways representations of blackness, including blackface, the three white escaped convicts have encountered. Within the film, Tommy Johnson's role is "wholly instrumental," as the cinema scholar Arthur Knight suggests, not only in facilitating the Soggy Bottom's populist success by providing the musical accompaniment for "Man of Constant Sorrow," but also by "providing his companions the occasion for their liberal heroism" (Knight 239). The Coens may be signifying on white blues fans' fetishization of Robert Johnson's "real" blackness. Nonetheless, the myth of the black bluesman overtakes the movie, augmented by the fact that the actor, Chris Thomas King, is also a musician who plays the songs he performs in the movie (Harries B15). The transformative effects of "au-

18. The Soggy Bottom Boys don hillbilly drag.

thentic" blackness for *O Brother*'s three main protagonists, and for *Sullivan's Travels*'s protagonist, may constitute one of the strongest links between the contemporary film and Sturges's precedent. Knight notes how black figures and voices traverse *O Brother* from beginning to end: "These imprisoned or isolated, yet connected figures make the case for the inescapable presence and importance of blacks in America . . . even as they suggest that the blithe, utopian integration . . . of the film is incomplete and far from fully accomplished." While Johnson's presence as the authentic, mythical black bluesman supplements the three white men's quest and transformation, blackface has assisted the group's recording of their ol'-timey song and has helped them liberate Johnson from the clutches of the Klan. Homeric references aside, the film is an allegory for the story of how "bluegrass, commercial country music and rock-and-roll" came to be, one that demonstrates white appropriations of blackness while also opening up the possibility for a "good" populist whiteness wrought out of the acknowledgment and recovery of the proverbial black guitarist in the band.[5]

Following Denning's critique of Depression-era racial populisms delimited to "a story of white Protestant 'plain people' " and even Sturges's equivocal enactment and refusal of this story, when *O Brother* consolidates "good" versus "bad" white racial populisms, we might ask what other political constellations and possibilities are ignored in the process (*Cultural Front*, 267). Yet, even in its current form, the film courts other political constellations and possibilities through its performances of whiteness. Importantly, in the scene when they win over the white crowd, the Soggy Bottom Boys don hillbilly drag in the form of ludicrous, shaggy gray beards that they mug with throughout their performance. Everett performs an impromptu buck-and-wing dance, quoting a pre–tap dance hybrid from the American minstrel stage that drew upon "the rapid toe and heel action of the Irish jig, the percussive sensibility of the Lancashire clog, and West African body movements and rhythms" (Hudson, "Tap Dance," para. 1). As "good" populist whiteness is secured in the audience's response, in their failing hillbilly masquerade —a kind of whiteface performance—the Soggy Bottom Boys reveal and send up the theatrical parameters of folksy whiteness and, by extension, the white racial parameters of the populism they call forth. They do this as their whiteness is repeatedly called into question by Stokes. Stokes, in fact, articulates a possibility the film seems to play with throughout in its accumulation of unstable racial signifiers that signify cultural, social, and political registers of blackness. This list obviously includes the men's familiarity with "Negro songs" but also the centrality of Dapper Dan pomade, hair nets, and male "coiffure"; Everett's, Pete's, and Delmar's incarceration on the chain gang at Parchman Farm; Pete's whipping and the threat of the noose at the hands of the sheriff/Satan; and the injunction directed at Everett after he has wrangled with his ex-wife's suitor in a five-and-dime store, "And stay out of Woolworth's" (Content, Kreider, and White 43–44). In the Klan scene that unnerved so many critics, Everett, Pete, and Delmar disguise themselves in the white robes of three Klansman they have rendered unconscious, only to have their hoods ripped off, revealing their sooty faces, recently blacked-up from their successful scheme to free Pete from Parchman. As their faces are revealed to the other Klansmen at the rally, in an almost Schuyler moment, one Klan member yells, "The color guard is colored!"

One might pause here and genuinely ask, what *if* the color guard was "colored"? What if the film had literalized Stokes's racial (mis)recognition in its lead protagonist? To take up the gambit of envisioning Sullivan's hypothetical film, had Schuyler, West, and Hurston written the script and Sturges directed *O Brother* (not Sullivan), we might have seen the film stage one of the most popular plotlines of the Jim Crow era: Clooney's Everett would have been a black man passing for white who, in a final twist, returns to his black family in the end. And if the Coen brothers had taken more risks with their own casting and plotting in 2000, they might have cast a black actor for Pete or Delmar. Clooney's performance as a black man passing for white would more boldly, even controversially unsettle notions of authentic, discretely racialized genres

19. The three white protagonists wear blackface and plot their rescue of Tommy Johnson from the Klan by posing as the Klan's color guard.

by exposing the performative dimensions of whiteness and blackness that are naturalized in those designations. I walk this possibility out with the caveat that passing does not transcend sedimented discursive categories of black and white, rather, in some ways, it conserves the status quo: in many passing narratives, whiteness and blackness operate as discrete identities that the passer volitionally performs (Wald, *Crossing*, 6–7). However, when it comes to notions of racial authenticity and the ways, in this case, that an authentic aura is produced within the standard story of folk music, Everett's passing would show whiteness to be a performance that covers over black sources and practitioners within the genre. With an African American actor playing the role of Delmar or Pete, the political contours of the film would change in other ways as well. When the men save Tommy from the KKK, the scene would constitute a fantastical enactment of interracial solidarity against the domestic fascist, racist power-structure, one closer to the radical energies of the Popular Front, instead of the film's recycling of the white liberal savior cliché (read "good" white populism). While this change would do little to trouble the masculine contours of the film and its Popular Front precedent, it would still represent a more compelling narrative than the current resolution. Finally, with this change of cast and characters, Johnson would no longer simply be the authentic black supplement to a group of white singers but a member of an integrated band. He might be given something to play and perform beyond the guitar, such as a personality at odds with the myth of the bluesman. These alterations not only would seize upon the anarchic energies of modernist burlesque but they would complicate and advance the film's central thesis about folk music and the politics of race and authenticity.

In its current structure, *O Brother Where Art Thou?* establishes the miscegenated origins of roots music through the sonic blending of black and white voices and different regional styles alongside the invocation of visually discrete, mythical black and white bodies (Robert Johnson and Ulysses, to name but a few). In my hypothetical version, the film would compound the invisible proximity, fluidity, even interchangeability of black and white voices with the inclusion of a character who in his racial passing confounds the actual audience's proclivities for reading race visually. Rather than rendering the music colorblind or universalist, the film in its "valentine to the music" would destabilize the notions of racial authenticity that blunt the music's historical complexity, political force, and emotional power (Joel Coen, qtd. in Turan, "With the Coens," para. 7). Such a move would sharpen the film's satirical edge, earning its Depression-era inheritance, not just on style points but in substance, by implicating the audience directly in the fun house mirror of authenticity, its immanent marketability, and its many performances. This is the legacy bequeathed us by Sturges, Hurston, West, Schuyler, and others. When we look back to the thirties, perhaps even with nostalgia, what may be most important to our new-millennial moment is not that period's noble folk, its populist purities, or its claim to authentic aesthetics but rather its deft critique of those constructs as they operate within the public sphere of politics, culture, and the marketplace.

Notes

1. "This 'rediscovery of culture' did not begin with the Depression," Jonathan Veitch reminds us, "rather, it was part of an ongoing response to the corrosive process of modernization that has . . . constituted American life since its very beginnings" (*American Superrealism*, 90).

2. Joseph Stalin's decree in 1932, "On the Reconstruction of Literature and Art Organization," paved the way for the adoption of socialist realism as the official state platform on cultural production during the First Congress of Soviet Writers held in Moscow in 1934 (Wood, "Realisms," 321).

3. Riffing on Jeffrey Weiss's term "music hall modernism" for the influence of the music hall on the art movements of the French avant-garde, Michael North uses the term "modernist burlesque" (152–53) in his brilliant *Reading 1922: A Return to the Scene of the Modern* to describe an irreverent, even "obscene" aesthetic "that linked modernism and popular culture in an alliance against the censor" (151). Championed by Gilbert Seldes, E. E. Cummings, and the group of friends and contributors who published and edited *The Dial*, modernist burlesque embraced "a model of ironic juxtaposition in which quick transitions between the high and the low, the comic and the bathetic, the artistic and the commercial deflate pretensions and level out specious distinctions" (152). Much to the delight of its practitioners, the "effrontery" and "impudence" of this mode infuriated state and regional censors who closely followed the movie and literary publishing industries in "the cultural war of 1922" (151). I am indebted to Alys Weinbaum and Gillian Harkins for suggesting the term "burlesque modernism" as a concept metaphor for reading the work of George Schuyler, Nathanael West, and other satirists of the period.

4. In Henry Louis Gates's famous elaboration of signifying, it is the trope of all tropes in the black vernacular tradition, one that "turns on repetition of formal structures and their differences" (*Figures*, 235–36). Speaking of Esu, the Signifying Monkey, Gates describes how he and other tricksters are "mediators, and their mediations are tricks" (237).

5. Here I follow the anthropologists George E. Marcus and Michael M. J. Fischer in their connection between ethnographic and documentary modes of representation in the thirties, finding them to be mutually related forms of cultural critique within the United States in the 1920s and 1930s. As they explain, both modes met the public's "hunger for reliable information"

(*Anthropology*, 125) with the "documentation or the description of reality," producing empirical evidence that was taken to be "more or less self-explanatory" (127).

6. In Cedric Robinson's formative conception, "The development, organization and expansion of capitalist society pursued essentially racial directions, and so too did social ideology. As a material force, then, it could be expected that racialism would inevitably permeate the social structures emergent from capitalism. I have used the term 'racial capitalism' to refer to this development and to the subsequent structure as a historical agency" (*Black Marxism*, 2).

7. Jeff Decker demonstrates how the phrase *the American Dream* was not a transhistorical concept but rather "a term invented *after* the 1920s" to represent "the moral vacuity of entrepreneurial self-making in the nation's past" (*Made in America*, 80).

8. This is not to confuse populist rhetoric with populist politics. Following Denning's distinction, liberals and radicals of the Popular Front deployed several "discordant" populist rhetorics of the folk and the worker but followed "a class-based labor politics" (*Cultural Front*, 125).

9. Though "the worker" and "the people" were distinct phrases, in the 1930s they resonated with each other enough to justify their substitution, at least to some on the Left, like Burke. At the same time, the reason Burke proposed this substitution had to do with the different popular valences of each phrase: "I am suggesting that an approach based upon the positive symbol of 'the people,' rather than upon the negative symbol of 'the worker,' makes more naturally for this kind of identification whereby one's political alignment is fused with broader cultural elements" (Burke, "Revolutionary Symbolism," 91).

10. Regina Bendix notes how Herder, "in his collection of folksongs, organized into ethnic categories . . . worked with national characterizations" (*In Search*, 41). She translates his assertion in *The Spirit of Hebrew Poetry* (1782): "To judge a nation, does one not need to step in its time, its country, its circle of thought and feeling" (qtd. in Bendix, 41). While he develops these national characterizations, he argues against historical presentism and prefigures a kind of temporal, cultural relativism that would take hold in the discipline of anthropology in the twentieth century. Herder claims, for example, in his *Another Philosophy of History for the Education of Mankind* (1774), that "it would be foolishness to tear *a single Egyptian virtue* away from the land, the time, and the boyhood of the human spirit and to measure it by the *standard of another time*! . . . It should be our first concern to see him in none but *his own place*" (14).

11. Edward B. Tylor's cultural evolutionary model postulated that all societies developed through four stages of progress: savagery, barbarism, civilization, and the yet to be realized enlightenment (McNeil, "Pre-Society American Folklorists," 3).

12. For example, Henry Rowe Schoolcraft assembled and eventually pub-

lished a collection of American Indian oral narratives in the 1840s; William Francis Allen collaborated with Charles Pickard Ware and Lucy McKim to assemble and publish *Slave Songs of the United States* in 1867; and Will W. Harney and Mary N. Murfee composed stories of Appalachia's "strangeness" in the 1870s and 1880s (McNeil 2–4; Zumwalt, *American Folklore Scholarship*, 6; Becker, *Selling Tradition*, 55).

13. Here, Du Bois departs from Herder's views on race—which is to say that Herder denied the very existence of race as such—as Ernest Allen points out ("On the Reading of Riddles," 59–62).

14. Stalin's expansive visual propaganda campaign presumed that folk iconography would appeal to the peasants from the countryside who were being compelled to join a labor force of either industrial workers or newly collectivized farm workers (Bonnell, *Iconography*, 111–12). As Victoria Bonnell explains, "The application of traditional folk styles to Soviet posters was a controversial issue in the 1930s, when artists and officials were eager to create an entirely new 'proletarian' style of political art. Despite the controversy, however, the *lubok* format, with such characteristic conventions as contrasting panels showing 'then and now' and 'we and they,' was commonly utilized in the 1930s" (111–12).

15. The term *documentary* was first used in 1926 by the British filmmaker John Grierson, the director of *Drifters* (1929) and producer of *Night Mail* (1936). In Grierson's review of Robert Flaherty's *Moana* (1926), he claims that the film, "being a visual account of events in the daily life of a Polynesian youth . . . has *documentary* value" (emphasis added; Stott, *Documentary Expression*, 9). As Abigail Solomon-Godeau establishes in her now-classic essay on documentary practice, "Who Is Speaking Thus? Some Questions about Documentary Photography": "Because the majority of photographic uses previous to the term's introduction were what we would now automatically designate as documentary, it becomes clear that the documentary concept is historical, not ontological. . . . The late arrival of the category documentary into photographic parlance implies that until its formulation, photography was understood as innately and inescapably performing a documentary function. . . . [T]o nineteenth century minds the very notion of documentary photography would have seemed tautological" (169–70).

16. This claim follows Raymond Williams's description of genre: "It is in the practical and variable combination and even fusion of what are, in abstraction, different levels of the social material process that what we have known as genre becomes a new kind of constitutive evidence" (*Marxism and Literature*, 185).

17. Gayle Wald's caveat with regard to the political work of performativity is crucial here. In a discussion of films of racial passing from the 1940s that feature white actors playing black characters who pass for white, Wald tracks the dizzying dismantling and consolidation of race in these performances: "Brandishing the performativity of race, [such films] do not provide the key to its undoing as a strategy of social power; rather, they drama-

tize the ability of racial discourse openly and self-consciously to display its performativity as merely one more demonstration of its power" (*Crossing the Line*, 95).

18. See Bakhtin, "Introduction," 15, for his elucidation of the carnivalesque.

19. Slavoj Žižek argues: "What characterizes populism is . . . the mere formal fact that, through their enchainment, 'people' emerges as a political subject, and all different particular struggles and antagonisms appear as parts of a global antagonistic struggle between 'us' (people) and 'them.' Again, the content of 'us' and 'them' is not prescribed in advance but, precisely [in] the stakes of the struggle for hegemony; even ideological elements like brutal racism and anti-Semitism can be enchained in a populist series of equivalences, in the way 'them' is constructed" ("Against the Populist Temptation," 553–54).

20. In making this critique, I join other scholars of liberal affect. See Hartman, *Scenes of Subjection*, 17–23; and G. Wald, *Crossing the Line*, 168–77, for example.

21. As is well known, over the course of the decade Schuyler would turn away from his consumer activism and his socialist perspective, becoming ever more entrenched in anticommunist dogma.

22. Here, I have in mind, among others, Rita Barnard's *The Great Depression and the Culture of Abundance* (1995), Sara Blair's *Harlem Crossroads* (2007), Michael Denning's *The Cultural Front* (1997), Brent Hayes Edwards's *The Practice of Diaspora* (2003), Barbara Foley's *Radical Representations* (1993) and *Spectres of 1919* (2008), Rena Fraden's *Blueprints for a Black Federal Theatre, 1935–1939* (1994), Robin D. G. Kelley's *Hammer and Hoe* (1990), William Maxwell's *New Negro, Old Left* (1999), Bill V. Mullen's *Popular Fronts* (1999), Cary Nelson's *Repression and Recovery* (1989), Paula Rabinowitz's *Labor and Desire* (1991) and *They Must Be Represented* (1994), James Smethurst's *The New Red Negro* (1999), Michelle Stephens's *Black Empire* (2005), Jonathan Veitch's *American Superrealism* (1997), and Alan Wald's trilogy of the American literary Left, including *Exiles from a Future Time* (2002) and *Trinity of Passion* (2007), and Mary Helen Washington's forthcoming *Recovering Black Radicalism(s)*.

CHAPTER 1: MADHOUSE, BURLESQUE SHOW,
CONEY ISLAND

1. Interestingly, Charles Houston, the black lawyer who would act as chief legal counsel for the NAACP and mastermind the civil rights cases leading up to the *Brown* decision of 1954, felt quite differently about the International Labor Defense's activism in the *Scottsboro* case. As the historian Patricia Sullivan describes, Houston predicted that the *Scottsboro* case would be a "milestone" in American history: Houston explained that "[the ILD's] uncompromising resistance to southern prejudice set a new standard for agita-

tion for equality" (qtd. in *Days of Hope*, 88). Sullivan observes that the *Scottsboro* case "exposed the inadequacy of the NAACP's approach to the South. When news of the arrest . . . reached New York in the spring of 1931, Walter White had no local contacts to call on for a direct report. The nearest NAACP branch, in Chattanooga, had collapsed in 1930. White followed the case in the press, which relied primarily on southern newspapers, and the NAACP remained aloof. [The NAACP would only later try] to wrest control of the case from [the ILD who] had acted boldly and decisively" (87).

2. In a November column of "Views and Reviews" in 1933, Schuyler cast a hopeful eye on Roosevelt's National Recovery Administration, asking, "Who, acquainted with the American scene and especially our history, will deny that the country is sweeping on steadily toward collectivism?" (10). Schuyler asserts that "in the success of the NRA . . . I see hope for a revived and stronger Socialist party." At the same time, he chastises other radicals who protest Roosevelt's policies, dismissing them as "lunatic fringe Communists" whose only difference from socialists is "their [prior] advocacy of violent revolution . . . ten years ago."

3. In Schuyler's 1924 review of Upton Sinclair's *The Goslings*, he bluntly states his political sympathies: "If the majority of people in this country, white and black, are to be anything besides propertyless, exploited morons, then all workers must unite in One Big Union and see that this country of the people, by the politicians, for the plutocracy, is returned to those who perform the useful labor—the Workers" ("New Books," 331).

4. One of Ward Connerly's more recent efforts was California's rejected Proposition 54, on the ballots in 2003. That measure promised to "end government's preferential treatment based on race . . . junk a 17th-century racial classification system that has no place in 21st-century America, [and] . . . signal America's first step towards a color-blind society" (Proposition 54: www.racialprivacy.org).

5. Patterson's claims seem so intentionally fantastical that they read as a kind of straight-faced sociological parody. Indeed, if his editorial was meant to be read in that spirit, it makes all the more sense to look to Schuyler's work as a literary precursor. Setting tone aside, Patterson's very formulation of the disappearance of race depends upon its conjoined operation with class—the affluence required for purchasing this genetic engineering—as well as the meeting of science and the marketplace. In essence, his positing of racial hybridism points to a new racial category to be capitalized upon within consumer culture. It also strangely echoes Ralph Ellison's claim that "the fantasy of an America free of blacks is at least as old as the dream of creating a truly democratic society" (qtd. in Roediger, *Black on White*, 160). While Patterson's answer to racist oppression in the United States is reductive in its binary logic and romance of the market as a place of self-determination, it is motivated by a desire, facetious or earnest, to imagine a way in which oppressed people might transcend racial differences to affiliate around common class interests.

6. Ironically, if Schuyler's *Black No More* were read through the lens of his later political beliefs and affiliations, he might appear as a consistent advocate of colorblindness as well. In fact, Schuyler's political transformation throughout his life, from iconoclastic socialist to outspoken John Birch Society member, strangely parallels the political spectrum between Orlando Patterson on one side, and the black neocons on the other.

7. Michael Denning defines the modern racial regime as a "formation that emerged in the years after the Civil War. The end of systems of forced labor in the 1860s . . . marked not only a remarkable expansion of global labor migration and the rise of the 'new imperialism' in the late nineteenth century, but also the birth of the modern racial systems with their legal codes of segregation, exclusion, reservations, and anti-miscegenation" (*Cultural Front*, 33).

8. For scholarship that examines the relationship between race, consumer culture, and capitalism in the Harlem Renaissance, see Carby's *Reconstructing Womanhood* (163–75) and *Cultures in Babylon* (7–63); Griffin, *Who Set You Flowin'*; and Mullen, "Optic White."

9. See, for example, Huggins's *Harlem Renaissance* and *Voices from the Harlem Renaissance*; Lewis, *When Harlem Was in Vogue*; Wintz, *Harlem Renaissance*; and the selection of Schuyler's writings offered in *The Norton Anthology of African American Literature*, 2nd ed. In noting Schuyler's peculiar absence, I sound a common refrain in the small body of criticism about the book. Michael E. Peplow makes this observation first in his 1974 article: "In this era of renewed interest in the Harlem Renaissance . . . *Black No More* is virtually ignored" ("George Schuyler," 242–43).

10. Several critics usefully track a sustained critique of the racial discourse of the period in *Black No More*. See, for example, Kuenz, "American Racial Discourse"; Morgan, " 'Strange and Wonderful' "; Favor, "Color"; and, most recently, Ferguson's literary history of Schuyler, which includes a chapter devoted to *Black No More*'s critique of race mythology (*Sage of Sugar Hill*, 212–44). The essay by Mills ("Absurdity of America") and the essay by Kuenz take up the links between race, capitalism, and nationalism, a rubric I take up in this chapter. Kuenz's fine essay asserts: "By recoding racial markers as class signs and showing throughout the novel their structural inability *as* signs, Schuyler situates both 'blackness' and 'whiteness' in relation to an industrial and market economy increasingly willing and able to manipulate and finally obliterate any semblance of culture, tradition and individual identity, racial or otherwise, among the people it needs to keep itself going" (171). In an excellent essay whose concerns also overlap with my own, Jason Haslam focuses on Schuyler's "economics of race" explicitly in terms of white privilege to demonstrate the ways "in which the class system and bigoted racial categories both create and are created by each other, in a seemingly endless cycle of reproduction" (" 'Open sesame,' " 16). My argument diverges from Keunz's and Haslam's and draws upon Harryette Mullen's brilliant essay "Optic White" in its emphasis on the mechanics of racial

reproduction and the relationship between Fordism, race, and commodity culture in the novel.

11. For works that read *Black No More* through Schuyler's later conservative politics, see, for example, Bone, *Negro Novelist*; Larson, "Introduction"; Faulkner, "Vanishing Race"; and Tucker, " 'Can Science Succeed?' " In regard to Schuyler's collusion with conservative interpretations of his earlier work, in *Black and Conservative*, an autobiography he publishes in the mid-sixties toward the end of his life, he downplays his leftist political affiliations (Peplow, *George Schuyler*, 20).

12. As Thomas Holt describes, "Henry Ford was a segregationist and an anti-Semite, but he set out to hire blacks for his plants, working through the Urban League and prominent black ministers in Detroit. Outstripping all other automakers, Ford's aggressive recruitment garnered about half of all blacks in the auto industry during the interwar period, peaking in the 1930s at 11 percent of the entire workforce at the infamous River Rouge Plant" (*Problem of Race*, 71).

13. Grace Hale's history of whiteness and segregation attributes white people's acute anxieties about black participation in mass consumer culture to the fact that consumption is "so central to changing conceptions of American citizenship" (*Making Whiteness*, 284). Greater standardization of and access to these goods threatened to merge the nation's consumers together as one body of buyers, sparking "white fears of a raceless consumer society" (203). As Hale argues, this integration signaled for southern whites the threat of another kind of bodily incorporation: miscegenation. Thus, within the social body of the nation, as increasingly defined at the turn of the century by its marketplace, white supremacist anxiety turns once again to narratives of biological reproduction and an attendant fixation on racial purity.

14. For a discussion of Jean Toomer's ambivalent formulation of the disappearance of "the Negro of the folk-song" with the advent of the modern New Negro of Seventh Street, see North (*Dialect of Modernism*, 166–74). For a discussion of Hurston's folklore collecting and her fears about the effects of commercialization upon rural, African American vernacular culture, see Hemenway (*Zora Neale Hurston*, 84–103).

15. My reading is indebted to Smith's brilliant analysis of Hughes's argument and, more generally, her assessment of the discourse of racial authenticity in relation to the black middle-class in films of the 1990s. See V. Smith, "Authenticity" (65–67).

16. Ian Haney Lopez includes an appendix to his *White By Law*, documenting the U.S. courts' decisions in the racial prerequisite cases from 1878 to 1952 according to an array of potentially contradictory rationales: "scientific evidence," "common knowledge," "legal precedent," "congressional intent," and "ocular inspection of the skin" (203–8).

17. Daphne Brooks provided this insight in correspondence, 21 July 2007.

18. The story of minstrelsy and blackface performance is thus the subject of

a variety of rich scholarly interpretations—in *Love and Theft*, Eric Lott locates in the form a volatile, complex relay between love and theft that amounted to a transgression of the color line; in *Blackface, White Noise*, Michael Rogin explores the ways in which newly immigrated Eastern European Jews in the early days of cinema used blackface performances to produce themselves as white; in *Raising Cain*, W. T. Lahmon Jr. investigates how the form's lore cycle deployed both for and against racial stereotyping and different class interests; in *Bodies in Dissent*, Daphne Brooks demonstrates how the subversive and incendiary performances of turn-of-the-century blackface entertainers such as George Walker and Bert Williams "scripted alien(ated) racial and gender narratives for a new era"; and in *The Last Darky*, Louis Chude-Sokei attends to the ways that Bert Williams's cross-cultural, intra-racial masquerade "reinvented and appropriated [blackface minstrelsy] to subversive effect" (Brooks, *Bodies*, 12; Chude-Sokei, *Last Darky*, 5).

19. Cohen, *Consumer's Republic*, 151–53; Cross, *All-Consuming Century*, 19.

20. In a certain sense, these products emerge out of an ipso facto "market segmentation" due to Jim Crow segregation. As such, they anticipate the turn away from a conception of a unified mass market toward a theory of a "segmented market" that will be capitalized on in the booming postwar economy of the 1950s. See Cohen, *Consumer's Republic*, 295.

21. Cohen, *Making a New Deal*, 154–55; Dinerstein, *Swinging the Machine*, 137–81; Du Bois, *Souls of Black Folk*, 162–64.

22. Cohen, *Making a New Deal*, 155–58. When segregation was legally mandated and many sites of consumption reflected this, producers assumed a unified mass consumer who was, contradictorily, both white and middle-class. On the heels of the *Brown* decision in 1954—the decision that in theory, if not in practice, would lead to an integrated consumer body—in 1957 marketers came upon the idea of "market segmentation," which cross-cuts the marketplace into many categories of social difference such as race, age, region, class, religion, and lifestyle. This convergence strikes me as more than coincidental. Cohen, *Consumer's Republic*, 292–344.

23. Once he becomes white, Schuyler's protagonist, Max Disher, thinks, "Now he could go anywhere, associate with anybody, be anything he wanted to be. . . . At last he felt like an American citizen" (27–29).

24. In the history of antebellum slavery it has long been understood that people of African descent were treated as objects of racialized property, bought and sold as commodities on the auction circuit. C. Harris's path-breaking analysis demonstrates the various ways that whiteness has been shored up as "a highly valued and exclusive form of property" from the nation's inception onward ("Whiteness as Property," 1724).

25. Weinbaum, *Wayward Reproductions*, 34–39, 15–60.

26. Alys Weinbaum pointed out the "uplift" resonance of the Black-No-More procedure in conversation, 22 March 2005. For more on the many valences of racial uplift, see Gaines, *Uplifting the Race*.

27. Here, I improvise on Orlando Patterson's conception of slavery as "social death" in his important *Slavery and Social Death* (38–45). Patterson claims that slavery represented "two modes of . . . social death . . . in the intrusive mode the slave was conceived of as someone who did not belong because he was an outsider, while in the extrusive mode the slave became an outsider because he did not (or no longer) belonged" (44). The intrusive mode of social death describes the slave who is thought to be the "enemy within." In *Black No More*, as we soon see, the African Americans who have undergone Crookman's process suffer a kind of social death in their newfound whiteness; they have committed a form of race suicide. Moreover, they are perceived by white supremacists as enemies within: "Why, one couldn't tell who was who!" (81).

28. The notion of whiteness as a mass-produced racial formation is reiterated by other African American writers as well. For example, James Baldwin compared the process of becoming white to remaining "trapped in [a] factory" (qtd. in Roediger, *Black on White*, 22).

29. In the character of Max, Schuyler satirizes the fiction of passing, in particular, James Weldon Johnson's *The Autobiography of an Ex-Colored Man* (1912), providing us with a trickster protagonist who revels in the joke played on the unwitting white public with far less ambivalence than Johnson's unnamed narrator (Wald, *Crossing the Line*, 36; Favor, "Color," 49).

30. For analyses of the state regulation of race, property, and sexuality, see Hartman, *Scenes*, 98–99, 183–91; Mullen, "Optic White," 73, 76–77, 81; and Weinbaum, *Wayward Reproductions*, 36, 15–60.

31. In an editorial titled "The Caucasian Problem," published in 1944, Schuyler would write, "Race, an anthropological fiction, has become a sociological fact" (49).

32. See Amy Robinson's nuanced discussion of the hegemonic dupe in her performative theory of reading identity ("It Takes One," 725–28, 734–36).

33. In a routine that brilliantly and efficiently send ups this idea, Chris Rock addresses a common complaint voiced by white people, "Affirmative action, illegal aliens . . . we're losing the country." He responds: "White people ain't losing shit. If y'all losing, who's winning? Shit, there ain't a white man in this room that would change places with me. None of you would change places with me. And I'm rich! That's how good it is to be white. There's a white, one-legged busboy in here right now . . . that won't change places with my black ass. He's going, 'No, man, I don't wanna switch. I wanna ride this white thing out. See where it takes me.' That's right, 'cause when you white, the sky's the limit. When you black, the limit's the sky!" *Chris Rock: Bigger and Blacker*. Daphne Brooks provided me with this reference in correspondence, 21 July 2007.

34. Schuyler himself "got up on speaking ladders and addressed the indifferent populace in the downtown area [of Syracuse]" when he was the educational director of the local Syracuse Socialist Party in the early 1920s (*Black and Conservative*, 113–15).

35. See George Lipsitz's elaboration of the "possessive investment in whiteness" and the ways it has produced racial hierarchies in the United States (*Possessive Investment*, 1–25).

36. Schuyler chooses obvious and absurd names for both characters, names that speak to the subtext of their life's work: Snobbcraft literally crafts laws that produce and maintain his own elitist, racist position. Buggerie's name alludes to sodomy between men as it was referred to in several state constitutions within colonial America (see "Rhode Island, Section 37" in Lutz's *Colonial Origins*). Not surprisingly, he develops statistics that eventually reveal the intimate, often subterranean interracial relationships that have made up America's population from its colonial beginnings onward.

37. Blum, *W. E. B. Du Bois*, 134–80.

38. In her important investigation of race and reproduction, Mullen describes how in Ellison's *Invisible Man*, Mohammed's myth of Yakub, and Schuyler's *Black No More*, these "technological fantasies feature mechanical production as an asexual reproduction of whiteness, which is not dependent upon the coupling of a black woman with a white man (thus excluding the black male) or upon the coupling of a black man with a white woman (thus risking the castration of the black male). In these technological metaphors/ fantasies, miscegenation is effected without sexual reproduction" ("Optic White," 77). In a related theoretical project, Weinbaum's *Wayward Reproductions* makes a crucial intervention in feminist scholarship about race and reproduction by excavating what she refers to as the "race/reproduction bind" (especially 5–14, 15–60, 187–226, 227–46).

39. Women's bodies were regulated within the racialized and patriarchal strictures of U.S. law due to their potentially unpredictable reproduction and transmission of racial property in the form of progeny, be they heirs, slaves, or both.

40. Teresa Zackodnik usefully complicates this legal history by tracing revisions within antimiscegenation law during the colonial period that accounted for the possibility of white mothers and black fathers alongside the more prevalent interracial coupling of white fathers and black mothers. In order to prevent mulattoes from claiming whiteness and its attendant privileges, these statutes stipulated that in the case of a biracial child born of a freeborn white mother and an enslaved black father, the child would be held in bond by the father's masters. Thus, the mother's claim to whiteness did not extend to her child. In fact, she could lose her white privilege as a result of her intimate association with a black man ("Fixing the Color Line," 426–29). See also Hartman, *Scenes*, 190; Weinbaum 41.

41. As Smith explains in her "Class and Gender in Narratives of Passing," the consequences of passing "are distributed differentially on the basis of gender (women in narrative are more likely to be punished for passing than are men)" (36).

42. Gayle Wald writes of *Pinky* and *Lost Boundaries*, Hollywood's famous

films in 1949 about racial passing: "Brandishing the performativity of race, they do not provide the key to its undoing as a strategy of social power; rather, they dramatize the ability of racial discourse openly and self-consciously to display its performativity as merely one more demonstration of its power" (95). This assessment pertains to the particular fungibility of race in the marketplace.

43. H. L. Mencken would also describe his readership of the *American Mercury*, the magazine he founded in 1924, as a "civilized minority," a shared usage that anticipates an intellectual exchange with Schuyler that would last until the late 1940s (Ferguson 163–64).

44. See Bone (*Negro Novelist*) and Larson ("Introduction") for an interpretation of the novel as assimilationist, and Rayson ("George Schuyler") for an overarching interpretation of Schuyler's career and *Black No More* within it, that asserts his priority of class over and above race. Conversely, Tucker's analysis sees Schuyler deconstructing essentialist definitions of race in *Black No More* in order to suggest that " 'race' just does not matter anymore" in a prefiguration of the work of the black neocons who espouse colorblindness (" 'Can Science Succeed?' " 148). This reading ignores Schuyler's trenchant critique of the ways race and class work together in the service of inequitable social and economic structures.

CHAPTER 2: INANIMATE HIDEOSITIES

1. Even during the height of West's revival by the New York intellectuals during the Cold War, a few writers refused to depoliticize his work. The leftwing writer Josephine Herbst, one of West's close friends, cautioned against this in an exceptionally perceptive appraisal of his work that she wrote for *Kenyon Review* in 1961. Specifically, she faults James Light for his tendency "to reflect more of the climate of the '50s than of the era in which West lived, felt or created. The penitents of that earlier decade have poured lava over some of the living elements which should once again be seen in their original verdure to make sense of the time and the place. No matter the eventualities—no matter the errors—the conflicting ideologies—the tragedies. To see what West used and discarded one must return to the Then and strip away the Now" (in Martin, *Nathanael West: A Collection*, 25). Similarly, in "Late Thoughts on Nathanael West" published in 1965, Daniel Aaron warns that "to see West as a misunderstood and neglected 'taker-outer' shouldered into obscurity by the more celebrated 'putter-inners' is to exaggerate his singularity. . . . Being a radical in the 1930's (and West was a faithful subscriber to Party manifestoes) did not necessarily mean that one had to write ritualistic proletarian novels or Whitmanesque exhortations to revolt. There was another kind of writing, Edward Dahlberg called it 'implication literature' tinged with 'just as deep radical dye.' West belonged to that select

company of socially committed writers in the Depression Decade who drew revolutionary conclusions in highly idiosyncratic and undoctrinaire ways" (in Martin, *Nathanael West: A Collection*, 162).

2. For a concise comparison of Barnard's, Irr's, and Veitch's treatments of West's fiction, see Eric Schocket's review "Revising the 1930s." Each of these critics valuably reads West's work in relation to the Frankfurt school. My analysis dovetails most closely with Rachel Rubinstein's fine examination of West's burlesque of the commercial and patriotic value of racial and ethnic commodities.

3. Given West's own dedication to burlesque and vaudeville, both as a fan and as a writer of the absurd and the grotesque, his purported dislike of "Jewish stage humor" is surprising and it raises useful questions about the grounds for his objection (Martin 237–38). Was West troubled by the commodification of Jewishness in the form of stereotypes played for laughs, a mode of representation he himself would throw in the face of his readers, or did he subscribe to a stereotypical equation of "commercial spirit" with Judaism such that the performance of Jewishness for a paying audience reinforced this belief for him? In either case, West's own line of work as a screenwriter would have presented him with a challenge.

4. Jay Martin suggests that "the Weinsteins gave up their Judaism with their emigration. . . . [N]ow they would become American" (25). To that end, Martin describes how "the assumptions at the heart of American life . . . told them they might escape from the pale of Jewishness through the equality of the informed mind and economic achievement. . . . Their hopes . . . admirably coincided with the American dream of success. It is not surprising that before West was ten, his parents gave him presents of Horatio Alger's books" (24). In retrospect, the gift of the Alger books made a deep impression on West, though clearly not the impression his parents were seeking.

5. I am indebted to Lloyd Michaels's essay "A Particular Kind of Joking" for its formulation of West's use of burlesque as "a stylistic device" and a "way of seeing life as a particular kind of theatrical performance" (149).

6. In aligning West's writing with his progressive political activism, his life's work seems to advocate for acting passionately, even in the face of potential futility. In this way, we might understand his leftist commitments as a politicized existentialism.

7. Though I disagree with Veitch's account of West "[attempting] to carve out a middle ground between 'radical presses' like the *New Masses* on the one hand and the 'literature boys' at *Partisan Review* on the other," I concur with Veitch's conclusion that West's fiction "offers one of the most insightful critiques of the inhumanity of capitalism during the thirties" (*American Superrealism*, xii, xvi).

8. Jerry Bryant makes a passing remark in his book *Victims and Heroes* (1997) that Schuyler's *Black No More* is a "mordant parody" set in a "zany, impossible pseudo-fiction world that anticipates Nathanael West's mad Horatio Alger travesty *A Cool Million*" (149).

9. Jonathan Veitch uses Thurman Arnold's term, "the folklore of capitalism," to describe the object of West's satire in *A Cool Million* (5, 94). I modify the phrase here to focus on "the folklore of racial capitalism" in the novel.

10. West focuses on the body as a key site of state-sanctioned violence. As the cultural critic Lauren Berlant and others have demonstrated, within a constitutional paradigm of citizenship the implicitly white, male, property-owning American subject is accorded "the disembodied entitlements of liberal citizenship" ("The Queen," 552). Thus, Lem's public embodiment is a sign of his inability to attain "abstract national 'personhood'" (553).

11. In its early years, the Farm Security Administration photographic file contained many photographs of women and children in migrant settlements that notably lacked a male presence. Instead of depicting unemployed, idle, and therefore emasculated men in direct juxtaposition with the women they would support in a heteronormative family structure, the most popular images in the file avoided picturing the men at all. As viewers, we are to assume that the men are out looking for work: thus, their very absence suggests that they are deserving of government aid. Consider Dorothea Lange's photograph of a woman and her child, chosen for the cover of the 1939 edition of Steinbeck's *The Grapes of Wrath*: while Lange took several photographs of the woman and child along with her husband, this was the image most widely used out of the series. The woman looks directly into the camera with a penetrating stare; the child's gaze mirrors his mother's as he nurses at her breast. The woman nourishes her child, even under these impoverished conditions; in keeping with a distribution of work based upon traditional gender roles, as she performs this sacrosanct maternal duty, we are to assume that her husband is either out working or looking for work. By cropping him out of the picture, the image reinforces a gendered private/public division based upon a configuration of domestic and work spaces as distinct feminine and masculine spheres. In photographs later in the decade portraying FSA success stories, the clients perform traditionally gendered labor, suggesting that capitalism and patriarchy are once again properly accommodating systems.

12. Rita Barnard concentrates on West's visit in 1933 to the Chicago World's Fair "A Century of Progress," while Jonathan Veitch focuses on West's failed attempt to mount a Broadway musical revue entitled *American Chauve Souris* (Barnard, *Great Depression*, 150–54; Veitch 88–91).

13. In view of the close relationship between popular theater and fiction in the nineteenth century, seen most overtly in the narrativization of stage productions into dime novels, the inclusion of both mediums in each novel is not surprising (Denning, *Mechanic Accents*, 24).

14. Interestingly, Jolson's famous blackface routine facilitated the assimilation of his immigrant Jewishness into unmarked American whiteness and Walker's successful cosmetics line provided the means for women of color and white ethnics to lighten their skin tone and straighten their hair in accordance with hegemonic standards of white beauty (Rogin, *Blackface*, 95).

15. Michael Denning writes of the "technological revolution [in printing] in the 1830s and 1840s; the spread of stereotyping eroded the skills of compositors and the new steam-powered presses not only displaced many pressmen but increased the capital necessary for the larger printing plants" (18). As a result, the small printers beset with failing newspapers in the wake of this new technology turned to printing "highly-advertised story papers" and "pamphlet novels for a dime [and thus became] the first successful entrepreneurs of the cheap fiction industry." Later Denning writes of the form as the "first cheap, mass-produced, and national cultural medium" (207).

16. By "racial," Denning seems to mean "nonwhite." *Mechanic Accents* was first published in 1987, a date that precedes the creation of the discipline of whiteness studies.

17. Jeffrey Louis Decker historicizes the term "American Dream," first used in 1931, showing how "the concept was deployed not to celebrate but to critique, from the standpoint of the Great Depression, the moral bankruptcy of self-made industrialists in the Gilded Age" (*Made in America*, xxix).

18. Hurston uses her metaphor of the "unnatural museum" to demonstrate the reductive, racist tastes of the white publishing industry.

19. At the same time, West undercuts these non-Anglo-Saxon stereotypes. At one point, Lem and a new acquaintance, John, wander into "Mott Street and its environs, observing with considerable interest the curious customs and outlandish manners of that neighborhood's large oriental population" (123). John makes a racist joke to an old Asian man in keeping with the touristic thrill of their walk—"no tickee, no washee"—and "laughed foolishly in the manner of his kind." With this subtle switch in narration, the focus rests on the typology of John, Lem's white companion and "his kind's" instinctual foolishness. Fittingly, the old man replies "with great dignity, 'By the blessed beard of my grandfather, you're the lousiest pimple faced ape I ever did see'" (123–24).

20. Tourist interest in such exhibits of "living history" had already been established with the construction of Colonial Williamsburg (1926).

21. Jonathan Freedman observes that "this conflation of Jew and Chinese as economic players has a long history. . . . Herder 'explicitly compare[d] the Chinese to the Jews' not only on such matters as 'a prideful refusal to intermix and interbreed with other nations' but also on the grounds of their 'cunning industriousness and their talent for imitating anything their greed finds useful.' There's good reason for this conflation: like Jews, Chinese merchants were traditionally active throughout East and South Asia and faced—again like Jews—resentment, discrimination, and even the occasional pogrom as a result. And, perhaps not coincidentally, a similar mixture of industriousness and avarice runs throughout the representations of both groups, even as it is, in both cases, accompanied by language stressing a debasing sense of their dirt, filth, sexual deviancy" (Freedman, "Transgressions," 83).

22. Around the start of the twentieth century, middle-class reformers

used the image of white slavery to condemn the power of corporate trusts, comparing the exploitation of the working class by such monopolies to the exploitation of enslaved African Americans at the hands of corrupt planters (Keire, "Vice Trust," 7).

23. Veitch notes that "the rediscovery of America's folkways is indistinguishable from their exploitation," while Barnard compares this textual instance to the stance taken by West's "more orthodox Marxist contemporaries, who typically (and rather puritanically) associated consumerism with prostitution" (Veitch 91, 93; Barnard 147–48).

24. West ironically plays on the fact that many economic analysts felt that the gold standard was to blame for the collapse of financial institutions and the start of the Depression.

25. Jonathan Veitch analyzes in detail the script adapted from *A Cool Million* (Veitch 105–12).

CHAPTER 3: THE LAST AMERICAN FRONTIER

1. When I refer to the New Deal's larger documentary project, I include in this endeavor the Farm Security Administration's Photographic Unit and lesser known photo projects from other government agencies such as the United States Department of Agriculture, the Civilian Conservation Corps, the Rural Electrification Administration, and the Agricultural Adjustment Association, as well as w p a arts projects such as the Federal Theater and the Public Works of Art Program. For a more detailed account, see *Official Images: New Deal Photography*, ed. Pete Daniel, Merry A. Foresta, Maren Stange, and Sally Stein, as well as Barbara Melosh's *Engendering Culture*.

2. The w p a poster states: "AMERICAN GUIDE WEEK: STATE BY STATE THE WPA WRITERS' PROJECTS DESCRIBE AMERICA TO AMERICANS: Through these guides to the forty-eight states, Alaska, Puerto Rico, the District of Columbia, and the principal cities and major regions of the United States, citizens and visitors to our country now have at their fingertips, for the first time in our history, a series of volumes that ably illustrate our national way of life, yet at the same time portray variants in local patterns of living and regional development—President Roosevelt" ("American Guide Week").

3. Occasional exceptions occurred within this logic when specific communities of émigrés, like Florida's Cuban population, were deemed too recent and too "other" to be fully assimilated into America's "melting pot," a popular notion at the time.

4. A perfect illustration of the Guide Series' desire to produce and preserve difference as a condensation of the real occurs in a proposal for the study of folklore in New Mexico by the FWP: "There was a time when standardization was rampant and all efforts, social and economic, converged on the idea of making the country uniform to the point where Southwestern

villages would be identical to Middletown. Our art, our literature, and our music became one. Since then, however, we have become more appreciative of the differences in the various localities of the United States. In fact, we welcome a genuine distinction as something that should be preserved. The more genuine manifestation of true regional culture is embodied in the folklore production throughout the United States" (Weigle, "Finding the 'True America,'" 67).

5. The Public Works Administration took on road building and improvement as part of its larger imperative to provide work for the unemployed, enhance public welfare, build up the nation's infrastructure, and revitalize American industry.

6. Classic works such as Jerre Mangione's *The Dream and the Deal* and Monty Penkower's *The Federal Writers' Project* lay a crucial foundation for textual exploration of the guidebooks' representational politics, a challenge few critics have taken up.

7. Woods notes how "South Florida was in the forefront of a modernizing South with its economy driven by tourism, modern media and factory farms" (*Beyond the Architect's Eye*, 203).

8. One of the more notable shifts in the tourism of the twenties and thirties was the emergence of "tin-can tourists," vacationers who toured in their cars, staying in campgrounds or in trailer courts in metal trailers, and who ate food from tin cans (Stronge, *Sunshine Economy*, 88–89; Woods 215). This group of travelers also included migrant laborers in search of work.

9. The WPA's "American Guide Manual" was a lengthy set of instructions written for the state-level editorial staff to guide them in the composition of their regional guides. These instructions included information about condensing their descriptions, checking their entries for accuracy, and achieving the correct tone in their reportage.

10. The expanded mobility of the middle class was quite literal. The middle class constituted a new group of tourists able to afford automobiles and take advantage of the new public works highways. The "motel"—"a contraction of *motor* and *hotel*, with *motor hotel* the implied full form"— was invented in response to the burgeoning market of automobile tourism (Jakle, Sculle, and Rogers, *The Motel*, 18). To facilitate this growth industry and provide jobs for unemployed workers, in 1934, the New Deal's Public Works Project erected signs and markers for tourists and embarked upon a program of roadside beautification throughout the country (Weigle 61).

11. The Federal Writers' Project was interested in the relationship between folklore, contemporary culture, and democracy as well as the (re)definition of the term "American." It embraced a notion of cultural pluralism based upon earlier formulations of a "trans-national America" and "a federation of cultures" (Hirsch, "Cultural Pluralism," 50–51). As part of the FWP's program of national incorporation, the national editors called for an interpretation of culture that would consider individuals and groups American while acknowledging their specific regional and ethnic identities. At least in

theory, the FWP subscribed to a philosophy of cultural relativism espoused by anthropologists such as Franz Boas and Ruth Benedict, viewing culture as plural and historically conditioned, instead of the opposing dogma of cultural evolution, which emphasized a universal and hierarchical culture. For more about the Guide Series' commitment to ideas of cultural pluralism and cultural relativism, see Hirsch.

12. In the preface of the guidebook for Washington, D.C., the editors state: "In plan and scope, this series goes beyond the general concept of the conventional guidebook. Its objective is to present as complete a picture as possible of American communities, their political, economic, industrial, and cultural history, their contemporary scene, as well as the specific points of interest ordinarily sought out by the tourist. . . . [T]he main series of regional, State, and local guides . . . has been assembled by the Nationwide organization of the Federal Writers' Projects" (v).

13. For further general discussion, see chaps. 4 and 5 of Penkower's *The Federal Writers' Project* ("Writing the American Guide Series" and "Censorship" respectively), 75–116. For a specific exchange in August 1938 over the terminology of the "Civil War" pertaining to the Florida guide, see the examples of the correspondence between the state FWP director, Corita Doggett Corse; the secretary for the United Daughters of the Confederacy in Florida, Mary Branham; and the federal director of the FWP American Guide Series, Henry Alsberg. Note how Branham insists in her letter that "the term Civil War would be very prejudicial to the popularity of the publications in Florida or anywhere else in the South. The U.D.C greatly prefers the title 'War Between the States.' " See the "correspondence" link in para. 2 of the *New Deal Narratives: Visions of Florida*, "Historical Controversies," section of the web site created by Juliet Gorman.

14. Bold describes how "the American Guide Series birthed a national populist style" (*WPA Guides*, 9).

15. Here, I reiterate a central claim of my dissertation, "The 'Real' Collective in New Deal Documentary and Ethnography," 86–92. This is a point that critics such as Christine Bold take up as well (see *WPA Guides*, 31–32).

16. As William Stott describes, "The series does present a huge quantity of facts—so many that every reader finds in every guide much to him that is useless. To *him*. To someone else, those useless facts will be the heart of the work, will touch the soul of the country. And this is the excellence of the Guide Series: it presents an America that really is quite like a nation" (author's italics, 118). Underscoring the masculine profile of the guide's ideal citizen-reader, individual facts stand in for the interests of individual men. Every fact and every man stands for and is, in turn, defined by the democratic nation. America is what each man thinks it is, simultaneously: in this paradigm, the specific signification of each man's vision is not as crucial to a definition of America as the possibility for the *simultaneity of vision*. What we see here is a crucial slippage between the collection of guides, their collecting narrative practice, and the collective of the American public. "The

American Guide Manual" states as one of its primary aims: "While much of the material to be used by us is undoubtedly available, the Guide can perform a unique service by collecting the authentic Americana of every region" (supplement 7742-8).

17. Robert Toll describes how, after 1820, "entertainment became less formal in tone and turned to regional American folk culture for material to construct heroes for common Americans" (*Blacking Up*, 6). He argues that "before audiences defined blacks, in minstrelsy, they forged positive stage images of themselves" (13). This popular entertainment relied upon "native white folk types" such as the debunking Yankee, the boastful frontiersman, and the belligerent but egalitarian "urban 'common man' . . . Mose the B'howery B'hoy" (14–16).

18. Marion Post Wolcott's photographs are notable in this regard (Woods 214).

19. Continually represented in essentialist and paternalistic terms, African Americans are depicted as physical and often primitive folk: the "Literature" chapter of the guide states that "the Negro's part in Florida literature has progressed from the simple recording of slave days to thoughtful self-expression," describing Zora Neale Hurston's *Jonah's Gourd Vine* as "a simple story about her people" (146–47). In the "Folklore" chapter, the guide proclaims: "Muscular prowess is a tradition with the Negro, and feats of strength have become an important part of his lore" (132). A third striking example of this deployment and affirmation of stereotypes occurs in the "Music and Theater" chapter. While praising the complexity of African American music, especially in comparison to the "primitive music of the Seminoles," the guide simultaneously situates this cultural production in terms of essential traits and organic process: "Music always has been an emotional outlet for the Florida Negro, and his songs have multiplied and shaped themselves to his tasks, his tribulations, and his irrepressible spirits. . . . Composed in time of sorrow, joy, work, or imprisonment, [the work songs] illustrate the Negro's relief in rhythm" (149–50).

20. To momentarily adhere to the Florida guidebook's quantifying tendencies, its index illustrates the guide's discrepancy in representation between Latin Americans and its other folk groups—Latin Americans receive four page references (584), but there are approximately ninety page references to "Negroes" (588), seventy page references to "Indians" (582), and twenty page references to "crackers" (574).

21. Here I borrow the term from Johannes Fabian in his elaboration of the anthropologist's use of time in relation to the cultural other: "I will call it a denial of coevalness. By that I mean a persistent and systematic tendency to place the referent(s) of anthropology in a Time other than the present of the producer of anthropological discourse. . . . The unusual coeval, and especially the noun coevalness, express a need to steer between such closely related notions as synchronous/simultaneous and contemporary. I take synchronous to refer to events occurring at the same physical time; contempo-

rary asserts the co-occurrence in what I call typological time. Coeval . . . covers both ('of same age, duration or epoch')" (*Time and the Other*, 31).

22. This political and cultural characterization of Florida's geography is repeated in the "Agriculture" chapter. After explaining that "the growing season progresses from south to north," the passage concludes: "General farming is a minor occupation in peninsula-Florida, where vast stretches of pine land are broken by few clearings; but in the ante-bellum plantation region of upper Florida the scene is strikingly northern: farmhouses line the highways, fields are fenced, and livestock graze on hills" (79). The northern part of Florida, which resembles the South's plantations, duplicates the general farming practices of the North. In this instance, Florida's microcosmic organic environment mirrors the larger agricultural geography of the nation: the north part of the state matches the northern part of the country, though architecturally and spatially, it resembles the South. Florida functions as a palimpsest of regions traditionally posed as binary opposites.

23. In its "Newspapers and Radio" chapter, the guide critiques Florida's contemporary newspapers for being "thoroughly respectable and soft-voiced in their sentiments, although intensely sectional. Local boosting and bias took the form of ignoring rather than disparaging other communities" (125). The guide's example of taking every region into account stands in implicit contradistinction to this biased model; by noting these journalistic failures, it reveals its own text as a paragon of inclusivity and accuracy. The guide's method of implicit, self-congratulatory comparison is all the more clear several passages later: observing the general "chamber of commerce" orientation of Florida's newspapers, the guide notes that this "trend began with a taboo on the news of hurricanes, freezes, and anything calculated to scare off visitors"; it softens its critique, claiming that "in recent years the Florida press has treated such events more in accordance with their news value. . . . Flamboyant claims have mostly given way to constructive criticism of local affairs." Again, the guide reinforces its own authority by evaluating the veracity of Florida's most popular "truth-telling" source, the newspaper.

24. In fact, as Christine Bold recounts, the *Pathfinder* magazine described the national editors as gatekeepers who prevented this kind of analysis: "The Washington office includes a policy editor whose duty is to watch for possible libel and make sure that the w p a's socially conscious writers stop at describing slums, instead of going on to theorizing about what has caused the slums" (qtd. in Bold 29).

25. The guide cannot ultimately repress the violence of this scene: in describing the Reconstruction period in Florida in its "History" chapter, a time "darkened by suffering and poverty," the guide notes that in "about 1870, Florida experienced a period of lawlessness, particularly in the turpentine sections of middle Florida, evidenced by an unusually active Ku Klux Klan" (58–59). Notably, though, that account of violence is located safely in the past, in spite of the Klan's continuing presence in the state in the 1930s.

26. Nancy Silber locates a similar set of representations in the travel literature of the 1870s: "In the eyes of the northern traveler, blacks became less of a problem and more of a 'picturesque' element on the southern scene" (*Romance*, 77–81, quotation from 78).

27. Stetson Kennedy, the state director of the Florida Writers' Project's Folklore, Oral History, and Ethnic Studies division from 1937 to 1942, clarifies the term *cracker* in an undated essay entitled "A Florida Treasure Hunt": "The term 'Cracker,' while now more widely known as a derogatory term for rural whites, has a more specific—and less insulting—definition in Florida. The Florida 'Crackers' are whites of Celtic descent who first settled South Florida around the mid-eighteenth century. 'Crackers' usually migrated to the Florida Everglades from Alabama, Georgia, and the Carolinas, drawn to the fertile land for ranching and farming, and the peninsula's plentiful resources for fishing. The name's origins have been disputed, but the Celtic nature of Cracker culture—from musical styles to occupational choices—is indisputable" (web site of American Memory, http://memory.loc.gov/ammem/index.html, accessed 29 June 2007).

28. The logic is somewhat ambiguous here—does the guide indicate that by virtue of being black in America, one experiences hardship and poverty, thus resulting in a strategy of "defensive guile," or, conversely, does the guide invest in an essentialist formulation, claiming that this is a "natural" African American posture, adopted and transformed into a sound business practice by poor, rural whites?

29. Another instance of this implied insider access occurs in the guide's discussion of voodooism in the African American and Afro-Cuban communities. The guide explains: "Since voodooism is an unwritten form of the occult, it varies greatly according to the environment. . . . Negro bean pickers from the Bahamas and the West Indies indulge in voodoo ceremonials and dances. . . . These manifestations are sincere and far removed from curious eyes. Voodoo rituals in Tampa have been witnessed up to their ultimate frenzies, from which outsiders are excluded" (131). This account poses a series of interesting questions pertinent to Hurston's *Mules and Men* as well: Who is witnessing and evaluating the sincerity of these rituals? How does the guide have access to these private ceremonials? If these forms are largely "unwritten," then what are the guide's primary sources? The passive voice and omnipotent narrator preserve the guide's authority and occlude this line of inquiry.

30. This trope is manifested in contemporary cinema. One need only consider films such as *Deliverance* (1972), *Breakdown* (1997), and others to contemplate its more modern manifestation of white, middle-class anxiety about travel into an American interior inhabited by hostile, poor, rural whites.

31. Beginning in the late nineteenth century, the term *Yankee* was used to indicate a racially "pure" Anglo-Saxon New Englander, a designation that ignored New England's vast immigrant populations as well as its African

American residents. The term still carried this meaning in the thirties. For more about the invention of New England as a tourist haven and the role a notion of ethnic homogeneity played in this process, see Dona Brown's fascinating *Inventing New England*; in particular, see 107–9, 190–93, 204, 215.

32. A web site that makes available the Federal Writers' Project's collection of Florida folkways (at the American Folklife Center, Library of Congress: http://memory.loc.gov/ammem//collections/florida/) offers a far more diverse and rich portrait of Florida's peoples, including sound recordings of African Americans, Bahamian Americans, British Americans (described as crackers in the Florida guide), Cuban Americans, Czech Americans, Greek Americans, Italian Americans, Minorcan Americans, Seminole Indians, Slovak Americans, and Syrian Americans. Yet the state's "folklore" is selectively reduced to "four strains" in the Florida guide: "the 'cracker,' the Negro, the Latin-American and the Seminole" (128).

33. A similar description of Yankees prevails in other guides as well. For example, *California: A Guide to the Golden State* (1939) proclaims: "The aggressive energy of the Yankees, against which the leisure-loving ways of the easy-going *Californios* could not prevail (with some few exceptions in the south) still moves a people who have built aqueducts from faraway mountains to reclaim whole deserts, strung power lines from mighty dams across inaccessible wilderness to distant cities, dredged one of the Nation's great harbors from mud flats and flung the world's biggest bridges across the bay" (7). Reifying the notion of the ever present frontier in relation to the American frontiersman, the guide describes "the unquenchable wanderlust with which [Californians] have taken to the automobile, thronging the highways with never-ending streams of traffic bound for the seashore, deserts, forests and mountain," suggesting that "they hope . . . that they can yet make of El Dorado the promised land that has fired men's imaginations for four hundred years."

34. While the nineteenth-century travelogue relied upon the reader's identification with its narrator's desire for exoticism, the travel guide promises the fulfillment of its reader's fantasy as an immediate and possible reality. The travel guide's excess of information mediates the reader's every possible fantasy at the same time that it bolsters the guide's truth-claims. It is not surprising, then, that the rise of the tourist guide around the beginning of the twentieth century coincided with the ascendancy of information media, such as newspapers, public notices, and governmental reports such as the Blue Books. In the 1930s, new information technologies such as the radio, film, and the photo magazine sped up the dissemination of "official" information, the authority of these technologies relying all the more on the promise of verisimilitude.

35. The supplementary instructions of the "American Guide Manual" for writing on "Indians and Indian Life" caution: "In writing of Indians and Indian life for the American Guide, we want first to emphasize those points of interest—scenic or cultural—which are most likely to capture the atten-

tion. . . . Every state has its landmarks in, and its associations with, Indian lore. . . . It will be necessary then to select, but care should be taken that the selection is made with a view to interesting the outsider who looks for the first time upon a strange landscape. . . . More often than not, [the visitor] will not be a specialist, and the information we give him, while it should be accurate from the anthropologist's point of view, will have to be palatable—simple but not sketchy" (supplement 7891-1).

36. Listed among its authoritative explorers, anthropologists, and archaeologists are the explorer Alvar Nunez Cabeza de Vaca; the curator of the National Museum of Anthropology, Dr. Ales Hrdlicka; F. H. Cushing of the Federal Bureau of Ethnology; and Henry B. Collins of the National Museum.

37. The practice of becoming an authority on authoritative sources shapes the contours of academic inquiry and authority as well.

38. Bold makes a similar point about the guidebook genre's tendency toward "a management of difference": "According to the conventions of this genre, the disruptions of difference are contained—or at least camouflaged—by the larger scheme of orderly diversity" (10).

CHAPTER 4: DE PRIVILEGE TO GO

1. Hurston's desire for this credibility is evident in her unflagging efforts to persuade her mentor, Franz Boas—the champion of cultural relativism and anthropological study at "home"—to write an introduction for the work and thereby publicly endorse the collection. In a letter written to Boas in August 1934, just six months before the publication of *Mules and Men* in 1935, Hurston wrote: "I am full of tremors, lest you decide that you do not want to write the introduction to my 'Mules and Men.' I want you to do it so very much. Also I want Dr. [Ruth] Benedict to read the ms. and offer suggestions" (qtd. in Hemenway, *Zora Neale Hurston*, 163).

2. Here I use the phrase "participant observer" to describe anthropologists of this school, even though it gained its currency in the 1960s, not the 1930s. Instead of the term "participant observation," Boas repeatedly used the phrase "intensive fieldwork"; Malinowski described the practice as "the method of statistic documentation by *concrete evidence*" in which one was supposed to observe "the imponderabilia of *actual life*" (*Argonauts*, 17–18; emphasis added).

3. Boas's generation of ethnographers viewed the field much like a laboratory, an area of controlled observation and experimentation; thus, dwelling in the field was crucial to any anthropological investigation (Clifford, *Routes*, 21). In *Anthropology and Modern Life* (1928), Boas claims that "the objective study of types of culture that have developed on historically independent lines or that have grown fundamentally distinct enables the anthropologist to differentiate clearly between those phases of life that are valid for all mankind and others that are culturally determined. Supplied with [that]

knowledge he [is able] to view our own civilization critically, and to enter into a comparative study of values with a mind relatively uninfluenced by the emotions elicited by the automatically regulated behavior in which he participates as a member of our society" (207). Branislaw Malinowski, in his seminal *Argonauts of the Western Pacific* (1922), frames the field experience in similarly positivist terms: "The collecting of concrete data over a wide range of facts is thus one of the main points of the field method. . . . The method of reducing information, if possible, into charts or synoptic tables ought to be extended to the study of practically all aspects of native life" (13–14). In his assessment, "the goal [of the ethnographer] is briefly to grasp the native's point of view, his relation to life, to realize *his* vision of *his* world" (25).

4. Several critics have insightfully commented on the spatial aspects of *Mules and Men*. Barbara Johnson claims, "Hurston's work itself was constantly dramatizing and undercutting . . . inside/outside oppositions, transforming the plane geometry of physical space into the complex transactions of discursive exchange" ("Thresholds," 279). Similarly attending to the space of discourse, Houston Baker begins his reading of Hurston's collection by defining the poetic image as "eulogized [potentially liberating] space"; through this concept, he demonstrates the book's "*instantiation* (a word that marks time and suggests place) of the conjure woman as a peculiar, imagistic, Afro-American space" ("Workings," 282).

5. The collection of folklore consists of the tales a community tells about itself *and* the tales the ethnographer tells about herself.

6. Cheryl Wall argues that "Hurston draws no connection between the sermon and the agon between Big Sweet and Ella Wall. Here and throughout the book her method is presentational, not analytical. Nevertheless, the reader's approbation of Big Sweet seems won in part by the juxtaposition between the two scenes" ("*Mules and Men*," 671). While my own argument may appear to rest on spurious claims of intentionality (i.e., Hurston intended the structure of the narrative to suggest certain kinds of folkloric analysis), the text enacts this analysis, whether or not Hurston calculated this effect.

7. As David Kadlec explains in his article "Zora Neale Hurston and the Federal Folk," when Hurston wrote for the Federal Writers' Project's Florida guidebook and the state's unpublished *The Florida Negro*, she documented a blues song entitled "East Coast Blues" that was eventually included in the Florida guide's "Music and Theater" chapter. Kadlec notes that Hurston originally included this song in the appendix of *Mules and Men* some four years earlier, in 1935, which means that she collected it sometime in the late twenties while she compiled her *Mules* manuscript. He then traces the song's lyrical tropes to several songs popular in the Harlem cabarets of the 1920s, songs that Hurston, in fact, sang out in the field to gain footing and credibility with her rural southern subjects. What emerges in this complex circuit is the fundamentally improvisational loop of cultural production, as the song is passed from urban commercial culture to rural southern culture and

back again, a paradigm that undercuts the preservationist theories of culture that she sometimes espoused.

8. Her concern about the loss of an essential blackness mirrors Malinowski's anxiety that the very subjects of ethnographic study were "dying out." In his introduction to *Argonauts*, he writes: "Ethnology is in the sadly ludicrous, not to say tragic, position, that at the very moment it begins to put its workshop in order . . . the material of its study melts away with hopeless rapidity. Just now, when the methods and aims of scientific field ethnology have taken shape, when men fully trained for the work have begun to travel into savage countries and study their inhabitants—these die away under our very eyes" (xv).

9. Boas writes: "Let us assume that there exists a society that has developed its culture according to certain laws discovered by a close scrutiny of behavior of diverse societies. For some reason, perhaps on account of hostile attacks that have nothing to do with the inner workings of the society, the people have to leave their home and migrate from the fertile country into a desert. They have to adjust themselves to new forms of life; new ideas will develop in the new surroundings. The fact that they have been transplanted from one region to another is just an accident. . . . [A]ccidents of this kind are the rule in every society, for no society is isolated but exists in more or less intimate relations to its neighbors" (210–11). In his estimation, cultural change occurs in every society but the intrusion by other groups (the geographic and social displacements caused by interactions with outsiders) determines the rapidity of this change.

10. Arjun Appadurai argues in "Putting Hierarchy in Its Place": "Natives, people confined to and by the places to which they belong, groups unsullied by contact with a larger world, have probably never existed" (39).

11. A similar deconstructive move occurs later in the essay, when Hurston states that "the Negro, the world over, is famous as a mimic. But this in no way damages his standing as an original. Mimicry is an art in itself. If it is not, then all art must fall by the same blow that strikes it down" ("Characteristics," 59).

12. Brian Carr and Tova Cooper astutely suggest that George Thomas undercuts Hurston's justification of salvage ethnography, the need to record the tales "before it's too late," when he retorts that there is "no danger of that" ("Zora Neale Hurston," 298). In their excellent reading, "while Zora seems at first to believe the commonsensical notion that these tales are valuable because they are potentially scarce or fading, George's refutation of both the value and scarcity of these 'lies' leads us to wonder if the relations between potential value and loss is not rather reversed. Is it not more the case here that the value of these 'lies' consists in construing them as lost?" Michael Elliot reads George's response as Hurston's subtle method of signifying on the "salvage imperative of her chosen profession" (*Culture Concept*, 173).

13. As Malinowski writes, "The third commandment of field-work runs:

Find out the typical ways of thinking and feeling, corresponding to the institutions and culture of a given community. . . . The best ethnographical writers . . . have always tried to quote verbatim statements of crucial importance. . . . One step further in this line can be made by the ethnographer who acquires a knowledge of the native language and can use it as an instrument of inquiry" (23).

14. Rosan Jordan points out that neither the *Journal of American Folklore* nor the *American Anthropologist* reviewed *Mules and Men* when it first came out ("Not into Cold Space," 128n2). Darwin Turner's introduction to *Mules and Men* in 1970 distinguishes Hurston's work from the usual concerns of anthropology when he warns: "The anthropologist will not find here an exhaustive and exhausting description of the traditions, mores, and living habits of a folk; he will not be provided with prescriptions for the future behavior of these folk or suggestions for further studies. The folklorist will not find a cataloguing of the tales with documented references to parallel tales in other cultures and other collections" (qtd. in Jordan 109). Larry Neal continues in this vein, asserting that Hurston approached folklore "with the engaged sensibility of the artist; she left the 'comprehensive' scientific approach to culture to men like her former teacher, Franz Boas, and to Melville Herskovits. . . . She would have been very uncomfortable as a scholar committed to 'pure' research" (qtd. in Jordan 128n4).

15. I use Malinowski's *Argonauts* as my primary source of comparison with *Mules and Men* because it is considered by most anthropologists to be *the* pioneering ethnography of the 1920s. In Susan Hegeman's estimation, "The new anthropology that emerged by the 1920s . . . was virtually embodied in the figure of Branislaw Malinowski . . . . [It] would be characterized by monographs on single cultures, based on information gathered by ethnographers acting as participant observers" (*Patterns*, 27). It helped entrench an ideal of fieldwork that became central to the discipline of anthropology by the 1930s, during which time Hurston was trained at Columbia and out in the field collecting. Fatimah Tobing Rony asserts that "if [Robert Flaherty's] *Nanook* [*of the North*] is the archetypal documentary/ethnographic/art film, *Argonauts* is without a doubt the archetypal written ethnography," primarily because Malinowski's work put forth a new conception of the anthropologist as fieldworker (*Third Eye*, 117). In his *Predicaments of Culture*, James Clifford sums up the effects of Malinowski's efforts in *Argonauts*: "The establishment of intensive participant observation as a professional norm . . . would have to await the Malinowskian cohort. . . . [He] gives us the image of the new 'anthropology.' . . . The story of research built into *Argonauts*, into Mead's popular work on Samoa, and into *We the Tikopia* became an implicit narrative underlying all professional reports on exotic worlds" (28–29). While Boas wrote much about the study of anthropology, he never produced a field account that would have the same impact as Malinowski's, in spite of the fact that "he made intensive fieldwork the sine qua non of serious anthropological discourse" (Clifford 27).

16. The contemporaneous genre of guidebooks, like the Federal Writers' Project's American Guide Series discussed in my third chapter, deployed a similar narrative strategy.

17. In *Dust Tracks*, Hurston illustrates the difficulties of collecting folklore when a rigid binarism of outsider-observer and native-informant is in place. In her description of her first collecting trip to Florida she states: "My first six months were disappointing. I found out later that it was not because I had no talents for research, but because I did not have the right approach. The glamour of Barnard College was still upon me. I dwelt in marble halls. I knew where the material was all right. But, I went about asking, in carefully accented Barnardese, 'Pardon me, but do you know any folk-tales or folk-songs?' The men and women who had whole treasuries of material just seeping through their pores looked at me and shook their heads. No, they had never heard of anything like that around here. Maybe it was over in the next county. Why didn't I try over there?" (127–28). What interests me about this statement is the implicit connection she makes between dwelling and traveling: because she still dwells in "marble halls," she cannot locate any folklore, even though she knows that she is in the right place. She must dwell as well as travel in the field to successfully collect her material.

18. Keith Walters expands upon Barbara Johnson's claim that Hurston signifies on Mrs. Mason, suggesting that Hurston also treats her mentor, Franz Boas, in her introduction and Mrs. Annie Nathan Meyer, the woman to whom the book is dedicated, to the same "feather-bed tactics." Hurston worked as a domestic for Meyer, the founder of Barnard College; eventually, Meyer helped Hurston procure a scholarship there. Walters reads the story of the Jew and the soul-piece not as generally anti-Semitic but rather a specific act of signifying on her Jewish patrons, Boas and Meyer (" 'He Can Read,' " 362). In a broader sense, Houston Baker reads the entire collection as a "pharmakon conceived as the script or spirit work of black creativity," one that "astutely defied King Boas and Queen R. Osgood Mason" (303).

19. Hurston's rendering of Eatonville as a "town [that] had not changed" reveals the ways she "privileges the nostalgic and freezes it in time" (Carby, "Politics," 79). But if Hurston does indeed perform "a metonymic freezing" of her hometown and its inhabitants, reconstructing it in allochronic terms (just as it was during her childhood) and insisting that it stand for an essential rural folk "Negroness," then how does she situate herself in temporal and spatial terms in relation to this static place and time? (See Arjun Appadarai's "Introduction: Place and Voice in Anthropological Theory" for an extended discussion of metonymic freezing.) I argue that Hurston "shares time" with her informants in her descriptions of ritualized spaces of exchange, consumption, and transmission and in her accounts of her travels with her informants.

20. Interestingly, Hurston's account deposes the church as the center of southern black life. In her alternative mapping, the market lies at the geo-

graphic and symbolic center of the township of Eatonville. Ed Blum, correspondence, 2 October 2006.

21. Michael Elliot rightly suggests that in this scene, "the narrator sounds almost like a parody of the naïve, uninitiated anthropologist," indicating a pattern of instability and dissemblance that will render Hurston "an unreliable narrator in the most literal sense" (173).

22. In contrast, Malinowski explains that the natives viewed him as a "necessary evil," his presence only mitigated by bribes. He writes: "As [the native Trobrianders] knew I would thrust my nose into everything, even where a well-mannered native would not dream of intruding, they finished by regarding me as part and parcel of their life, a necessary evil or nuisance, mitigated by donations of tobacco" (8).

23. Arna Bontemps lodged a similar critique of *Mules and Men*, claiming that it was impossible to know where the anthropology "left off and where Zora began" (Hemenway, *Zora Neale Hurston*, 166).

24. Hurston heeds this rule in the beginning of chapter 2. She sums up the import of the overfamiliar stories and moves on to recount a conversation that begins with a discussion of church and preachers and ends on the topic of the difference between men and women. She states: "They told enough for a volume by itself. Some of the stories were the familiar drummer-type of tale about two Irishmen, Pat and Mike, or two Jews as the case might be. Some were the European folk-tales undiluted, like Jack and the Beanstalk. Others had slight local variations, but the Negro imagination is so facile that there was little need for outside help" (20). Her summary foregrounds her process of selection and editing as an ethnographer and storyteller in her own right.

25. Johannes Fabian argues that the early discipline of anthropology consistently deploys allochronic time in its representations of the other (see *Time and the Other*). In other words, in the classic ethnographic account, the native and the anthropologist do not share time together; the primitive is located outside of history. Leigh Ann Duck deploys this concept in *Mules and Men* by showing how Hurston first depicts Eatonville as "deny[ing] the coevalness of other regions . . . yet . . . [modeling] possibilities for 'intersubjective time.' Indeed, Hurston's text is structured to emphasize her own experiences of coevalness—the ways she and the Floridians share in the same time" ("'Go there,'" 274–75).

26. At the same time, the "toe-party" isn't all that unfamiliar. In Benigno Sanchez-Eppler's persuasive reading, the party is a "carnivalesque" echo of the slave auction. As it both remembers and transforms the memory of slavery, it enacts a "comprehensive reshuffling of subject positions": white men are excluded from the exchange and there is a seeming parity between the black man who "buys" a toe and the black woman who is then treated to "everything she want" and can sell her toe again and again ("Telling Anthropology," 479). Sanchez-Eppler is careful to point out that "the women re-

main objects for sale." He teases out the gendered implications of this ritual for Hurston's position as an ethnographer.

27. Both Robert Hemenway and Cheryl Wall have commented on the strangely subdued character of "Zora," the narrator, in this chapter. Hemenway states that "to display this art in its natural folk setting she created a narrator who would not intrude on the folklore event. A semi-fictional Zora Neale Hurston is our guide to southern black folklore, a curiously retiring figure who is more art than life. The exuberant Zora Hurston . . . is seldom in evidence in *Mules and Men*" (164). Cheryl Wall complicates this formulation by suggesting that the narrative traces the transformation of the narrator Zora from a "naive and diffident" initiate to an empowered ethnographer and hoodoo conjurer. Wall notes that in this first chapter, "the totally passive Zora . . . defers to someone else for every decision made" (664–65). When reading the chapter within the context of the traditional field account of the time, I draw slightly different conclusions. Hurston's willingness to be led by her informants to her material is a typical trope, though she portrays herself as a surprisingly active presence in this scene when compared to the depictions of folklorists in other accounts. As a narrative strategy, the informants' presence as guides bolsters the ethnography's authority and draws the reader into the drama of collecting and observing.

28. Here, I use the term "fixed" only in its most literal sense. In keeping with Doreen Massey's assertions that place is process, I view a place like Armetta Jones's house as fluid, its meanings slightly shifting with every social interaction (Massey, *Space*, 155).

29. In the introduction to *Mules and Men*, Hurston's stated reasons for going to Eatonville were simple: "I knew that the town was full of material and that I could get it without hurt, harm or danger" (2). In Polk County, there are no such guarantees.

30. For excellent scholarship on Hurston's treatment of migrant labor in the text, see Nicholls, "Migrant Labor," and Meisenhelder, "Conflict and Resistance."

31. In Courtney Love's famous phrasing in the song "Doll Parts," recorded with her band Hole: "I fake it so real I am beyond fake."

32. The power of these stories is expressed in chapter 5 when one of Hurston's informants, Larkins White, says to the rest of the storytellers: "Y'all been wearin' Ole Massa's southern-can out dis mornin'. Pass him over here to me and lemme handle some grammar with him" (85). The figure of "Ole Massa" in the tales becomes corporeal, an almost physical subject that can be handled with language. In this way, storytelling becomes a forceful act of retribution.

33. Big Sweet is the first woman in the quarters to claim that she has the "law in her mouth." As she lectures to Joe Willard about the rules of their relationship, she asserts "*any* time Ah shack up wid any man Ah gives myself de privilege to go wherever he might be, night or day. Ah got de law in my mouth" (124). Whereas Gene and Gold have a domestic arrangement, Big

Sweet takes the liberty to move freely, paying no heed to sexist designations of public and private space. (It comes as no surprise that if Joe disappoints her, she will put his name "in de streets"; that space is no more off limits to her than any other.)

34. Hemenway writes that "since the publisher [Lippincott] wanted a '$3.50 book,' [Hurston] also selected and condensed from her earlier hoodoo article to add to the volume, the hoodoo section forming the last third of the book" (163).

35. Hurston must initially pay her tutors. In return, one of them helps ensure "that a certain influential white woman . . . would never lose interest in [her] as long as she lived" (227). In this insular loop, that woman is most probably Mrs. Mason, who has presumably funded Hurston's hoodoo tutelage in the first place.

36. See, for example, Johnson, "Thresholds"; Willis, "Wandering"; Boxwell, "Sis Cat"; Baker, "Workings"; and Walters, " 'He Can Read.' "

CHAPTER 5: AM I LAUGHING?

1. If we were to imagine their final product *The Forgotten Boys*, it might have approximated William Wellman's *Wild Boys of The Road* (1933), a sentimental story of adolescent hobos who leave their families to look for work and discover new forms of communal life on the road (Moran and Rogin, " 'What's the Matter,' " 118). In fact, according to the authorized biography of William Wyler by Axel Madsen and Wyler, John Huston and Wyler "threw themselves on another Universal property, Daniel Ahearn's story *The Wild Boys of the Road* . . . [until] the property was sold to First National from under their noses and ended up being directed by William Wellman" (82–83).

2. Of course, this is, in many ways, a false opposition, which Sturges well knew. Satires such as Charlie Chaplin's *The Idle Class* (1920), *The Gold Rush* (1925), *City Lights* (1931), and *Modern Times* (1936) illustrate the razor's edge of comedy's capacity for political critique, as does *Sullivan's Travels*.

3. The American Film Institute lists *Sullivan's Travels* as its thirty-ninth entry in its list of America's Hundred Funniest Movies, and the Writers' Guild of America lists it as its twenty-ninth entry in its "101 Greatest Screenplays" (from the AFI and WGA web sites, www.afi.org/ and www.wga.org/, both accessed 13 November 2006).

4. Christopher Ames focuses on *Sullivan's Travels'* self-referential commentary on filmmaking and audience in chap. 3 of his *Movies about the Movies* (80–107). See also DePastino, *Citizen Hobo*, 210–11; Levine, *Unpredictable*, 311–13; Moran and Rogin, " 'What's the Matter,' " 106–34; Pfister, *Complicity*, 616–17; Susman, *Culture as History*, 192–97; and Vidal, "Sullivan's Travels," 216–19.

5. Interestingly, though every critic agrees that Sullivan makes lighthearted fare—that much is evident in the plot—there is some difference of

opinion about the exact nature of those films. Arthur Knight refers to Sullivan as a director of musicals, a theory bolstered by the script's references to the producers' cry for Sullivan to continue to make films about "nice clean young people who fell in love, with *laughter* and *music* and ... *legs*" and their idea for a sequel to one of Sullivan's prior hits: "How about 'Ants in Your Pants of 1941'? You can have Bob Hope, Mary Martin ... Bing Crosby. . . . the Abbey Dancers. . . . [and] a big-name band" (Knight, *Disintegrating the Musical*, 240; Henderson, *Five Screenplays*, 544, emphasis in the original, 547).

6. In 1941, the question of representing the people was posed to Hollywood once again, this time animated by patriotic and nationalist concerns within an international theater of war: in Franklin D. Roosevelt's Oscar night address, he called upon Hollywood to tell "the unfortunate people under totalitarian governments [about] the truths of our democracy" (Spoto, *Madcap*, 163–66). Throughout his career, Sturges chafed at such directives and constraints by flouting the Hays production code and overzealous bosses such as Buddy DeSylva—he was ever the auteur in this respect.

7. I am indebted to Heather Lukes for clarifying this point in conversation, July 2009.

8. In her book *Bodies in Dissent*, on the incendiary theatrics of African American performers in the transatlantic performance culture of the nineteenth century and the early twentieth, Daphne Brooks argues for attending "to the significance of minstrelsy's particular role in the making of a spectacularly incongruous body as a performance strategy unto itself" (25). This performance strategy, originated in minstrelsy's discordant and grotesque theatrics, wends its way through the modernist burlesque of George Schuyler, Nathanael West, and Preston Sturges.

9. In Diane Jacobs's account, "While true radicals like Dashiell Hammett contemplated going off to Spain to fight Franco, while even moderates like Preston's friend Paul Kohner, with Ernst Lubitsch and Salka Viertal, established the European Film Fund to find work for émigrés fleeing Hitler, and while most every important writer in Hollywood was joining either the liberal Screen Writers Guild or the more conservative Screen Playwrights, Preston joined nothing and sided with no one. . . . Preston avoided political movements as he avoided religions, and for somewhat the same reason: because so much evil was done in their names" (183).

10. In the 1930s, Kenneth Burke developed a notion of the grotesque that Denning uses as the basis for his trope of the proletarian grotesque; Burke's theories illuminate this register of cultural front social critique as well. Accounting for Erskine Caldwell's grotesques, Burke explains Caldwell's use of "caricature and humor, [how] the mental state of 'refusal' here [creates] *extravagant incongruities* that sometimes can be received with laughter, but are frequently so closely connected with degradation and acute suffering that the effect is wholly grim" (*Philosophy*, 351; emphasis added).

11. Though large-scale vaudeville performances were dying out by 1932,

much of Sturges's physical comedy is derived from its slapstick maneuvers. *Sullivan's Travels* is particularly indebted to the segments of the variety show devoted to minstrelsy and male impersonation (Michaels, "Particular Kind," 152, 155–56).

12. In one literal register of meaning, we might understand Sullivan's arrest for driving a car that is presumably not his as further evidence of the degree to which he successfully passes as a tramp. In yet another, Althusserian register, in this scene of misrecognition by the law, the officer apprehends him first as a thief, paradoxically naming a kind of disavowed truth—Sullivan is not the thief of a car but rather of an identity not his own, conveyed in his tramp disguise. At the same time, when the law initiates him (once again) into his proper, privileged subject position, we see its juridical and social contours in the ease with which he speaks to authority and evades punishment (Butler, *Bodies*, 121–24).

13. Moran and Rogin pick up this reference in the scene that marks Sullivan's true descent into powerlessness and poverty, when he distributes money to the poor as an act of thanks and is later knocked unconscious and robbed by a tramp, who then dies in the path of an oncoming train. They explain, "As in early silent film's cinema of attractions, the locomotive that will kill the tramp comes straight into the audience at the same time. . . . [T]he train that breaks the fourth wall to kill the tramp forces us to confront our own spectator stake in vicarious pleasure" (120).

14. Initially, a drama of capital and labor is the subject of the realist film Sullivan would like to direct and the source of the conflict between him and his producers. Sullivan's only mode of escape from the studio system is to become an amnesiac prisoner through a series of misrecognitions, a non-wage laborer, around the same time that the Girl, not surprisingly, becomes even more incorporated within the labor of Hollywood as an actress.

15. Baz Lhurmann describes this as "heightened audience-participation style. I call it 'contract playing': you sign a contract with the audience in which they agree to participate in your film" ("Ants in His Pants").

16. Sturges himself had faced accusations of promoting communist sentiment in his screenplay *If I Were a King* (1938), which had to be publicly defended by Paramount (Ames, *Movies*, 83).

17. Christopher Ames cites Neal Gabler's account of the early pioneers of motion pictures, most of whom were eastern European immigrants who had, indeed, experienced a peculiarly American kind of success and thus were invested in presenting the nation's bootstrap mythology in a positive light. As Ames suggests, the producers in *Sullivan's Travels* are second-generation; they invoke "the rags-to-riches past as a pretense" (85).

18. Is this an ironic reference to the fifteen-minute silent comedy *The Panther Woman of the Needle Trades*, made by Ralph Steiner for the fashion show in 1933 of the dress designer Elizabeth Dawes (Denning, *Cultural Front*, 146)? Or a reference to Ralph Ince's earlier silent film, *The Panther Woman*

(1919)? Or Kathleen Burk's role as Lota the Panther Woman in *Island of the Lost Souls* (1933), Paramount's masterpiece of horror based upon H. G. Wells's *The Island of Dr. Moreau* (1896)?

19. Todd DePastino writes of the segregating practices of the hobo "main stem," the lodging house neighborhoods that had developed in urban centers with the tramp crisis of the 1870s (71–85). African American and Asian American migratory workers were routinely barred from the "cheap hotels and employment agencies of hobohemian neighborhoods" (77). While "southern and eastern European laborers did not face legal exclusion from hobo districts . . . these immigrants rarely turned to . . . the main stem. . . . For hoboes, the main stem was a domain of the racially privileged, for regardless of their homeless condition, they enjoyed an individual mobility and access not shared by their excluded counterparts" (77–78).

20. Michael Denning writes, "The quintessential depression stories were stories of downward mobility, of stockbrokers leaping to their deaths: it was a crash, a comeuppance of the established classes" (244).

21. The Girl's unnamed status emphatically refers to her function in the plot as what Judith Butler calls "a forcible citation of a norm": "The naming of a 'girl' is transitive, that is [it] initiates the process by which 'girling' is compelled, the term or, rather, its symbolic power, governs the formation of a corporeally enacted femininity that never fully approximates the norm" (*Bodies*, 232). That she is interpellated as the "girl in the picture" in the exchange between the cop and Sullivan only heightens this operation.

22. As Richard Dyer notes in the chapter titled "The White Man's Muscles," "Clothes are barriers of prestige, notably of wealth, status and class: to be without them is to lose prestige. . . . At the same time, there is value in the white male body being seen. . . . [T]he body often figures very effectively as a point of final explanation of social difference" (*White*, 146–47).

23. Cheryl Harris asserts that white identity "became a line of protection and demarcation from the potential threat of commodification. . . . White identity and whiteness were sources of privilege and protection" ("Whiteness," 1721).

24. As Judith Butler suggests, what is "masked by masquerade" remains a pivotal point in a range of psychoanalytic interpretations (*Gender*, 47, 53).

25. Extending the logic of the film-within-the film and the Girl's ingénue act, we could say that Sullivan's performance as a tramp ironically consolidates his actual life as millionaire director as "authentic" by comparison, thereby countering narratives of the "unreality" of the Hollywood dream machine.

26. James Harvey extols McCrea's comic aplomb, noting that he is direct, gruff, and "unflappably good-natured . . . with the threat of something irascible as well" (*Romantic Comedy*, 294).

27. In an article on Carson McCuller's use of the interracial chain gang in her fiction, Margaret Whitt notes that "although the Southern prison system was segregated, the chain gang from its inception was integrated. . . . [A]

1946 government document (Prisoners in State and Federal Prisons and Reformatories) indicates that 50.3% of new felony convicts in the South were black. . . . In Georgia, there were 1,062 white men to 1,710 black men received in the prison system during this year of statistical gathering. . . . It is safe to conjecture that black men outnumbered white men on most chain gangs throughout the first half of the century" (119–22). In Jacobs's biography of Sturges, she explains how "[he] researched precisely what prisoners wore, in what states they were still chained, under what circumstances their privileges could be removed, whether they went to church or worked on Sunday" (257).

28. When Miz Zeffie asks Ursula, "Did you notice his torso?," as Sullivan chops wood for room and board, Ursula replies, "I notice that you noticed it."

29. For scholarship on the relation between sentimentality and white liberal political discourse, see Hartman, *Scenes of Subjection*, 17–23; and Wald, *Crossing the Line*, 168–77.

30. These tonal oddities were probably exacerbated by the feedback Sturges received from the studio. Buddy DeSylva took over Paramount just as Sturges was working on *Sullivan's Travels*. DeSylva and Sturges wrangled over control of the film. Jacobs describes how in one of these contests, DeSylva expressed concern that the montage was "too long and too explicit. 'Soft peddle misery,' he . . . advised Sturges after the first preview" (259). Interestingly, Lawrence Levine uses the montage as a linchpin in his argument about "open texts," suggesting that "there is a great deal of room for audiences to insert themselves" in the production of textual meaning (*Unpredictable*, 310). In his interpretation of *Sullivan's Travels*, he writes: "What is arresting . . . is that the film itself did much more than [just make people laugh]: it helped to inform its audiences about the nature and extent of suffering in the United States. No final ending, no ultimate apologia could automatically erase the images of misery, despair, and hopelessness the film made available to the audience" (*Unpredictable*, 311).

31. Heather Lukes drew my attention to this aspect of the scene, July 2009.

32. Ed Blum provided this insight in correspondence, 10 November 2006. Interestingly, the film's depiction of an interracial audience in a church coincided with a turn away from the segregating practices of many of the nation's religious institutions in the 1940s, as "a host of voices arose from the Christian communities assailing racial discrimination in society and in the churches" (Emerson and Blum, "Dreams," 18).

33. For more discussion of discordant populisms, see Denning 125, 123–36.

34. The communist cultural critic Mike Gold articulated this concept in his introduction to Langston Hughes's *A New Song*, a volume of poetry dedicated to the International Workers Order. As William Maxwell describes in his *New Negro, Old Left*, Gold claimed that "the best African American literature was thus a kind of volk-proletarian composite, both 'a folk literature, close to the joys and sorrows of [black] people' and a voice for

the freedom of black and white workers, 'brothers in suffering and struggle'" (111).

35. The "backstager" is a metagenre about the making of a show in which characters sing and dance as they rehearse for a performance.

36. Neil Young in his online "film lounge" review castigates Sturges for "never [letting] any of the underprivileged tramps and prisoners speak for themselves. . . . [T]he tramps pass in front of the camera with a mournful expression, the chain-gang prisoners laugh like moronic jackasses." Yet, Young still praises the scene in the black church: "It's a pivotal, serious, almost overwhelmingly moving scene in which the process of watching a film becomes a heightened, baroque religious ritual. If everything afterwards seems trivially anti-climactic, that's a small price to pay for one of the most astonishing scenes in American movies, quite unlike anything else before or since" (from www.jigsawlounge.co.uk, accessed 15 April 2009).

37. These shots closely resemble the grotesques pictured in Caldwell's and Bourke-White's *You Have Seen Their Faces*.

38. Indeed, Sturges was very much invested in the auteur theory, down to the industry mechanics of filmmaking. One night he ran into John Huston at the famous Hollywood bar, the Brown Derby, and spent two hours advising him on how to convince Warner Brothers to allow Huston to direct his own screenplays. Sturges was upset by the fact that Huston's first directing assignment was Dashiell Hammett's *The Maltese Falcon*; "The point, he lectured Huston, was that a film should have a single creator" (Jacobs, *Christmas in July*, 243–44). According to Brian Henderson, "With *Sullivan's Travels* for the first time Sturges, as a working director, conceived and wrote a script which he knew he would direct, which he was indeed under contract to write and direct, with even the likely casting and approximate production schedule already in mind. *Sullivan's Travels* thus marks, arguably, Sturges's full attainment of the status of writer-director" (*Five Screenplays*, 517).

39. Kenon Breazeale describes this constellation of attitudes about female consumers in an article about *Esquire*'s strategic cultivation of the male consumer during the magazine's inception in 1930s: "Not only New Deal rhetoric but the dynamic of attitudes about gender specific to the magazine industry circa 1930 created an opportune moment for *Esquire*'s founding. Understanding that occasion means understanding how rigidly sex-linked the ideology of consumption had become during the 1920s. In a narrow sense that industry functioned on the interplay between two presumptions: the socially appropriate aim of women is to cultivate themselves as consumers; and shopping is what is wrong with women and women shoppers are what is wrong with the world" ("In Spite of Women," 228). Barbara Melosh, in her book *Engendering Culture*, describes how "ironically, despite women's increasing importance in the work force of a consumer economy, cultural images of women emphasized their role as shoppers. In the 1920s and 1930s, images of the female shopper embodied the considerable ambiva-

lence that surrounded consumption. . . . Both within and beyond the rhetoric of advertising, consumption was associated with sexual desire. The image of the female shopper embodied this wide-spread conflation of erotic and consumer desire. Just as women represented both temptation and purity in cultural images of sexuality, so they came to represent both excess and regulation of consumer desire" (183–84). In keeping with this iconography, Melosh points out how Sinclair Lewis mocks his character, Babbit, by demonstrating Babbit's reliance on commodity culture: consumption is a sign of "diminished manhood" (184).

40. Since Sturges and all directors are exacting about the composition of their crowds, the historical fact of white-only or racially segregated theaters only heightens the import of his pivotal, integrated audience.

1. In the words of Charles Taylor, *O Brother* "invokes the images familiar from the photographs of Walker Evans and Dorothea Lange—shanty images, ragamuffin children, big-bellied bosses in summer suits—as well as books and movies of the era, like *The Grapes of Wrath* and *I am a Fugitive From a Chain Gang* and the musicals of Busby Berkeley" ("O Brother," para. 1). Benjamin Filene develops an insightful account of the ways that the contemporary folk revival initiated by *O Brother* owes so many of its assumptions to the folk revival of the thirties ("O Brother, What Next?").

2. In a metasense, Clooney exuberantly plays with the disjuncture between his lip-synching and the actual soundtrack, a freedom he can revel in, given that the actual singing was done by the contemporary talented musician Dan Tyminksi, as Martin Harries notes ("Coen Brothers' New Film," B14); he also observes that, in this shell game of authenticity and artificiality, old and new, obviously neither of the men hails from the 1930s.

3. Richard Middleton notes how "Tommy's guitar fits effortlessly into the marvelously intricate textures of a full bluegrass band sound" ("O Brother, Let's Go Down," 48). As he makes this assessment, he underscores the irony that in the late 1930s, the bluegrass sound of the song did not yet exist as tradition: "Already 'tradition' is being read back into the past and presented as more traditional than the real thing—a characteristic of revivals" (61n2).

4. Hugh Ruppersburg describes how Governor Pappy O'Daniel is based upon one W. Lee "Pappy" O'Daniel, a man who owned the company Hillbilly Flour, "sponsored a country-music radio show in the 1920s and 1930s, wrote country music and performed with a group called 'The Hillbilly Boys.' . . . [H]e was elected governor of Texas in 1938 and senator in 1941" ("'Oh, So Many,'" 13).

5. Edward O'Neill puts forth a more dismissive account: "By inserting the 'old-timey' folk musical style that white musicians liven up by employing

black musicians (the historical figure of Robert Johnson) and by appropriating their musical styles, the film tries to criticize this very process of borrowing while at the same time congratulating itself for recognizing the history of black exploitation, oppression and marginalization" (157). I am not convinced that the film, rightly or wrongly, condemns this process of borrowing or sees it as starkly unidirectional.

Bibliography

Aaron, Daniel. "Late Thoughts on Nathanael West." *Massachusetts Review* 6 (Winter–Spring 1965): 307–16. Rpt. *Nathanael West: A Collection of Critical Essays*, edited by Jay Martin. Englewood Cliffs: Prentice-Hall, 1971.

Abrahams, Roger D. "Phantoms of Romantic Nationalism in Folkloristics." *Journal of American Folklore* 106, no. 419 (1993): 3–37.

The African Queen. Directed by John Huston. 20th Century Fox, 1951.

Agee, James. *Agee on Film: Criticism and Comment on the Movies*. 1958; New York: Modern Library, 2000.

Agee, James, and Walker Evans. *Let Us Now Praise Famous Men*. 1939; New York: Houghton Mifflin, 1988.

Allen, Ernest, Jr. "On the Reading of Riddles: Rethinking Du Boisian 'Double Consciousness.'" In *Existence in Black: An Anthology of Black Existential Writing*, edited by Lewis Ricardo Gordon, 49–68. Routledge: New York, 1997.

Alpers, Benjamin L. *Dictators, Democracy, and American Public Culture: Envisioning the Totalitarian Enemy, 1920s–1950s*. Chapel Hill: University of North Carolina, 2002.

"American Guide Week, Nov. 10–16: Take Pride in Your Country: State by State the WPA Writers' Projects Describe America to Americans." Processed by Pennsylvania Art Program, WPA [1941]. Work Projects Administration Poster Collection, American Memory, Library of Congress. Web site of American Memory, http://memory.loc.gov/ammem/index.html, accessed 14 September 2007.

Ames, Christopher. *Movies about the Movies: Hollywood Reflected*. Lexington: University Press of Kentucky, 1997.

Anderson, Benedict. *Imagined Communities: Reflections on the Origin and Spread of Nationalism*. 1983; New York: Verso, 1991.

Appadurai, Arjun. "Introduction: Place and Voice in Anthropological Theory." *Cultural Anthropology* 3 (1988): 16–20.

———. "Putting Hierarchy in its Place." *Cultural Anthropology* 3 (1988): 36–49.

Arnold, Thurman. *The Folklore of Capitalism*. 1937; New Haven: Yale University Press, 1962.

Baker, Houston A., Jr. *Modernism and the Harlem Renaissance*. Chicago: University of Chicago Press, 1989.

———. "Workings of the Spirit: Conjure and the Space of Black Women's Creativity." In *Zora Neale Hurston: Critical Perspectives Past and Present*, edited by Henry Louis Gates Jr. and K. A. Appiah, 280–308. New York: Amistad, 1993.

Bakhtin, Mikail M. Introduction to *Rabelais and His World*. Translated by Helene Iswolsky. Bloomington: Indiana University Press, 1984.

Balibar, Etienne, and Immanuel Wallerstein. *Race, Nation, Class: Ambiguous Identities*. Translated by Chris Turner. New York: Verso, 1991.

Barnard, Rita. *The Great Depression and the Culture of Abundance: Kenneth Fearing, Nathanael West and Mass Culture in the 1930s*. New York: Cambridge University Press, 1995.

Bazin, André. *The Cinema of Cruelty from Bunuel to Hitchcock*. Edited by François Truffaut and translated by Sabine d'Estree. 1975; New York: Seaver Books, 1982.

Becker, Jane S. *Selling Tradition: Appalachia and the Construction of an American Folk*. Chapel Hill: University of North Carolina Press, 1998.

Behar, Ruth. "Introduction: Women Writing Culture: Another Telling of the Story of American Anthropology." *Critique of Anthropology* 13 (1993): 307–25.

Behdad, Ali. *Belated Travelers*. Durham: Duke University Press, 1994.

Belosi, Thomas. " 'Indian Self-Government' as a Technique of Domination." *American Indian Quarterly* 15, no. 1 (Winter 1991): 23–28.

Ben Hur. Directed by William Wyler. Warner Bros., 1959.

Bendix, Regina. *In Search of Authenticity: The Formation of Folklore Studies*. Madison: University of Wisconsin Press, 1997.

Benjamin, Walter. "The Author as Producer" (1966). In *Reflections: Essays, Aphorisms, Autobiographical Writings*, edited and with an introduction by Peter Demetz. New York: Schocken Books, 1978.

———. "Unpacking My Library: A Talk about Book Collecting" (1931). In *Illuminations: Essays and Reflections*. New York: Schocken Books, 1968.

———. "The Work of Art in the Age of Mechanical Reproduction" (1936). In *Illuminations: Essays and Reflections*. New York: Schocken Books, 1968.

Berlant, Lauren. *The Queen of America Goes to Washington City: Essays on Sex and Citizenship*. Durham: Duke University Press, 1997.

———. "The Queen of America Goes to Washington City: Harriet Jacobs, Frances Harper, Anita Hill." *American Literature* 65, no. 3, Subjects and Citizens: Nation, Race, and Gender from Oroonoko to Anita Hill (September 1993): 549–74.

Blair, Sara. *Harlem Crossroads: Black Writers and the Photograph in the 20th Century*. Princeton: Princeton University Press, 2007.

Blum, Edward J. *Reforging the White Republic: Race, Religion, and American Nationalism, 1865–1898*. Baton Rouge: Louisiana State University Press, 2005.

———. *W. E. B. Du Bois, American Prophet*. Philadelphia: University of Pennsylvania Press, 2007.

Boas, Franz. *Anthropology and Modern Day Life*. 1928; Westport, Conn.: Greenwood Press, 1984.

Bold, Christine. *The* wpa *Guides: Mapping America*. Jackson: University Press of Mississippi, 1999.

Bolnick, Deborah Weiss. "Showing Who They Really Are." Paper presented at the annual meeting of the American Anthropological Association, November 2003.

Bone, Robert. *The Negro Novelist in America*. New Haven: Yale University Press, 1968.

Bonnell, Victoria. *Iconography of Power: Soviet Political Posters under Lenin and Stalin*. Berkeley: University of California Press, 1999.

Borowitz, Andy. Interviewed by Liane Hansen. *Weekend Edition Sunday*. National Public Radio. Segment from radio station kuow, Seattle, 10 October 2004.

Boxwell, D. A. "Sis Cat as Ethnographer: Self-Presentation and Self-Inscription in Zora Neale Hurston's *Mules and Men*." *African American Review* 26 (1992): 605–17.

Boyd, Valerie. *Wrapped in Rainbows: The Life of Zora Neale Hurston*. New York: Scribner, 2003.

Brady, Mary Pat. *Extinct Lands, Temporal Geographies: Chicana Literature and the Urgency of Space*. Durham: Duke University Press, 2002.

Breakdown. Directed by Jonathan Mostow. Paramount Pictures, 1997.

Breazeale, Kenon. "In Spite of Women: *Esquire* and the Male Consumer." In *The Gender and Consumer Culture Reader*, edited by Jennifer Scanlon, 226–44. New York: New York University Press, 2000.

Brecht, Bertolt. "Alienation Effects in Chinese Acting." In *Brecht on Theater*, 91–100. 1957; New York: Hill and Wang, 1986.

——. "The Popular and the Realistic." In *Brecht on Theater*, 107–14. 1957; New York: Hill and Wang, 1986.

Brody, Jennifer DeVere. *Impossible Purities: Blackness, Femininity, and Victorian Culture*. Durham: Duke University Press, 1998.

Bronner, Simon J. *Following Tradition: Folklore in the Discourse of American Culture*. Logan: Utah State University Press, 1998.

Brooks, Daphne A. *Bodies in Dissent: Spectacular Performances of Race and Freedom, 1850–1910*. Durham: Duke University Press, 2006.

——. "Burnt Sugar: Post-Soul Satire and Rock Memory." In *This Is Pop: In Search of the Elusive at Experience Music Project*, edited by Eric Weisbard, 103–16. Cambridge: Harvard University Press, 2004.

Brooks, Van Wyck. "On Creating a Usable Past." In *The Early Years*, edited by Claire Sprague, 219–26. New York: Harper and Row, 1968.

Brown, Dona. *Inventing New England: Regional Tourism in the Nineteenth Century*. Washington: Smithsonian Institution Press, 1995.

Bryant, Jerry. *Victims and Heroes: Racial Violence in the African American Novel*. Amherst: University of Massachusetts Press, 1997.

Buck-Morss, Susan. "Envisioning Capital: Political Economy on Display." In *Visual Display: Culture beyond Appearances*, edited by Peter Wollen and Lynne Cooke, 110–42. Seattle: Bay Press, 1995.

Bunzl, Matti. "Franz Boas and the Humboldtian Tradition: From Volksgeist and Nationalcharakter to an Anthropological Concept of Culture." In *Volksgeist as Method and Epic: Essays in Boasian Ethnography and the German Anthropological Tradition*, edited by George W. Stocking, 17–78. Madison: University of Wisconsin Press, 1996.

Burke, Kenneth. *The Philosophy of Literary Form: Studies in Symbolic Action*. Baton Rouge: Louisiana State University Press, 1941.

———. "Revolutionary Symbolism in America." In *American Writers' Congress*, edited by Henry Hart, 87–94. New York: International Publishers, 1935.

Burma, John H. "An Analysis of the Present Negro Press." *Social Forces* 26, no. 2 (December 1947): 172–80.

Burnett, Gene. *Florida's Past: People and Events That Shaped the State*. Sarasota, Fl.: Pineapple Press, 1998.

Butler, Judith. *Bodies That Matter: On the Discursive Limits of "Sex."* New York: Routledge, 1993.

———. *Gender Trouble: Feminism and the Subversion of Identity*. New York: Routledge, 1990.

———. "Performative Acts and Gender Constitution: An Essay in Phenomenology and Feminist Theory." In *Performing Feminisms: Feminist Critical Theory and Theatre*, edited by Sue-Ellen Case, 270–82. Baltimore: Johns Hopkins University Press, 1990.

Buzard, James. "On Auto-Ethnographic Authority." *Yale Journal of Criticism* 16 (2003): 61–91.

Caldwell, Erskine, and Margaret Bourke-White. *You Have Seen Their Faces*. New York: Viking Press, 1937.

California State. Federal Writers' Project of the Works Projects Administration for the State of California. *California: A Guide to the Golden State*. New York: Hastings House, 1939.

Carbado, Devon. "Racial Naturalization." *American Quarterly* 57, no. 3 (September 2005): 633–58.

Carby, Hazel V. *Cultures in Babylon: Black Britain and African America*. New York: Verso, 1999.

———. "The Politics of Fiction, Anthropology, and the Folk: Zora Neale Hurston." *New Essays on Their Eyes Were Watching God*, edited by Michael Awkward, 71–93. New York: Cambridge University Press, 1990.

———. *Reconstructing Womanhood: The Emergence of the Afro-American Woman Novelist*. New York: Oxford University Press, 1987.

Carlson, Leonard. "Federal Policy and Indian Land: Economic Interests and the Sale of Indian Allotments, 1900–34." *Agricultural History* 57, no. 1 (January 1983): 33–45.

Carr, Brian, and Tova Cooper. "Zora Neale Hurston and the Modernism at the Critical Limit." *MFS Modern Fiction Studies* 48 (2002): 285–313.

Cawelti, John. *Apostles of a Self-Made Man*. Chicago: University of Chicago Press, 1965.

Chadwell, Sean. "Inventing That 'Old-timey' Style: Southern Authenticity in *O Brother, Where Art Thou?*" *Journal of Popular Film and Television* 32, no. 1 (Spring 2004): 2–9.

Cherniavsky, Eva. *Incorporations: Race, Nation and the Body Politics of Capital*. Minneapolis: University of Minnesota Press, 2006.

Chris Rock: Bigger and Blacker (1999). Directed by Keith Truesdell. HBO Home Video, 2000.

Christmas in July. Directed by Preston Sturges. Paramount, 1940.

Chude-Sokei, Louis. *The Last Darky: Bert Williams, Black-on-Black Minstrelsy, and the African Diaspora*. Durham: Duke University Press, 2006.

Clarke, Deborah. " 'The porch couldn't talk for looking': Voice and Vision in *Their Eyes Were Watching God*." *African American Review* 35 (2001): 599–613.

Clifford, James. *The Predicament of Culture: Twentieth-Century Ethnography, Literature, and Art*. Cambridge: Harvard University Press, 1988.

———. *Routes: Travel and Translation in the Late Twentieth Century*. Cambridge: Harvard University Press, 1997.

Cohen, Lizabeth. *A Consumer's Republic: The Politics of Mass Consumption in Postwar America*. New York: Vintage, 2003.

———. *Making a New Deal: Industrial Workers in Chicago, 1919–1939*. Cambridge: Cambridge University Press, 1990.

Colbert, Stephen. Interview with Charlie Rose. *Charlie Rose*. PBS, 8 December 2006.

Cole, John Y. "Amassing American 'Stuff': The Library of Congress and the Federal Arts Projects of the 1930s." *Library of Congress Quarterly Journal* 41, no. 4 (1983): 356–89.

Conrad, Joseph. *Lord Jim*. 1900; New York: Penguin, 1986.

Content, Rob, Tim Kreider, and Boyd White. "*O Brother, Where Art Thou?*" (Reviews). *Film Quarterly* 55 (Fall 2001): 41–48.

Crimp, Douglas. *On the Museum's Ruins*. Cambridge: MIT Press, 1995.

Cripps, Thomas. *Slow Fade to Black: The Negro in American Film, 1900–1942*. 1977; New York: Oxford University Press, 1993.

Cross, Gary. *An All-Consuming Century: Why Commercialism Won in Modern America*. New York: Columbia University Press, 2000.

Curtis, Barry, and Claire Pajaczkowska. " 'Getting There': Travel, Time and Narrative." In *Traveler's Tales: Narratives of Home and Displacement*, edited by George Robertson, Melinda Mash, Lisa Tickner, Jon Bird, Barry Curtis, and Tim Putnam, 198–215. Routledge: New York, 1994.

Daniel, Peter, Merry Foresta, Maren Stange, and Sally Stein, eds. *Official Images: New Deal Photography*. Washington: Smithsonian Institution Press, 1987.

de Certeau, Michel. *The Practice of Everyday Life*. Translated by Steven Rendall. Berkeley: University of California Press, 1984.

Debord, Guy. *Society of the Spectacle*. Translated by Ken Knabb. London: Rebel Press, 1967.

Decker, Jeffrey Louis. *Made in America: Self-styled Success from Horatio Alger to Oprah Winfrey.* Minneapolis: University of Minnesota Press, 1997.

Deliverance. Directed by John Boorman. Warner Brothers. 1972.

Denning, Michael. *The Cultural Front.* New York: Verso, 1997.

——. *Mechanic Accents: Dime Novels and Working-Class Culture in America.* Revised edition. New York: Verso, 1998.

DePastino, Todd. *Citizen Hobo: How a Century of Homelessness Shaped America.* Chicago: University of Chicago Press, 2003.

Dickinson, Emily. "1129: 'Tell all the Truth but tell it slant—.'" *The Norton Anthology of Modern Poetry,* 2nd ed., edited by Richard Ellmann and Robert O'Clair. New York: Norton, 1988.

Dickson-Carr, Darryl. *African American Satire: The Sacredly Profane Novel.* Columbia: University of Missouri Press, 2001.

Diffee, Christopher. "Sex and the City: The White Slavery Scare and Social Governance in the Progressive Era." *American Quarterly* 57, no. 2 (June 2005): 411–37.

Dimock, Wai Chee. "Introduction: Genres as Fields of Knowledge." Special Topic: Remapping Genre. *PMLA* 122, no. 5 (October 2007): 1377–88.

Dinerstein, Joel. *Swinging the Machine: Modernity, Technology and African American Culture between the World Wars.* Boston: University of Massachusetts Press, 2003.

Doane, Mary Ann. *Femmes Fatales: Feminism, Film Theory, Psychoanalysis.* New York: Routledge, 1991.

Dolby-Stahl, Sandra. "Literary Objectives: Hurston's Use of Personal Narrative in *Mules and Men.*" *Western Folklore* 51 (1992): 51–63.

Dorson, Richard M. *Folklore and Folklife: An Introduction.* Chicago: University of Chicago Press, 1982.

Du Bois, W. E. B. *Black Reconstruction in America: 1860–1880.* 1935; New York: Free Press, 1998.

——. *Dusk of Dawn: An Essay towards the Autobiography of the Race Concept.* New York: Transaction Publishers, 1983.

——. *The Souls of Black Folk.* 1903; New York: Dover Publications, 1994.

Duck, Leigh Anne. "'Go there tuh *know* there': Zora Neale Hurston and the Chronotope of the Folk." *American Literary History* 13 (2001): 265–94.

Dyer, Richard. *White.* New York: Routledge, 1997.

Easy Living. Directed by Mitchell Leisen. Paramount, 1937.

Edward, Brent Hayes. *The Practice of Diaspora: Litearture, Translation, and the Rise of Black Internationalism.* Cambridge: Harvard University Press, 2003.

Eilperin, Juliet. "Palin's 'Pro-America Areas' Remark: Extended Version." *Washington Post,* 17 October 2008. The Trail: Election Day 2008.

Elliot, Michael. *The Culture Concept: Writing and Difference in the Age of Realism.* Minnesota: University of Minnesota Press, 2002.

Elsner, John, and Roger Cardinal. *The Cultures of Collecting.* Cambridge: Harvard University Press, 1994.

Emerson, Michael O., and Edward J. Blum. "Dreams." In *People of the Dream*, 5–27. Princeton: Princeton University Press, 2006.

Emrich, Duncan. "'Folk-Lore': William Jon Thoms." *California Folklore Quarterly* 5 (October 1946): 355–74.

Fabian, Johannes. *Time and the Other: How Anthropology Makes Its Object.* New York: Columbia University Press, 1983.

Fanon, Frantz. *Black Skin, White Masks.* Translated by Charles Lam Markmann. New York: Grove Weidenfeld, 1967.

Faulkner, Howard J. "A Vanishing Race." *CLA Journal* 37, no. 3 (1994): 284–87.

Favor, J. Martin. "Color, Culture and the Nature of Race: George S. Schuyler's *Black No More.*" In *Authentic Blackness: The Folk in the New Negro Renaissance*, 111–36. Durham: Duke University Press, 1999.

Federal Writers' Project. *American Stuff: An Anthology of Prose & Verse by Members of the Federal Writers' Project; with Sixteen Prints by the Federal Art Project.* New York: Viking Press, 1937.

Feintuch, Burt, ed. *The Conservation of Culture: Folklorists and the Public Sector.* Lexington: University of Kentucky Press, 1988.

Ferguson, Jeffrey B. *The Sage of Sugar Hill: George S. Schuyler and the Harlem Renaissance.* New Haven: Yale University Press, 2005.

Fiedler, Leslie A. *Love and Death in the American Novel.* 1960; Champaign: Dalkey Archive Press, 2003.

Filene, Benjamin. "O Brother, What Next? Making Sense of the Folk Fad." *Southern Cultures* 10, no. 2 (2004): 50–69.

——. *Romancing the Folk: Public Memory and American Roots Music.* Chapel Hill: University of North Carolina Press, 2000.

Findlay, James A., and Margaret Bing. "Touring Florida through the Federal Writers' Project." *Journal of Decorative and Propaganda Arts* 23, Florida Theme Issue (1998): 289–305.

Fisher, Rudolph. *Walls of Jericho.* 1928; Ann Arbor: University of Michigan Press, 1994.

Fleischhauer, Carl, and Beverly W. Brannan, eds. *Documenting America: 1935–1943.* Los Angeles: University of California Press, 1988.

Florida Folklife from the WPA Collections, 1937–1942. The American Folklife Center, American Memory, Library of Congress. Web site of American Memory, http://memory.loc.gov/ammem/index.html, accessed 29 June 2007.

Florida State. Federal Writers' Project of the Works Projects Administration for the State of Florida. *Florida: A Guide to the Southernmost State.* New York: Oxford University Press, 1939.

Foley, Barbara. *Radical Representations: Politics and Form in U.S. Proletarian Fiction, 1929–1941.* Durham: Duke University Press, 1993.

——. *Specters of 1919: Class and Nation in the Making of the New Negro.* Chicago: University of Illinois Press, 2008.

Foucault, Michel. *The Archaeology of Knowledge & the Discourse on Language.* New York: Pantheon Books, 1972.

Fraden, Rena. *Blueprints for a Black Federal Theater, 1935–39*. New York: Cambridge University Press, 1994.

Freedman, Jonathan. "Transgressions of a Model Minority." *Shofar: An Interdisciplinary Journal of Jewish Studies* 23, no. 4 (Summer 2005): 69–97.

Frow, John. "Tourism and the Semiotics of Nostalgia." *October* 21 (1991): 123–51.

Fuller, Thomas. " 'Go West, young man!'—An Elusive Slogan." *Indiana Magazine of History* 100, no. 3 (2004): 19.

Gaines, Kevin K. *Uplifting the Race: Black Leadership, Politics and Culture in the Twentieth Century*. Chapel Hill: University of North Carolina Press, 1996.

Gates, Henry Louis, Jr. *Figures in Black: Words, Signs, and the "Racial" Self*. New York: Oxford University Press, 1987.

——. "Harlem on Our Minds." *Critical Inquiry* 24, no. 1 (autumn 1997): 1–12.

Gates, Henry Louis, Jr., and K. A. Appiah, eds. *Zora Neale Hurston: Critical Perspectives Past and Present*. New York: Amistad, 1993.

Gehring, Wes D., ed. *Handbook of American Film Genres*. New York: Greenwood Press, 1988.

Gilbert, Matthew. "Speaking Truthiness to Power." *Boston Globe*, 11 November 2007, Sunday, Living Arts section, N16.

Gilroy, Paul. *Against Race: Imagining Political Culture beyond the Color Line*. Cambridge: Belknap Press of Harvard University Press, 2000.

——. "Modern Tones." In *Rhapsodies in Black: Art of the Harlem Renaissance*, edited by Richard J. Powell and David A. Bailey, 102–9. Berkeley: University of California Press, 1997.

Glassman, Steve, and Kathryn Lee Seidel. *Zora in Florida*. Orlando: University of Central Florida Press, 1991.

Glenn, Susan. *Female Spectacle: The Theatrical Roots of Modern Feminism*. Cambridge: Harvard University Press, 2000.

——. "Taking Burlesque Seriously." *Reviews in American History* 21, no. 1 (March 1993): 93–100.

Gordon, Deborah. "The Politics of Ethnographic Authority: Race and Writing in the Ethnography of Margaret Mead and Zora Neale Hurston." In *Modernist Anthropology: From Fieldwork to Text*, edited by Marc Manganaro, 146–62. Princeton: Princeton University Press, 1990.

Gorman, Juliet. "Historical Controversies." *New Deal Narratives: Visions of Florida*. May 2001. In "The Thirties" section of "Jukin' It Out: Contested Visions of Florida in New Deal Narratives," web site of Oberlin College Library at www.oberlin.edu/library/, accessed 18 September 2007.

Gramsci, Antonio. *Selections from the Prison Notebooks of Antonio Gramsci*. Edited and translated by Quintin Hoare and Geoffrey Nowell Smith. New York: International Publishers, 1971.

Grant, Madison. *The Passing of the Great Race*. New York: Scribner's, 1916.

The Grapes of Wrath. Directed by John Ford. 20th Century Fox, 1940.

The Great McGinty. Directed by Preston Sturges. Paramount, 1940.

Green, Archie. *Torching the Fink Books and Other Essays on Vernacular Culture*. Chapel Hill: University of North Carolina Press, 2001.

Greenberg, Jonathan. "Nathanael West and the Mystery of Feeling." *MFS: Modern Fiction Studies* 52, no. 3 (2006): 588–612.

Grider, Sylvia. "Salvaging the Folklore of 'Old English' Folk." *100 Years of American Folklore Studies: A Conceptual History*. Edited by William M. Clements. Washington: American Folklore Society, 1988.

Griffin, Farah Jasmine. *Who Set You Flowin'?: The African-American Migration Narrative*. New York: Oxford University Press, 1995.

Griffin, Sean. "The Gang's All Here: Generic versus Racial Integration in the 1940s Musical." *Cinema Journal* 42, no. 1 (Fall 2002): 21–45.

Halberstam, Judith. *Female Masculinity*. Durham: Duke University Press, 1998.

Hale, Grace. *Making Whiteness: The Culture of Segregation in the South, 1890–1940*. New York: Pantheon Books, 1998.

Hall, Stuart. "Race, Articulation and Societies Structured in Dominance." *Sociological Theories: Race and Colonialism*, 305–45. Paris: UNESCO, 1980.

Harries, Martin. "In the Coen Brothers' New Film, the Dark, Utopian Music of the American South." *Chronicle of Higher Education*, 2 February 2001, B14–5.

Harris, Cheryl. "Whiteness as Property." *Harvard Law Review* 106 (June 1993): 1707–91.

Harris, Trudier. *Exorcising Blackness: Historical and Literary Lynching and Burning Rituals*. Bloomington: University of Indiana, 1984.

Hartman, Saidiya A. *Scenes of Subjection: Terror, Slavery and Self-Making in Nineteenth-Century America*. New York: Oxford University Press, 1997.

Harvey, David. *The Condition of Postmodernity*. Cambridge: Blackwell Publishers, 1990.

Harvey, James. *Romantic Comedy in Hollywood, from Lubitsch to Sturges*. New York: De Capo Press, 1998.

Haslam, Jason. " 'The open sesame of a pork-colored skin': Whiteness and Privilege in *Black No More*." *Modern Language Studies* 32, no. 1 (2002): 15–30.

Hegeman, Susan. *Patterns for America: Modernism and the Concept of Culture*. Princeton: Princeton University Press, 1999.

Hemenway, Robert E. *Zora Neale Hurston: A Literary Biography*. Chicago: University of Chicago Press, 1980.

Henderson, Brian, ed. *Five Screenplays by Preston Sturges*. Los Angeles: University of California Press, 1985.

Hendler, Glenn. "Pandering in the Public Sphere: Masculinity and the Market in Horatio Alger." *American Quarterly* 48, no. 3 (1996): 415–38.

Herbst, Josephine. "Nathanael West." *Kenyon Review* 23 (Fall 1961): 611–30. Rpt. in *Nathanael West: A Collection of Critical Essays*, edited by Jay Martin, 13–30. Englewood Cliffs: Prentice-Hall, 1971.

Herder, Johann Gottfried. *Another Philosophy of History and Selected Political Writings*. Translated, with introduction and notes by Ioannis D. Evrigenis and Daniel Pellerin. Indianapolis: Hackett Publishing, 2004.

Herman, Jan. *A Talent for Trouble: The Life of Hollywood's Most Acclaimed Director, William Wyler*. New York: G. P. Putnam's Sons, 1995.

Hernandez, Graciela. "Multiple Mediations in Zora Neale Hurston's *Mules and Men*." *Critique of Anthropology* 13 (1993): 351–62.

Hirsch, Jerrold. "Cultural Pluralism and Applied Folklore: The New Deal Precedent." In *The Conservation of Culture: Folklorists and the Public Sector*, edited by Burt Feintuch, 46–67. Lexington: University of Kentucky Press, 1988.

Hoefel, Roseanne. " 'Different by Degree': Ella Cara Deloria, Zora Neale Hurston, and Franz Boas Contend with Race and Ethnicity." *American Indian Quarterly* 25, no. 2 (Spring 2001): 181–202.

Hoffman, Joel M. "From Augustine to Tangerine: Florida at the U.S. World Fairs." *Journal of Decorative and Propaganda Arts* 23, Florida Theme Issue (1998): 48–85.

Hole. "Doll Parts." On the album *Live through This*. Geffen Records, 1994.

Holloway, Jonathan Scott. *Confronting the Veil: Abram Harris Jr., E. Franklin Frazier, and Ralph Bunche, 1919–1941*. Chapel Hill: University of North Carolina Press, 2002.

Holloway, Karla F. C. *The Character of the Word: The Texts of Zora Neale Hurston*. Westport, Conn.: Greenwood Press, 1987.

Holt, Thomas C. *The Problem of Race in the 21st Century*. Cambridge: Harvard University Press, 2000.

Hudson, Peter. "Tap Dance." In *Africana: The Encyclopedia of the African and African American Experience*. On www.mywire.com/, the MyWire Knowledge web site of Oxford University Press, dated 1 January 2008, accessed 22 November 2009.

Huggins, Nathan. *Harlem Renaissance*. New York: Oxford University Press, 1973.

——. *Voices from the Harlem Renaissance*. New York: Oxford University Press, 1995.

Hughes, Langston. *The Big Sea: An Autobiography*. 1940; 2nd ed., New York: Hill and Wang, 1993.

——. "The Negro Artist and the Racial Mountain" (1926). In *The Norton Anthology of African American Literature*, 2nd ed., edited by Henry Louis Gates Jr. and Nellie McKay, 1311–14. New York: Norton, 2004.

——. *The Ways of White Folks*. 1934; New York: Vintage, 1990.

Humphries, David T. *Different Dispatches: Journalism in American Modernist Prose*. New York: Routledge, 2006.

Hurston, Zora Neale. "Characteristics of Negro Expression." In *The Sanctified Church: The Folklore Writings of Zora Neale Hurston*, 41–78. 1934; Berkeley: Turtle Island, 1981.

——. *Dust Tracks on a Road*. 1942; New York: Harper Perennial, 1991.

———. *Go Gator and the Muddy Water: Writings by Zora Neale Hurston and the Federal Writer's Project.* Edited and with a biographical essay by Pamela Bordelon. New York: W. W. Norton, 1999.

———. *Mules and Men.* 1935; New York: Harper Perennial, 1990.

———. *The Sanctified Church: The Folklore Writings of Zora Neale Hurston.* Berkeley: Turtle Island, 1981.

———. "What White Publishers Won't Print." In *I Love Myself When I Am Laughing . . . And Then Again When I Am Looking Mean and Impressive: A Zora Neale Hurston Reader,* 169–73. New York: Feminist Press, 1979.

Huston, John. *An Open Book.* London: Columbus Books, 1988.

Hutchinson, George. *The Harlem Renaissance in Black and White.* Cambridge: Belknap Press of Harvard University Press, 1997.

I Am a Fugitive from a Chain Gang. Directed by Mervyn LeRoy. Warner Bros., 1932.

Irr, Caren. *The Suburb of Dissent: Cultural Politics in the United States and Canada in the 1930s.* Durham: Duke University Press, 1998.

Jacobs, Diane. *Christmas in July: The Life and Art of Preston Sturges.* Los Angeles: University of California Press, 1992.

Jacobson, Matthew Frye. *Whiteness of a Different Color: European Immigrants and the Alchemy of Race.* Cambridge: Harvard University Press, 1998.

Jakle, John A., and Keith A. Sculle. *Motoring: The Highway Experience in America.* Athens: University of Georgia Press, 2008.

Jakle, John A., Keith A. Sculle, and Jefferson S. Rogers. *The Motel in America (The Road and American Culture Series).* Baltimore: Johns Hopkins University Press, 1996.

Jarrett, Gene Andrew. *Deans and Truants: Race and Realism in African American Literature.* Philadelphia: University of Pennsylvania, 2007.

Johnson, Barbara. "Metaphor, Metonymy and Voice in *Their Eyes Were Watching God.*" In *A World of Difference,* 155–71. Baltimore: Johns Hopkins Press, 1987.

———. "Thresholds of Difference: Structures of Address in Zora Neale Hurston." *Critical Inquiry* 12 (1985): 278–89.

Johnson, Charles S. "The New Frontage on American Life" (1925). In *The New Negro,* 278–98. New York: Atheneum, 1968.

Johnson, Guy B. "Newspaper Advertisements and Negro Culture." *Journal of Social Forces* 3, no. 4 (May 1925): 706–9.

Jordan, Rosan Augusta. "Not into Cold Space: Zora Neale Hurston and J. Frank Dobie as Holistic Folklorists." *Southern Folklore* 49 (1992): 109–31.

Joseph, Philip. "The Verdict from the Porch: Zora Neale Hurston and Reparative Justice." *American Literature* 74 (2002): 455–83.

Kadlec, David. "Zora Neale Hurston and the Federal Folk." *Modernism/Modernity* 7 (2000): 471–85.

Kaplan, Carla, ed. *Zora Neale Hurston: A Life in Letters.* New York: Doubleday, 2002.

Kazin, Alfred. *On Native Grounds: An Interpretation of Modern American Prose Literature*. 1942; New York: Harcourt Brace, 1995.

Keire, Mara. "The Vice Trust: A Reinterpretation of the White Slavery Scare in the United States, 1907–1917." *Journal of Social History* 35, no. 1 (2001): 5–41.

Kelly, Robin D. G. "AHR Forum: Notes on Deconstructing the 'Folk.'" *American Historical Review* 97 (December 1992): 1400–408.

———. *Hammer and Hoe: Alabama Communists during the Great Depression*. Chapel Hill: University of North Carolina Press, 1990.

Kennedy, Stetson. "A Florida Treasure Hunt." *Florida Folklife from the WPA Collections, 1937–1942*. American Folklife Center, American Memory, Library of Congress. Web site of American Memory, http://memory.loc.gov/, accessed 29 June 2007.

———. *Palmetto Country* (1942). Rpt. Tallahassee: Florida A & M University Press, 1989.

———. "Working with Zora." In *All About Zora: Proceedings of the Academic Conference of the First Annual Zora Neale Hurston Festival of the Arts, January 26–27, 1990*, edited by Alice Morgan Grant, 26–27. Winter Park, Fl.: Four-G Publishers, 1991.

King, Edward. *The Great South*. Hartford, Conn.: American Publishing Company, 1875.

Knight, Arthur. *Disintegrating the Musical: Black Performance and American Musical Film*. Durham: Duke University Press, 2002.

Krugman, Paul. "Desperately Seeking Seriousness." *New York Times*, 26 October 2008.

Kuenz, Jane. "American Racial Discourse, 1900–1930: Schuyler's *Black No More*." *Novel* 30, no. 2 (1997): 170–92.

The Lady Eve. Directed by Preston Sturges. Paramount, 1941.

Lamothe, Daphne. *Inventing the New Negro: Narrative, Culture and Ethnography*. Philadelphia: University of Pennsylvania Press, 2008.

Larsen, Nella. *Quicksand and Passing* (1928). Rpt. in *American Women Writers Series*. Foreword by Deborah McDowell. New Brunswick: Rutgers University Press, 1986.

Larson, Charles A. "Introduction to *Black No More*." In George Schuyler, *Black No More*. New York: Macmillan, 1971.

Leak, Jeffrey B., ed. *Rac[e]ing to the Right: Selected Essays of George S. Schuyler*. Knoxville: University of Tennessee Press, 2001.

Lears, T. J. Jackson. *No Place of Grace: Antimodernism and the Transformation of American Culture, 1880–1920*. New York: Pantheon, 1981.

Levine, Lawrence. "The Historian and the Icon: Photography and the History of the American People in the 1930s and 1940s." In *Documenting America, 1935–1943*, edited by Carl Fleischauer and Beverly Brannan, 15–42. Los Angeles: University of California, 1988.

———. *The Unpredictable Past: Explorations in American Cultural History*. New York: Oxford University Press, 1993.

Lewis, David Levering. *When Harlem Was in Vogue*. New York: Penguin, 1997.

Lewis, Robert M. *From Traveling Show to Vaudeville: Theatrical Spectacle in America, 1830–1910*. Baltimore: Johns Hopkins University Press, 2003.

Lhamon, W. T. *Raising Cain: Blackface Performance from Jim Crow to Hip Hop*. Cambridge: Harvard University Press, 1998.

Lhurmann, Baz, et al. "Ants in His Pants." Sight and Sound, May 2000. Web site of the British Film Institute, www.bfi.org.uk, accessed 6 August 2005.

Lippmann, Walter. *Men of Destiny*. New York: Macmillan, 1927.

———. *Public Opinion*. New York: Macmillan, 1922.

Lipsitz, George. *The Possessive Investment in Whiteness: How White People Profit from Identity Politics*. Philadelphia: Temple University Press, 1998.

Littell, Robert. "Putting America on Paper." *Today* 5 (30 November 1935): 6–9.

The Little Foxes. Directed by William Wyler. RKO, 1941.

Locke, Alain. "The New Negro." *The New Negro*, 3–16. 1925; New York: Atheneum, 1968.

———. *"Their Eyes Were Watching God*—Review." *Opportunity*, 1 June 1938. Rpt. in *Zora Neale Hurston: Critical Perspectives Past and Present*, edited by Henry Louis Gates Jr. and K. A. Appiah. New York: Amistad, 1993.

Lopez, Ian F. Haney. *White by Law: The Legal Construction of Race*. New York: New York University Press, 1996.

Lott, Eric. *Love and Theft: Blackface Minstrelsy and the American Working Class*. New York: Oxford University Press, 1993.

Lutz, Donald. "Rhode Island, Section 37: Acts and Orders of 1647." In *Colonial Origins of the American Constitution: A Documentary History*. Indianapolis: Liberty Fund, 1998. Web site of *The Online Library of Liberty*, http://oll.libertyfund.org/, 2005, accessed 30 June 2006.

MacCannell, Dean. *Empty Meeting Grounds: The Tourist Papers*. New York: Routledge, 1992.

———. *The Tourist: A New Theory of the Leisure Class*. New York: Schocken Books, 1975.

Madsen, Axel, and William Wyler. *William Wyler: The Authorized Biography*. New York: Thomas Y. Crowell, 1973.

Malinowski, Branislaw. *Argonauts of the Western Pacific: An Account of Native Enterprise and Adventure in the Archipelagoes of Melanesian New Guinea*. 1922; Prospect Heights, Ill.: Waveland Press, 1984.

Malone, Bill. *Country Music, USA*. 2nd rev. ed. Austin: University of Texas Press, 2002.

The Maltese Falcon. Directed by John Huston. Warner Bros., 1941.

Mancini, J. M. "'Messin' with the Furniture Man': Early Country Music, Regional Culture, and the Search for Anthological Modernism." *American Literary History* 16, no. 2 (2004): 208–37.

Mangione, Jerre. *The Dream and the Deal: The Federal Writers' Project, 1935–1943*. 1972; Philadelphia: University of Pennsylvania Press, 1983.

Mao, Douglas, and Rebecca L. Walkowitz. "The New Modernist Studies." *PMLA* 123, no. 3 (May 2008): 737–48.

Marcus, George E., and Michael M. J. Fischer. *Anthropology as Cultural Critique: An Experimental Moment in the Human Sciences.* Chicago: University of Chicago Press, 1986.

Marcus, Greil. *Mystery Train: Images of America in Rock 'n' Roll.* 1975; 5th ed., New York: Plume, 2008.

Martin, Charles D. *The White African American Body: A Cultural and Literary Exploration.* New Brunswick: Rutgers University Press, 2002.

Martin, Jay. *Nathanael West: The Art of His Life.* New York: Farrar, Straus and Giroux, 1970.

——, ed. *Nathanael West: A Collection of Critical Essays.* Englewood Cliffs: Prentice-Hall, 1971.

Marx, Karl. *Capital: A Critique of Political Economy.* Edited by Frederick Engels. 1916; New York: International Publishers, 1967.

Massey, Doreen. *Space, Place and Gender.* Minneapolis: University of Minnesota Press, 1994.

Maxwell, William J. *New Negro, Old Left: African American Writing and Communism between the Wars.* New York: Columbia University Press, 1999.

McCallum, Todd. "The Tramp Is Back." *Labour/Le Travail* 56 (Fall 2005). Web site at www.historycooperative.org/, accessed 26 October 2006.

McCausland, Elizabeth. "Save the Arts Projects." *The Nation* 145, no. 3 (17 July 1937). Web site of New Deal Network, http://newdeal.feri.org/, accessed 4 September 2007.

McDonogh, Gary, ed. *The Florida Negro: A Federal Writers' Project Legacy.* Jackson: University Press of Mississippi, 1993.

McElvaine, Robert S. *The Great Depression: America, 1929–1941.* 1983; New York: Times Books, 1993.

McIntyre, Rebecca C. "Promoting the Gothic South." *Southern Cultures* 11, no. 2 (Summer 2005): 33–61.

McNeil, W. K. "Pre-Society American Folklorists." In *100 Years of American Folklore Studies: A Conceptual History*, edited by William M. Clements, 2–5. Washington: American Folklore Society, 1988.

Meet John Doe. Directed by Frank Capra. Frank Capra Productions Inc., 1941.

Meisenhelder, Susan. "Conflict and Resistance in Zora Neale Hurston's *Mules and Men.*" *Journal of American Folklore* 109 (1996): 267–88.

Melosh, Barbara. *Engendering Culture: Manhood and Womanhood in New Deal Public Art and Theater.* Washington: Smithsonian Institution Press, 1991.

Michaels, Lloyd I. "A Particular Kind of Joking: Burlesque, Vaudeville, and Nathanael West." *Studies in American Humor* 1, no. 3 (January 1975): 148–60.

Middleton, Richard. "O Brother, Let's Go Down Home: Loss, Nostalgia and the Blues." *Popular Music* 26, no. 1 (January 2007): 47–64.

Miller, James. "Inventing the 'Found' Object: Artifactuality, Folk History and the Rise of Capitalist Ethnography in 1930s America." *Journal of American Folklore* 117 (2004): 373–93.

Mills, Joseph. "Absurdity of America in Schuyler's *Black No More*." *EnterText* 1, no. 1 (Winter 2000): 127–48. Joseph Mill's personal page on web site of Brunel University, http://people.brunel.ac.uk/, accessed 18 March 2005.

Miracle of Morgan's Creek. Directed by Preston Sturges. Paramount, 1944.

Moon, Henry Lee. "Mules and Men." (Review). *New Republic*, December 11, 1935. Rpt. in *Zora Neale Hurston: Critical Perspectives Past and Present*, edited by Henry Louis Gates Jr. and K. A. Appiah. New York: Amistad, 1993.

Moran, Kathleen, and Michael Rogin. "Mr. Capra Goes to Washington." *Representations* 84, In Memory of Michael Rogin (Autumn 2003): 213–48.

——. " 'What's the Matter with Capra?': *Sullivan's Travels* and the Popular Front." *Representations* 71 (Summer 2000): 106–34.

Morgan, Stacey. " 'The Strange and Wonderful Workings of Science': Race Science and Essentialism in George Schuyler's Black No More." *CLA Journal* 42, no. 3 (1999): 331–52.

Mormino, Gary R. "Sunbelt Dreams and Altered States: A Social and Cultural History of Florida, 1950–2000." *Florida Historical Quarterly* 81, no. 1, The Best Laid Plans: Community, History, and Urban Development in Central Florida (Summer 2002): 3–21.

Moten, Fred. *In the Break: The Aesthetics of the Black Radical Tradition*. Minneapolis: University of Minnesota Press, 2003.

Mr. Deeds Goes to Town. Directed by Frank Capra. Columbia, 1936.

Mr. Smith Goes to Washington. Directed by Frank Capra. Columbia, 1939.

Mullen, Bill V. *Popular Fronts: Chicago and African American Cultural Politics, 1935–1946*. Urbana and Chicago: University of Illinois Press, 1999.

Mullen, Bill V., and James Smethurst. *Left of the Color Line: Race, Radicalism, and Twentieth-Century Literature of the United States*. Chapel Hill: University of North Carolina Press, 2003.

Mullen, Harryette. "Optic White: Blackness and the Production of Whiteness." *diacritics* 24, nos. 2–3 (Summer–Fall 1994): 71–89.

Muñoz, José Esteban. " 'The White to Be Angry': Vaginal Davis's Terrorist Drag." *Social Text* 52/53, Queer Transexions of Race, Nation and Gender (Fall–Winter 1997): 80–103.

Muscio, Giuliana. *Hollywood's New Deal*. Philadelphia: Temple University Press, 1997.

Nakamura, Lisa. "Race in/for Cyberspace: Identity Tourism and Racial Passing on the Internet." In *The Cybercultures Reader*, edited by David M. Bell and Barbara M. Kennedy, 712–20. London: Routledge, 2000.

"National Annenberg Election Survey, 2004." News release of 21 September 2004, Annenberg Public Policy Center of the University of Pennsylvania. Web site of Ragan newsletters, www.employeecomm.com/, accessed 12 August 2007.

Newell, William Wells. "On the Field and Work of a Journal of American Folk-Lore." *Journal of American Folklore* 1 (June 1888): 3–7.

Nicholls, David G. "Migrant Labor, Folklore and Resistance in Hurston's Polk County: Reframing *Mules and Men.*" *African American Review* 33 (Fall 1999): 467–79.

North, Michael. *The Dialect of Modernism: Race, Language and Twentieth-Century Literature.* New York: Oxford University Press, 1994.

——. *Reading 1922: A Return to the Scene of the Modern.* New York: Oxford University Press, 1999.

O Brother, Where Art Thou? Directed by Joel Coen and Ethan Coen (uncredited). Written by Homer, Ethan Coen, and Joel Coen. Touchstone Pictures, 2000.

O Brother, Where Art Thou? Soundtrack. Produced by T-Bone Burnett. Various artists. Mercury Nashville/Lost Highway Records, 2000.

Oermann, Keith K. "*O Brother, Where Art Thou?* Musical Background." Web site of Lost Highway, www.losthighwayrecords.com/, accessed 23 November 2009.

O'Neill, Edward R. "Traumatic Postmodern Histories: *Velvet Goldmine*'s Phantasmatic Testimonies." *Camera Obscura* 19, no. 3 (2004): 156–85.

Orvell, Miles. *The Real Thing: Imitation and Authenticity in American Culture, 1880–1940.* Chapel Hill: University of North Carolina Press, 1989.

Our Daily Bread. Directed by King Vidor. Viking Productions Inc., 1934.

The Palm Beach Story. Directed by Preston Sturges. Paramount, 1942.

Patterson, David. "Inventing Nathanael West." *Washington Times,* 31 August 1997, B7.

Patterson, Orlando. "Race Over." *New Republic,* 10 January 2000, 6.

——. *Slavery and Social Death.* Cambridge: Harvard University Press, 1982.

Pearce, Susan M., ed. *Interpreting Objects and Collections.* New York: Routledge, 1994.

——. *Museums, Objects and Collections: A Cultural Study.* Washington: Smithsonian Institution Press, 1992.

Peiss, Kathy L. "American Women and the Making of Modern Consumer Culture." *Journal of MultiMedia History* 1, no. 1 (Fall 1998): 33. Web site of journal, www.albany.edu/jmmh, accessed 2 November 2006..

Pells, Richard. *Radical Visions and American Dreams: Culture and Social Thought.* Rpt. 1973; Chicago: University of Illinois Press, 1998.

Penkower, Monty N. *The Federal Writers' Project: A Study in Government Patronage of the Arts.* Urbana: University of Illinois Press, 1977.

Peplow, Michael W. "George Schuyler, Satirist: Rhetorical Devices in Black No More." *CLA Journal* 18, no. 2 (1974): 242–57.

——. *George Schuyler.* Boston: Twayne Publishers, 1980.

Pfister, Joel. "Complicity Critiques." *American Literary History* 12, *History in the Making.* (Autumn 2000): 610–32.

——. *Individuality Incorporated: Indians and the Multicultural Modern.* Durham: Duke University Press, 2004.

Podhoretz, Norman. "Nathanael West: A Particular Kind of Joking." *New*

Yorker, 18 May 1957: 155–65. Rpt. in *Nathanael West: A Collection of Critical Essays*, edited by Jay Martin, 154–60. Englewood Cliffs, N.J.: Prentice-Hall, 1971.

"Proposition 54." *The Racial Privacy Initiative*. www.adversity.net/RPI, accessed 1 January 2005.

Raban, Jonathan. "A Surfeit of Commodities: The Novels of Nathanael West." In *The American Novel and the Nineteen Twenties*, edited by Malcolm Bradbury and David Palmer, 215–232. London: Edward Arnold, 1971.

Rabinowitz, Paula. *Labor and Desire: Women's Revolutionary Fiction in Depression America*. Chapel Hill: University of North Carolina Press, 1991.

———. *They Must Be Represented: The Politics of Documentary*. New York: Verso, 1994.

Rahv, Philip. "The Cult of Experience in American Writing." *Partisan Review* (1940). Rpt. in *Essays on Literature and Politics: 1932–1972*, 8–22. Boston: Houghton Mifflin, 1978.

Rampersad, Arnold. "Harlem Renaissance, 1919–40." In *The Norton Anthology of African American Literature*, 2nd ed., edited by Henry Louis Gates Jr. and Nellie McKay, 953–62. New York: Norton, 2004.

———. *The Life of Langston Hughes*, vol. 1, *1902–1941: I, Too, Sing America*. New York: Oxford University Press, 1986.

Rayson, Ann. "George Schuyler: Paradox among 'Assimilationist' Writers." *Black American Literature Forum* 12 (1978): 102–6.

Renov, Michael, ed. *Theorizing Documentary*. New York: Routledge, 1993.

Retman, Sonnet. "The "Real" Collective in New Deal Documentary and Ethnography: The Federal Writers' Project, the Farm Security Administration, Zora Neale Hurston's *Mules and Men* and James Agee's and Walker Evans' *Let Us Now Praise Famous Men*." Ph.D. dissertation, University of California, Los Angeles, 1997.

Rhodes, Gary Don, and John Parris Springer. *Docufictions: Essays on the Intersections of Documentary and Fictional Filmmaking*. Jefferson, N.C.: McFarland, 2006.

Roadside America. "Wigwam Village Motel #2." Web site of Roadside America, www.roadsideamerica.com, accessed 21 September 2007.

Roberts, Matthew. "Bonfire of the Avant-Garde: Cultural Rage and Readerly Complicity in *The Day of the Locust*." *Modern Fiction Studies* 42, no. 1 (1996): 61–90.

Robinson, Amy. "It Takes One to Know One: Passing and Communities of Common Interest." *Critical Inquiry* 20 (Summer 1994): 715–36.

Robinson, Cedric. *Black Marxism: The Making of the Black Radical Tradition*. London: Zed Press, 1983. Rpt. with foreword by Robin D. G. Kelley, new preface by author. Chapel Hill: University of North Carolina, 2000.

Roediger, David. *Black on White: Black Writers on What It Means to Be White*. New York: Schocken Books, 1998.

———. *The Wages of Whiteness: Race and the Making of the American Working Class*. New York: Verso, 1991.

——. *Working toward Whiteness: How America's Immigrants Became White.* New York: Basic Books, 2005.

Rogin, Michael. *Blackface, White Noise: Jewish Immigrants in the Hollywood Melting Pot.* Berkeley: University of California Press, 1996.

Rony, Fatimah Tobing. *The Third Eye: Race, Cinema, and Ethnographic Spectacle.* Durham: Duke University Press, 1996.

Rooks, Noliwe M. *Hair Raising: Beauty, Culture, and African American Women.* New Brunswick: Rutgers University Press, 1996.

Roosevelt, Franklin Delano. "Fireside Chat on the National Recovery Administration" (24 July 1933). In *The Essential Franklin Delano Roosevelt,* edited, with an introduction, by John Gabriel Hunt, 61–69. New York: Gramercy Books, 1995.

Rosen, A. T. "Sonnet #2: Of wretchedness, of passion, and of travail." In *American Stuff: An Anthology of Prose & Verse by Members of the Federal Writers' Project; with Sixteen Prints by the Federal Art Project,* by Federal Writers' Project, 232–34. New York: Viking Press, 1937.

Rourke, Constance. *American Humor: A Study of the National Character.* Introduction by Greil Marcus. 1931; New York: New York Review of Books, 2004.

Roza, Mathilde. "American Literary Modernism, Popular Culture, and Metropolitan Mass Life: The Early Fiction of Robert M. Coates." In *Uneasy Alliance: Twentieth Century American Literature, Culture and Biography,* edited by Hans Bak, 109–42. Amsterdam: Rodopi Editions, 2004.

Rozgonyi, Jay. *Preston Sturges's Vision of America: Critical Analyses of Fourteen Films.* Jefferson, N.C.: McFarland, 1995.

Rubinstein, Rachel. "Nathanael West's Indian Commodities." *Shofar: An Interdisciplinary Journal of Jewish Studies* 23, no. 4 (2005): 98–120.

Ruppersburg, Hugh. "'Oh, So Many Startlements . . .': History, Race, and Myth in *O Brother Where Art Thou?*" *Southern Cultures* 9, no. 4 (2003): 5–26.

Sanchez-Eppler, Benigno. "Telling Anthropology: Zora Neale Hurston and Gilberto Freyre Disciplined in Their Field-Home-Work." *American Literary History* 4 (1992): 464–88.

Sanford, John. "Remembering West: Novels and Other Writings." (Review.) *Los Angeles Times,* 3 August, 1997, 6.

Schocket, Eric. "Modernism and the Aesthetics of Management, or T. S. Eliot's Labor Literature." In *Left of the Color Line: Race, Radicalism, and Twentieth-Century Literature of the United States,* edited by Bill V. Mullen and James Smethurst, 13–37. Chapel Hill: University of North Carolina Press, 2003.

——. "Revising the 1930s in the 1990s, or the Work of Art in the Age of Diminished Expectations." *American Quarterly* 52, no. 1 (March 2000): 159–67.

——. "Undercover Explorations of the 'Other Half,' or the Writer as Class Transvestite." *Representations* 64 (Fall 1998): 109–33.

———. *Vanishing Moments: Class and American Literature.* Ann Arbor: University of Michigan Press, 2006.

Schuyler, George. *Black and Conservative: The Autobiography of George S. Schuyler.* New Rochelle, N.Y.: Arlington House Publishers, 1966.

———. *Black No More* (1931). Rpt. New York: Modern Library, 1999.

———. "The Caucasian Problem" (1944). In *What the Negro Wants*, edited by Rayford Logan, 281–98. Chapel Hill: University of North Carolina Press, 1944. Rpt. in *Rac[e]ing to the Right: Selected Essays of George S. Schuyler*, edited by Jeffrey B. Leak, 37–50. Knoxville: University of Tennessee Press, 2001.

———. "The Negro and Nordic Civilization." *The Messenger* 7 (May 1925). In *Rac[e]ing to the Right: Selected Essays of George S. Schuyler*, edited by Jeffrey B. Leak, 3–12. Knoxville: University of Tennessee Press, 2001.

———. "The Negro-Art Hokum" (1926). In *The Norton Anthology of African American Literature*, 2nd ed., edited by Henry Louis Gates Jr. and Nellie McKay, 1221–22. New York: Norton, 2004.

———. "New Books: Who Owns the Schools and Colleges—and Why?" *The Messenger* 6 (1924): 322.

———. "Our White Folks" (1927). In *Black on White: Black Writers on What It Means to Be White*, edited by David Roediger, 71–84. New York: Schocken Books, 1998.

———. "Views and Reviews." *Pittsburgh Courier*, 16 April 1927, 25 November 1933, 17 October 1936, and 30 August 1941.

Schuyler, George, and Theophilus Lewis. "Shafts and Darts: The Civilized Minority." *The Messenger* 6 (1924): 288.

Scott, A. O. "Hail, Ulysses, Escaped Convict." (Review.) *New York Times*, 22 December 2000. Reviews page of web site of *New York Times*, http://movies.nytimes.com/, accessed 22 November 2009.

Scott, Clive. *Street Photography: From Atget to Cartier-Bresson.* London: Tauris, 2007.

Scruggs, Charles. *The Sage in Harlem: H. L. Mencken and the Black Writers of the 1920s.* Baltimore: Johns Hopkins University Press, 1984.

Shaffer, Marguerite S. *See America First: Tourism and National Identity, 1880–1940.* Washington: Smithsonian Institution Press, 2001.

Shea, Rachel Hartigan. "The Honest Untruth." *Washington Post*, 9 October 2007, Style section, C07.

Silber, Nancy. *The Romance of Reunion: Northerners and the South, 1865–1900.* Chapel Hill: University of North Carolina Press, 1993.

Singh, Nikhil Pal. "Retracing the Black-Red Thread." *American Literary History* 15, no. 4 (2003): 830–40.

Smethurst, James. *The New Red Negro: The Literary Left and African American Poetry, 1930–1946.* New York: Oxford University Press, 1999.

Smith, Terry. *Making the Modern: Industry, Art and Design in America.* Chicago: University of Chicago Press, 1993.

Smith, Valerie. "Authenticity in Narratives of the Black Middle Class." In *Not*

Just Race, Not Just Gender: Black Feminist Readings, 63–86. New York: Routledge, 1998.

———. "Class and Gender in Narratives of Passing." In *Not Just Race, Not Just Gender: Black Feminist Readings*, 35–62. New York: Routledge, 1998.

———. "Reading the Intersection of Race and Gender in Narratives of Passing." *diacritics* 24, nos. 2–3 (Summer–Fall 1994): 43–57.

Soja, Edward, and Barbara Hopper. "The Spaces That Differences Make: Some Notes on the Geographical Margins of the New Cultural Politics." In *Place and the Politics of Identity*, edited by Michael Keith and Steve Pile, 183–205. New York: Routledge, 1993.

Solomon, William. *Literature, Amusement, and Technology in the Great Depression*. Cambridge: Cambridge University Press, 2002.

Solomon-Godeau, Abigail. *Photography at the Dock*. Minneapolis: University of Minnesota Press, 1991.

Spillers, Hortense. "Notes on an Alternative Model: Neither/Nor." In *The Year Left 2: An American Socialist Yearbook*, edited by Mike Davis et al., 176–94. London: Verso, 1997.

———. "A Tale of Three Zoras: Barbara Johnson and Black Women Writers." *diacritics* 34, no. 1 (Spring 2004): 94–97.

Spoto, Donald. *Madcap: The Life of Preston Sturges*. Boston: Little, Brown, 1990.

Stange, Maren. "'The Record Itself': Farm Security Administration Photography and the Transformation of Rural Life." In *Official Images: New Deal Photography*, edited by Peter Daniel, Merry Foresta, Maren Stange, and Sally Stein, 1–35. Washington: Smithsonian Institution Press, 1987.

———. *Symbols of Ideal Life: Social Documentary Photography in America, 1890–1950*. New York: Cambridge University Press, 1989.

Stanley, Alessandra. "Bringing Out the Absurdity of the News." *New York Times*, 25 October 2005, Arts section. Web site of *New York Times*, www.nytimes.com/, accessed 14 November 2008.

Steichen, Edward, "The F.S.A. Photographers." In *U.S. Camera Annual 1939*, edited by T. J. Maloney, 44–63. New York: William Morrow, 1938.

Steinbeck, John. *The Grapes of Wrath*. 1939; New York: Viking Books, 1997.

Steinberg, Jacques. "2005: In a Word; Truthiness." *New York Times*, 25 December 2005, Week in Review section, web site of *New York Times*, www.nytimes.com/, accessed 18 January 2009.

Steiner, Christopher. "Museums and the Politics of Nationalism." *Museum Anthropology* 19, no. 2 (1995): 3–6.

Stephens, Michelle. *Black Empire: The Masculine Global Imaginary of Caribbean Intellectuals in the United States, 1914–1962*. Durham: Duke University Press, 2005.

Stewart, Donald Odgen, ed. *Fighting Words*. New York: Harcourt, Brace, 1940.

Stewart, Jon. Interview with Bill Moyers. *Bill Moyers' Journal*. PBS, 27 April 2007. Web site of PBS, www.pbs.org.

Stewart, Susan. *Crimes of Writing: Problems in the Containment of Representation.* Durham: Duke University Press, 1994.

———. *On Longing: Narratives of the Miniature, the Gigantic, the Souvenir, the Collection.* Durham: Duke University Press, 1984.

Stites, Richard. *Russian Popular Culture: Entertainment and Society since 1900.* Cambridge: Cambridge University Press, 1992.

Stoddard, Lothrop. *The Rising Tide of Color against White World-Supremacy.* New York: Scribner, 1920.

Stott, William. *Documentary Expression and Thirties America.* 1983; Chicago: University of Chicago Press, 1986.

Stowe, Harriet Beecher. *Palmetto Leaves* (1873). Rpt. Gainsville: University Press of Florida, 1999.

Stronge, William B. *The Sunshine Economy: An Economic History of Florida since the Civil War.* Gainesville: University Press of Florida, 2008.

Stryker, Roy, and Nancy C. Wood. *In This Proud Land: America, 1935–1943, as Seen in the FSA Photographs.* New York: Galahad Books, 1973.

Studlar, Gaylyn. *This Mad Masquerade: Stardom and Masculinity in the Jazz Age.* New York: Columbia University Press, 1996.

Sturges, Preston. *Preston Sturges.* Adapted and edited by Sandy Sturges. New York: Simon and Schuster, 1990.

Sullivan, Patricia. *Days of Hope: Race and Democracy in the New Deal Era.* Chapel Hill: University of North Carolina Press, 1996.

Sullivan's Travels. Directed by Preston Sturges. Paramount, 1941; The Criterion Collection, 2001.

Sunshine, Sylvia (Abbie M. Brooks). *Petals Picked from Sunny Climes.* 1880; Gainesville: University Press of Florida, 1976.

Susman, Warren. *Culture as History: The Transformation of American Society in the Twentieth Century.* New York: Pantheon Books, 1984.

Szalay, Michael. *New Deal Modernism: American Literature and the Invention of the Welfare State.* Durham: Duke University Press, 2000.

Tagg, John. *The Burden of Representation: Essays on Photographies and Histories.* Minneapolis: University of Minnesota Press, 1988.

Talalay, Kathryn. *Composition in Black and White: The Tragic Saga of Harlem's Biracial Prodigy.* New York: Oxford University Press, 1995.

Taylor, Charles. "O Brother, Where Art Thou? Dogpatch Rapture!" *Salon,* 22 December 2000. Salon Media Group 2009, web site of *Salon,* www.salon.com/, accessed 26 November 2009.

Thorpe, Thomas Bangs. *Picturesque America.* Centennial edition, edited by William Cullen Bryant. 1874; New York: Lyle Stuart, 1974.

Thurman, Wallace. *Infants of the Spring* (1932). Rpt. The Northeastern Library of Black Literature edition, edited by Richard Yarborough. Boston: Northeastern University Press, 1992.

Toll, Robert. *Blacking Up: The Minstrel Show in Nineteenth-Century America.* New York: Oxford University Press, 1974.

Trachtenberg, Alan. "From Image to Story: Reading the File." In *Document-*

ing America, 1935–1943, edited by Carl Fleischhauer and Beverly Brannan,. Los Angeles: University of California, 1988.

——. *The Incorporation of America: Culture and Society in the Gilded Age.* New York: Farrar, Straus and Giroux, 1982.

Trouble in Paradise. Directed by Ernst Lubitsch. Paramount, 1932.

Tucker, Jeffrey A. "'Can Science Succeed Where the Civil War Failed?': George S. Schuyler and Race." In *Race Consciousness: African American Studies for the New Century*, edited by Judith Jackson Fossett and Jeffrey A. Tucker, 136–53. New York: New York University Press, 1997.

Turan, Kenneth. "With the Coens, You Get Homer Plus Honky-Tonk." *Los Angeles Times*, 15 May 2000. Web site of *Los Angeles Times* Article Collection, http://articles.latimes.com/, accessed 27 November 2009.

Veitch, Jonathan. *American Superrealism: Nathanael West and the Politics of Representation in the 1930s.* Madison: University of Wisconsin Press, 1997.

Vidal, Gore. "Sullivan's Travels." In *Past Imperfect: History According to the Movies*, edited by Ted Mico, John Miller-Monzon, and David Rubel, 216–19. New York: Henry Holt, 1995.

Wald, Alan M. *Exiles from a Future Time: The Forging of the Mid-Twentieth-Century Literary Left.* Chapel Hill: University of North Carolina Press, 2002.

——. *Writing from the Left: New Essays on Radical Culture and Politics.* New York: Verso, 1994.

Wald, Gayle. *Crossing the Line: Racial Passing in Twentieth-Century U.S. Literature and Culture.* Durham: Duke University Press, 2000.

Wald, Priscilla. "Becoming 'Colored': The Self-Authorized Language of Difference in Zora Neale Hurston." *American Literary History* 2, no. 1 (1990): 79–100.

——. *Constituting Americans: Cultural Anxiety and Narrative Form.* Durham: Duke University Press, 1995.

Walker, Alice, ed. *I Love Myself When I Am Laughing . . . And Then Again When I Am Looking Mean and Impressive: A Zora Neale Hurston Reader.* New York: Feminist Press, 1979.

——. "Looking for Zora." In *I Love Myself When I Am Laughing . . . : A Zora Neale Hurston Reader*, 297–313. New York: Feminist Press, 1979.

Wall, Cheryl. "*Mules and Men* and Women: Zora Neale Hurston's Strategies of Narration and Visions of Female Empowerment." *Black American Literature Forum* 23 (Winter 1989): 661–80.

Walters, Keith. "'He Can Read My Writing but He Sho' Can't Read My Mind': Zora Neale Hurston's Revenge in *Mules and Men*." *Journal of American Folklore* 112, Theorizing the Hybrid (Summer 1999): 343–71.

Washington, Mary Helen. "Alice Childress, Lorraine Hansberry, and Claudia Jones: Black Women Write the Popular Front." In *Left of the Color Line: Race, Radicalism, and Twentieth-Century Literature of the United States*, 183–204. Chapel Hill: University of North Carolina Press, 2003.

Washington, D.C. (Federal Writers' Project of the Works Projects Administration for the District of Columbia). *Washington: City and Capitol.* Washington: United States Government Printing Office, 1937.

Washington State (Federal Writers' Project of the Works Projects Administration for the State of Washington). *Washington: A Guide to the Evergreen State.* Portland, Or.: Binfords and Mort, 1941.

Watkins, Mel. *On the Real Side: Laughing, Lying, and Signifying.* New York: Simon and Schuster, 1994.

Weems, Robert. *Desegregating the Dollar: African American Consumerism in the Twentieth Century.* New York: New York University Press, 1998.

Weigle, Marta. "Finding the 'True America': Ethnic Tourism in New Mexico During the New Deal." In *Folklife Annual '88–89,* edited by James Hardin and Alan Jabbour, 58–73. Washington: Library of Congress, 1989.

Weinbaum, Alys. "Racial Aura: Walter Benjamin and the Work of Art in a Biotechnological Age." *Literature and Medicine* 26, no. 1 (2007): 207–89.

——. *Wayward Reproductions: Genealogies of Race and Nation in Transatlantic Modern Thought.* Durham: Duke University Press, 2004.

West, Nathanael. *Nathanael West: Novels and Other Writings.* Edited by Sacvan Bercovitch. New York: Library of America, 1997.

——. *Two Novels by Nathanael West: A Cool Million and The Dream Life of Balso Snell.* 1931; New York: Farrar, Straus and Giroux, 1991.

Whitt, Margaret. "From Eros to Agape: Reconsidering the Chain Gang's Song in McCullers's 'Ballad of the Sad Café.'" *Studies in Short Fiction* 33 (Winter 1996): 119–22.

Wild Boys of the Road. Directed by William Wellman. Warner Bros., 1933.

Williams, Linda. *Playing the Race Card: Melodramas of Black and White from Uncle Tom to O. J. Simpson.* Princeton: Princeton University Press, 2001.

Williams, Raymond. *Marxism and Literature.* New York: Oxford University Press, 1977.

Willis, Susan. "Wandering: Hurston's Search for Self and Method." In *Zora Neale Hurston: Critical Perspectives Past and Present,* edited by Henry Louis Gates Jr. and K. A. Appiah, 110–29. New York: Amistad, 1993.

Winders, Jamie. "Imperfectly Imperial: Northern Travel Writers in the Postbellum U.S. South, 1865–1880." *Annals of the Association of American Geographers* 95, no. 2 (June 2005): 391–410.

Wintz, Cary, ed. *The Harlem Renaissance, 1920–40.* Vol. 4. New York: Garland, 1996.

Wollen, Peter. "Introduction." In *Visual Display: Culture beyond Appearances,* edited by Peter Wollen and Lynne Cooke, 8–12. Seattle: Bay Press, 1995.

Wood, Paul. "Realisms and Realities." In *Realism, Rationalism, Surrealism: Art between the Wars,* edited by Briony Fer, David Batchelor, and Paul Wood, 250–333. New Haven: Yale University Press, 1993.

Woods, Mary N. *Beyond the Architect's Eye: Photographs and the American Built Environment.* Philadelphia: University of Pennsylvania Press, 2009.

Wordsworth, William. "Preface to the Lyrical Ballads." In *Prefaces and Pro-logues*, vol. 39. The Harvard Classics. New York: Collier and Son, 1909–14.

Works Progress Administration. Federal Writers' Project. "*The American Guide Manual.*" Washington: Works Progress Administration, 1935.

Wray, Matt. *Not Quite White: White Trash and the Boundaries of Whiteness.* Durham: Duke University Press, 2006.

Wright, Richard. "Blueprint for Negro Writing" (1937). In *The Norton Anthology of African American Literature*, 2nd ed., edited by Henry Louis Gates Jr. and Nellie McKay, 1403–10. New York: Norton, 2004.

Young, Nancy K., and William H. Young. *The Great Depression: A Cultural Encyclopedia.* Santa Barbara: Greenwood Press, 2007.

Young, Neil. "Sullivan's Travels." (Review.) *Film Lounge*, 7 August 2005. Web site of Jigsaw Lounge, www.jigsawlounge.co.uk/.

Zackodnik, Teresa. "Fixing the Color Line: The Mulatto, Southern Courts and Racial Identity." *American Quarterly* 53 (September 2001): 420–51.

Zimring, Carl A. " 'Neon, Junk, and Ruined Landscape': Competing Visions of America's Roadsides and the Highway Beautification Act of 1965." In *The World beyond the Windshield: Roads and Landscapes in the United States and Europe*, edited by Christof Mauch and Thomas Zeller, 94–107. Athens: Ohio University Press, 2008.

Žižek, Slavoj. "Against the Populist Temptation." *Critical Inquiry* 32, no. 3 (Spring 2006): 551–74.

———. *Enjoy Your Symptom! Jacques Lacan in Hollywood and Out.* New York: Routledge, 1992.

———. *The Sublime Object of Ideology.* London: Verso, 1989.

Zumwalt, Rosemary Levy. *American Folklore Scholarship: A Dialogue of Dissent.* Bloomington: Indiana University Press, 1988.

Index

Aaron, Daniel, 78
African Americans: authenticity and, 24, 43–46, 160, 268n19; commu-nism's view of, 12; as consumers, 41–44, 46–49, 51–52; in Florida, 124–28, 136, 169–88; folk identity and, 10, 12–14, 27, 42; folklore of, 149–50, 158–69; slavery and, 65, 96, 133; ste-reotypes of, 120, 155; symbolism and, 224. *See also* blackface routines; gender; Great Migration; min-strelsy; music; race; women; *specific authors and works*
African American Satire (Dickson-Carr), 40
The African Queen (Huston), 191
Agee, James, 29, 88, 90, 121, 193, 230
Alger, Horatio, 76–77, 80–83, 86–88, 91, 105–6, 108–9, 142, 206
Alsberg, Harry, 118–19, 148, 267n13
America: communism in, 33; consumer-citizenry in, 41–42, 46–47, 79, 122, 138; folk identity and, 1, 4, 16, 140–43; immigrants and, 45, 58, 76, 91, 100, 107, 110, 125, 218; mythologies of, 5, 64–80, 83–87, 93, 99, 107–9, 126–28; nationalism in, 11–12, 94, 96–97, 100–102, 107; pulp fiction in, 80–86; racialized identity and, 8, 64–71. *See also* capitalism; class; fascism; folk; whiteness; *spe-cific works, authors, agencies, organi-zations, politicians*
America First (group), 80
American Document (Graham), 16
American Dream, 7–8, 73, 76, 78, 99, 252n7, 263n17
An American Exodus (Lange and Tay-lor), 16
American Folklore Society, 10
American Guide Series (FWP), 3, 113–51

American Humor (Rourke), 21, 124
American Mercury (publication), 35
American Negro Slavery (Phillips), 55
Ames, Christopher, 205
Anderson, Nels, 192
Anderson, Sherwood, 90
anthropology, 120–21, 156–57, 252n10, 272n3, 275n14; allochronic time in, 24, 183, 276n19, 277n25; coeval time in, 130, 145, 151, 175, 183, 187, 268n21, 277n25; imperialism and, 54–56; insider/outsider dynamic in, 23–24, 28, 154–55, 162–67, 178–81, 192, 275n15; salvage paradigm, 13, 154–55, 159–60, 170, 274n12. *See also* ethnography
Anthropology and Modern Life (Boas), 159
anti-semitism, 76
Appalachian Spring (Graham), 16
Archive of American Folk-Song, 3, 13
Argonauts of the Western Pacific (Mal-inowski), 163, 272n3
Arrival of a Train at the Station (Lumi-ère), 202
audiences: as amateur anthropologists, 113–14, 117, 119–20, 135–38, 143–46; authenticity and, 24, 201, 221, 236, 245, 250; coerced spectatorship of, 63; as duped majority, 22, 56–57; empathy and, 22, 29, 75, 105, 198, 212, 222, 237, 254n20; fascism and white supremacy and, 5, 21–22, 26, 56, 62–63, 67, 80, 106–9; as femi-nized, 231–34, 236; as insiders and outsiders, 153, 172; as interracial constellation, 227–31, 236, 283n32, 285n40; middlebrow taste and, 194–95, 197–99, 201, 204–5, 218–20, 231–34, 237; race spectacles and, 21, 45, 56, 62–63, 80, 85, 220–21, 237, 245,

audiences (*cont.*)
283n32; role of, with respect to works of art, 28–29, 109, 122–23, 198, 237, 281n15; as white collective, 122–23, 242, 245–46, 248. *See also* interpellation; minstrelsy; passing; performativity; *Sullivan's Travels* (Sturges)
authenticity: antiques craze and, 93–97; folk's relation to, 1–3, 8, 16, 99, 101, 103, 120, 140–43, 237; genre considerations and, 201, 204; Harlem Renaissance debates on, 44–46; *O Brother, Where Art Thou?* and, 244; performativity and, 21, 24, 175–83, 187, 195, 199, 210, 213, 216; stereotypes and, 96. *See also* class; drag; gender; masquerade; passing; performativity; race; vernacular
automobiles, 114–15, 131, 134, 155, 174, 177, 266n8

Baker, Josephine, 45
Barnard, Rita, 24, 73, 81
Barnum, P. T., 124
Bazin, André, 231, 238
Ben Hur (Wyler), 191
Big John (folklore character), 149–50
Big Sweet, 182, 278n33
Black and Conservative (Schuyler), 33–34
blackface routines, 45, 58–59, 88, 110, 217, 249, 257n18
Black Legion, 80
blackness: authenticity and, 24, 43–46, 160, 268n19; class's relation to, 79, 124–25, 129–31; gender and, 38, 53, 64–68, 96, 156, 175, 260n38; production and reproduction of, 22, 33–35, 44–49, 55–56, 85, 103; stereotypes of, 120, 155. *See also* African Americans; blackface routines; gender; minstrelsy; miscegenation; race; whiteness; *specific artists and works*
Black No More (Schuyler): masquerading and, 38; passing in, 26, 49–52, 54–56, 58–60; plot of, 21–22, 36–38; racial essentialism in, 60–64; satirical elements of, 36–37, 40, 58–59, 61, 65, 67, 79, 88. *See also* Schuyler, George

Black Swan Records, 47
Blair, Sara, 24
blues (genre), 44, 47, 57
Blume, Peter, 20
Boas, Franz, 42, 153–63, 175, 272n1, 274n9
bodies (as consumer good), 83, 89–92, 96–97, 99, 101, 106. *See also* gender; performativity; race
Bold, Christine, 115, 121
bootstrap myth, 5, 40, 81, 195, 238, 281n17. *See also* America; class
Bordelon, Pam, 148
Botkin, B. A., 13, 120, 123
Bourke-White, Margaret, 16–17, 88, 90, 220, 222
Brady, Mary Pat, 155
Breazeale, Kenon, 232, 284n39
Brecht, Bertolt, 18, 109
Brooks, Daphne, 45, 59, 258n18, 280n8
Brooks, Van Wyck, 1
Brothers Grimm, 9
Buchman, Sidney, 110
Burke, Kenneth, 8, 19, 198, 223, 252n9, 280n10
burlesque, 20, 75, 87, 109, 195, 202. *See also* genre; modernist burlesque; *specific writers and works*
Bush, George W., 2

Caldwell, Erskine, 16–17, 88, 90, 220, 222
capitalism: absurdities within, 36, 38, 93; folk as deployed by, 4, 6–7, 14, 24, 40, 77, 238; gender and, 64–71, 90–91, 101, 172–74, 207–9; geography and, 113–51; identity and, 37; music and, 242–50; nostalgia and, 93–95, 114, 243, 250; racial, 6, 14, 23–29, 38–57, 68–77, 82–84, 90–92, 99, 103, 108–9, 131, 155, 160, 188, 197, 199, 211, 222, 245–50, 252n6, 256n10, 261n43, 263n9, 282n23; tourism's relation to, 137–38, 140–43. *See also* America; class; consumerism; gender; race; tourism; whiteness
Capra, Frank, 105, 195, 197, 218–19, 226, 236
Carbado, Devon, 13, 125, 127
Carby, Hazel, 159, 177

Cawelti, John, 86
Certeau, Michel de, 146
Chadwell, Sean, 244
Chain Gang (White), 225
chain gangs, 225, 282n27
Chaplin, Charlie, 192
"Characteristics of Negro Expression"
(Hurston), 150, 158
Cherniavsky, Eva, 177
The Chocolate Dandies (Baker), 45
Christmas in July (Sturges), 193
Citizen Hobo (DePastino), 217
Citizen Kane (Welles), 19
Civil War, 123, 133, 267n13
class: in Florida, 129; gender issues
and, 211, 215; intersections of, with
race, 25, 43, 53–54, 56–60, 79, 124–
25, 129–31, 137, 180–81, 259n33,
282n19; mythologies of mobility
and, 26, 72–73, 79–81, 83, 85, 87, 93,
110, 195, 209–10, 238, 281n17; passing
and, 38, 85, 88, 107–8, 206, 208, 210,
213, 281n12. *See also* authenticity;
capitalism; gender; hobos; passing;
race
Clifford, James, 158
Clooney, George, 241, 285n2
Coates, Robert M., 77
Coen, Ethan and Joel, 241–50
Cogdell, Josephine, 35
Cohen, Lizabeth, 41
Colbert, Stephen, 2
The Colbert Report (program), 2
Cole, Lester, 73
Coleridge, Samuel Taylor, 9
Collecting: culture of, 81–82, 85, 90,
92–95, 113–14, 136, 185, 192, 267n16;
ethnographic, 159, 162, 170, 173, 185,
272n3; folklore, 9, 155, 165–66, 179,
257n14, 278n27; pulp fiction, 85–86
Collier, Joan, 128
Colonial Williamsburg, 93–94, 136
Columbia (music co.), 47
Commins, Saxe, 26
communism, 8, 12, 24
Communist Party USA, 33
Connerly, Ward, 36
Conrad, Joseph, 163
consumerism: the body's relation to,
83, 87–88, 91–92; democracy and,

46; femininity of, 192, 207, 209,
284n39; folk's creation and, 6, 14,
78–80; gender and, 231–33; race and,
6, 23, 41–44, 49–50, 92, 257n13. *See
also* capitalism; class; gender; race
Coolidge, Calvin, 82, 94
A Cool Million (West): class in, 54, 67,
81; critical receptions of, 72, 104–5;
fascism in, 80–81, 83, 92, 99–107,
109; gender considerations in, 94–
96; passing of, for pulp, 87–88; plot
of, 82–85; pulp fiction and, 85–87,
89–91, 97; racialization in, 81, 94–
96; satirical nature of, 78–79, 82–85;
stereotypes and, 77, 82, 85, 92–97,
108–9. *See also* West, Nathanael
Corse, Carita Doggett, 146–47
Coughlin, Father Charles, 8, 11
Cowley, Malcolm, 74
crackers (term), 124–25, 129–31, 136,
138–43, 182, 270n27
Cripps, Thomas, 225
The Crisis (publication), 35
Cronyn, George, 119
Cross, Gary, 115
Crowther, Bosley, 239
Cubans (immigrants), 125, 129, 265n3
Cullen, Countee, 46
The Cultural Front (Denning), 19
Cunard, Nancy, 158

The Daily Show (program), 2
Daily Worker (publication), 33
Dave Chappelle Show (program), 2
Dawes Act, 128
The Day of the Locust (West), 73
Debord, Guy, 137
Decker, Jeffrey, 85–86, 263n17
Denning, Michael, 8, 19–20, 68, 74,
86–89, 116, 194–99, 226–29, 239, 247,
256n7
DePastino, Todd, 217, 282n19
DeSylva, Buddy, 205, 227, 283n30
Dickson-Carr, Darryl, 40
Dime Novel Round-Up (publication),
86
Dime Novels (Pearson), 86
Dimock, Wai Chee, 19
disavowal, 45, 59, 62–63
documentary: in *Black No More*, 62;

documentary (*cont.*)
definitions of, 15, 253n15; Federal
Writers' Project and, 113–51; folk as
subject of, 1–3, 15–19, 108, 192, 220–
22; genre, 2–4, 6, 15–19, 24–25, 75,
82, 88, 104, 156, 192, 199–200, 202–4,
220–22, 230, 235, 251n5, 253n15; photographs, 1, 3, 13, 16–17, 220–22,
253n15, 265n1; social realism's
reliance upon, 7, 156; voice of, 7, 62,
104. *See also* genre; hybridity; signifying ethnography; social realism
(genre); *specific works and artists*
Dos Passos, John, 79
drag, 208–10, 212–13, 215–16, 247. *See
also* gender; masquerade; passing;
performativity
The Dream Life of Balso Snell (West),
73
Du Bois, W. E. B., 10–11, 46, 48, 165
Duck, Leigh Ann, 161, 185, 277n25
Durante, Jimmy, 77
Durning, Charles, 245
Dust Tracks on the Road (Hurston),
152–53, 276n17
Duvall, Wayne, 245

Easy Living (Leisen), 200
Edwards, Brent Hayes, 25
Elliot, Michael, 181, 274n12, 277n21
Emerson, Ralph Waldo, 9–10
Eternal City (Blume), 20
ethnography, 113, 118, 120, 139, 192–94.
See also anthropology; Boas, Franz;
documentary; Hurston, Zora Neale;
signifying ethnography; *specific
works and scholars*
eugenics movement, 50
Evans, Walker, 3, 29, 88, 90, 121

Fanon, Frantz, 58
Farm Security Administration, 13, 105,
129, 211
fascism: in *Black No More*, 22; folk's
deployment by, 8; performativity
and, 68; race and, 26–27, 36, 49–50,
70–71, 106–7; West on, 73, 80, 99–
105
Fearing, Kenneth, 79
Federal Writers' Project: American

Guide Series of, 3; conflicts within,
118–23, 148; purposes of, 13–14, 27,
113–14, 118–19, 123, 154, 158, 265n2,
267n12, 269nn22–23; signifying ethnography and, 27–28. See also *Florida* (F W P); Hurston, Zora Neale;
tourism
The Federal Writers' Project (Penkower), 122
Ferguson, Jeffrey B., 38, 51
Fiedler, Leslie, 97–98
Filene, Benjamin, 244
film (medium). See *O Brother, Where
Art Thou?* (Coen brothers); Sturges,
Preston; *Sullivan's Travels* (Sturges)
Fireside Chats (Roosevelt), 3
Fisher, Rudolph, 39
Florida: African Americans in, 126–27,
133; assimilationism in, 125–26, 141;
colonization of, 140–44, 146; economic disparity in, 129–30, 133; history's romanticization in, 136–37;
Hurston's view of, 152–88; tourism
in, 116–17, 130–37, 139, 142,
145
Florida (F W P): as compilation, 28, 147,
149, 267n16; documentary method
of, 117–19, 122; folk's construction
in, 27, 119–21, 124–28, 135–36,
268n19; history's romanticization in,
136–37; Hurston's role in, 117–18,
149–51; sectional reconciliation and,
132–33, 136–37, 140–43; tourist out-
look of, 133–35. *See also* Hurston,
Zora Neale; tourism
The Florida Negro (Hurston), 118, 148
Foley, Barbara, 25
folk: authenticity attributed to, 1–3, 8,
16, 99, 101, 103, 120, 140–43, 237; class
issues and, 14, 40, 43, 77, 100–101,
137, 238; as commodity, 44, 57–59,
90–91, 94–99, 101; consumerism's
role in creating, 6–7, 24, 26, 40, 67,
78–80, 116–17, 140–43, 156, 160; definitions of, 1–3, 252n10; documentary considerations of, 1–3, 15–19,
108, 192, 220–22; in *Florida*, 27, 119–
21, 124–30, 135–36, 268n19; as folksy,
26, 44, 105, 124–25, 151, 214, 248;
Hurston's deployment of, 5, 155–56,

159, 173, 177, 187, 188; media and, 1; nation and, 8–14, 117–18, 131, 146, 151, 156, 161, 188; nationalism and, 2–4, 8–14, 26–28, 41, 70, 77, 82, 94, 114; nostalgic temporalities of, 27, 116, 131; origins of, terminologically speaking, 4; in other nations' cultural imaginaries, 3–4, 8–10; populism's deployment of, 15–19, 67, 75, 108, 110, 113, 117, 125–26, 226, 235–36; racialization of, 4, 10–12, 14, 44, 114, 124–30, 136–40, 141, 151, 220, 226–27, 248; as readers and audiences, 56, 67, 172–74, 223–30, 236; representations of, 7–8, 195; romanticization of, 40, 59, 67, 75, 94, 96–97, 113–14, 117–21, 137, 192; Schuyler's deployment of, 5, 36; stereotypes of, 77, 82, 90, 105, 113, 145–46, 155, 220; in *Sullivan's Travels*, 192–95; as tourist commodity, 113–14, 124, 130–32, 137–38, 155–56; West's deployment of, 5. *See also* African Americans; capitalism; class; gender; Native Americans; race; tourism; whiteness; *specific works and authors*

folklore, 8–11, 13, 28, 120, 140–43, 158–69, 187

folksy (term), 3

Ford, Henry, 93–94, 107, 114, 131, 136, 158, 257n12

Ford, John, 219–21

Fordism, 6, 26, 37–49, 70, 78–79, 92, 114, 158

Foucault, Michel, 18

Fraden, Rena, 25

Freedman, Jonathan, 95, 263n21

Friends of Negro Freedom, 34

Frontline (program), 2

Fuchs, Daniel, 74

Garvey, Marcus, 59

Gates, Henry Louis, 5–6, 251n4

Gellert, Lawrence, 225

gender: audiences and, 231–32, 237, 263n11; capitalism and, 23, 64–71, 90–91, 101, 142, 207–9; class and power and, 211–12, 215; consumer culture and, 192, 231–33, 284n39; cross-dressing and, 195–96, 216;

Hurston and, 166–67, 172–74; passing and, 85, 88, 196, 234; performativity and, 69, 196–97, 199, 210, 212–15, 223, 234; race and, 6, 38, 54, 64–71, 83, 95–99, 108, 260n38, 260nn38–39, 278n33; stereotypes and, 95–98; tourism's marketing and, 120. *See also* class; masculinity; passing; performativity; race; whiteness; *specific works and artists*

genre: audiences knowledge of, 203–4, 226–27; definition of, 253n16; gender and, 196; hybridity in, 2–3, 17–21, 25, 193, 198, 200, 244; masquerade, 191–240; modernist burlesque, 4–5, 20–23, 58–62, 77–81, 195–99, 252n3, 280n8; music and, 44–45; *Sullivan's Travels* and, 28. *See also* authenticity; documentary; gender; hybridity; performativity; signifying ethnography; *specific genres, artists, and works*

Georgia Fiddlin' John Carson, 243

Germany, 3, 8–9

Gilroy, Paul, 44

Girls of the Road (film), 193

Gold, Mike, 35, 74, 283n34

Graham, Martha, 16

Gramsci, Antonio, 78–80

Grant, Cary, 214

Grant, Madison, 55, 99

The Grapes of Wrath (Ford), 197, 220–21, 226–27, 235

The Grapes of Wrath (Steinbeck), 3, 105, 218

Great Depression, 1; literary norms of, 5–6, 14; nativist movements' relation to, 11–12; politics and politicians of, 2–3, 7, 13; road construction projects and, 115; satire as response to, 4; signifying ethnography's place in, 154–56

The Great McGinty (Sturges), 193

Great Migration, 41–42, 159, 218

Greenfield Village, 93–94, 136

Grierson, John, 15

Griffin, Sean, 226

Grimm, Jacob and Wilhelm, 9

Gulliver's Travels (Swift), 199, 202

Guthrie, Woody, 3, 12

Halberstam, Judith, 216
Hale, Grace Elizabeth, 123, 136–37, 257n13
Hall, Stuart, 69
Harlem Renaissance, 24, 36, 38–40, 70, 153, 156
Harris, Cheryl, 49, 79
Hartman, Saidiya, 54, 65
Harvey, James, 209
Hearst, William Randolph, 94–95
Hegeman, Susan, 73, 96, 154
hegemony, 78–80
Hellman, Lillian, 73
Hemenway, Robert, 168, 278n27
Herbst, Josephine, 73–74, 78, 91, 261n1
Herder, Johann Gottfried, 8–10, 252n10, 263n21
Hernandez, Graciela, 182
Herndon, Angelo, 33–34
Heyward, Du Bose, 46
Himes, Chester, 79
Hitler, Adolf, 73, 108
hobohemia, 192, 209, 237
hobos, 192, 196, 208–13, 217, 219, 221, 281n12, 282n19
Home to Harlem (McKay), 46
Home Town (Anderson), 90
hoodoo, 183–87
Hoover, Herbert, 7
Hoovervilles, 216, 219, 220, 221–22, 227
Hughes, Langston, 35, 38–41, 43–44, 46–47, 79
Hurston, Zora Neale: biography of, 156, 272n1; ethnographical technique of, 23, 118, 121, 151, 153–54, 156–72, 175–88, 221, 275n14; FWP work of, 118, 147–52, 154–55; gender and, 166–67, 172–74, 181; Jewishness in, 167–68; performativity of, 23–24, 161, 163–65, 170, 175–83, 187–88, 205, 213; photos of, *112*; politics of, 24; Schuyler's professional relationship with, 35; on stereotypes, 92, 141; whiteness and, 164, 166. *See also* performativity; signifying ethnography; *specific works*
Huston, John, 191–92, 279n1, 284n38
hybridity: authenticity and, 165; gender and, 195–97; generic, 2, 4, 6, 17–21, 25, 39, 194–95, 198; genetic, 35;

music and, 242–44. *See also* authenticity; gender; genre; miscegenation; modernist burlesque; passing; performativity; signifying ethnography; *specific works and genres*

I Am a Fugitive from a Chain Gang (film), 225
identity, as commodity, 37
immigrants, 45, 59, 62, 91, 94–96, 100, 107, 110, 125, 218
imperialism, 36, 140–44, 146
the Indian (folk type). *See* Native Americans
Indian Reorganization Act, 128–29
Infants of the Spring (Thurman), 39–40
Ingster, Boris, 110
interpellation, 22, 195, 205, 216, 219–22, 229–31, 237, 243
Irr, Caren, 73

Jacobs, Diane, 197, 224, 280n9
Jakle, John, 137
jazz, 44, 47
The Jazz Singer (film), 45
Jewishness, 59, 75–76, 91, 100, 110, 167, 263n14, 263n21
Jim Crow laws, 6, 26, 40–42, 50, 99, 108, 126–34, 187, 226
John Birch Society, 34, 38
"John Henry" (song), 178–79
Johnson, Charles S., 42
Johnson, Guy B., 51
Johnson, Robert, 241, 246, 250
Johnson, Tommy, 241
Jolson, Al, 45, 58–59, 87, 110, 263n14
Jones, Vere, 48
Joseph, Philip, 155
Journal of American Folklore (journal), 10

Kazin, Alfred, 15–16
Kelley, Robin D. G., 25
Kellock, Katherine, 119
Kennedy, Stetson, 137, 148, 270n27
King, Chris Thomas, 241, 246
King, Edward, 132
Knight, Arthur, 246–47
Ku Klux Klan, 11, 58, 80, 245, 269n25

The Lady Eve (Sturges), 193, 200, 205
Lake, Veronica, *190*, 202, 209, 214–15, 221
Lamothe, Daphne, 24
Lange, Dorothea, 16, 192, 218, 263n11
Larsen, Nella, 39
laughter, 191, 198–99, 201, 221, 223–31, 238
Lawson, John, 198
Leadbelly (folk singer), 3, 225
Leisen, Mitchell, 200
Let Us Now Praise Famous Men (Agee and Evans), 29, 88, 90, 121
Levine, Lawrence, 194
Lévi-Strauss, Claude, 146
Lewis, John L., 11
Lewis, Sinclair, 79, 104
Lewis, Theophilus, 69
Lhamon, W. T., 45
Life (magazine), 15–16
Lippman, Walter, 89, 94
The Little Foxes (Wyler), 191
Locke, Alain, 42, 188
Lomax, Alan, 3, 13
Long, Huey, 8, 245
Look (magazine), 16
Lord Jim (Conrad), 163
Lorentz, Paul, 7
Lubitsch, Ernst, 193, 200, 202, 236
Lumière brothers, 202
lynching, 53, 56, 62–63, 69, 80, 100, 104

Madame C. J. Walker (cosmetics entrepreneur), 6, 50–51, 87
Malinowski, Branislaw, 154, 163, 169–70, 176, 272n3, 275n15
The Maltese Falcon (Huston), 191
"Mammy" (Jolson), 58
Mancini, J. M., 245
Mao, Douglas, 22
mapping, 113–51
Martin, Jay, 72, 77, 262n4
Marx Brothers, 77
masculinity: consumer culture and, 192, 232; embodiments and, 211; performative nature of, 28, 199–201, 210, 213–15, 217, 223, 238–39; racialization of, 26, 54, 65–66, 69, 77, 82, 93; threats to, 95, 105–7, 181, 206–7, 263n22; women and, 99, 196, 209–

10, 212; working-class, 199, 206, 208, 210, 214–17, 236. *See also* capitalism; gender; patriarchal structures; race; whiteness
Mason, Charlotte Osgood, 156
masquerade (genre), 192, 209–15, 217–22, 238–39, 242. *See also* drag; gender; passing; performativity
Massey, Doreen, 165
Maxwell, William, 25
McCarthy, Mary, 73
McCoy, Horace, 73, 198
McCrea, Joel, 192, 202, 208, 214
McElvaine, Robert, 14
McKay, Claude, 46
Mead, Margaret, 154
"Me and My Captain" (Gellert), 225
Mechanic Accents (Denning), 86
media: consumerism and, 6, 42; folk imagery and, 1, 16
Medicine Show, Huntington (Shahn), 32
Meet John Doe (Capra), 105, 195
Mein Kampf (Hitler), 73
Mencken, H. L., 35, 37, 261n43
The Messenger (journal), 35, 51
The Midnight Special and Other Prison Songs (Leadbelly), 225
migrant workers, 175–78
minstrelsy, 46, 59, 62, 124, 244, 248, 257n18; *See also* blackface; blackness; performativity
The Miracle of Morgan's Creek (Sturges), 193
miscegenation, 11, 35, 53, 60–71, 246, 260nn38–40
Miss Lonelyhearts (West), 72–73, 91
modernist burlesque, 4–5, 20–22, 37–41, 62, 72–78, 80–87, 195–99, 251n3, 252n3, 252n3, 280n8; Harlem Renaissance and, 39–41, 70, 79; postmodernist burlesque and, 241, 249–50; Schuyler and, 4–5, 37–41, 62, 70, 79–81, 151; *Sullivan's Travels* and, 195–99, 219, 231, 236, 238–40; West and, 4–5, 72–78, 80–87, 109–10, 151. *See also* performativity; satire; *specific authors and works*
Modern Quarterly (publication), 35
Moon, Henry Lee, 163

Moran, Kathleen, 194–95, 209, 220, 229, 233, 235
Moten, Fred, 21
Moyers, Bill, 2
Mr. Deeds Goes to Town (Capra), 105, 195
Mr. Smith Goes to Washington (Capra), 105, 195
Mules and Men (Hurston): critical reception of, 163, 275n14; folk's depiction in, 90, 194; Hurston's avatar in, 153, 159, 164, 169–79, 187, 273n4, 278n27; narrative structure of, 157–58, 162, 169–72, 185, 277n21; readership of, 172; signifying in, 5, 23, 121, 147, 149, 166, 169, 175–82, 276n18; Sis Cat tale, 186–88. *See also* Hurston, Zora Neale; signifying ethnography
Mullen, Bill V., 25
Mullen, Harryette, 256n10, 260n38
Murrow, Edward R., 15
music: authenticity and, 45, 245, 273n7; film scores and, 221, 224–27, 241, 280n5; folk musicians and, 3; "ol'-timey," 242–50; race and, 10–11, 44–45, 47, 57, 225, 243–44

NAACP (National Association for the Advancement of Colored People), 36, 56, 224
Naked City (Weegee), 19–20
The Nation (publication), 35, 38, 43
Native Americans: anthropological views of, 143–45; assimilationist agendas and, 125–26, 136; displacement of, historically, 123; federal government's relation to, 128–29; folk identity and, 10, 13–14, 27, 144–45; FWP guides' treatments of, 123; tourism and, 3, 120, 138, 140–46. *See also* folk; primitivism; race
Negro: An Anthology (Cunard), 158
"The Negro Art Hokum" (Schuyler), 43
"The Negro Artist and the Racial Mountain" (Hughes), 43–44
Negro Digest (publication), 35
Negro Liberator (publication), 33
Nelson, Cary, 25

Nelson, Tim Blake, 241
New Deal. *See* Great Depression; Roosevelt, Franklin D.
New Deal Modernism (Szalay), 115
Newell, William Wells, 10
New Masses (publication), 35
New Negro movement, 40, 49, 70
New Orleans, 183–86
New Republic (publication), 37, 163
"Newspaper Advertisements and Negro Culture" (Johnson), 51
New York Evening Post (newspaper), 36
Nicholls, David, 178
nostalgia, 14, 59, 81–82, 93–95, 102, 114, 243, 250

Obama, Barack, 2
O Brother, Where Art Thou? (Coen brothers), 241–50
Okeh (label), 47, 243
On Native Grounds (Kazin), 15
Opportunity (publication), 35
Our Daily Bread (Vidor), 226
Overmyer, Grace, 113
Owner, Chandler, 35

Palin, Sarah, 2
The Palm Beach Story (Sturges), 200
Palmetto Leaves (Stowe), 132
Paramount (label), 47
Parchman Farm, 241
participant observation (ethnography technique), 24, 153–54, 156–69, 188, 272n2
"A Particular Kind of Joking" (Podhoretz), 73
Partisan Review (publication), 74
passing: *Black No More* and, 49–68; class and, 38, 85, 88, 107–8, 206, 208, 210, 213, 281nn12–13; definitions of, 49–50, 68, 106; gender and, 38, 196, 234; racial, 26, 37, 49, 68, 209–10, 242, 248–49. *See also* authenticity; class; gender; hybridity; masquerade; performativity; race
The Passing of the Great Race (Grant), 55, 99
patriarchal structures, 26, 64–65, 68, 76, 81, 83, 99, 107
Patterns for America (Hegeman), 154

Patterson, Orlando, 37, 57, 255n5, 259n27
Pearson, Edmund, 86
Peiss, Kathy, 232
Pelley, Dudley, 100
Penkower, Monty, 122
Perelman, Sid, 77
performativity: authenticity and, 21, 24, 134, 195, 199, 204, 210, 213; in *Florida*, 134–35, 137–38; gender and, 69, 196–97, 212–13, 215–16, 223, 234; Hurston's ethnography and, 23–24, 154, 213; passing and, 68, 88; race and, 217, 242, 248–49, 253n17, 274n11. *See also* authenticity; class; drag; gender; masquerade; race
Petals Plucked from Sunny Climes (Sunshine), 132
Pfister, Joel, 128
Phillips, Ulrich, 55
photography, 2–3
Phylon (publication), 35
Picturesque America (Thorpe), 132
Pittsburgh Courier (newspaper), 35–36
Playful Pluto (film), 227
The Plow That Broke the Plains (Lorentz), 7
Podhoretz, Norman, 73
Popular Front, 8, 20, 74, 120, 195, 249, 252n9
populism (political), 7–8, 15–19, 27, 108, 156, 197, 252n8, 254n19
Porgy (Heyward), 46
Preseley, James, 178–79, 182
primitivism, 46, 59, 130, 139, 145, 156, 160, 184
proletarian grotesque (genre), 20, 198–99, 229, 236
pulp fiction, 80–87, 89, 97. *See also* Alger, Horatio; West, Nathanael

Quicksand (Larsen), 39

Rabinowitz, Paula, 25, 207
race: American mythologies and, 40, 125–28; capitalism and, 6, 26, 37–49, 51–60, 68–72, 77–92, 103, 108–9, 131, 155, 160, 188, 197–99, 211, 222, 245–50, 252n6, 256n10, 257n13, 261n43, 263n9, 282n23; class's intersections

with, 25, 40, 43, 53–60, 79, 131, 137–43, 180, 187, 259n33, 282n19; crackers and, 124–25, 129–31, 136–43, 182, 270n27; essentialism and, 42–43, 54, 57, 60–71, 255n5, 268n19; ethnographic explorations of, 156–69; fascism and, 26–27, 36, 49–50, 70–71, 106–7; folk identity and, 4, 10–12, 14, 44, 114, 124–30, 136–41, 151, 220, 226–27, 248; FWP guides' treatments of, 122–23; gender and, 38, 54, 64–71, 95, 98–99, 108, 278n33; literary production and, 38–40; music and, 10–11, 44, 47, 57, 225, 242–50; passing and, 26, 37–38, 88, 248–49; performativity and, 80, 85, 106, 217, 231–34, 247–49, 253n17, 274n8, 274n11; political separatism and, 10–11; as produced, 44–49, 55–56, 85, 103; Schuyler on, 22, 33–35; Schuyler's definition of, 55; segregation as function of, 34, 42, 50, 85, 127, 226; stereotypes and, 92–93, 120; in *Sullivan's Travels*, 217–22, 224–27; temporality and historicity and, 121–22, 125–26, 130, 135; tourism and, 122; violence and, 37. *See also* capitalism; class; folk; gender; Jim Crow laws; lynching; miscegenation; music; segregation; *specific artists and works*
"Race Over" (Patterson), 37
Rahv, Philip, 16
Randolph, A. Philip, 35
the reader. *See* audiences
Reitman, Ben, 208–9
Renov, Michael, 17
reproduction: of racialized bodies, 11, 35, 37–38, 50–53, 60–71, 99, 246, 256n10, 260nn38–40; in satire and documentary, 16, 75, 89, 100. *See also* African Americans; miscegenation; race; satire; social realism (genre)
"Revolutionary Symbolism in America" (Burke), 8
Rising Tide against White World-Supremacy (Stoddard), 99
The River (Lorentz), 7
Roberts, Matthew, 73
Robinson, Amy, 68, 106

Robinson, Cedric, 6, 252n6
Rockefeller, John D., Jr., 93, 136
Rogin, Michael, 45, 58, 88, 121, 194–95, 209, 220, 224, 229, 233, 235
Romanticism, 8–10
Roosevelt, Franklin D., 3, 7, 11–12, 123–24, 129, 218, 280n6
Rourke, Constance, 21, 81, 109, 124, 140–44
Routes (Clifford), 158
Rubinstein, Rachel, 73, 100, 103
Rural Electrification Administration, 129

The Sage of Sugar Hill (Ferguson), 38
satire: burlesque as form of, 4–5, 37–41, 81–82, 88, 231; critique of misogyny in, 38, 66–69; documentary's fusion in, 2–4, 6, 18–19, 25, 29; Harlem Renaissance and, 39–40; Juvenalian, 61–63; literary Left and, 79; political power of, 39–40, 57, 79, 279n2; Swift's version of, 199, 202. *See also* genre; laughter; modernist burlesque; signifying ethnography; *specific artists and works*
Schuyler, George: burlesque and satire of, 20, 23, 77, 205; criticisms of, 33, 38, 46, 256n9; journalism of, 35–36; parody in, 5, 21, 40, 51, 57–62, 65, 67, 69, 73, 75; plotting of, 21–22; political activism of, 23–24, 33–35, 38–39, 43, 46, 48, 254n21, 255nn2–3, 256n6
Scottsboro trial, 33–34, 254n1
screwball comedy (genre), 193–200, 207–18, 231, 238, 244
Scribner's Monthly (publication), 132
Sculle, Keith, 137
See America First (Shaffer), 115
Seeger, Charles, 13
segregation, 34, 42–43, 50, 85, 137, 226
The Service (publication), 34
sexuality, 202, 209–11, 213–15
Shaffer, Marguerite, 115, 117, 131
Shahn, Ben, 32
signifying ethnography: definitions of, 4–6, 154, 251n4; difficulties for, 158–61; in the Federal Writers' Project, 28; Hurston's use of, 5, 147, 157, 169–78; relation of, to traditional eth-

nography, 23, 169–70, 176, 251nn4–5, 272n3. *See also* Gates, Henry Louis; Hurston, Zora Neale; *Mules and Men* (Hurston)
Silas, Rachel, 184
Silver Shirts, 80, 100
Slaves Today (Schuyler), 36
Smethurst, James, 25
Smith, Terry, 17
Socialist Party, 34
social realism (genre), 3, 7, 14, 24, 75, 104, 124, 192–93, 209, 214–18, 238. *See also* class; documentary; genre; populism (political); whiteness; *specific works and artists*
The Souls of Black Folks (Du Bois), 10
Southern Exposure (White), 225
Soviet Union, 3, 12
Sowell, Thomas, 36
Spiller, Hortense, 96
Stagecoach (film), 235
Stalin, Joseph, 3, 12, 251n2, 253n14
Steele, Shelby, 36
Steinbeck, John, 3, 75, 105, 218
Stephens, Michelle, 25
stereotypes, 77, 82, 85, 89–96, 108–9, 124, 144–45, 167, 188. *See also* capitalism; class; consumerism; folk; gender; race; tourism
Stewart, Jon, 2–3
Stoddard, Lothrop, 99
Stott, William, 15–18
Stowe, Harriet Beecher, 132–33
Sturges, Preston: avatars of, in his films, 205, 207; capitalism's limitations and, 38; casting decisions of, 214; critical reception of, 193–95, 225, 231–34; photos of, *190*; politics of, 24, 197–98, 280n9; screenwriting of, 191–93. See also *Sullivan's Travels* (Sturges)
Sullivan's Travels (Sturges): audiences in and of, 28, 192, 197, 202–5, 219, *228*, 229–34, 236–37; critical reception of, 192–95, 225, 229–34; folk's depiction in, 90, 194, 203; gender in, 195–97, 207–11, 232; hybrid genres of, 193, 195–96, 198, 200–201, 212–20, 223–31, 235–36, 238, 244; laughter as catharsis in, 223; masquerade

in, 192, 209–15, 217–22, 242; photos
of, *190, 202, 207, 211, 213, 216, 220,
225, 228, 233*; plot of, 194, 198–203,
206–7, 234–36; race in, 217–18, 224–
27; research for, 191–92, 225; vaudeville's influence on, 217–19
Sunshine, Sylvia, 132
Susman, Warren, 194
Swift, Daniel, 199, 202
Szalay, Michael, 115, 118

Taylor, Paul, 16, 92, 131
Their Eyes Were Watching God
(Hurston), 155, 188
Thomas, George, 161–62, 170, 174
Thomas, William, 9
Thoreau, Henry David, 10
Thorpe, Thomas Bang, 132
Thurman, Wallace, 39–40
Toggery, Milton, 100
Toomer, Jean, 42
tourism: automobile's relation to, 114–
15, 131, 134, 155, 266n8; Florida's
dependence on, 116–17, 119, 132–33,
135–36, 144–45; folk's exoticism and,
114, 120–21, 126, 131–32, 144–45, 176,
271n34; middle class's emergence
and, 119–20; whiteness of, 27, 113–
14, 120, 126, 137–38, 140–43. *See also*
Federal Writers' Project; Hurston,
Zora Neale
Trachtenberg, Alan, 87
tramps. *See* hobos
Trouble in Paradise (Lubitsch), 200
Trumbo, Dalton, 198
truthiness (term), 2
turpentiners (folk), 135–37, 149
Turturro, John, 241
12 Million Black Voices (Wright), 90

Uncle Tom's Cabin (Stowe), 133
United States. *See* America
usable past, 1, 85, 92

vaudeville, 38, 75, 77, 202, 230
Veitch, Jonathan, 25–26, 73–74, 100,
251n1, 263n9
ventriloquism, 87–88, 90
vernacular, 13, 40–46, 163
Victor (label), 47

Vidor, King, 226
der Volk, 3–4, 8, 108

Wainwright, Mary, 147
Wald, Alan, 25
Wald, Priscilla, 12–13
Walker, Alice, 118
Walkowitz, Rebecca, 22
Wall, Cheryl, 157, 273n5, 278n27
The Walls of Jericho (Fisher), 39
Watson, John, 35
The Ways of White Folks (Hughes), 40
Weems, Robert, 41
Weinbaum, Alys, 11, 65, 251n3, 258n26,
260n38
Welles, Orson, 40, 68
West, Mae, 215
West, Nathanael: biography of, 83–85,
198, 262nn4–5; burlesque and satire
of, 20, 23, 72–110, 205, 262n3; critical
receptions of, 26, 72–74, 261n1; on
fascism, 26–27, 82–83; Jewishness
of, 76, 262n3; nostalgia's evocation
and, 81–82; parodic style of, 5, 73,
75–76; plotting of, 21–22; political
activities of, 23–24, 72–75; stereotypes' role in, 77, 82, 85. *See also A
Cool Million* (West)
"What White Publishers Won't Print"
(Hurston), 92, 188
White, Josh, 225
White, Viney, 184
White, Walter, 56
whiteface, 55–56, 217–18, 248
whiteness: blackface's relation to, 45,
58–59, 263n14; class as partial deter-
minant of, 79, 124–25, 129–31; consumerism and, 42–44, 57, 91; "folk"
identity and, 10; gender and, 64–71,
83, 260n38; Hurston's college career
and, 164; as implicit norm, 44–52,
55–56, 58–59, 62–64, 92–93, 100,
110, 218–19, 247, 263n10; suffering
and, 104–6, 197, 219, 236; supremacy
movements based on, 11–12, 22, 43,
46, 58, 99, 106–7; tourism and, 27,
114, 120, 134, 140–43, 226. *See also*
authenticity; capitalism; class; gender; performativity; race
white slavery, 95–98

Wild Boys of the Road (film), 193, 279n1
Willard, Joe, 182
Williams, William Carlos, 73
Wilson, Edmund, 74, 77
The Wizard of Oz (film), 235
women: black, 65–66; as masculine
  foils, 211–16; reproduction and,
  260nn38–39
Woods, Mary, 116–17, 131
Wordsworth, William, 9
The WPA *Guides* (Bold), 115
Wray, Matt, 138

Wright, Richard, 39, 90, 192
Wyler, Willie, 191–92, 279n1

Yankee (type), 126, 130, 134, 139,
  268n17, 270n31, 270n33
You Have Seen Their Faces (Bourke-
  White and Caldwell), 16–17, 88, 90,
  220, 222
Young Communist League, 33
Young Negroes' Cooperative League,
  48

SONNET RETMAN is an associate professor of African
American Studies and an adjunct associate professor of Women's
Studies and English at the University of Washington.
This is her first book.

Library of Congress Cataloging-in-Publication Data
Retman, Sonnet H., 1966–
Real folks : race and genre in the Great Depression /
Sonnet Retman.
p. cm.
Includes bibliographical references and index.
ISBN 978-0-8223-4925-9 (cloth : alk. paper)
ISBN 978-0-8223-4944-0 (pbk. : alk. paper)
1. American literature—20th century—History and criticism.
2. Literature and folklore—United States—History—20th
century. 3. Folklore—United States—History—20th century.
4. American literature—African American authors—History
and criticism. 5. United States—History—1933–1945. I. Title.
PS228.F64R486 2011
810.9'0052—dc22
2011006516